A·N·N·U·A·L E·D·I·T·I·O·N·S

Mike Scalzo

Adolescent Psychology

Fifth Edition

W9-AWX-570

EDITOR

Fred E. Stickle

Western Kentucky University

Fred E. Stickle received his B.S. degree from Cedarville University where he majored in Social Science Secondary Education. He completed his graduate study in counseling at Wright State University (M.S.) and Iowa State University (Ph.D.). He is a professor at Western Kentucky University where he teaches adolescent counseling. Dr. Stickle maintains a private practice where he provides counseling for adolescents and their families.

Contemporary Learning Series

http://www.mhcls.com

Credits

1. **Perspectives on Adolescence**
   Unit photo—© Ryan McVay/Getty Images
2. **Puberty, Physical Development, and Health**
   Unit photo—© PunchStock/Creatas
3. **Cognitive Development and Education**
   Unit photo—© PhotoLink/Getty Images
4. **Identity and Socio-Emotional Development**
   Unit photo—© Digital Vision
5. **Family Relationships**
   Unit photo—© Amos Morgan/Getty Images
6. **Peers and Contemporary Culture**
   Unit photo—© PunchStock/Brand X Pictures
7. **Teenage Sexuality**
   Unit photo—© Kirk Weddle/Getty Images
8. **Problem Behaviors and Intervention**
   Unit photo—© Getty Images/Doug Menuez

Copyright

Cataloging in Publication Data
Main entry under title: Annual Editions: Adolescent Psychology. 2006/2007.
1.Adolescent Psychology—Periodicals. I. Fred E. Stickle., Title: Adolescent psychology.
ISBN-10: 0-07-351610-4   ISBN-13: 978-0-07-351610-3   658'.05   ISSN 1094-2610

Fifth Edition

Cover image © Creatas/Punchstock, Scenics of America/PhotoLink/Getty Images and Photos.com
Printed in the United States of America   1234567890QPDQPD9876   Printed on Recycled Paper

Editors/Advisory Board

Members of the Advisory Board are instrumental in the final selection of articles for each edition of ANNUAL EDITIONS. Their review of articles for content, level, currentness, and appropriateness provides critical direction to the editor and staff. We think that you will find their careful consideration well reflected in this volume.

Staff

Preface

In publishing ANNUAL EDITIONS we recognize the enormous role played by the magazines, newspapers, and journals of the public press in providing current, first-rate educational information in a broad spectrum of interest areas. Many of these articles are appropriate for students, researchers, and professionals seeking accurate, current material to help bridge the gap between principles and theories and the real world. These articles, however, become more useful for study when those of lasting value are carefully collected, organized, indexed, and reproduced in a low-cost format, which provides easy and permanent access when the material is needed. That is the role played by ANNUAL EDITIONS.

The word adolescence is Latin in origin, derived from the verb adolescere, which means to grow into adulthood. Growing into maturity involves change. Most would argue that except for infancy, adolescence is the most change-filled period of life. The traditional definition was based largely on physical growth, as evident in the marked increase in height and weight.

Most researchers define the period of life between age 10 to 20 as adolescence. It is a period of transition in which a person moves from the immaturity of childhood into the maturity of adulthood. There is a growing realization that characteristics of adolescent behaviors do not result simply from the physical changes, but include a variety of psychological and social factors. Environmental settings such as family, peer, and school influence the development and the numerous and dynamic changes that take place.

It is commonplace to hear a discussion concerning adolescence as the "story years" with new crazes and fads or the problems of teenagers involving crime or sexuality. However, there are many strengths and even advantages to the teen-age years.

This anthology of readings will help you understand the bases of the developmental changes young people experience and appropriate aspects of individuals, families, communities, and cultures that give richness to adolescent development. The selection of articles includes opinions of various authors. You may agree with some articles and disagree with others. Some articles may even spur classroom debate.

The anthology has been organized into eight units. The units cover issues related to the biological, cognitive, socio-emotional, family, and adolescent development. In keeping with this perspective that the ecological context of adolescent development is crucial to understanding, we also incorporated articles that examine the impact of socio-economic, gender, ethnic, and cultural influences on adolescent development. Unit 1 looks at adolescence in historical and contemporary perspectives. Unit 2 examines the biological and physical impact of puberty. Unit 3 explores issues related to cognitive growth and education, and unit 4 addresses identity and socio-emotional development. Unit 5 covers family relationships during adolescence, while unit 6 focuses on peers and contemporary culture. Teen sexuality issues are examined in unit 7. Problem behaviors like teen violence, self-injurious individuals, bullying, drug use, delinquent behavior and suicide, and the consequences of adolescent maltreatment are included in unit 8.

I trust that the articles of Annual Editions: Adolescent Psychology will increase your understanding of adolescent development, and that you will find articles that are both interesting and thought-provoking. I want to know what you think of this edition; please take a few moments to complete the article rating form at the back of this volume. I need your help to improve future editions of Annual Editions: Adolescent Psychology.

Fred E. Stickle

Fred E. Stickle
Editor

Contents

The concepts in bold italics are developed in the article. For further expansion, please refer to the Topic Guide and the Index.

UNIT 3
Cognitive Development and Education

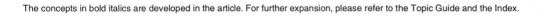

The concepts in bold italics are developed in the article. For further expansion, please refer to the Topic Guide and the Index.

UNIT 4
Identity and Social-Emotional Development

The concepts in bold italics are developed in the article. For further expansion, please refer to the Topic Guide and the Index.

UNIT 5
Family Relationships

UNIT 6
Peers and Contemporary Culture

The concepts in bold italics are developed in the article. For further expansion, please refer to the Topic Guide and the Index.

UNIT 7
Teenage Sexuality

UNIT 8
Problem Behaviors and Intervention

The concepts in bold italics are developed in the article. For further expansion, please refer to the Topic Guide and the Index.

The concepts in bold italics are developed in the article. For further expansion, please refer to the Topic Guide and the Index.

Topic Guide

This topic guide suggests how the selections in this book relate to the subjects covered in your course. You may want to use the topics listed on these pages to search the Web more easily.

On the following pages a number of Web sites have been gathered specifically for this book. They are arranged to reflect the units of this *Annual Edition*. You can link to these sites by going to the student online support site at *http://www.mhcls.com/online/.*

ALL THE ARTICLES THAT RELATE TO EACH TOPIC ARE LISTED BELOW THE BOLD-FACED TERM.

Abstinence
33. What to Tell Kids About Sex
34. Should Congress be Giving More Financial Support to Abstinence-Only Sex Education? YES
35. Should Congress Be Giving More Financial Support to Abstinence-Only Sex Education? NO
36. Choosing Virginity

Academic achievement
12. Healthier Students, Better Learners

Academic dishonesty
18. The New Cheating Epidemic

Adulthood
3. The Future of Adolescence: Lengthening Ladders to Adulthood

Aggression
10. Sense of Belonging to School: Can Schools Make a Difference?
11. Challenges and Suggestions for Safe Schools

Anxiety
10. Sense of Belonging to School: Can Schools Make a Difference?
25. A Nation of Wimps

Attention deficit
6. What Makes Teens Tick
7. Medicating Young Minds

Autonomy
14. Safe Schools for the Roller Coaster Years

Body image
5. Body Image: How Do You See Yourself?
21. A Mother's Story

Brain
6. What Makes Teens Tick
13. The 100 Best High Schools in America

Bullying
11. Challenges and Suggestions for Safe Schools
42. Bullying at School Among Older Adolescents

Capital punishment
40. Too Young to Die

Career
21. A Mother's Story

Cheating
18. The New Cheating Epidemic

College
15. The New College Dropout
17. Studies Reveal Strengths, Weaknesses in Improving Rates of High School Graduation and College Completion for Low-Income

Conflict
23. Support Network Eases Problems for Parents and Out-of-Control Teens

Culture
13. The 100 Best High Schools in America

Depression
7. Medicating Young Minds
15. The New College Dropout
25. A Nation of Wimps

Deviant behavior
38. Teenage Fatherhood and Involvement in Delinquent Behavior

Diet
4. Why do Kids Eat Healthful Food?

Disobedience and noncompliance
23. Support Network Eases Problems for Parents and Out-of-Control Teens

Diversity
1. Harnessing the Energies of Youth

Domestic violence
26. Prevention of Domestic Violence During Adolescence
27. Adolescents from Maritally Violent Homes

Drinking
16. The Perils of Higher Education
30. Family, Religious, School, and Peer Influences on Adolescent Alcohol Use
31. Alcohol Use Among Adolescents

Drugs and drug use
7. Medicating Young Minds
23. Support Network Eases Problems for Parents and Out-of-Control Teens

Emotional intelligence
20. Fostering Social-Emotional Learning in the Classroom

Emotions and emotional concerns
6. What Makes Teens Tick
7. Medicating Young Minds
8. The Biology of Risk Taking
14. Safe Schools for the Roller Coaster Years

UNIT 1

Perspectives on Adolescence

Unit Selections

1. **Harnessing the Energies of Youth**, Isaac C. Lamba
2. **On (not) "Coloring in the Outline" (Transformations from Youth Through Relationships)**, Linda C. Powell
3. **The Future of Adolescence: Lengthening Ladders to Adulthood**, Reed Larson

Key Points to Consider

- When in a person's development does the individual emerge as an adult rather than an adolescent?

- How has technology altered the way teens interact with each other and the rest of the world?

- How do wars and epidemics affect youth worldwide?

- Are today's teens prepared to become adults?

Student Website

www.mhcls.com/online

Internet References

Further information regarding these websites may be found in this book's preface or online.

Facts for Families
http://www.aacap.org/info_families/index.htm

The Opportunity of Adolescence
http://www.winternet.com/~webpage/adolescencepaper.html

Exactly what characterizes adolescence is not clearly established. G. Stanley Hall, who is credited with founding the scientific study of adolescence in the early part of the 1900s, saw adolescence as corresponding roughly with the teen years. He believed individuals of this age had great potential but also experienced extreme mood swings. He labeled adolescence as a period of "storm and stress." Because of their labile emotions, Hall believed that adolescents were typically maladjusted. But what did he believe was the cause of this storm and stress? He essentially believed the cause was biological. Hall's views had a profound effect on the subsequent study of adolescence. Biological factors that underlie adolescence and direct the transition from childhood to adulthood have been repeatedly studied and refined.

Historically, other researchers hold very different views on the causes and characteristics of adolescence. For example, Erik Erikson (1902-1994), a psychologist interested in how people formed normal or abnormal personalities, believed that adolescence was a key period in development. He theorized that during adolescence, individuals develop their identity. Just as Hall did, Erikson believed that there was some biological basis underlying development. Unlike Hall, however, Erikson emphasized the role society plays in the formation of the individual. Erikson proposed that adolescents must confront a number of conflicts (for example, understanding gender roles and understanding oneself as male or female) in order to develop an identity. The form of these conflicts and the problems the adolescent faced coping with them were influenced by the individual's culture. If adolescents were successful in meeting the conflicts, they would develop a healthy identity; if unsuccessful, they would suffer role diffusion or a negative identity. Similar to Hall, Erikson saw adolescence as a period where the individual's sense of self is disrupted, so it was typical for adolescents to be disturbed. Today, Erikson's ideas on identity formation are still influential. The stereotype that all adolescents suffer because of psychological problems has been called into question.

Margaret Mead, an anthropologist who started studying adolescents in the 1920s, presented a perspective on adolescence that differs from both Hall's and Erikson's. She concluded that culture, rather than biology, was the underlying cause of the transitional stage between childhood and adulthood. In cultures that held the same expectations for children as for adults, the transition from childhood to adulthood was smooth; there was no need for a clearly demarcated period where one was neither child or adult. In addition, adolescence did not have to be a period of storm and stress or of psychological problems. Although some of Mead's work has since been criticized, many of her ideas remain influential. Today's psychologists concur with Mead that adolescence need not be a time of psychological maladjustment. Modern anthropologists agree that biology alone does not define adolescence. Rather, the sociocultural environment in which an individual is raised affects how adolescence is manifested and characterized.

A cogent question is, what social and cultural factors lead to the development of adolescence in our society? Modern scholars believe that adolescence as we know it today did not even exist until the end of the 1800s. During the end of the nineteenth century and the beginning of the twentieth century, societal changes caused the stage of adolescence to be "invented." In this period, job opportunities for young people doing either farm labor or apprenticeships in factories were decreasing. For middle-class children, the value of staying in school in order to get a good job was stressed. Since there were fewer job opportunities, young people were less likely to be financially independent and had to rely on their families. By the beginning of the twentieth century, legislation ensuring that adolescents could not assume adult status was passed, child labor laws restricted how much time young people could work and compulsory education laws required adolescents to stay in school. In the 1930s, for the first time in this country's history, the majority of high school age individuals were enrolled in school. The teenagers were physically mature people who were dependent on their parents—they were neither children nor adults.

The articles in this unit focus on the images of adolescence in our culture as well as around the world. The first article by Isaac Lamba, provides a global perspective on adolescence. American adolescents are indeed different from others who are experiencing wars, epidemics, and other serious social upheavals. In the second article by Linda Powell, we hear from the adolescents themselves. Through their voices, Powell introduces us to themes in adolescent development such as the centrality of schools, the role of justice in their lives, and other issues that transform youth. In the final article, Reed Larson guides us through a look at the future of adolescence. He addresses a seminal question, "Are today's youth prepared to become adults?" His answer is "yes," despite the many challenges that face our teenagers such as terrorism and the AIDS epidemic.

Harnessing the Energies of Youth

Isaac C. Lamba

Any discussion of children and youth now must inevitably relate to the United Nations Millennium Development Goals, which provide the road map for human development. The recent United Nations Special Session on Children exposed failures of Governments in creating an enabling environment for youth within the Millennium Goals. Heads of State and Government reaffirmed the crucial importance of recognizing the rights of youth for any development agenda to work. As they conceded, children's greatest needs and aspirations point to a world that facilitates a rich human development based on "principles and democracy, equality, non-discrimination, peace, social justice and the universality, indivisibility, interdependence and interrelatedness of all human rights, including the right to development. Children and adolescents are resourceful citizens capable of building a better future for all" [A World Fit for Children]. The Special Session sounded a wake-up call to address the continuing neglect of children and youth in an uncaring world.

For a long time, the general public has viewed youth as a category wasteful of opportunity through frustration and lawlessness. The negative images of youth, who now form close to a half of the world's population, exclude and ignore the great potential in them which needs only to be given opportunity, cultivation and guidance.

The goal of a productive world of peace is often marred by selfish individuals in positions of influence, who have no tangible commitment or concern for the enrichment of the human condition of youth in order to launch them into meaningful adulthood. The quality of our young will depend on the bequest they receive; this forms a basic challenge of the twenty-first century. The identified and recognized needs of youth will constitute the agenda of the United Nations to be translated into action through its various agencies. Children need to be listened to for their proper participation in charting out their future as important partners in the custodianship of the world. Productivity in every nation originates from children and youth properly grounded in the cultural, social and economic virtues and aspirations of the nation,

which must exclude the dehumanizing and traumatic abduction into training as child soldiers in conflict situations or into forced child labour and prostitution.

In preparation for the Special Session, held from 8 to 10 May 2002, the youth in Malawi convened a "Children's Parliament" on 16 and 17 August, with the theme "A Malawi Fit for Children".

Areas of great concern defined by the children, whose recommendations the main Parliament adopted in toto, included education, HIV/AIDS, child participation in decision-making, poverty and the problem of orphans. The enormous challenge for lawmakers in Malawi was the realization of the children's desire and ability to eloquently articulate concerns affecting them, which called for relevance in policy formulation. Malawian children's concerns are repeated everywhere in the world, with the problem of violence against children on the list.

According to the Malawi National Youth Policy, factors contributing to the vulnerability of youth include inadequate educational and training facilities, exacerbated by social and cultural practices, early pregnancies and marriages, sexual harassment, violence and exploitation, HIV/AIDS and sexually transmitted diseases, drug and alcohol abuse, marginalization and non-involvement in decision-making, homelessness, unemployment and lack of sporting and proper entertainment facilities. These areas of preoccupation dovetail with the interests related to the UN mission.

However, for the UN to help harness the energies and potential of youth, Member States need to demonstrate the political and general will to assist them. Malawi President Bakili Muluzi, in a "State of the Nation" address on 31 May, called upon "all people in the country to work on giving our boys and girls equal opportunities to participate in the development of this country. They are our future. This is the time to prepare them for meaningful contribution".

In Africa, the situation of children and youth has been quite troubling: one in three children suffers from malnutrition; the AIDS pandemic has created huge numbers of orphans; and child labour, sex exploitation and child soldiers in war crises, with their terrible humanitarian tragedies, have impacted negatively the prospects of a humane, educated and enlightened society. Efforts by national governments to address these problems have failed to register much notable success because of the lack of financial resources and capacity. The United Nations has an important role to play here, but we must also recognize its successful performance often depends on the level of investment by the international community in societies riddled by poverty.

If education represents the backbone of socioeconomic empowerment and development, UN agencies, such as the UN Educational, Scientific and Cultural Organization (UNESCO), the International Bureau of Education and, to some extent the International Labour Organization (ILO) in the area of vocational training, can make a significant contribution by way of different programmes and projects. The Education for All concept was launched in Jomtien, Cambodia in the early 1990s with great expectations. The United Nations Children's Fund (UNICEF) and the United Nations Population Fund (UNFPA) continue to play important supporting roles in addressing the problem of physical infrastructure in education to promote some of the goals of Jomtien. The task for Government is extremely challenging in a poverty stricken country. In Malawi, universal primary education, introduced in 1994 by the United Democratic Front (UDF), has increased enrollment from 1.9 million to about 3.4 million today. This has brought enormous logistical and infrastructural problems which, however, should be seen as a stepping stone. Attempts to reduce the gap of educational opportunity to equally empower both girls and boys have formed an important agenda in countries such as Malawi, which has attained sex parity, although as yet only in the first five years of primary school. Out of the 100 million children out of school worldwide, 60 per cent are girls. The United Nations can continue to support the development of physical facilities and appropriate school curriculum, accompanied by incentives for girls. UNICEF has demonstrated conspicuous practical interest in funding curriculum revision, which must now include cross-cutting areas, such as gender and HIV/AIDS.

HIV/AIDS today constitutes the greatest threat to human development. The negative impact comes not just from the loss of millions of lives and the reversal of economic development efforts and insecurity, but also from the plight inflicted on children and youth, most of them in the poverty-ridden developing world. Of the close to 11 million children and youth living with AIDS, 70 per cent are in sub-Saharan Africa, while 12.1 million struggle as AIDS orphans in need of institutionalized care, about 90 per cent of them in sub-Saharan Africa (1.2 million in Zambia and 1 million in Malawi). Youth, for their part, need education, information and services that will emphasize self-respect, rights and informed choices to reduce their vulnerability to HIV infection, in order to assist the pledges by Governments to visibly cut HIV prevalence among 15- to 24-year-olds by 25 per cent by 2005. HIV/AIDS is a shared concern in the work of UNICEF, UNESCO and UNFPA. UN partnerships with Governments in financial support and technical assistance aim at arresting the scourge through training, public education and other interventions, which most Governments, given their poverty, are unable to mount on their own.

The fundamental issue of addressing alternatives that can engage youth profitably to supplement verbal messages through the curriculum and traditional forums must be addressed.

Every child or youth has a right to a dignified life free from exploitation and discrimination in a world that needs to be protected for them. Education without gainful occupation fails to appeal to the youth who see schooling as a gateway to a better economic life.

Governments may have the will to improve the welfare of youth, but lack of resources cripples the optimism. As the UN Secretary-General has noted, goals for youth improvement have been hampered by inadequate government funding—a most critical factor in developing youth capabilities and capacities, and a serious challenge for the UN global agenda in the creation of a world fit for children.

Lack of employment has frequently created a negative incentive to education and has given rise to pursuits, such as substance (drugs) abuse, premarital sex, violence and even crimes of theft. Training youth for self-employment would reduce deviance and promote balanced socio-economic development and dignified ambitions. A UN agency such as the ILO could contribute to this training through support to a college or even setting up a vocational training centre. Skills for building self-reliance would help to reduce youth indiscipline on the streets and in cities.

Youth have enormous mental and physical energy that seek expression. Quite often, official attention to the physical requirement has been minimal. Government investment in community youth recreational centres constitutes positive action as a potent strategy to build self-esteem among them, particularly in the absence of sufficient youth employment.

Support for small business enterprise has sometimes been dubbed risky for funding agencies. Malawi's experience in giving loans to youths has revealed promise through training. President Muluzi has declared his government's support for youth employment and entrepreneurship projects and programmes that will assist youth in developing not only skills for sustainable livelihood but also the leadership potential and confidence which the youth of Malawi exhibited during the children's parliament. As concerns projects and vocational training, the supportive role of the ILO and other UN agencies cannot be overemphasized.

In Bolivia, a moral leadership training programme, with a coverage that includes youth, has shown great promise in the development of character and leadership among young. (One Country, Bahai Magazine, Jan-March 2002). Small youth groups have been organized to undertake community projects, drawing the youth away from unworthy engagements. UNESCO could assist in leadership training.

If youth represent the custodians of the future of the world, they are the determinants of the quality of the world today, which must reflect our contribution to them. Our role is to enrich the process of developing youth into useful, productive and responsible architects of a world of peace. The United Nations in this process must take on and execute a partnership with Governments to ensure the raising of youth well grounded in the commendable socio-economic and cultural virtues for the sustainability of humankind.

Ambassador Isaac C. Lamba is Permanent Representative of the Republic of Malawi to the United Nations. In addition to a distinguished diplomatic career, he has an extensive background in academia.

On (not) "coloring in the outline"

(Transformations From Youth Through Relationships)

Linda C. Powell

This article provides an overview and analysis of 10 studies on violence and injustice from the perspective of youth. These articles are contained in the issue of Journal of Social Issues entitled Youth Perspectives on Violence and Injustice and, in the articles, the authors offer a unique opportunity to go far beyond the current discursive terrains of youth and violence. Through a reinterpretation of what is conceptualized as normative, an expansion of the conceptualization of "youth" and an exploration of a broad range of topics, contexts and methods, the issue explores five provocative and significant critical themes. These themes are: methodology is critical; youth as subject, not object; girl and danger of a clinical approach; centrality of schools? and at the intersection of social justice and development. The impact of popular culture on youth and violence and the importance of examining what adults value as "entertainment" are discussed also.

Adding a new voice to a conversation, a new point of view, does more than just increase the content in a linear way (Walkerdine, 2002). Including a voice that has previously been excluded contains the potential for changing the entire discussion. "Facts" and other notions once taken for granted are opened to scrutiny. "Natural" connections and causalities yield to new ways of organizing ideas and relationships. Notions assumed "settled" lead to new questions and implicate new players. In scientific terms (Kuhn, 1962), science moves forward not by careful and gradual research programs, but by huge new ideas that replace old ones. The action of moving youth voices toward the center of the study of violence is such a paradigm shift.

Daiute and Fine (this issue), the editors of this issue, report 10 studies that go beyond what Mahiri and Conner (this issue) describe as the public discourse about Black youth violence or "the outline" which sets boundaries of a somewhat proscribed conversation that adults have about young people and violence. Daiute and Fine (this issue) echo Mahiri and Conner's desire to go beyond this kind of "coloring in the outline" (Mahiri and Conner). This issue offers an opportunity to color far beyond the lines of the currently overlapping terrains of youth and violence. The 10 studies featured reinterpret what counts as normative, expand the conceptualization of "youth," and explore a broad range of topics, contexts and methods. The editors and contributors to this issue assume that there are ongoing, multiple systems that influence the lives of young people, that these systems can interact in paradoxical and counterintuitive ways and that when we listen, young people can describe their expe-

riences in ways that are multi-layered and complex. As the studies report, listening to these stories can dramatically enlarge our sense of and the nature of the "problem" of violence and the "meaning" of youth. In taking an important theoretical turn that young people have something to say about their own lives, and these young people do not disappoint—this issue creates the possibility of shifting the conversation and public discourse about youth and violence.

Lewin (1951) and Fallis and Opotow (this issue) remind us that social behavior is a function of both persons and their environments. From a youth-based perspective, this issue's ambitious task is to begin to make the function of both individual and contextual elements of youth and violence clearer and more precise. Youth narratives and experiences map in detail and in color the connections between their internal lives and their environmental context—looking at interactions, relationships, causality, and influences between the multiple ways they describe their experiences, and their life contexts and behaviors and the impact of social institutions. In many of these studies, the authors have, as Phoenix, Frosh, and Pattman (this issue) describe it, "gotten out of our way," giving us the actual words of young people. They let us decide whether or not we agree with the researchers' interpretation. In others, the authors (e.g., Cross, this issue) have carefully interwoven history with present day realities so we may re-view youth and violence.

Coloring outside of the line is not simply about the shape of the boundaries, but also about the hues and textures around the boundaries. The authors offer not just studies of "kids of color" but they enter the more dangerous area of seeing the experiences of kids of all colors through the prisms of race, gender and class. We begin to see the ways in which social identity matters in the social construction and attributions of behavior and the development of identities. In particular, young people have different experiences of similar stimuli and different consequences of their behavior depending on race, ethnicity, gender, or class (Bailey, 1992-93; Giles, 2001; Style & Powell, 1995; Wellesley College, 1992). These "embodied" studies give us additional insights into the experiences of youth that are always influenced by status, history, and position. For instance, we learn that violence is not something that "Black young men do," but violence becomes a phenomenon affecting all young people, but with potentially differential impact and consequence based on race and class. In this issue, we hear the voices of girls and of boys; of young people from elementary school through adolescence and early adulthood; of young people living in and migrating to the United States, Israel, and Britain. We meet these youth in their classrooms, in community organizations, on the streets, and in history. We see them through the lenses of psychology and sociology, through feminism, and through antiracist analyses. Some of these young people live in circumstances of war, racism, or tremendous social dislocation. Some studies dare to ask youth about "violence," itself. And they respond by telling us about their relationships, their homes, and their schools. More frightening, when they are asked about their relationships or about school, we learn how violence and the antecedents to violence weave into the everyday fabric of friendships, romance, and learning. Conducting research that surfaces youth perspectives in an authentic way requires a cognitive shift, a move away from the idea of "youth as problem" to an empathic entering into and with the experience of young people themselves. Making this cognitive shift leads to a set of theoretical and methodological "taken for granteds" that are provocative, significant, and subtly understated. In the following section, I discuss these shifts as critical themes that run across these papers.

Critical Themes

Methodology Is Critical

The studies are explicit in generating methods that allow researchers to "hear," theorize, interpret, and analyze critically what youth say about violence and how they say it. This may require some departures from more typical research methods. These methodological investments and innovations come in many forms and at every stage of research. Writers such as Phoenix et al. (this issue) and Tolman, Spencer, Rosen-Reynoso, and Porche (this issue) create research situations in which adults must listen deeply to youth, following their lead in inquiry and interpretation. Daiute, Stem, and Lelutiu-Weinberger (this issue) designed their project so that youth talk to adults could be contrasted to youth talk with peers, while studying the values of adults and students. Fine et al. (this issue) build research and survey questions with young people, turning over unexpected rocks in the differences between adult and youth experience. Using historical and sociological methods, Cross (this issue) excavates and examines the myths that generate and potentially pervert approaches to youth problems today. Spencer,

Dupree, Cunningham, Harpalani, and Munoz-Miller (this issue) use a specific theoretical framework that "integrate[s] salient issues of context and development". In exploring young people's experience with victimization via their thoughts, fears, and physical symptoms they attempt to "[capture] the meaning-making processes underlying foundational identity development and outcomes" (Spencer et al.). Hertz-Lazarowitz (this issue) applies concepts from a model of Social Drama (Harre, 1979) that seems uniquely useful in understanding the action and intergroup dynamics on a university campus.

These approaches are a far cry from the traditional approaches to studying youth violence. First, these studies investigate the experiences of "normal" kids, those not officially identified as violent or "at risk" for violence. In this way, these are truly studies "of" violence from the perspective "of" youth. Secondly, these studies care about development as a dynamic. Violence is not conceived as a one time event. Rather, it is viewed as an experience that will influence what occurs next in their lives, coming at a vulnerable time in the lifespan and having impact on learning, relational development, feelings of engagement/alienation, etc. Finally, each of these studies comments in some way on the "essentialist versus systemic perspective" (Cross). For instance, Cross (this issue) states that observers essentialize problems when Blacks (or youth) are involved and those same problems are perceived as more systemic when Whites and other social groups (like adults) are studied. Most of these studies are interdisciplinary, including the methods of social, developmental and clinical psychology, sociology, history, public health, and education. Fine et al. (this issue) worked with young people at the outset of the research to generate questions, discovering a vein of experience that the adults could not access. Most of the studies used multiple methods, including clinical interviewing. Phoenix et al. (this issue) remind us that since "we 'make' our identities through our autobiographical narratives", we can learn from young people by having them tell rich, complex potentially contradictory stories about their experience. Tolman et al. (this issue) describe this process as creating a "… dialogue between theory and youth perspectives…". Solis's (this issue) theoretical framework holds that violence is "a dialectical process that is constantly unfolding between social structures and individuals". Therefore, for her, violence has social, rather than natural or individual, origins. Fallis and Opotow (this issue) included dissemination as a critical part of their data analysis; this phase challenged student researchers to become conceptually clear about their work and allowed each stage of the project to generate new questions.

Youth as Subject, Not Object

What each of these studies indicates is the potential for empowerment and, hence, new results when young people are involved as subject and even researcher, rather than simply objects of someone else's inquiry. As Hertz-Lazarowitz (this issue) sums up, "… we sought to document young people in conflict and confrontation using events of injustice and surveillance to develop critical and political thinking". The phenomenology of meaning making rather than remaining object in someone else's study requires new kinds of supportive and interpretive research environments. The results of these studies suggest (not counter-intuitively) that young people tell different stories when they trust that their authentic experiences are genuinely valued and respected. This may be an inadvertent "metafinding" of these studies. Wells (1985) has usefully given us the "radio" meta-phor for thinking about multiple levels of analysis, and how to think usefully about group-level variables. Daiute and Fine (this issue) state that youth today are growing up with a sense of adult betrayal and alienation. If we imagine that many stations are playing all the time, it becomes possible to "tune in" to a single station and listen. This is not to say that no young people have good relationships with adults, but that when we tune in on the "youth station" we hear the absence of sufficient holding environments constructed and honored by adults for youth.

Group relations theory (Rioch, 1975; Shapiro and Carr, 1991; Wells, 1985) uses psychoanalysis and social psychology to build complex understandings of individuals, groups, and social systems. It can help with the interactions between institutional and personal factors and how these influences conspire to create identities and connecting individual lives, personal narrations and institutional effects. Fallis and Opotow (this issue) introduce the notion of multiple levels of analysis (individual, interpersonal, and institutional) when identifying what gets addressed and what remains latent within a system. They offer a sophisticated interpretation of school cutting, an activity they conceive of as challenging the authority of the school to avoid conflict or direct challenges of systems and processes they see as alienating. A purely behavioral and individual focus protects the system from investigating its own contributions, dynamics, and interests. Systemic failure (disengagement, alienation due to the nature of school) is handled by individual interventions. As long as we see only individuals, the systemic or group level problem will persist, unfettered and unaddressed.

Fallis and Opotow's (this issue) complex definition of "boring" as a reason to cut class is instructive as we think about young people and violence. When students describe something as boring, they are not just describing the absence of something or being disinterested. Upon investigation, they mean something very specific: a one way, top down, unengaged relationship with a teacher whose pedagogy feels disrespectful because it is not designed to "tempt, engage or include" them. From a youth perspective, boring is not a naturally occurring phenomenon. It is the predictable outcome of specific decisions and actions of the teacher and school.

The third major assumption of these writings, again refreshing and understated, is that the social world is not necessarily neutral for young people. Researchers must be willing to suspect that some young person isn't personally troubled or some issue isn't just "pesty...." We have to be willing to look at institutional structures that contribute to youth behavior. Fallis and Opotow (this issue) note that "moral exclusion is the alchemy that transforms intransigent, unaddressed conflict into structural violence [and] ... situates responsibility for negative outcomes in victims rather than those with institutional resources and power". This notion indicts our adult, researcher at-

tention, spotlighting what it emphasizes or what it doesn't seem to notice.

Institutions cannot be taken as helpful or supportive simply because adults intend for them to be. Young people develop a variety of ways of navigating their complex social world. These studies document how much can be learned by listening to the experiences of young people as they challenge public institutions. From the perspective of young people, history, schools, and communities can oppress and create inequity. As an example, many policing programs are allegedly designed to protect citizens. However, Fine et al. (this issue) discovered that young people experience themselves as a population at risk of police targeting. That is a youth perspective on adult surveillance.

What is the impact on identity development when receiving a constant message that you are untrustworthy, suspicious and potential criminals and it "shows" on you—your look determines your criminality, not your behavior? As Fine et al. (this issue) note, even good behavior does not protect Black youth from police surveillance. Similarly, the voices of young people have rarely been heard in discussions of police violence, despite being a target of more aggressive policing initiatives.

Finally, these essays recognize that adult definitions of social problems can be social defenses (Jaques, 1955; Menzies, 1975; Powell, 1994) against the anxiety stirred by youth perspectives on social problems. Why is it still an unusual idea to take students' concerns seriously when planning school reform efforts or to work with them collaboratively in creating youth policy? This avoidance of authentic engagement serves as a psychological defense for adults. For example, what happens when we look beyond cutting class as an individual issue to the systemic issues giving rise to cutting? What happens when we consider youth behavior as data and even a critique, not just as individual errant behavior (Fine, 1991)? When teachers see cutting class as a disciplinary matter, it protects them from the hypothesis that it is a comment on their teaching.

Girl and Danger of a Clinical Approach

The authors of these studies honor young people's experiences with and explanations about the risks of violence to their physical and psychological well-being. For the purpose of this issue, youth violence is not a "disease" and violence against and by young people must be addressed as a social and political problem. This moves beyond individual behavior, into the realm of phenomenology, or the meaning making systems that young people employ to understand and organize their experiences. These studies require stepping back from individually framed behavior and looking at the big picture of affective experiences of young people. This issue assumes that youth do have internal worlds that are products, reflections, and defenses against their experiences.

Across these essays we hear a psychoanalytic or clinical language through which researchers stretch to recognize the relation of adult fetishes and youth behavior; adult anxieties and our projections onto youth. Further, the researchers seek to move into the internal world which inevitably brings us into the world of clinical dynamics. For example, Daiute and Fine (this issue) note that "Research in the field of youth violence … rarely reports from the standpoints of youths themselves who may look at the world around them as problematic … Adults project onto youth our growing concerns about violence [emphasis added]". Mahiri and Conner (this issue) use the notions of displacement and scapegoats (Banet and Hayden, 1977; Wells, 1985). In addition to the practical mechanism they quote from Chomsky (1995), in psychoanalysis this is the most extreme form of projective identification. Parallel process (Smith and Berg, 1987; Smith, Simmon, and Thames, 1989) is intimated by Hertz-Lazarowitz when she considers the possibility that lessons learned from the conflict on campus can be considered data about the university as a whole, as well as in Israel. Fallis and Opotow (this issue) remind us of Apples' (1996) poignant insight about students' "almost unconscious realization that … schooling will not enable them to go much farther than they already are", which provides a powerful glimpse into a student's internal world. Tolman et al. (this issue) organize their inquiry around Rich's (1983) definition of heterosexuality as a universally pervasive institution, with mechanisms that "insure that it functions unconsciously and imperceptibly for most individuals" (Tolman et al.).

Using clinical language about the unconscious gives us incredible firepower to more authentically construct the complexity within and between individuals and groups. It allows us to account for that which is apparent, and that which operates below the surface. Organizations, too, have an unconscious (Obholzer and Roberts, 1994), with manifest and latent content, conflict and defensive strategies. Daiute et al. (this issue) note this: "When violence prevention programs are placed in contexts where children are presumed to have experienced discrimination conflicts, it should not be surprising that they may need or want to express life experiences that the curriculum actually represses [emphasis added]". Fallis and Opotow (this issue) also comment on this, noting that "intransigent conflicts that resist standard solutions are often characterized by misdiagnoses that miss deeper issues such as the basic need for consistency, security, respect, justice, and a sense of personal control". And, above all, it lets us enter the terrain of the imagination, of dreams and images, which are developmentally and politically critical in the identities of youth.

There remains the difficulties of capturing and measuring the inner world in any respectful way: One major danger is that we have all been boys and girls. Transference—clinical, research, and theoretical—appears as a likely problem. First, we have to attempt to make some meaning out of the experiences youth share and the stories they tell. We must wonder about the questions that adults have not asked. While this is always true of the research adventure, our absences make an interesting pattern. Like Tolman's wondering why (all) the research on dating violence hasn't inquired into why there is so much violence? There is significant research on gender differences in dating behavior but a marked absence of gendered analysis (for counterexamples see Leadbeater and Way, 1996). This is similar to Fine et al. (this issue) not conceding the possibility of sexual harassment of young women by the police. Or in Phoenix et al. (this issue) wondering about repressed material in adults

leading to Black boys being seen as super-masculine. Perhaps these are the kinds of arenas we may not have conscious access to and are not eager (or encouraged) to excavate.

Hertz-Lazarowitz (this issue) looks specifically at meaning making in her study of Palestine and Israeli dynamics at Haifa University. First, she shifts the question away from personal behavior to personal experiences. One of her central interview questions clearly seeks internal meaning: Has someone in authority controlled or acted toward you in an unjust way? In this question, the research puts the question of justice right at the forefront. Her study focuses also on the social meaning, potentially offering a new understanding of the interplay between personal and collective factors.

Solis (this issue) hypothesizes a "dialectical relationship [as] a cycle between the societal abuse faced by Mexican immigrants, and the personal acts of violence and abuse enacted by Mexican immigrants". From this perspective, violence is a tool youth use to make sense of themselves, other people and institutions. She uses the term "violenced" (Solis, this issue) to describe those who have had violence perpetrated upon them as a result of their "illegal" status.

Centrality of Schools?

Schools are the only social institution that can compel young people to be present. For that reason alone, schools are important in any discussion of youth perspectives on violence. In this issue, all of the studies mention schools; six are specifically situated within them. Tragically, schools are increasingly a place where some young people enact violence. We believe, also, that schools are a key site where young people negotiate their understanding in the world and develop their capacity for social engagement and meaning making. Schools have been considered important as an agency of indoctrination, reproduction of social relations, and sites of social violence (Block, 1997). It is an important social institution where the emotional aspects of the youth social system and adult social system interact on a daily basis.

Cross (this issue) provides a complete rereading of Frazier's 1939 work about delinquency in Chicago with a systemic rather than essentialist perspective. While Frazier sought explanations for the behavior in family and community dynamics, Homel (1984) found a more persuasive systemic argument in the schools and their maladaptive attempts to deal with racism and overcrowding. These (systemic) facts undercut the myth that African Americans were crippled in some way by slavery, and yet the (essentialist) myth continues to influence our thinking about Black youth and violence today. Do we still think, as Cross (this issue) asks, that schools are designed "… to prevent delinquency through educational engagement"? Or have we given up on that?

School can be a site of violence, and the task of schools is influenced by young people's experiences of violence. Phoenix et al. (this issue) remind us that experiences of school influence how young people see their worlds. Tolman et al. (this issue) note that school is the context in which much of teen dating takes place, between people who are known to one another, and in a context where adults fail to interrupt and may even encourage harassing behaviors. Spencer et al. (this issue) note an important finding in their study: each of the post-traumatic stress disorder (PTSD) symptoms that were predicted by experience with violence was related to focus of attention. They rightly note that feelings of fear, distraction and self-consciousness in response to experiences with violence can interfere with normative learning processes.

This concern about violence in schools is not simply about social interactions, but also occurs in the pedagogy of the school. For example, in explicating the ways that teachers and students struggled together to produce a set of values, Daiute et al. (this issue) remind us that an emphasis on mastery discourages critique or transformation; from this perspective, all questions and challenges emerge as individual failures. Tolman et al. (this issue) discover that school policies that provoke individual discussion about sexual harassment and dating violence, without a critique of the larger systems which produce and perpetuate violence in intimate relationships, leave girls feeling scared and boys feeling unfairly accused.

Mahiri and Conner's (this issue) study findings reflected three broad, highly related themes that clearly contrasted with public discourse on Black youth. In particular, the lives of the youth closely correspond to the circumstances of many of the Black youth that U.S. society has characterized as violent "others" (Fordham, 1996; Payne, 2001; Ward, 2001), with one key difference. Those youth that attended small schools with teachers that were interested in and capable of teaching a unique curriculum unit engaged young people in ways that match their experiences about violence. The impact of school size (Wasley et al., 2000; Fine and Soimerville, 1998) was noted also by Fine et al. (this issue). Small schools give the opportunity for innovative curriculum. In the Mahiri and Connor article (this issue) students research and document aspects of their own lives; they interview members of their community and assess positive and negative aspects of their community. Academic work is used to mirror and explore their experience, developing their intellectual ability to think about what actually happens in their world. This schooling experience starts with the lived experience of young people, and does not demand that students create a separate school self. This integrating, unitive approach could be for young people the opposite of Fallis and Opotow's (this issue) "boring" aspects of school. Why is it still news to us that young people bring complex and competing worlds into their classrooms, worlds which require respect and negotiation for the learning task to proceed?

At the Intersection of Social Justice and Development

Unlike the linear and unidimensional "outline" that is much of the public conversation about youth and violence, the young people in these studies emerge in colorful, vivid, and complex terms. They inhabit a world which they must accept as routinely unpredictable and violent by necessity, a world where public policy may make you unsafe, and a world where huge forces like history and war will determine daily interactions with others. And as several researchers discovered, young people describe this simply as "the way things are." A world where boys must struggle to act like "real men," and romance requires violence, where girls must balance being desirable, vulnerable, and acceptable. A world where language has no meaning and homophobia is "just" a joke (although boys will go to great lengths to avoid being called "gay"). Not surprisingly, many young people, in several of the studies, "just decide not to care about it" or "to simply ignore it." The numbing burdens of this world become monotonous and debilitating. And too often the responses of adults imply that it is up to the individual young person to take action. Despite our intent, our educational and social policies often operate as if young people are our enemy rather than our future.

As a whole, these studies expand our definitions of "violence." Myth making robs and lies and distorts—and is a form of violence against the history and culture of African Americans. Being termed "illegal" is violence against the self and the identity of Mexican immigrant children and families. Microaggressions of disrespect and suspicion (Toussaint, Boyd-Franklin, & Franklin, 2000) are experienced as forms of interpersonal violence. Organizational structures and practices that diminish the sense of self and deny resources are a form of violence. The cumulative impact of these processes on identity development can be devastating. A person or a group can suffer real damage if the world mirrors back to them a confining or demeaning or contemptible picture of themselves. As Solis (this issue) notes, "… as long as violence continues to be lived privately and ignored publicly, and as long as the means to respond to violence other than with violence remains unfamiliar to [them]", young people will find themselves in a bind. The 10 studies in this issue suggest that interventions with the power to solve the intransigent problems youth face will require youth perspectives leveled "at the intersection of social justice and development" (Daiute and Fine, this issue) situated front and center. What does this issue have to say to the school reform, youth development, and violence prevention literatures? It calls into question new interpretations of seemingly straightforward data; it offers methodologies and syntheses. It makes us wonder whether perhaps we should we be interrogating "adulthood" the way we eventually had to interrogate Whiteness? If sampling the internal world of young people is important, then like psychotherapy, it is labor intensive work. It requires relationship and clinical skill, respect and courage.

An Afterthought

In a recent address to the Public Education Network national convention, Nobel laureate Toni Morrison (2002) used her own narrative as a student to inspire and provoke her audience to think about education in a post-9/11 world. Her earliest desire for academic achievement was fueled, she said, by a "terror" or desire that she wouldn't be competent in an adult world. This is the world that no longer exists for young people. In the absence of adult engagement with youth voices and experiences, popular culture (Lash, 2000; Wolff, 1999) sells a version of adult life that always feels in reach. There is less and less that schools or real adults have to teach that TV and movies don't provide a more powerful and immediate "curriculum." That terror she felt has now been assuaged by a plastic sense of order and certainty; no problem exists that is not solved by the end of the episode (with suitable commercial breaks) or turned into a meme of stimulation.

Cross (this issue) notes that it is unclear how Frazier (1939/1948) missed the role of schools overcrowding and double-shift schools in understanding youth problems in Chicago. Are researchers also overlooking the impact of popular culture now? Will we look back and wonder about the unrestrained impact of violence as entertainment on issues of identity and violence; depictions of this violence are easily found on television, in video games, and in films. Interesting that it may elude us too if we do not recognize it as a force (Daspit and Weaver, 1999; Minow and LeMay, 1995). If we fail to consider it as a potential variable-the way Frazier may never have thought about the structure of the day—then we will miss the potential impact of this multibillion-dollar, saturating industry (Daspit, 1999). The challenge is that popular culture lives in our imaginations, in our unconscious, away from our immediate awareness and public selves. The major power of advertising is its ability to convince us that we are not influenced by it (Kilbourne, 1999).

Cross (this issue) imagines the comments from the 1940s: "yes, now that you point it out to me, double-shifting probably does not help matters, but there must be some cultural or genetic reasons why so many Black teens keep getting into trouble". We ruminate in the same way about the steady diet of stimulating images fed to all of us, with young people perhaps more vulnerable than others; we know that it affects brain chemistry; we sense that it is changing the ways that we relate to ourselves and each other, we know that our consuming behaviors are sustainable only at the costs of lives around the globe, and then we look away. Like the adults that Cross describes, we assume that it must be about something else: bad genes, the education system, the mental health system, racism, etc. And while all of these contribute to our understanding of youth violence, there is a strange silence in this issue and in general about what de Zengotita (2002) calls "The Numbing of The American Mind" and the particular impact that has on children and youth. We, too, struggle with the addictive properties of popular culture; however, we would rather project all of our concern on young people. Hertz-Lazarowitz reminds us of McLaren and Giroux's (1994) reflection: "education has to be viewed as a political matter related to the power structure of the society". Maybe schools are less potent as critical sites for identity development, and popular culture reigns. Mahiri and Connor (this issue) allude to this when they suggest that "elements of hip-hop culture and rap music constituted a kind of 'pop culture pedagogy' that extended, offered alternatives to, or challenged the pedagogy of schools".

However, I would go further. The images and values of popular culture have colonized the imagination, subtly defining what is important, the ways in which we interact and the meanings we construct. Certain images, especially those that link sexuality and violence (the critical link of the last two articles in this issue) take up a place in our imaginations, whether we consciously "know" or acknowledge it. The preponderance of violence as entertainment does at least three things: First, the very medium of television, movies, video games, and the Internet pulls us into an external focus and risks making us passive and "receptive" in the most intimate areas of our own lives. This contributes to the sense reported by many young people that "this is just the way things are," and "you get used to it…" This passivity develops separate from the "content" of specific films or music. This is a metaeffect, provoked by intensity and saturation. Secondly, popular culture teaches an amazingly consistent and "standardized" curriculum of consumerist and materialist values. In a world of harsh policy battles about what young people should be taught in schools, there is a seemingly clear consensus in the curriculum of popular culture that individualism, efficiency, and materialism are the keys to a happy life. And that violence is a common, legitimate, and sometimes glamorous way of handling conflict and difference. And finally, popular culture holds identity development processes hostage to a false reality, away from the human, interactive, social field. This may be why the focus in so many of these studies on actual experience—shared between adults and young people—proved to be so riveting. Several studies note that relationships over time with youth participants led to deeper levels of comfort with process and reflection on their involvement in the study. This proves especially important in Solis's (this issue) case study of her work with one student over time.

While there is much additional research to chart this new terrain, it seems likely that popular culture has some impact on issues of youth and violence and it has some impact on how adults view and engage with issues of youth and violence. For instance, in my most recent work with educators, it has become clear that adults are often quite clear about the implications of consumerist values on the young people with whom they work. They are usually quite enthusiastic about the need for critical media training and coursework about advertising and marketing. Although they say that young people are rarely initially engaged by these ideas, believing themselves to be about this kind of influence—while they wear the clothes, buy the music, and incorporate the values of the culture that surrounds them. However, these educators are routinely less interested in exploring their own reaction to popular culture and the ways in which issues of consumption, externalization, and ambition affect them on a daily basis.

Studying this new terrain will be fraught with methodological, psychological and political difficulties. One of the greatest challenges may be the requirement that adults, researchers, and educators examine our own values about popular culture, examine our own values about "entertainment," and not simply lump it into some larger vague category called "the media." The simple fact that a multi-billion dollar industry exists and thrives on images of violence seemingly unfettered may communicate to young people what we really believe.

References

Apple, M. (1996). Cultural politics and education. New York: Teachers College Press.

Bailey, S. (1992-93). Gender equity: The unexamined basic of school reform. Stanford Law & Policy Review, 4, Winter.

Banet, A. G., Jr., & Hayden, C. (1977). The Tavistock primer. In J. E. Jones, & J. W. Pfeiffer (Eds.), The 1977 handbook for group facilitators (pp. 155-167). La Jolla, CA: University Associates.

Block, A. (1997). I'm only bleeding: Education as the practice of social violence against children. New York: Peter Lang.

Chomsky, N. (1995). A dialogue with Noam Chomsky. Harvard Educational Review, 65(2).

Daspit, T. (1999). Rap pedagogies: "Bring(ing) the noise of knowledge born on the microphone" to radical education. In T. Daspit & J. A. Weaver (Eds.), Popular culture and critical pedagogy. Reading, constructing, connecting (pp. 163-181). New York: Garland Publishing.

Daspit, T., & Weaver, J. A. (Eds). (1999). Popular culture and critical pedagogy. Reading, constructing, connecting. New York: Garland Publishing.

de Zengotita, T. (2002). Numbing of the American mind. Harper's Magazine, 304 (1823), 33-41.

Fine, M. (1991). Framing dropouts: Notes on the politics of an urban public high school. Albany, NY: State University of New York Press.

Fine, M., & Somerville, J. I. (Eds.). (1998). Small schools, big imaginations: Creative look at urban public schools. Chicago: Cross City Campaign for Urban School Reform.

Fordham, S. (1996). Blacked out. Dilemmas of race, identity, and success at Capital High. Chicago: University of Chicago Press.

Frazier, E. F. (1939). The Negro family in the United States. Chicago: University of Chicago Press; revised edition 1948. New York: Dryden Press.

Giles, H. C. (2001). Transforming the deficit narrative: Race, class and social capital in parent-school relations. In C. Korn & A. Bursztyn (Eds.), Case studies in cultural transition: Re-thinking multi-cultural education. Wesport, CT: Greenwood Press.

Harre, R. (1979). Social being. London: Blackwell.

Homel, M. W. (1984). Down from equality: Black Chicagoans and the public schools, 1920-1940. Champaign-Urbana, IL: University of Illinois Press.

Jaques, E. (1955). Social systems as a defense against persecutory and depression anxiety. In M. Klein, P. Heimann, & R. E. Money-Kyrle (Eds.), New directions in psychoanalysis (pp. 277-299). London: Tavistock.

Kilbourne, J. (1999). Can't buy my love: How advertising changes the way we think and feel. New York: Simon & Schuster.

Kuhn, T. (1962). Structure of scientific revolutions. Chicago: University of Chicago Press.

Lasn, K. (2000). Culture jam: How to reverse America's suicidal consumer binge—And why we must. New York: Quill.

Leadbeater, B. J. R., & Way, N. (Eds.). (1996). Urban girls: Resisting stereotypes, creating identities. New York: New York University Press.

Lewin, K. (1951). Field theory in social science: Selected papers (D. Cartwright, Ed.). New York: Harper.

McLaren, P., & Giroux, H. A. (1994). Between borders: Pedagogy and the politics of cultural studies. New York: Routledge.

Menzies, I. E. P. (1975). A case-study in the functioning of social systems as a defense against anxiety. In A. D. Colman & W. H. Bexton (Eds.), Group relations reader I. Washington, DC: A.K. Rice Institute.

Minow, N. N., & LeMay, C. L. (1995). Abandoned in the wasteland: Children, television, and the first amendment. New York: Hill & Wang.

Morrison, T. (2002). Freeing the imagination of America. Keynote address, PEN Annual Conference. Assessment and Accountability: The Great Equity Debate 11/11/02-11/13/02.

Obholzer, A., & Roberts, V. Z. (Eds.). (1994). The unconscious at work: Individual and organizational stress in the human services. London, New York: Routledge.

Payne, Y. A. (2001). Black men and street life as a site of resiliency: A counter story for Black scholars. International Journal of Critical Psychology (4), 109-122.

Powell, L. C. (1994). Interpreting social defenses: Family groups in an urban setting. In M. Fine (Ed.), Chartering urban school reform: Reflections on public high schools in the midst of change. New York: Teachers College Press.

Rich, A. (1983). Compulsory heterosexuality & lesbian existence. In A. Snitow, C. Stansell, & S. Thompson (Eds.), Power of desire: The politics of sexuality (pp. 177-205). New York: Monthly Review Press.

Rioch, M. J. (1975). "All we like sheep—" [Isaiah 53:6]: Followers and leaders. In A. D. Colman & W. H. Bexton (Eds.), Group relations reader I. Washington, DC: A. K. Rice Institute.

Shapiro, E. R., & Carr, A. W. (1991). Lost in familiar places: Creating new connections between the individual and society. New Haven, CT: Yale University Press.

Senge, P. M. (1990). The fifth discipline: The art and practice of the learning organization. New York: Doubleday.

Smith, K. K., & Berg, D. N. (1987). Paradoxes of group life: Understanding conflict, paralysis, and movement in group dynamics. San Francisco: Jossey Bass.

Smith, K. K., Simmons, V. M., & Thames, T. B. (1989). "Fix the women": An intervention into an organizational conflict based on parallel process thinking. The Journal of Applied Behavioral Science, 25(1), 11-29.

Style, E., & Powell, L. C. (1995). In our own hands: A diversity primer. Transformations (2), 65-84.

Toussaint, P., Boyd-Franklin, N., & Franklin, A. J. (2000). Boys into men: Raising our African American teenage sons. New York: Dutton/Penguin Books.

Walkerdine, V. (2002). Challenging subjects. London: Palgrave Publishers.

Ward, J. (2001). Raising resisters. In M. Fine & L. Weis (Eds.), Constructions sites. New York: Teachers College Press.

Wasley, P., et al. (2000). Executive summary: Small schools: Great strides: A study of new small schools in Chicago. New York: Bank Street College.

Wellesley College, C. f. R. o. W. (1992). How schools shortchange girls: A study of major findings on girls in education. AAUW Educational Foundation.

Wells, L. (1985). The group-as-a-whole perspective and its theoretical roots. In A. D. Colman & M. H. Geller (Eds.), Group relations reader 2. Sausalito, CA: GREX.

Wolff, M. J. (1999). The entertainment economy: How media forces are transforming our lives. New York: Crown Publishing Group.

LINDA C. POWELL is a Clinical Psychologist and an internationally-known group relations consultant, in the tradition of the Tavistock Institute of Human Relations in London, England. Currently, she is Visiting Professor at the Graduate Center of the City University of New York as well as Affiliated Faculty at the Leadership Institute, University of San Diego. Using an interdisciplinary set of skills as Educator, Organizational Consultant, and Psychotherapist, Dr. Powell has been working with groups and individuals on issues of power and change for almost thirty years. In addition to her corporate consultation and coaching efforts, she works in education reforms, most recently with the nationally-noted research report on the impact of Chicago small-schools movement, "Small Schools, Great Strides." Dr. Powell has authored several articles and book chapters on leadership and urban school reform, most recently, "Savage inequalities indeed: Irrationality and urban school reform" with Maggie Barber and "From charity to justice: Toward a theology of urban school reform." She is the co-editor of Off-

White: Reading on race, power and society (Routledge Press). She is currently working on a book-length exploration of the dilemmas of social identity, leadership, and organizational change and is the President of Resources for Change, Inc., a consulting firm specializing in organizational transformation.

From *Journal of Social Issues*, Spring 2003, pp. 197-211. © 2003 by Blackwell Publishers, Ltd. Reprinted with permission.

The Future of Adolescence:
Lengthening Ladders to Adulthood

BY REED LARSON

Navigating the social and economic complexities of adult life requires more savvy and education than ever.

The life stage of adolescence is a crucial link in the future of society. It is a period when young people either become prepared for and enthusiastic about taking over adult roles, or they rebel against the expectations and responsibilities of adulthood. When things go right, adolescents enter adulthood with new energy and ideas that revitalize society and its institutions.

As we move into the twenty-first century, this life stage is changing rapidly across the world due to globalization, shifting job markets, and transformations in the family, among other things. It is crucial to learn how these changes affect young people's preparedness for the social and economic complexities of the adult world. The Study Group on Adolescence in the 21st Century, composed of a consortium of international scholars, examined the various contours of adolescents' preparation for the years ahead. The Group found that, although the demands on adolescents and the hazards they face in reaching adulthood are increasing, many young people are rising to the challenge.

A Raised Bar for Adulthood

What we expect of young people is extraordinary. First, we expect them to attend school for 12 to 18 years or longer without any guarantee that this education will match what they will need for career success. We ask them to make a leap of trust based on the assumption that the skills they are learning will be relevant when they eventually enter adulthood. Furthermore, we expect them to study without financial remuneration, accept a generic identity defined by their student role, and delay starting a family while in school. These circumstances put young people in a kind of limbo status for years.

As society evolves, this period of limbo continues to lengthen. Young people around the world are being expected to delay entry into adulthood ever longer. This is happening, in large part, because the platform one needs to reach for suc-

cessful adulthood is getting higher. An information society requires that young people learn more to become full members.

In postindustrial societies, we expect people to attend school until they're at least 22 years old—with no guarantee that their studies will lead to future employment, says author Reed Larson.

Education tops the list of new demands for adulthood, as more and more jobs, including manufacturing and service jobs, require literacy, numeracy, and computer skills. Brains are increasingly valued over brawn: In the United States, entry-level wages for people with only a high-school education have fallen by more than 20% since the 1970s. Job prospects are bleaker than ever for youths who do not continue their education after high school, and while there are exceptions—like the teenager who starts a basement computer business and becomes a multimillionaire—working a string of low-paying service jobs with no medical insurance is a much more common scenario for those with limited education.

The growing need for literacy skills in adult life extends beyond the workplace. Literacy is required to navigate complex insurance papers, retirement packages, legal regulations, and countless other complicated bureaucracies that are part of everyday life. Adults must be literate just to keep up with their own health care. Whereas 40 years ago patients were simply told what to do by their doctors, today patients are expected to be partners in their health management and to keep up with ever-changing research on diet, exercise, and disease prevention and treatment.

In addition to literacy, adolescents need to develop more versatile interpersonal skills to navigate the different worlds of home, work, and school—worlds of increasing complexity and diversity. Adult relationships are becoming less scripted and more transient, and teens need to develop skills for negotiating more *ad hoc* associations. Adults also must be able to operate in more-diverse social worlds. On the job, around the neighborhood, even within families, there is an increased likelihood that young people will need to know how to relate with people from different cultural and religious backgrounds. In developing the knowledge and vernaculars to move smoothly and communicate effectively across various social worlds, adolescents will need to acquire skills to change language, posture, tone, and negotiation strategies to adapt to multiple milieus. The adolescent who is able to function in only one world is increasingly ill-prepared for adult life.

Obstacles to Adulthood

As the platform of adulthood rises, the ladders required to get there lengthen. These boosted demands and longer ladders can increase the precariousness of adolescence, since a longer climb to adulthood creates new disadvantages for those who lack the financial means, emotional support, or mental capacity to keep climbing.

At work, at home, and at play, the human landscape increasingly features the co-mingling of individuals from different cultural, religious, and economic backgrounds. It is crucial for teens to develop social skills that will enable them to be comfortable and effective communicating with a variety of people in multiple milieus, suggests the author.

Acquiring advanced education and opportunities for learning diverse life skills often requires family wealth. In the United States, for example, annual college tuition generally ranges from $16,000 to $36,000—a full year's salary for many parents. Even when tuition is covered by grants and scholarships, families must have sufficient wealth to be able to forgo the income their college-bound children would otherwise provide; many poor families, especially in developing countries, cannot afford this sacrifice. By contrast, middle- and upper-class youths throughout the world are gaining access to new resources, such as after-school programs, camps, tutors, travel opportunities, computers and new technologies, which will prepare them for both the literacy and life skills of modern adulthood.

Education and Earnings in the United States

High School	$1.2 million
Bachelor's	$2.1 million
Master's	$2.5 million
Ph.D.	$3.4 million
Professional	$4.4 million

Average lifetime work earnings by educational degree, based on 1999 earnings projected over a typical adult work life from age 25 to 64.

Source: U.S. Census Bureau

Girls are at a particular disadvantage in many nations, facing sex discrimination as an obstacle to obtaining even basic education and social skills. In the Middle East and South Asia, girls are more likely to be pulled from school at an early age and are thus less likely to develop critical literacy skills. Across most of the world, girls face more demands for work in the home and restrictions on movement that constrain their opportunities to gain direct experience with diverse social worlds. As rates of divorce and abandonment rise worldwide, so do the risks for young women who fail to obtain skills to function independently. As they reach adulthood, uneducated women are increasingly vulnerable to poverty and exploitation.

Even academically skilled youths from middle-class families are subject to new perils on the climb to adulthood. The rapidly changing job market makes it difficult to predict what opportunities will be available when these adolescents finally seek employment. Entire sectors can disappear on short notice when industries move their operations abroad or close shop altogether.

High school and college curricula in the United States, many critics argue, provide a poor fit to the job market. Schools in many developing countries in South Asia and Africa are using curricula that have changed little since they were colonies of Western nations, focusing on memorization rather than critical thinking and on areas such as classics rather than marketable skills in computer technology or business. The result is growing numbers of youths who are educated but unemployed.

Backlash against Limbo

It is also the case that a longer climb to adulthood, resulting in a longer period of limbo, can increase the stress experienced by adolescents. Even worse, it can lead to behaviors that arrest their process of preparation. In the United States, the experience of stress among young people has been steadily increasing. In 1999, 30% of college freshmen reported being "frequently overwhelmed," up from 16% in 1985.

The lengthening of ladders, then, increases the risk that more youths will "fall off." Adolescents who, for whatever reason, do not continue in education increasingly find themselves stuck in a low-paying and unstable labor pool.

Young people tend to live in the present moment and find immediate attractions much more appealing than long-term goals—especially when the achievement of those goals is abstract and being pushed further and further away. There is increasing possibility that adolescents will respond to the high-pressure, competitive worlds they are being asked to take on by turning off or turning away.

Societies must be concerned with a major unknown: whether young people, as a group, might rebel against the increasing demands placed upon them and the longer period of limbo they must endure. This result is increasingly probable as adolescents are spending more time with peers than they did in the past, which is creating distinct youth cultures in many societies. These youth cultures might become vehicles of mass resistance to adult society, like the hippie culture of the 1960s.

In New Zealand, Maori adolescents have drawn on American rap and hip-hop culture to resist assimilation into the mainstream. The attraction of radical Islam to many youths reflects a reaction against the competition and materialism of the new global world. In some cases these adolescents' resistance may lead to their joining militant groups, while in others it may simply mean that they enter adulthood unprepared to hold a job and raise a family.

However, we should not be too alarmist. Resistance is most likely when the ladders to adulthood are uninviting, poorly marked, and when the outcomes are uncertain—all things we can do something about. There is also a strong likelihood that the new youth cultures in the twenty-first century will lead society in positive directions. Often youth movements are inspired by pursuit of core human values: compassion, authenticity, and renewal of meaning. It is possible that generational "revolt" will pull societies away from the frantic lifestyles, shallow materialism, and divisive competitiveness that are accompanying globalization. It should be kept in mind that youths in most cases are a positive force.

Rising to the Challenge

The Study Group found that youths in most parts of the world report being optimistic about their lives and that, despite the greater demands and longer ladders, the majority of young people are rising to the challenge. Rates of illiteracy among 15-year-olds have fallen from 37% to 20% since 1970, UNESCO statistics show. Rates of high school and college graduation across most nations continue to climb. And there is little question that many young women have more versatile skills for taking care of themselves and navigating public environments today than 50 years ago. In the United States, teenage rates of pregnancy and violence have fallen substantially across the last decade, indicating that fewer teens are getting off track.

The most convincing scientific evidence of the increasing abilities of youth comes from IQ test scores. New Zealand political scientist James Flynn gathered intelligence test scores of young people over the last 70 years. Because new norms for the

tests are established every few years, the publicly reported scores have shown little change. Once Flynn went back to the unadjusted scores, however, he found the IQs of young people rose dramatically over this period: The average IQ of a young adult today is 20 points higher than in 1940. There is no way to pinpoint what accounts for this increase, but it seems likely that youths' abilities have grown as they have responded to the increased complexity of modern life.

Web Resources on Youth Trends

- **Search Institute**, www.search-institute.org
  Social science organization focuses on youth development in multiple community and society settings.
- **2001 Monitoring the Future Study**,
  www.nida.nih.gov/Infofax/HSYouthtrends.html
  Study on the extent of drug abuse among eighth, tenth, and twelfth graders, conducted annually by the University of Michigan's Institute for Social Research and funded by the National Institute on Drug Abuse.
- **Ewing Marion Kauffman Foundation**,
  www.emkf.org
  Researches and identifies unfulfilled needs in society, then develops, implements, and/or funds solutions to help young people achieve success in school and life.
- **Youth Values 2000**, www.youthvalues.org
  International project, initiated by the International Sport and Culture Association, exploring young people's self-image, values, and beliefs about the world around them.
- **European Youth Forum**, www.youthforum.org
  Youth platform in Europe, composed of youth councils and nongovernmental youth organizations, that works to facilitate communication between young people and decision makers.

The general decrease in family size also contributes to youths' better preparedness for adulthood. Smaller families mean that parents can devote more attention and resources to each child. Parents in many parts of the world are adopting a more responsive and communicative parenting style, which research shows facilitates development of interpersonal skills and enhances mental health.

Other new supports and opportunities have also brightened the outlook for adolescents. Young people receive better health care than they did 50 years ago; consequently, youths around the world are much less likely to die from disease. The Internet provides an important new vehicle for some young people (though as yet a very small percentage of the world's youth) to access a wealth of information. Via the Net, adolescents can also run businesses, participate in social movements, and develop relationships; they are less handicapped by traditional barriers of age.

As a result of these opportunities and their own initiative, the current generation of youth is smarter, more mature, and more socially versatile than any generation in human history. They are better able to function in multiple worlds, collaborate in teams, and solve unstructured problems. We must not underestimate the ways in which adolescents in all parts of the world and of all social classes may draw on their youthful reservoirs of energy and optimism to forge fresh directions and develop new skills.

However, it would be a mistake to be too sanguine. Adolescence in the twenty-first century provides many opportunities for youths to make wrong turns or just become turned off, never to realize their true potential. In order to keep adolescents on the right track, society needs to provide more diverse kinds of ladders for people with different learning styles and socioeconomic backgrounds, regardless of sex or ethnicity. Many jobs involve skills that do not correspond to those tested in school, and we need to provide avenues for them to receive non-academic opportunities to grow and shine—internships, job skills workshops, even art classes, to name a few.

There should also be way stations along the climb that allow young people to rest, gather themselves, and consider alternatives. The success of government, business, the arts, and private life in 2050 and beyond depends on how well we nurture and inspire the next generation to take over and give their best.

About the Author
Reed Larson leads the Study Group on Adolescence in the 21st Century, which was sponsored by the Society for Research on Adolescence and the International Society for Behavioral Development. He is a professor in the Department of Human and Community Development at the University of Illinois, 1105 West Nevada Street, Urbana, Illinois 61801. E-mail larsonR@uiuc.edu.

For more information on the Study Group, visit its Web site, www.s-r-a.org/studygroup.html.

UNIT 2

Puberty, Physical Development, and Health

Unit Selections

Key Points to Consider

- How can teens be encouraged to actively engage in physical activity and a good diet? What factors lead teens to abuse their bodies?

- How does the media influence teen body image and how can this influence be minimized?

- How do hormones and the developing brain affect the emotions of teens?

- Is the use of prescription drugs for adolescent disorders out of control?

- How can educators guide teens into healthy adulthood and help them not take the road to risk-taking behavior?

- What can be done to reduce serious health injuries caused from teenage sports?

Student Website

www.mhcls.com/online

Internet References

Further information regarding these websites may be found in this book's preface or online.

Developmental Psychology
  http://www.psy.pdx.edu/PsiCafe/Areas/Developmental/Puberty/

Adolescent Health
  http://www.ama.org/ama/pub/category/1947.html

The physical changes accompanying the onset of puberty are usually the first clear indicators that a child is entering the period of adolescence. The changes can be a source of both pride and humiliation for the developing adolescent. These physiological changes are regulated by a structure in the brain known as the hypothalamus. The hypothalamus is responsible for stimulating increased production of hormones that control development of the primary and secondary sex characteristics. Primary sex characteristics include physical changes in the reproductive system. Examples include growth of the ovaries and testicles. Secondary sex characteristics are physical changes not directly involved in reproduction. Examples include voice changes, height increases, growth of facial hair in males and breast development in females.

The hypothalamus signals the pituitary gland which in turn stimulates the gonads to produce hormones (androgens and estrogens). The hypothalamus then detects the level of sex hormones present in the bloodstream and calls for either more or less hormone production. During childhood the hypothalamus is very sensitive to sex hormones and keeps production at a low level. For some reason that is not yet completely known, the hypothalamus changes its sensitivity to the sex hormones in adolescence. As a result, significantly greater quantities of sex hormones are needed before the hypothalamus signals the pituitary gland to shut down production. The thyroid and adrenal glands also play a role in the development of secondary sex characteristics.

The physiological changes themselves occur over a 5 to 6 year span. Girls generally start to undergo puberty 18 to 24 months before boys, with the typical onset at 10 or 11. The earliest pubertal changes in girls are breast budding, height spurt, and sparse pubic hair. Experiencing a first menstrual cycle is a midpubertal event, with the average age of menarche in the United States currently being 12 years old. For boys, initial signs of puberty are that the testicles begin to increase in size and the height spurt begins—facial hair, deepening voice, and first ejaculation occur later.

The sequence of pubertal changes is fairly constant across individuals; however, the timing of puberty varies greatly from one person to the next. Some adolescents are out of step with their peers because they mature early, whereas others are late-maturers. The advantages and disadvantages of early versus late maturation have been the subject of much research, so a few readings touch on this topic. One conclusion is that early maturation is correlated with earlier involvement in risk-taking behaviors like alcohol use and sexual activity. In extreme cases, biological disorders result in delayed or precocious puberty, but there are new medications for treating these conditions.

The onset of puberty is affected by diet, exercise, and genetic history. Largely due to improved nutrition and to better control of illnesses, puberty occurs 3 to 4 years earlier in the twenty-first century than it did 150 years ago. Adolescents today also grow several inches taller and weigh more. A visit to historical homes will show that the doorways and beds were much smaller in previous centuries. This trend toward earlier maturation is a worldwide phenomenon that has presumably reached a leveling off point. Adolescents experience psychological and social challenges related to puberty. For example, sexual arousal increases and the teenager must learn how to handle sexual situations. Likewise, gender-typical behavior is more expected by others observing the youth. The adolescent must also incorporate bodily changes into his or her self-image. Concerns about physical appearance become a major preoccupation and play a significant role in self-esteem at this time. These issues are addressed in this unit. In particular, the readings examine the body image concerns adolescents experience. This contributes to adolescents' anxiety about their bodies and how "normal" they are. On the other hand, other cultures employ rites of passage to mark entrance into manhood or womanhood. Many such rites of passage involve physical markings on the adolescent—such as circumcision or body tattooing.

The first two selections in this unit discuss health and body image. The first article by Jennifer O'Dea describes a study of teens and their eating and exercise habits. The participants in the study reported that when they practice healthy habits they do so to enhance their endurance and performance in sporting events. For those participants who don't practice healthier life styles, the article also explores barriers to good teen health. The final essay in this unit pertains to adolescent body image. Body image is very important to most adolescents because it is closely tied to self-esteem or self-worth. The article would be incomplete if it did not provide information on how teens can improve their own feelings about themselves.

Claudia Wallis presents an interesting examination of the brain and explains the origin of attention-deficit and hyperactivity. The effect that the developing brain and hormones have on the emotions of youth is examined.

Jeffrey Kluger states that some physicians believe that medication use is out of control. Although prescription drugs can ease the symptoms of a number of adolescent disorders the long-term effects are unknown.

Some adolescents seek intense emotional experiences which result in risk-taking behaviors. Lisa Price provides suggestions to educators that will guide teens into healthy adulthood. Risk-taking behaviors that are unhealthy are sometimes encouraged by tough training for athletes in some sports. This can cause serious health issues years later.

Why do kids eat healthful food?

Perceived benefits of and barriers to healthful eating and physical activity among children and adolescents.

Jennifer A. O'Dea

The goal was to have children and adolescents identify and rank the major perceived benefits of and barriers to healthful eating and physical activity and to suggest strategies for overcoming barriers. Semistructured, in-depth focus groups were undertaken using standardized questions and prompts. Students in grades 2 through 11 (ages 7 through 17; N=213) from 34 randomly selected schools participated in 38 focus groups. Major benefits of healthful eating included improvements to cognitive and physical performance, fitness, endurance, psychological benefits, physical sensation (feeling good physically), and production of energy. Barriers included convenience, taste, and social factors. Benefits of physical activity included social benefits, enhancement of psychological status, physical sensation, and sports performance. Barriers included a preference for indoor activities, lack of energy and motivation, time constraints, and social factors. Suggested strategies for overcoming barriers included support from parents and school staff, better planning, time management, self-motivation, education, restructuring the physical environment, and greater variety of physical activities. J Am Diet Assoc. 2003; 103: 497-501.

Health education theories (1-2) suggest that health behaviors are influenced in part by the perceived benefits of and barriers to a specified action. Social learning theory (3) emphasizes the importance of understanding personal beliefs and motivations underlying different behaviors, and the need to emphasize short-term and tangible benefits of behaviors. Obtaining a detailed understanding of the perceived benefits of and barriers to healthful eating and physical activity among children and adolescents forms the first step in designing appropriate dietary counseling and would be very valuable in the planning of health and nutrition education treatment and prevention programs, particularly obesity prevention programs.

There is a paucity of published studies about children's and adolescent's perceived benefits of healthful eating together with their perceived barriers to these practices. Several studies (4-8) have explored barriers to healthful eating, typically asking children and adolescents why they do not eat healthful foods and drinks, but few have investigated why they do eat healthful foods or what factors motivate this behavior.

Barriers to healthful eating, identified in previous studies, include a lack of sense of urgency about personal health; undesirable taste, appearance and smell of healthful food; lack of time; limited availability of choice; and convenience (5-8).

The major goal of this study was to answer the question, "Why do children and adolescents eat healthful foods and engage in physical activity?"

METHODS

The focus groups included 213 school students (51% female) from school grades 2 through 11 in 34 schools representing all states and territories of Australia and including a representative mix of ethnicity and socioeconomic status. Forty school principals were invited to participate, and two declined because of time constraints. Participants were randomly selected from class lists and given parental consent forms to return (98.3% response rate). A total of 38 focus group discussions were conducted, each lasting 20 to 30 minutes. A total of 15.8 hours of tape-recorded interviews were obtained and transcribed verbatim to produce a manuscript. The data were then analyzed using content analysis (9-12), which involved the systematic examination of the transcripts to identify and group emergent clusters and themes, and then code, classify, and develop major categories of themes.

RESULTS

Healthful foods were frequently defined by grade 3 through 11 students as fruits, vegetables, juice, pasta, rice, milk, and cheese, and less frequently as bread, cereals, meat, chicken, and water.

The most important benefits of healthful eating (Table 1) were enhancement of cognitive function, physical performance, psychological factors, and physical sensation, and production of energy. These five themes were consistently described by both sexes from all school grades and ethnic groups.

Older participants in grades 6 through 11 were able to clearly articulate the "refreshing" effect of healthful foods, particularly fruits and vegetables, as they related to the enhanced function of the body, mind, and psyche. Participants commonly used descriptive words such as "clean" "refresh," "feeling good," and "revived." Contrasting themes about the benefits of healthful eating included descriptions about the adverse effects of "junk foods" (defined as candy, chocolate, soda, fast foods, fried foods), which were described as slowing down the mind and body, draining the body of energy, making the body and mind feel "slow" and "heavy," and "clogging up the system." Eating "junk foods" was accompanied by guilt that contrasted with the psychological benefits of healthful eating, including personal pride, self-reward, and a sense of accomplishment and self-efficacy.

An overlapping theme was the clearly articulated link between healthful eating and physical performance. Participants clearly reported that the benefits of healthful eating enabled physical fitness, endurance, and physical well-being, whereas the impact of "junk food" reversed the beneficial physical effects and caused a "draining of energy" and subsequently resulted in more physical inactivity.

The benefits of healthful eating to appearance, weight control, immunity, longevity, and future health were articulated by males and females of all ages, but were ranked as moderately important, well below the importance of the other benefits.

The major barriers to healthful eating are given in Table 1. The theme of parental control over the food supply was notable, with the vast majority of participants of all ages indicating that they eat what is available and allowable at home, at school, and at friends' homes. Advertising for "junk foods" and price were identified as minor barriers.

Participants in grades 5 through 11 were able to suggest strategies for overcoming the barriers to healthful eating, but younger children could not. The major strategies included the following:

- Parental support, as described above;
- Planning to eat more healthful foods and drinks—carrying healthful foods to school; not taking money to school; reducing the availability of 'junk food" at home, school, and community; increasing the availability of healthful foods at home and school to reduce boredom and to motivate interest;
- Cognitive strategies—using self-motivation strategies to remind oneself of the many benefits of healthful eating and the undesirable short-term impact of "junk foods"; and
- Educational strategies—-increasing information and education about food and nutrition; increasing advertising of healthful foods to make them more appealing; receiving personal advice from a doctor or dietitian about healthful eating habits.

The major benefits of and barriers to physical activity are given in Table 2. Minor benefits included health protection (eg, heart health, bone strength, weight control).

The theme of feeling tired, sluggish, and lazy was clearly linked to the consumption of "junk food." Minor barriers included disinterest in current physical education activities, teasing, self-consciousness, lack of transport, and unsuitable outdoor environment.

Suggested strategies to increase physical activity were identified by participants in grades 5 through 11. These included the following:

- Planning/organization—making arrangements to play with friends, becoming involved in a team, prioritizing physical activity as important and fun;
- Increase variety and excitement of physical activity—participants, particularly teenagers, indicated boredom with existing physical education programs and expressed interest in new and unusual activities such as aerobics, martial arts, Tai Bo, yoga, archery, hiking, rock climbing, and water sports;
- Parental support and involvement—participants of all ages indicated that they would like to do outdoor games and activities with parents and they would like their parents to encourage them to become involved in various physical activities;
- Time management—participants of all ages indicated that they needed to rearrange the amount of time spent on homework, chores, part-time work, and family activities to make time for physical activities; and
- Restructure physical environment—female adolescents indicated that they would like female-ori-

Table 1

Major reported perceived benefits of and barriers to healthful eating identified by children and adolescents[a]

Major benefits (in descending order of importance)	Typical comments
Cognitive function/cognitive performance	
Enhanced concentration and mental function. Mental alertness/mental activity. Improved school performance.	"After eating healthy, it just cleans out the system and you focus better ... I focus better on school work and everything." (11th-grade female)[b]
Physical sensation	
Feel good physically. Feel "fresh and clean" physically, not "clogged up".	"I feel good ... I feel more refreshed ... lighter ... cleaner ... I feel cleaner on the inside." (9th-grade female) "Eating healthy foods is like taking a shower." (8th-grade male)
Psychological benefits	
Self reward—have done something good for self. Cleans, refreshes, and clears mental function. Enhances self-esteem. Reduces guilt and anxiety.	"It's just a personal achievement ... it's my personal feeling like I've done something for myself ..." (8th-grade male) "I like feeling that I've done something good for myself, feeling good about myself ... not feeling guilty." (11th-grade female)
Physical performance	
Enhanced fitness and sports performance. Enhanced strength, energy, endurance.	"It helps me run ... it can make me do things like run ... skip ... jump ... hop ... walk a long way." (3rd-grade female) "It keeps you fit ... like I've got heaps of energy and I eat healthy foods if I want energy ..." (6th-grade male)
Increases production of energy	
"Creates" energy. Sustains energy and endurance. Regulates energy throughout the day.	"... I eat a salad and I feel ... fresh and I feel like going out and doing stuff ... but if I sit there and pig out on junk food, I feel like a blob ... I can't move ..." (9th-grade female) "Every time I eat fruit, I feel revived ... it's energizing." (7th-grade male)
Major barriers to healthful eating (in descending order of importance)	**Typical comments**
Convenience of less healthful alternatives	
Availability of "less healthful" alternatives. Easy and quick preparation of "less healthful" alternatives. Time costs involved in healthful foods.	... and when I get home from school, I think 'I should eat some fruits,' but then I see the chips ... they're easier ... it just feels like the easier thing to do." (6th-grade male)
Internal/physiologic preference	
Prefer taste of "less healthful" alternatives. Satiety of "less healthful" alternatives. Cravings for "less healthful" alternatives. Healthful food "looks and smells dull and boring."	"The sugar is ... a tasty food and sometimes healthy food is kind of yucky and smelly..." (3rd-grade female) "Temptation for all those nutty chocolate things ..." (5th-grade female)
Social reinforcement	
Peer pressure. Parental control over food. Lack of parental/ school support and modeling.	"My parents buy the food ... I think it's the availability of food that's around at the time ..." (11th-grade male) "We have lots of junk food ... my dad's into junk food ..." (5th-grade female)
Reward driven/mood enhancement	
Treating oneself with unhealthful alternatives. Eating when bored/emotional eating. Relieve stress with less healthful alternatives. Less healthful alternatives improve mood and are more fun/exciting.	"Sometimes it all depends on your mood ... if I'm feeling depressed, I just feel like eating chocolate ..." (11th-grade female) "Sometimes I just have to have some junk food ... it makes me feel better ..." (9th-grade male)

[a] Results in Table 1 were obtained by using the following semistructured focus group questions and prompts: What does healthy eating do for you? How? What stops you from having healthy foods and drinks? How? Why? Can you vote on which benefit/barrier is most important or has the greatest effect on you?

[b] Approximate age ranges (in years) for school grade levels: 3rd grade=8 to 9; 4th=9 to 10; 5th=10 to 11; 6th=11 to 12; 7th=12 to 13; 8th=13 to 14; 9th=14 to 15; 10th=15 to 16; 11th=16 to 17; 12th=17 to 18.

Table 2

Major reported, perceived benefits of and barriers to physical activity among childrenand adolescents[a]

Major benefits (in descending order of importance)	Typical comments
Social benefits	
Fun/enjoyment. Socializing with friends. Enjoyment of teamwork, team identity. Fitness aids other areas of life (eg, coping). Development of life skills. Parental approval.	"It's fun ... just playing with your friends." (4th-grade male) [b] "At physical culture ... I just have all these friends that I've known for a long time and to have a social group outside of school ... it just makes me feel better." (9th-grade female) "It's the social part of it that's most important ... having friends in the team is really important so that you have fun and you learn to get on with people ... and the life skills help with the social side." (11th-grade male)
Psychologic enhancement	
Sense of achievement, pride, self-esteem, confidence. Enhanced mood. Develop discipline. Sense of balance in life. Reduces guilt. Enjoyment of challenges and goals, excitement, adrenaline rush.	"You feel better physically and it increases your self-esteem ... because you know you're doing something good for your body ..." (11th-grade female) "Feelings about yourself ... in the mind ... the feeling that you've done something good for yourself ... feeling good about yourself ... not feeling guilty ..." (9th-grade female)
Physical sensation (feeling good physically)	
Feel refreshed, "cleansed." Enjoy sensation of movement. Creation of energy, reduces fatigue. Sensation of well-being, strength, and fitness. Enhanced sleep.	"When you're dancing ... you're sweaty but you don't care ... you just keep on going and then when you go out you feel so good ... you feel so health ..." (11th-grade male) "It makes me feel good ... afterwards my body just feels better..."(9th-grade female) "It uses my energy so I'm not restless in the night and I get good sleep." (6th-grade male)
Sports performance	
Improved sports performance. Skill development. Improved coordination, agility, flexibility, reflexes. Improved fitness, strength, endurance.	"It keeps you being able to play well for the whole game ..." (8th-grade male) "Being able to turn and breathe after you run ..." (10th-grade female)
Cognitive benefits	
Clears mind and thinking. Enhances concentration and brain function.	"It clears my mind for studying ...if I go for a run I can come back and be sharper ...better concentration ..." (11th-grade male)
Coping strategy	
Stress relief, relaxation, distraction from worries, mental break. Outlet for aggression, frustration, and anger. Physical break.	"You get your mind off school, like all the pressures of school ... you just forget about it ... so that's relief." (9th-grade male) "If I'm really, really angry, I can go outside and go for a big walk ..." (11th-grade female) "Sometime I just need to go and punch the punching bag and kick it and it makes me feel heaps ..." (8th-grade female)
Preference for indoor activities	
Prefer to watch television, videos, play on computer. Prefer to play with toys, games, books, music indoors.	"I'm stuck to the television somethimes ... lots of movies ..." (3rd-grade female)
Low energy level	
Feeling tired, lazy, and sluggish. "Junk food" snacks drain energy. Lack of energy.	"I just can't move ... I just don't feel like moving ... I feel tired or I feel lazy ..." (6th-grade male) "Junk food makes you slow-down ... really lazy ... you don't feel like doing anything ..." (3rd-grade female)
Time constraints	
Homework, jobs consume spare time. Other plans, commitments consume time.	"Sometimes I just don't have time because I've got school and I've got homework or I've got to go to work ..." (11th-grade female)
Social factors	
Peer pressure—friends are involved in sedentary activities. Parental control/preferences. Lack of parental support. Lack of playmates or suitable playmates. Teasing/bullying from peers. Criticism from others (peers, teachers).	"... it's like my social life as well ... I just like to go and hang around with friends ... sit and talk ..." (9th-grade female) ...if I want to play with my best friend ... my mom has to drive me there ..." (5th-grade female)"... I hate physical education with boys ... they hog the gear and they laugh at you and tease you ..." (9th-grade female)
Motivation	
Low level of self-motivation. Low level of motivation from others. Low perceived rewards.	"... I'd do more stuff it I had someone to do it with me ... because you'd motivate each other ..." (10th-grade male)

[a]Results in Table 2 were obtained by using the following semistructured focus group questions and prompts: What does physical activity do for you? How? What stops you from being physically active? Why? Can you vote on which benefit/barrier is most important or has the greatest effect on you?

[b]Approximate age ranges (in years for school grade levels: 3rd grade = 8 to 9; 4th =9 to 10; 5th = 10 to 11; 6th = 11 to 12; 7th = 12 to 13; 8th = 13 to 14; 9th = 14 to 15; 10th = 15 to 16; 11th = 16; 11th = 16 to 17; 12th = 17 to 18.

ented sports and activities taught by female teachers in private facilities. They suggested having doors on private showers and changing rooms, and self-selected physical education uniforms.

Children of all ages expressed the need for parents and teachers to help with these strategies.

DISCUSSION

This study presents rich new data on a somewhat neglected area of research, namely, the specific benefits children and adolescents obtain from healthful eating and physical activity.

The study results suggest that the greatest motivator of healthful eating among children and adolescents in grades 5 through 11 is the desire to create a "cleansed," "refreshed," and "energized" mind, body, and emotional state. Participants of both sexes and all ages and ethnicities consistently reported having experienced short-term mental, physical, and psychological benefits from healthful eating as well as similar benefits from physical activity. In agreement with previous findings (5-7), motivating factors of less importance were health protection, benefits to appearance, and weight control, although these benefits were certainly not considered unimportant.

The strong social, psychological, and cognitive benefits of physical activity reported by participants add to the paucity of literature on this topic (13-16) and have the potential to help clinicians, educators, administrators, and parents better understand the strongest motivating factors behind children's health behaviors.

Overlapping themes between the benefits of healthful eating and physical activity included beliefs that both food and exercise have a "cleansing" effect on the body, mind, and emotional state and that "junk food" has the reverse effect. Children and adolescents report that the combination of healthful eating and physical activity confers many benefits to schoolwork by enhancing clear thinking, concentration, sleep, stress control, and energy. Findings about barriers concur with those of previous studies (48, 13-16) with the expansion of themes and addition of a new barrier related to parental control, parental expectations, lack of parental and school support, and lack of role modeling.

Results clearly show that children and adolescents are looking to their parents and teachers to encourage, support, and enable them to be involved in more healthful behaviors.

APPLICATIONS

The combination of these findings, applied within appropriate theoretical frameworks, could be a powerful way of motivating children to seek the health benefits that they identify as most important. In particular, the finding that children and adolescents believe that healthful eating and physical activity confer many interrelated cognitive, physical, and psychological benefits is a new and interesting result that has vast implications for motivating children and adolescents in clinical, community, and educational settings.

This research was supported by a Kellogg Australia Nutrition Research Grant.

Many thanks to the school staff and students who participated in this national research study.

References

1. Ajzen I, Fishbein M. Understanding Attitudes and Predicting Social Behaviour. Englewood Cliffs, NJ: Prentice-Hall; 1980.
2. Ajzen I. The Theory of Planned Behaviour. Organizational Behaviour and Human Decision Processes. 1991;50:179-211.
3. Bandura A. Social Foundations of Thought and Action: A Social Cognitive Theory. Englewood Cliffs, NJ: Prentice-Hall; 1966.
4. Ling A. Perceived benefits and barriers of increased fruit and vegetable consumption: Validation of a decisional balance scale. J Nutr Ed. 2001;33:257-265.
5. Gracey D, Stanley N, Burke V, Corti B, Beilin LJ. Nutritional knowledge, beliefs, and behaviours in teenage school students. Health Ed Res. 1996;11:187-204.
6. Neumark-Sztainer D, Story M, Perry C, Casey MA. Factors influencing food choices of adolescents: Findings from focus group discussions with adolescents. J Am Diet Assoc. 1999;99:929-934,937.
7. California Project Lean. Food on the Run Campaign. Key informant interviews with students, experts and LEAN regional coordinators about healthful eating and physical activity in multicultural youth. Sacramento, CA: Food on the Run Campaign; 1998.
8. Glanz K, Basil M, Maibach 2, Goldberg J, Snyder D. Why Americans eat what they do: Taste, nutrition, cost, convenience and weight control concerns as influences on food consumption. J Am Diet Assoc. 1998;98:1118-1126.
9. Miles MB, Huberman AM. Qualitative Data Analysis: An Expanded Sourcebook. Thousand Oaks, CA: Sage; 1994.
10. Pope C, Maya N. Reaching the parts other methods cannot reach: An introduction to qualitative methods in health and health service research. BMJ. 1995;311:42-45.
11. Britten N. Qualitative interviews in medical research. BMJ. 1995;311:251-253.
12. Mays N, Pope N. Rigour and qualitative research. BMJ. 1995;311:109-112.
13. Heath GW, Pratt M, Warren CW, Kann L. Physical activity patterns in American high school students: Results from the 1990 youth risk behavior survey. Arch Pediatr Adolesc Med. 1994;148:1131-1136.
14. Thompson JL, Davis SM, Gittlesohn J, Going S, Becenti A, Metcalfe L, Stone 2, Harnack L, Ring K. Patterns of physical activity among American Indian children: An assessment of barriers and support. J Community Health. 2001;26:423-445.
15. Wu TY, Pender N. Determinants of physical activity among Taiwanese adolescents: An application of the health promotion model. Res Nurs Health. 2002;25:25-36.
16. Leslie J, Yancy A, McCarthy W, Albert S, Wert C, Miles 0, James J. Development and implementation of a school-based nutrition and fitness promotion program for ethnically diverse middle-school girls. J Am Diet Assoc. 1999;99:967-970.

J A. O'Dea is a faculty member, Department of Education, University of Sydney, Australia, and a visiting scholar, Center for Weight and Health, Department of Nutritional Sciences, University of California, Berkeley, CA. Address correspondence to: Jennifer A. O'Dea, MPH, PhD, RD, University of Sydney, Faculty of Education, ASS, NSW 2006, Australia. E-mail: j.o'dea@edfac.usyd.edu.au

Body Image: How do you see yourself?

**How you feel about your body has a big impact on your health.
Learn to like the person you see in the mirror!**

Kathiann M. Kowalski

Brianna slipped quietly out of the house before dawn. She had lost 30 pounds by dieting, but now the weight was creeping back. She decided to try non-stop exercising for three days. Brianna wasn't thinking about missing school or even being alone by herself on the street. She would start walking and just keep going.

Fifteen hours later, Brianna walked into a police station. Her feet ached, and her sweat-pants were covered with burrs from wandering through a park. She was exhausted, scared, and hungry.

A poor body image had led to Brianna's eating disorder and depression. Her grand exercise plan failed, but it had one good outcome. Brianna finally got help dealing with her problem.

What You See and Feel

Body image is the way you see your body and how you feel about it. People with a healthy body image view themselves realistically and like their physical selves. People with a poor body image feel dissatisfied with their bodies, regardless of whether they are objectively healthy.

Different factors influence a teen's body image. "Certainly the media are setting standards for how girls and boys should look, defining what is beautiful in our culture," says Mimi Nichter. When the University of Arizona professor interviewed girls for her book, Fat Talk: What Girls and Their Parents Say About Dieting, most girls chose a "Barbie-doll" look: tall, thin, and large-breasted.

That same image pervades many ads on television and in magazines. When it comes to males, the media emphasize a tall, lean, muscular look. "People are paid to create an image or an illusion," says Sarah Stinson, head of the eating disorders program at Fairview Red Wing Health Services in Minnesota.

Only about 2 percent of women are as thin as most models, says the National Eating Disorders Association. Models work full-time with exercise trainers, makeup artists, and others to maintain their appearance. At photo shoots, clips and weights mold clothes to flatter a model's body. Once images are shot, computer artists take over. They airbrush pictures to remove any flaws. They can even change the shape of the bodies in the pictures. Thus, the standard media images of beauty often aren't true to life.

Faced with such unrealistic ideals, most teens feel worse about their bodies after reading teen fashion magazines. For those who felt unaccepted or unappreciated in their social environment—up to one-third of girls in one study—the effects lasted longer, according to Eric Stice at the University of Texas at Austin.

"From my perspective," says Stice, "this study is very damning for the mass media." In real life, he adds, most boys think a starved waif look is ugly for girls. And most girls don't like seeing mega-muscles on guys.

Peer pressure also influences a teen's body image. "Teasing can be very painful," says Nichter. "Kids seem to remember that for a very long time."

Frequently talking about weight can wear down someone's body image too. "I guess I started thinking I was fat at the start of high school," says Brianna. "Girls talk about it all the time at school—who's on diets. I would compare myself to other people, and I guess I thought I was fat."

"The majority of young women feel insecure," says Stinson. "What's happening is they're projecting those insecurities on each other, and you're getting this very competitive environment."

Families factor in too. When Brianna was little, her father sometimes commented on her eating a lot. Her brother sometimes called her a "fat pig." In other families, parents may tell a boy to eat so he grows up "big and strong." Or they may wistfully say that a daughter has "such a pretty face"—implying that the rest of her body is ugly.

Growing Pains

Young people internalize those messages. In a study by the Centers for Disease Control and Prevention (CDC), around 30 percent of students thought they were overweight. In reality, less than 14 percent of students were "at risk for becoming overweight." (The term refers to students whose body mass index was above the 85th percentile.)

Yet the 14 percent figure is also a problem. Nearly one-third of students get little or no physical activity, reports the CDC. Higher weight and a sedentary lifestyle increase the risks for diabetes, heart disease, and other health problems. Meanwhile, young people at the higher ranges of the weight scale often feel more frustrated by the gap between what they see in the mirror and what they see in the media.

Puberty complicates things. Girls get taller and gain an average of 25 pounds. They need the added fat for breast development and to enable them to conceive and carry babies as adults.

"Young women don't believe that they should gain fat," says Stinson. "They're terrified of it and don't understand the healthy role of natural body fat in development."

Boys get taller and more muscular as their bodies mature. That's generally consistent with our culture's ideal for males. But not all boys mature at the same rate. And not everyone gains muscle like the images featured in sports and fitness magazines.

When Problems Arise

When teens have a poor body image, self-esteem dips. Relationships suffer too. Conversations with friends may center on dieting and exercise, to the exclusion of other topics. Teens focus more on how they look than on what they want to accomplish in life. Instead of bonding with each other, teens often become competitive. That fuels feelings of isolation.

In the worst cases, eating disorders and other unhealthy behaviors develop. Eating disorders are more common among females than males. Yet the National Eating Disorders Association says about 10 percent of patients are male. (Besides a poor body image, other factors are often to blame. These include feelings of being out of control and, in some cases, a history of physical or sexual abuse.)

Brianna had anorexia nervosa. She did not eat enough to maintain a normal weight for her height. Besides looking very thin, she felt weak and had dizzy spells. Because girls need a certain level of body fat to menstruate, she stopped getting her period regularly. With her immune system weakened, Brianna came down with pneumonia during her sophomore year. Plus, Brianna recalls, "I lost hair. And I was cold all the time."

In addition to these problems, anorexia can cause loss of bone density, dehydration, and downy hair on the skin. When the heart muscle weakens and blood pressure drops too low, fatal heart failure can happen. By experimenting with diet pills, Brianna added to that risk. Even "natural" weight loss products can over-stimulate the heart and cause heart attacks.

Binge eating disorder involves frequent episodes of uncontrolled eating, without regard to physical hunger or fullness. Patients suffer from guilt, shame, or disgust with their behavior. They often gain weight, which adds to any body image problems.

A person with bulimia experiences cycles of binging and purging. Even if a patient's weight stays normal, frequent vomiting causes decaying tooth enamel, swollen glands, a sore throat, and a puffy face. If patients take laxatives, they risk damage to their digestive systems and suffer from nutrient deficiencies.

Exercise bulimia compensates for eating with excessive physical activity. In her junior year of high school, actress Jamie Lynn Sigler exercised every day for hours. Her weight dropped to 90 pounds.

"As time went on, it began to take over my life and interfere with other things that were important to me," Jamie recalled, "like hanging out with my friends, my family, dance and theatre, and even my health." When she began thinking about suicide, Jamie finally confided in her parents. The book Wise Girl: What I've Learned About Life, Love, and Loss tells the story of her recovery.

Body dysmorphia, a distorted body image, can also lead to excessive bodybuilding, especially among boys. Some also abuse steroids—drugs that unnaturally mimic the hormone testosterone to spur muscle growth. Risks of steroid abuse include possible outbreaks of violence during use and depression after cycling off the drugs, plus other physical and psychological consequences.

"When you have an eating disorder, you really don't want to talk about it," said Sigler. "You get very defensive. You isolate yourself a lot." If you're concerned about a friend, keep telling that person, "I'm here for you when you're ready to talk about it."

Building a Healthier Body Image

A doctor specializing in eating disorders gave Brianna a thorough check-up and prescribed medicine to help her clinical depression. Brianna also meets regularly with a psychologist, who has given her strategies to build a healthier body image.

"She had me write a list of things I like about myself," says Brianna. "When I start comparing myself to people, I think of one of those things rather than thinking, 'Oh, she looks so good and I look so bad.'" Among other things, Brianna is very intelligent. She is a hard worker. She is great at ballet. She plays the flute beautifully. And she likes her pretty blonde hair and blue eyes.

Dance class can still be a challenge, since the other advanced students are very thin. Brianna is learning to accept that people have different body shapes: ectomorphic, mesomorphic, and endomorphic. Ectomorphic people are very thin. Mesomorphic people are muscular. Endomorphic people tend to carry more fat. Many people's bodies mix these characteristics. Thus, one part of the body may be muscular, while another part may gain fat easily.

Brianna also met with a dietitian. When she was constantly dieting, she skipped meals. By nighttime she was so hungry that she might eat half a box of cereal. Now she's eating regular meals and including a reasonable amount of fat. She feels healthier and stronger. Now that she's eating regular meals again, she socializes more with other students at lunchtime too.

Another helpful strategy is to change the pattern of "fat talk" among friends. Sometimes teens join in the talk as a way to fit in. Other times, "I feel fat" can be code for other feelings that young people feel uncomfortable talking about: loneliness, disappointment, anger, insecurity, and so on. If teens encourage each other to talk about what's really bothering them, they can break the cycle of putting their bodies down. Clearer communication also frees teens to help each other deal with problems constructively.

Taking Charge

The media emphasize unrealistic standards of beauty. But, says Stinson, "You don't have to buy into these messages." She encourages young people to become activists: Write letters to companies praising ads that show normal teens with different body shapes and sizes. Conversely, send complaints and boycott companies that exploit young people by sexualizing them or glorifying thinness.

Don't fall prey to the dieting industry either.

Even "natural" weight-loss pills can contain stimulants that cause serious health problems. And despite "money-back guarantees," diet gizmos and gimmicks don't work. If any one did work, would Americans continue to spend $40 billion a year on books, diet programs, pills, gadgets, and everything else the dieting industry produces?

You can help educate other young people about having a healthy body image. In Minnesota, teen members of Red Wing GO GIRLS! make frequent presentations to help other young people develop a positive body image. By teaching others, the teens have become role models who are very proud of their own bodies.

Your Body, Your Health

"It's not your weight that determines your health," says Stinson. "It's your lifestyle." Here are some tips for a healthy lifestyle:

- Eat a variety of foods when you're physically hungry. Refer to the U.S. Department of Agriculture's Food Guide Pyramid www.nal.usda.gov:8001/py/pmap.htm).
- Don't forget the calcium: The Food and Drug Administration (FDA) recommends four servings of calcium-rich foods a day for teens.

- Enjoy regular physical activities. Aim for at least 30 minutes a day most days of the week. Set realistic goals for yourself, and have a good time. The more your body can do, the better you'll feel about it.

Brianna is enjoying dance more now. She also has joined her school's swim team and enjoys the camaraderie with her teammates. When the team members feel tired after a practice, it's a good feeling. "As long as you're healthy and active, and your body is doing everything it's supposed to do, there's nothing wrong with your body shape," she says.

Based on her experience, Brianna adds this message to teens: "You're OK the way you are. Think of the many great things you are—you're like no one else. Just don't ever try to compare yourself with anyone because it's not worth it. You have to be yourself."

Reality Check: Show YOUR Appreciation

Real life heroes aren't people who stand around looking good. They're people who accomplish things and share their talents with others. In fact, you may be surprised about the things other people admire in you.

Try the following exercise:

1. Sit down with a group of classmates. Let each person take turns telling every other person something positive that they sincerely appreciate about the other person. The positive thing must be something other than physical appearance.
2. When group members hear something positive about themselves, they must look directly at the speaker and say thank you. No mumbling allowed!
3. Promise aloud to go for a week without commenting at all on anyone's weight or physical appearance. Enforce the agreement among yourselves.
4. For an added challenge, avoid looking at yourself in the mirror for two days. Talk with classmates about how hard or easy it was.

How WEIGHT CHANGES Can Affect You

If you think losing 10 or even 20 pounds will make life wonderful, think again. The standard media images of beauty are not realistic. Even if you lost weight, you probably still would not match that ideal.

Initially, people who lose weight often feel proud of themselves. When many people hit a plateau, they feel frustrated. Weight levels off, despite continued dieting. The body naturally resists losing more than a small percentage of its weight too quickly. The metabolism slows down.

The National Eating Disorders Association says that 95 percent of people who diet gain back the weight within one to five years. That yo-yo effect places physical stress on the body. Gaining the weight back can further damage self-esteem.

More important, weight loss won't make all of life's problems go away. Dating and other social encounters can still be rocky. Family relationships can still be perplexing. School and work remain challenging.

Before you try to lose any weight, talk to your doctor or a dietitian. Body mass index (BMI) varies tremendously. Health professionals usually recommend weight loss only for people at the high end of the range. (BMI equals weight in pounds divided by height in inches, divided by height in inches again, multiplied by 703.)

Instead of going on a diet, many health professionals stress a healthy lifestyle. That includes a reasonable amount of enjoyable physical activity. It also includes healthy eating behaviors. Instead of wolfing down food on the run, for example, try slowing down and enjoying what you're eating. You can also learn to make smart nutrition choices by watching serving sizes and keeping the USDA's Food Guide Pyramid in mind.

From *Current Health 2*, Vol. 29, No. 7, March 2003, pp. 6-12. © 2003 by Weekly Reader Corporation. Reprinted with permission.

What Makes Teens Tick

A flood of hormones, sure. But also a host of structural changes
in the brain. Can those explain the behaviors that make
adolescence so exciting—and so exasperating?

Claudia Wallis

Five young men in sneakers and jeans troop into a waiting room at the National Institutes of Health Clinical Center in Bethesda, Md., and drape themselves all over the chairs in classic collapsed-teenager mode, trailing backpacks, a CD player and a laptop loaded with computer games. It's midafternoon, and they are, of course, tired, but even so their presence adds a jangly, hormonal buzz to the bland, institutional setting. Fair-haired twins Corey and Skyler Mann, 16, and their burlier big brothers Anthony and Brandon, 18, who are also twins, plus eldest brother Christopher, 22, are here to have their heads examined. Literally. The five brothers from Orem, Utah, are the latest recruits to a giant study that's been going on in this building since 1991. Its goal: to determine how the brain develops from childhood into adolescence and on into early adulthood.

It is the project of Dr. Jay Giedd (pronounced *Geed*), chief of brain imaging in the child psychiatry branch at the National Institute of Mental Health. Giedd, 43, has devoted the past 13 years to peering inside the heads of 1,800 kids and teenagers using high-powered magnetic resonance imaging (MRI). For each volunteer, he creates a unique photo album, taking MRI snapshots every two years and building a record as the brain morphs and grows. Giedd started out investigating the developmental origins of attention-deficit/hyperactivity disorder (ADHD) and autism ("I was going alphabetically," he jokes) but soon discovered that so little was known about how the brain is supposed to develop that it was impossible to figure out where things might be going wrong. In a way, the vast project that has become his life's work is nothing more than an attempt to establish a gigantic control group. "It turned out that normal brains were so interesting in themselves," he marvels. "And the adolescent studies have been the most surprising of all."

Before the imaging studies by Giedd and his collaborators at UCLA, Harvard, the Montreal Neurological Institute and a dozen other institutions, most scientists believed the brain was largely a finished product by the time a child reached the age of 12. Not only is it full-grown in size, Giedd explains, but "in a lot of psychological literature, traced back to [Swiss psychologist Jean] Piaget, the highest rung in the ladder of cognitive development was about age 12—formal operations." In the past, children entered initiation rites and started learning trades at about the onset of puberty. Some theorists concluded from this that the idea of adolescence was an artificial construct, a phenomenon invented in the post—Industrial Revolution years. Giedd's scanning studies proved what every parent of a teenager knows: not only is the brain of the adolescent far from mature, but both gray and white matter undergo extensive structural changes well past puberty. "When we started," says Giedd, "we thought we'd follow kids until about 18 or 20. If we had to pick a number now, we'd probably go to age 25."

Now that MRI studies have cracked open a window on the developing brain, researchers are looking at how the newly detected physiological changes might account for the adolescent behaviors so familiar to parents: emotional outbursts, reckless risk taking and rule breaking, and the impassioned pursuit of sex, drugs and rock 'n' roll. Some experts believe the structural changes seen at adolescence may explain the timing of such major mental illnesses as schizophrenia and bipolar disorder. These diseases typically begin in adolescence and contribute to the high rate of teen suicide. Increasingly, the wild conduct once blamed on "raging hormones" is being seen as the byproduct of two factors: a surfeit of hormones, yes, but also a paucity of the cognitive controls needed for mature behavior.

In recent years, Giedd has shifted his focus to twins, which is why the Manns are such exciting recruits. Although most brain development seems to follow a set plan, with changes following cues that are preprogrammed into genes, other, subtler changes in gray matter reflect experience and environment. By following twins, who start out with identical—or, in fraternal twins, similar—programming but then diverge as life takes them on different paths, he hopes to tease apart the influences of nature and nurture. Ultimately, he hopes to find, for instance, that Anthony Mann's plan to become a pilot and Brandon's to study law will lead to brain differences that are detectable on future MRIs. The brain, more than any other organ, is where experience becomes flesh.

Throughout the afternoon, the Mann brothers take turns completing tests of intelligence and cognitive function. Between sessions they occasionally needle one another in the waiting room. "If the other person is in a bad mood, you've got to provoke it," Anthony asserts slyly. Their mother Nancy Mann, a sunny paragon of patience who has three daughters in addition to the five boys, smiles and rolls her eyes.

Shortly before 5 p.m., the Manns head downstairs to the imaging floor to meet the magnet. Giedd, a trim, energetic man with a reddish beard, twinkly blue eyes and an impish sense of humor, greets Anthony and tells him what to expect. He asks Anthony to remove his watch, his necklace and a high school ring, labeled KEEPER. Does Anthony have any metal in his body? Any piercings? Not this clean-cut, soccer-playing Mormon. Giedd tapes a vitamin E capsule onto Anthony's left cheek and one in each ear. He explains that the oil-filled capsules are opaque to the scanner and will define a plane on the images, as well as help researchers tell left from right. The scanning will take about 15 minutes, during which Anthony must lie completely still. Dressed in a red sweat shirt, jeans and white K-Swiss sneakers, he stretches out on the examining table and slides his head into the machine's giant magnetic ring.

MRI, Giedd points out, "made studying healthy kids possible" because there's no radiation involved. (Before MRI, brain development was studied mostly by using cadavers.) Each of the Mann boys will be scanned three times. The first scan is a quick survey that lasts one minute. The second lasts two minutes and looks for any damage or abnormality. The third is 10 minutes long and taken at maximum resolution. It's the money shot. Giedd watches as Anthony's brain appears in cross section on a computer screen. The machine scans 124 slices, each as thin as a dime. It will take 20 hours of computer time to process the images, but the analysis is done by humans, says Giedd. "The human brain is still the best at pattern recognition," he marvels.

Some people get nervous as the MRI machine clangs noisily. Claustrophobes panic. Anthony, lying still in the soul of the machine, simply falls asleep.

CONSTRUCTION AHEAD

One reason scientists have been surprised by the ferment in the teenage brain is that the brain grows very little over the course of childhood. By the time a child is 6, it is 90% to 95% of its adult size. As a matter of fact, we are born equipped with most of the neurons our brain will ever have—and that's fewer than we have in utero. Humans achieve their maximum brain-cell density between the third and sixth month of gestation—the culmination of an explosive period of prenatal neural growth. During the final months before birth, our brains undergo a dramatic pruning in which unnecessary brain cells are eliminated. Many neuroscientists now believe that autism is the result of insufficient or abnormal prenatal pruning.

The last area of the brain to mature is the part capable of deciding, I'll finish my homework, take out the garbage, and then I'll IM my friends.

What Giedd's long-term studies have documented is that there is a second wave of proliferation and pruning that occurs later in childhood and that the final, critical part of this second wave, affecting some of our highest mental functions, occurs in the late teens. Unlike the prenatal changes, this neural waxing and waning alters not the number of nerve cells but the number of connections, or synapses, between them. When a child is between the ages of 6 and 12, the neurons grow bushier, each making dozens of connections to other neurons and creating new pathways for nerve signals. The thickening of all this gray matter—the neurons and their branchlike dendrites—peaks when girls are about 11 and boys 12½, at which point a serious round of pruning is under way. Gray matter is thinned out at a rate of about 0.7% a year, tapering off in the early 20s. At the same time, the brain's white matter thickens. The white matter is composed of fatty myelin sheaths that encase axons and, like insulation on a wire, make nerve-signal transmissions faster and more efficient. With each passing year (maybe even up to age 40) myelin sheaths thicken, much like tree rings. During adolescence, says Giedd, summing up the process, "you get fewer but faster connections in the brain." The brain becomes a more efficient machine, but there is a trade-off: it is probably losing some of its raw potential for learning and its ability to recover from trauma.

Most scientists believe that the pruning is guided both by genetics and by a use-it-or-lose-it principle. Nobel prizewinning neuroscientist Gerald Edelman has described that process as "neural Darwinism"—survival of the fittest (or most used) synapses. How you spend your time may be critical. Research shows, for instance, that practicing piano quickly thickens neurons in the brain regions that control the fingers. Studies of London cab drivers, who must memorize all the city's streets, show that they have an unusually large hippocampus, a structure involved in memory. Giedd's research suggests that the cerebellum, an area that coordinates both physical and mental activities, is particularly responsive to experience, but he warns that it's too soon to know just what drives

MRI machine tests brain

the buildup and pruning phases. He's hoping his studies of twins will help answer such questions: "We're looking at what they eat, how they spend their time—is it video games or sports? Now the fun begins," he says.

No matter how a particular brain turns out, its development proceeds in stages, generally from back to front. Some of the brain regions that reach maturity earliest—through proliferation and pruning—are those in the back of the brain that mediate direct contact with the environment by controlling such sensory functions as vision, hearing, touch and spatial processing. Next are areas that coordinate those functions: the part of the brain that helps you know where the light switch is in your bathroom even if you can't see it in the middle of the night. The very last part of the brain to be pruned and shaped to its adult dimensions is the prefrontal cortex, home of the so-called executive functions—planning, setting priorities, organizing thoughts, suppressing impulses, weighing the consequences of one's actions. In other words, the final part of the brain to grow up is the part capable of deciding, I'll finish my homework and take out the garbage, and *then* I'll IM my friends about seeing a movie.

"Scientists and the general public had attributed the bad decisions teens make to hormonal changes," says Elizabeth Sowell, a UCLA neuroscientist who has done seminal MRI work on the developing brain. "But once we started mapping where and when the brain changes were happening, we could say, Aha, the part of the brain that makes teenagers more responsible is not finished maturing yet."

RAGING HORMONES

Hormones, however, remain an important part of the teen-brain story. Right about the time the brain switches from proliferating to pruning, the body comes under the hormonal assault of puberty. (Research suggests that the two events are not closely linked because brain development proceeds on schedule even when a child experiences early or late puberty.) For years, psychologists attributed the intense, combustible emotions and unpredictable behavior of teens to this biochemical onslaught. And new research adds fresh support. At puberty, the ovaries and testes begin to pour estrogen and testosterone into the bloodstream, spurring the development of the reproductive system, causing hair to sprout in the armpits and groin, wreaking havoc with the skin, and shaping the body to its adult contours. At the same time, testosterone-like hormones released by the adrenal glands, located near the kidneys, begin to circulate. Recent discoveries show that these adrenal sex hormones are extremely active in the brain, attaching to receptors everywhere and exerting a direct influence on serotonin and other neurochemicals that regulate mood and excitability.

The sex hormones are especially active in the brain's emotional center—the limbic system. This creates a "tinderbox of emotions," says Dr. Ronald Dahl, a psychiatrist at the University of Pittsburgh. Not only do feelings reach a flash point more easily, but adolescents tend to seek out situations where they can allow their emotions and passions to run wild. "Adolescents are actively looking for experiences to create intense feelings," says Dahl. "It's a very important hint that there is some particular hormone-brain relationship contributing to the appetite for thrills, strong sensations and excitement." This thrill seeking may have evolved to promote exploration, an eagerness to leave the nest and seek one's own path and partner. But in a world where fast cars, illicit drugs, gangs and dangerous liaisons beckon, it also puts the teenager at risk.

That is especially so because the brain regions that put the brakes on risky, impulsive behavior are still under construction. "The parts of the brain responsible for things like sensation seeking are getting turned on in big ways around the time of puberty," says Temple University psychologist Laurence Steinberg. "But the parts for exercising judgment are still maturing throughout the course of adolescence. So you've got this time gap between when things impel kids toward taking risks early in adolescence, and when things that allow people to think before they act come online. It's like turning on the engine of a car without a skilled driver at the wheel."

DUMB DECISIONS

Increasingly, psychologists like Steinberg are trying to connect the familiar patterns of adolescents' wacky behavior to the new findings about their evolving brain structure. It's not always easy to do. "In all likelihood, the behavior is changing because the brain is changing," he says. "But that is still a bit of a leap." A critical tool in making that leap is functional magnetic resonance imaging (fMRI). While ordinary MRI reveals brain structure, fMRI actually shows brain activity while subjects are doing assigned tasks.

At McLean Hospital in Belmont, Mass., Harvard neuropsychologist Deborah Yurgelun-Todd did an elegant series of FMRI experiments in which both kids and adults were asked to identity the emotions displayed in photographs of faces. "In doing these tasks," she says, "kids and young adolescents rely heavily on the amygdala, a structure in the temporal lobes associated with emotional and gut reactions. Adults rely less on the amygdala and more on the frontal lobe, a region associated with planning and judgment." While adults make few errors in assessing the photos, kids under 14 tend to make mistakes. In particular, they identify fearful expressions as angry, confused or sad. By following the same kids year after year, Yurgelun-Todd has been able to watch their brain-activity pattern—and their judgment—mature. Fledgling physiology, she believes, may explain why adolescents so frequently misread emotional signals, seeing anger and hostility where none exists. Teenage ranting ("That teacher hates me!") can be better understood in this light.

Hormone surges make them emotional tinderboxes. An immature cortex gives them shaky judgment. Melatonin throws their sleep schedules out of whack.

At Temple University, Steinberg has been studying another kind of judgment: risk assessment. In an experiment using a driving-simulation game, he studies teens and adults as they decide whether to run a yellow light. Both sets of subjects, he found, make safe choices when playing alone. But in group play, teenagers start to take more risks in the presence of their friends, while those over age 20 don't show much change in their behavior. "With this manipulation," says Steinberg, "we've shown that age differences in decision making and judgment may appear under conditions that are emotionally arousing or have high social impact." Most teen crimes, he says, are committed by kids in packs.

Other researchers are exploring how the adolescent propensity for uninhibited risk taking propels teens to experiment with drugs and alcohol. Traditionally, psychologists have attributed this experimentation to peer pressure, teenagers' attraction to novelty and their roaring interest in loosening sexual inhibitions. But researchers have raised the possibility that rapid changes in dopamine-rich areas of the brain may be an additional factor in making teens vulnerable to the stimulating and addictive effects of drugs and alcohol. Dopamine, the brain chemical involved in motivation and in reinforcing behavior, is particularly abundant and active in the teen years.

Why is it so hard to get a teenager off the couch and working on that all important college essay? You might blame it on their immature *nucleus accumbens*, a region in the frontal cortex that directs motivation to seek rewards. James Bjork at the National Institute on Alcohol Abuse and Alcoholism has been using fMRI to study motivation in a challenging gambling game. He found that teenagers have less activity in this region than adults do. "If adolescents have a motivational deficit, it may mean that they are prone to engaging in behaviors that have either a really high excitement factor or a really low effort factor, or a combination of both." Sound familiar? Bjork believes his work may hold valuable lessons for parents and society. "When presenting suggestions, anything parents can do to emphasize more immediate payoffs will be more effective," he says. To persuade a teen to quit drinking, for example, he suggests stressing something immediate and tangible—the danger of getting kicked off the football team, say—rather than a future on skid row.

Persuading a teenager to go to bed and get up on a reasonable schedule is another matter entirely. This kind of decision-making has less to do with the frontal lobe than with the pineal gland at the base of the brain. As nighttime approaches and daylight recedes, the pineal gland produces melatonin, a chemical that signals the body to begin shutting down for sleep. Studies by Mary Carskadon at Brown University have shown that it takes longer for melatonin levels to rise in teenagers than in younger kids or in adults, regardless of exposure to light or stimulating activities. "The brain's program for starting nighttime is later," she explains.

PRUNING PROBLEMS

The new discoveries about teenage brain development have prompted all sorts of questions and theories about the timing of childhood mental illness and cognitive disorders. Some scientists now believe that ADHD and Tourette's syndrome, which typically appear by the time a child reaches age 7, may be related to the brain proliferation period. Though both disorders have genetic roots, the rapid growth of brain tissue in early childhood, especially in regions rich in dopamine, "may set the stage for the increase in motor activities and tics," says Dr. Martin Teicher, director of developmental biopsychiatry research at McLean Hospital. "When it starts to prune in adolescence, you often see symptoms recede."

Schizophrenia, on the other hand, makes its appearance at about the time the prefrontal cortex is getting pruned. "Many people have speculated that schizophrenia may be due to an abnormality in the pruning process," says Teicher. "Another hypothesis is that schizophrenia has a much earlier, prenatal origin, but as the brain prunes, it gets unmasked." MRI studies have shown that while the average teenager loses about 15% of his cortical gray matter, those who develop schizophrenia lose as much as 25%.

WHAT'S A PARENT TO DO?

Brain scientists tend to be reluctant to make the leap from the laboratory to real-life, hard-core teenagers. Some feel a little burned by the way earlier neurological discoveries resulted in *Baby Einstein* tapes and other marketing schemes that misapplied their science. It is clear, however, that there are implications in the new research for parents, educators and lawmakers.

In light of what has been learned, it seems almost arbitrary that our society has decided that a young American is ready to drive a car at 16, to vote and serve in the Army at 18 and to drink alcohol at 21. Giedd says the best estimate for when the brain is truly mature is 25, the age at which you can rent a car. "Avis must have some pretty sophisticated neuroscientists," he jokes. Now that we have scientific evidence that the adolescent brain is not quite up to scratch, some legal scholars and child advocates argue that minors should never be tried as adults and should be spared the death penalty. Last year, in an official statement that summarized current research on the adolescent brain, the American Bar Association urged all state legislatures to ban the death penalty for juveniles. "For social and biological reasons," it read, "teens have increased difficulty making mature decisions and understanding the consequences of their actions."

Most parents, of course, know this instinctively. Still, it's useful to learn that teenage behavior is not just a matter of willful pigheadedness or determination to drive you crazy—though these, too, can be factors. "There's a debate over how much conscious control kids have," says Giedd, who has four "teenagers in training" of his own. "You can tell them to shape up or ship out, but making mistakes is part of how the brain optimally grows." It might be more useful to help them make up for what their brain still lacks by providing structure, organizing their time, guiding them through tough decisions (even when they resist) and applying those time-tested parental virtues: patience and love.

From *Time*, May 10, 2004 pp. 56, 58–59, 61–62, 65. Copyright © 2004 by Time Inc. Reprinted by permission.

MEDICATING YOUNG MINDS

Drugs have become increasingly popular for treating kids with mood and behavior problems. But how will that affect them in the long run?

By Jeffrey Kluger

GETTING BY IS HARD ENOUGH when you're 13. it's harder still when you've got other things on your mind—and Andrea Okeson had plenty to distract her. There were the constant stomach pains to consider; there was the nervousness, the distractibility, the overwhelming need to be alone. And, of course, there was the business of repeatedly checking the locks on the doors. All these things grew, inexplicably, to consume Andrea, until by the time she was through with the eighth grade, she seemed pretty much through with everything else too. "Andrea," said a teacher to her one day, "you look like death."

The problem, though neither Andrea nor her teacher knew it, was that her adolescent brain was being tossed by the neurochemical storms of generalized anxiety, obsessive-compulsive disorder (OCD) and attention-deficit/hyperactivity disorder (ADHD)—a decidedly lousy trifecta. If that was what eighth grade was, ninth was unimaginable.

But that was then. Andrea, now 18, is a freshman at the College of St. Catherine in St. Paul, Minn., enjoying her friends and her studies and looking forward to a career in fashion merchandising, all thanks to a bit of chemical stabilizing provided by a pair of pills: Lexapro, an antidepressant, and Adderall, a relatively new anti-ADHD drug. "I feel excited about things," Andrea says. "I feel like I got me back."

So a little medicine fixed what ailed a child. Good news all around, right? Well, yes—and no. Lexapro is the perfect an-

swer for anxiety all right, provided you're willing to overlook the fact that it does its work by artificially manipulating the very chemicals responsible for feeling and thought. Adderall is the perfect answer for ADHD, provided you overlook the fact that it's a stimulant like Dexedrine. Oh, yes, you also have to overlook the fact that the Adderall has left Andrea with such side effects as weight loss and sleeplessness, and both drugs are being poured into a young brain that has years to go before it's finally fully formed. Still, says Andrea, "I'm just glad there were things that could be done."

Those things—whether Lexapro or Ritalin or Prozac or something else—are being done for more and more children in the U.S. and around the world. In fact, they are being done with such frequency that some people have justifiably begun to ask, Are we adults raising Generation R$_x$?

Just a few years ago, psychologists couldn't say with certainty that kids were even capable of suffering from depression the same way adults do. Now, according to PhRMA, a pharmaceutical trade group, up to 10% of all American kids may suffer from some mental illness. Perhaps twice that many have exhibited some symptoms of depression. Up to a million others may suffer from the alternately depressive and manic mood swings of bipolar disorder (BPD), one more condition that was thought until recently to be an affliction of adults alone. ADHD rates are exploding too.

According to a Mayo Clinic study, children between 5 and 19 have at least a 7.5% chance of being found to have ADHD, which amounts to nearly 5 million kids. Other children are receiving diagnoses and medication for obsessive-compulsive disorder, social-anxiety disorder, post-traumatic stress disorder (PTSD), pathological impulsiveness, sleeplessness, phobias and more.

Has the world—and Western societies in particular—simply become a more destabilizing place in which to raise children? Probably so. But other factors are at work, including sharp-eyed parents and doctors with a rising awareness of childhood mental illness and what can be done for it. "The scientific community thought that mental illness did not just start at 15 or 20 years old, but we didn't have the proper tools to diagnose it," says Rémi Quirion, director of the Institute of Neuroscience, Mental Health and Addiction of Canada. "Now we have developed more sophisticated tools and are more aware that these disorders could exist in young kids."

Also feeding the trend for more diagnoses is the arrival of whole new classes of psychotropic drugs with fewer side effects and greater efficacy than earlier medications, particularly the selective serotonin reuptake inhibitors (SSRIS), or antidepressants. While an earlier generation of antidepressants-tricyclics like Tofranil—didn't work in kids, SSRIS do. But the benefits of these SSRIS may not outweigh their risks. Last month British drug regulators recommended against the use of Paxil, Zoloft and three other SSRIS for children, citing links to suicidal thoughts and self-harm. Health Canada is now reviewing that link that has warned health-care professionals against prescribing Paxil to anyone 18 and under. It has also warned against the pediatric use of Effexor, a selective serotonin and norepinephrine reuptake inhibitor (SNRI).

"OUR USAGE EXCEEDS OUR KNOWLEDGE BASE. **WE'RE LEARNING WHAT THESE DRUGS ARE** TO BE USED FOR, BUT LET'S FACE IT: **WE'RE EXPERIMENTING ON THESE KIDS.**"

—**DR. GLEN ELLIOTT**
UCSF Psychiatric Institute

For now, nobody, not even the drug companies, argues that pills alone are the ideal answer to mental illness. Most experts believe that drugs are most effective when combined with talk therapy or other counseling. Nonetheless, the American Academy of Child and Adolescent Psychiatry now lists dozens of medications available for troubled kids, from the comparatively familiar Ritalin (for ADHD) to Zoloft and Celexa (for depression) to less familiar ones like Seroquel, Tegretol, Depakote (for bipolar disorder), and more are coming along all the time—though not all are approved for use in Canada. There are stimulants, mood stabilizers, sleep medications, antidepressants, anticonvulsants, antipsychotics, antianxieties and narrowcast drugs to deal with impulsiveness and post-traumatic flashbacks. A few of the newest meds were developed or approved specifically for kids. The majority have been okayed for adults only, but are being used "off label" for younger and younger patients. In 2002, for example, Canadian doctors made 141,000 recommendations for Paxil to patients under 19, says drug-policy researcher Alan Cassels, who calculated data provided by IMS Health Canada. The practice is common and perfectly legal but potentially risky, some believe. "For kids, we don't know as much about what

dose we should use and what could be the long-term impact of the treatment we're giving," says Quirion.

Within the medical community—to say nothing of the families of the troubled kids-concern is growing about what psychotropic drugs can do to still developing brains. Few people deny that mind pills help—ask the untold numbers who have climbed out of depressive pits or shaken off bipolar fits thanks to modern pharmacology. But few deny either that Western culture is a quick-fix culture, and if you give people a feel-good answer to a complicated problem, they will use it with little thought of long-term consequences.

"The problem," warns Dr. Glen Elliott, director of the Langley Porter Psychiatric Institute's children's center at the University of California, San Francisco, "is that our usage has outstripped our knowledge base. Let's face it, we're experimenting on these kids without tracking the results."

THE CASE FOR MEDICATION

THOSE EXPERIMENTS, HOWEVER, ARE OFTEN driven by dire need. When a child is suffering or suicidal, is it fair not to turn to the prescription pad in conjunction with therapy? Is it even safe? Untreated depression has a lifetime suicide rate of 15%—with still more deaths caused by related behaviors like self-medicating with alcohol and drugs. Kids with severe and untreated ADHD have been linked, according to some studies, to higher rates of substance abuse, dropping out of school and trouble with the law. Bipolar kids have a tendency to injure and kill themselves and others with uncontrolled behavior like brawling or reckless driving. They are also more prone to suicide.

Which is why Teresa Hatten of Fort Wayne, Ind., hesitated little when it came time to put her granddaughter Monica on medication. Hatten's grown daughter, Monica's mom, suffers from bipolar disorder, and so does Monica, 13. To give Monica a chance at a stable upbringing, Hatten took on the job of raising her, and one of the first things she had to do was get the violent mood swings of the bipolar disorder under con-

trol. It's been a long, tough slog. An initial drug combination of Ritalin and Prozac, prescribed when Monica was 6, simply collapsed her alternating depressed and manic moods into a single state with sad and wild features. By the time she was 8, her behavior was so unhinged, her school tried to expel her. Next Monica was switched to Zyprexa, an antipsychotic, that led to serious weight gain. "At 12 years old she had stretch marks," says Hatten. Now, a year later, Monica is taking a four-drug cocktail that includes Tegretol, an anticonvulsant, and Abilify, an antipsychotic. That, at last, seems to have solved the problem. "She's the best I've ever seen her," says Hatten. "She's smiling. Her moods are consistent. I'm cautiously optimistic." Monica agrees: "I'm in a better mood." Next up in the family's wellness campaign: Monica's 8-year-old cousin Jamari, who is on Zyprexa for a mood disorder.

Jonathan Singh, 18, of Toronto, has also come out of the darkness. "I had known for a long time something was wrong, but I didn't know what," he says. "I felt like there was this big, black fog in my brain that I couldn't fix." Exhausted and emaciated, Jonathan was finally given a diagnosis of major depression a year ago and was immediately put on Zoloft. Today, he has more energy and focus, his grades have improved, and he takes better care of himself. For his family, this has been a huge relief. "He has the look of someone who has come back to life," says his mother Jackie Beaurivage.

"**WE KNOW THAT FRONTAL LOBES,** WHICH MANAGE BOTH **FEELING AND THOUGHT, DON'T FULLY MATURE UNTIL** AGE 30."

—**STEPHEN HINSHAW,**
University of California

All along the disorder spectrum there are such pharmacological success stories. In the October issue of the *Archives of General Psychiatry*, Dr. Mark Olfson of the New York State Psychiatric Institute reports that every time the use of antidepressants jumps 1%, suicide rates among kids 10 to 19 decrease, although

WORK	HOW THEY	Children are just as vulnerable as adults to mental illness. But though the pharmaceutical pantry is filling up with more medications designed and tested for kids, in some cases they still have to settle for smaller doses of drugs made for adults	
	HOW IT WORKS	**SIDE EFFECTS**	**TESTED/ APPROVED**
ADDERALL	A once-a-day amphetamine, it puts the brake on areas of the brain responsible for organizing thoughts	Rapid heartbeat, high blood pressure and, in rare cases, overstimulation. It can also become addictive	✔ Approved to treat ADHD in children 3 and older
CONCERTA	It keeps neurons bathed in norepinephrine and dopamine, which reduce hyperactivity and inattention	Headache, stomach pain, sleeplessness and, in rare cases, overstimulation	✔ Approved for treatment of ADHD in children 6 to 12
STRATTERA	Approved in the U.S. a year ago, it's the first nonstimulant for ADHD: it enhances norepinephrine levels in the brain	Decreased appetite, fatigue, nausea, stomach pain	✔ Approved to treat ADHD in children 6 and older
RITALIN	Its active agent, methylphenidate, stimulates the brain to filter and prioritize incoming information	Headache, lack of appetite, irritability, nervousness, insomnia	✔ Approved to treat ADHD in children 6 and older
METHYPATCH	The patch form of the stimulant methylphenidate for ADHD, it delivers continuous low doses through the skin	Similar to those for oral methylphenidate	Not approved. In the U.S., the FDA has deemed the ADHD drug "unapprovable" until further study
PROZAC	Approved in the U.S. in 1987; the first antidepressant aimed at regulating serotonin, a brain chemical involved in mood	Insomnia, anxiety, nervousness, weight loss, mania	✔ Not approved for pediatric use but prescribed for children in Canada
ZOLOFT	It enhances the levels of serotonin in the brain to maintain feelings of satisfaction and stability	Upset stomach, dry mouth, agitation, decreased appetite	Not approved for kids. In Britain, regulators recently recommended against the use of SSRIs for children
PAXIL	Like Prozac and Zoloft, it elevates levels of serotonin in the brain	Nausea, drowsiness, insomnia	Not approved for kids. Health Canada has warned of an increase in suicidal thoughts for children on the drug
EFFEXOR	It targets two brain chemicals, serotonin and norepinephrine, to regulate mood	Nausea, constipation, nervousness, loss of appetite, drowsiness	Not approved for kids. Health Canada has warned of an increase in suicidal thoughts among children on the drug
DEPAKOTE	This antiseizure medication is particularly effective in treating the grandiose, hyperagitated state of mania	Liver and white blood cell abnormalities, headache, nausea, drowsiness	Not approved for kids, but used to treat childhood bipolar mania and seizures
ZYPREXA	It's a mood stabilizer designed to balance levels of serotonin and dopamine in the brain	Weight gain, drowsiness, dry mouth, seizures	Not approved for kids but prescribed pediatrically for bipolar disorder, psychotic depression and schizophrenia
LITHIUM	It stabilizes the episodes of elated, intensely joyous moods associated with mania	Nausea, loss of appetite, trembling of the hands	Not approved for kids but prescribed pediatrically for bipolar disorder and as an agent for suicide prevention

only slightly. But that doesn't include the nonsuicidal depressed kids whose misery is eased thanks to the same pills.

ARE ADULTS MEDDLING WITH NORMAL DEVELOPMENT?

FOR CHILDREN WITH LESS SEVERE problems—children who are somber but not depressed, antsy but not clinically hyperactive, who rely on some repetitive behaviors for comfort but are not patently obsessive compulsive—the pros and cons of using drugs are far less obvious. "Unless there is careful assessment, we might start medicating normal variations [in behavior]," says Stephen Hinshaw, chairman of psychology at the University of California, Berkeley.

The world would be a far less interesting place if all the eccentric kids were medicated toward some golden mean. Besides, there are just too many unanswered questions about giving mind drugs to kids to feel comfortable with ever broadening usage. What worries some doctors is that if you medicate a child's developing brain, you may be burning the village to save it. What does any kind of psychopharmacological meddling do, not just to brain chemistry but also to the acquisition of emotional skills-when, for example, antianxiety drugs are prescribed for a child who has not yet acquired the experience of managing stress without the meds? And what about side effects, from weight gain to jitteriness to flattened personality—all the things you don't want in the social crucible of grade school and, worse, high school.

Adding to the worries is a growing body of knowledge showing just how incompletely formed a child's brain truly is. "We now know from imaging studies that frontal lobes, which are vital to executive functions like managing feelings and thought, don't fully mature until age 30," says Hinshaw. That's a lot of time for drugs to muck around with cerebral clay.

For that reason, it may not always be worth pulling the pharmacological rip cord, particularly when symptoms are relatively mild. Child psychologists point out that often nonpharmaceutical treatments can reduce or eliminate the need for drugs. Anxiety disorders such as phobias can respond well to behavioral

therapy-in which patients are gently exposed to graduated levels of the very things they fear until the brain habituates to the escalating risk.

Depression too may respond to new, streamlined therapy techniques, especially cognitive therapy—a treatment aimed at helping patients reframe their view of the world so that setbacks and losses are put in less catastrophic perspective. "Cognitive behavioral therapy helps kids learn to manage their thoughts," says Dr. Miriam Kaufman, a professor of pediatrics at the University of Toronto and author of Helping Your Teen Overcome Depression: A Guide for Parents.

For kids with more serious symptoms, experts are worried that undermedicating is a bigger risk than overmedicating. "Say you've got a kid who's severely obsessive and literally can't leave the home because of the fears and rituals he's got to perform," says UCSF's Elliott. "Think about what anyone age 2 to age 16 has to learn to function in our society. Then think about losing two of those years to a disorder. Which two would you choose to lose?" Also on the side of intervention is the belief that treating more kids with mental illness could reduce its incidence in adults.

Dr. Kiki Chang at Stanford University is trying to show that this is true with bipolar kids. He recently published a study in the Journal of Clinical Psychiatry that looked at kids from bipolar families who had only early signs of the disease. Preemptive doses of Depakote eased early symptoms in 78% of cases before the illness ever had a chance to take hold. "You can sit and watch it develop or intervene and possibly prevent the disorder," says Chang. While the researcher is excited about his results, he admits that treating kids who are not yet truly sick is controversial. "There's a chance some of the kids might not develop bipolar at all," says Chang. "We need to have more genetics, more brain imaging, more biological markers to know which direction the kids are going."

HOW CAN WE MEASURE THE RESULT?

PREVENTING SYMPTOMS, OF COURSE, IS NOT everything. A sleep-

ing child is completely asymptomatic, for example, but that's not the same as being fully functioning. If the drugs that extinguish symptoms also alter the still developing brain, the cure may come at too high a price, at least for kids who are only mildly symptomatic. To determine if this kind of damage is being done, investigators have been turning more and more to brain scans such as magnetic resonance imaging (MRI). The results they're getting have been intriguing.

MRIs had already shown that the brain volumes of kids with ADHD are 3% smaller than those of unafflicted kids. That concerned researchers since nearly all those scans had been taken of children already being medicated for the disorder. Were the anatomical differences there to begin with, or were they caused by the drugs? Attempting to answer that, Dr. F. Xavier Castellanos of the New York University Child Studies Center took other scans, this time using only kids with ADHD and comparing those who were taking medication with those who were not. Reassuringly, he discovered that they all shared the same structural anomaly, a finding that seems to exonerate the drugs.

Dr. Steven Pliszka, chief of child psychiatry at the University of Texas Health Center in San Antonio, went further. He conducted scans that picked up not just the structure but the activity of the brains of untreated ADHD children, and compared these images with those from children who had been medicated for a year or more. The treated group showed no signs of any deficits in brain function as measured in blood flow. In fact, he says, "we saw hints of improvement toward normal."

What nobody denies is that more research is needed to resolve all these questions—and that it won't be easy to get it started. The first problem is one of time. It was only in the early 1990s that the antidepressant Prozac exploded into pharmacies. It's hard to do a lifetime of longitudinal studies on a drug that's been widely used for just over a decade. And each time the industry invents a new medication, the clock rewinds to zero for that particular pill.

Even if it were possible to conduct extended studies, getting volunteers for the work is difficult. The attrition rate is high in any years—-long research, especially so when the subjects are kids, who bore easily and, at any rate, eventually go away to college. On average, 40% of children will drop out of a long-term study before the work is done. And that assumes their parents will even sign them up in the first place. Some brain scans involve at least a little bit of radiation—something most parents are reluctant to expose their children to, particularly if those kids have no emotional disorders and are simply being used as a baseline to establish the look of a healthy brain. Getting good scans from kids who have diagnosable conditions isn't easy, as any radiologist who has ever tried to conduct a lengthy MRI on a child with ADHD can attest. "Holding still is not exactly what they do well," says Elliott.

"YOU CAN'T SCREEN FOR SIDE EFFECTS IN A 10-YEAR-OLD IN FIVE MINUTES. MANY DOCTORS DON'T LISTEN TO KIDS."

Ethical questions hamstring research too. Any gold-standard study requires that some of the kids who are suffering from a disorder receive no drugs so that they can be compared with the kids who

do. But if you believe the medications are helpful, how can you withhold them from a group of symptomatic children who need them?

Despite such obstacles, research is moving ahead, if haltingly. The U.S. National Institute of Mental Health is conducting a study called the Preschool ADHD Treatment Study, in which researchers will track ADHD kids between 3 and 8 years old to determine the benefits and side effects of stimulant medications. Castellanos and N.Y.U. colleague Rachel Klein are taking things further, calling back subjects who were enrolled in an ADHD-treatment study that began in 1970 to scan their now late-30s and early-40s brains for the long-term effects of drugs. Castellanos is also planning a study of young rats treated with varying amounts of psychotropic drugs, conducting dosing and anatomical studies that cannot be performed on humans.

THE RISK OF HASTY PRESCRIPTIONS

JUST AS IMPORTANT AS GETTING THE research rolling is fixing the health-care system on which kids rely. Like adults taking mind meds, Canadian children often get their drugs not from a specialist in psychiatry but from a pediatrician or family doctor. Part of the reason for the hurried drugging, experts say, is that there is a shortage of qualified

physicians in most regions of the country, particularly rural areas. In a perfect, or at least better, world more doctors would be trained in psychotherapy and more specialists and clinics would be located in remote areas. "We're probably at 20% of where we should be," says Dr. Tatyana Barankin, head of continuing medical education, division of child psychiatry, at the University of Toronto.

The pharmaceutical companies could be doing better too—and if they don't, governments must push them to do it. There is a lot of money to be made in developing the next Prozac, but there is less profit if you test it for longer than the law demands.

Until all these things happen, the heaviest lifting will, as always, be left to the family. Perhaps the most powerful medicine a suffering child needs is the educated instincts of a well-informed parent—one who has taken the time to study up on all the pharmaceutical and nonpharmaceutical options and pick the right ones. There will always be dangers associated with taking too many drugs-and also dangers from taking too few. "Like every other choice you make for your kids," says Chang, "you make right ones and wrong ones." When the health of a child's mind is on the line, getting it wrong is something that no parent wants.

The Biology of Risk Taking

*For help in guiding adolescents into healthy adulthood,
educators can look to new findings in the fields of
neuroscience and developmental psychology.*

Lisa F. Price

> *I celebrate myself,*
> *And what I assume you shall assume,*
> *For every atom belonging to me as good belongs to you.*
> —Walt Whitman, *Leaves of Grass*

Adolescence is a time of excitement, growth, and change. Whitman's words capture the enthusiasm and passion with which teenagers approach the world. Sometimes adolescents direct this passion toward a positive goal, such as a creative essay, an art project, after-school sports, or a healthy romance. At other times, they divert their passions to problematic activities, such as drug experimentation, reckless driving, shoplifting, fights, or school truancy.

Why do adolescents take risks? Why are teens so passionate? Are adolescents just young adults, or are they fundamentally different? Advances in developmental psychology and neuroscience have provided us with some answers. We now understand that adolescent turmoil, which we used to view as an expression of raging hormones, is actually the result of a complex interplay of body chemistry, brain development, and cognitive growth (Buchanan, Eccles, & Becker, 1992). Moreover, the changes that teenagers experience occur in the context of multiple systems—such as individual relationships, family, school, and community—that support and influence change.

Educators are in a pivotal position to promote healthy adolescent growth. Understanding the biological changes that adolescents undergo and the behaviors that result can provide the foundation for realistic expectations and effective interventions.

The Impact of Puberty

The hormonal changes of adolescence are often considered synonymous with puberty. The word *puberty* comes from the Latin term *pubertas*, meaning "age of maturity." As implied by the word's etymology, the changes of pu-

berty have long been understood to usher in adulthood; in many cultures, puberty and the capacity to conceive continue to mark entry into adulthood. In contrast, puberty in modern Western culture has become a multistep entry process into a much longer period of adolescence (King, 2002).

Hormonal changes of adolescence include adrenarche, gonadarche, and menarche (Dahl, 2004; King, 2002). Adrenarche refers to the increased production of adrenal hormones and occurs as early as age 6-8. These hormones influence skeletal growth, hair production, and skin changes. Gonadarche refers to the pulsatile production of a cascade of hormones and contributes to driving the growth spurt and genital, breast, and pubic hair development. Menarche refers to the beginning of girls' menses, which generally occurs late in girls' pubertal development.

The Stages and Ages of Puberty

The clinician J. M. Tanner developed a system for classifying male and female pubertal growth into five stages (Tanner I-V). In the 1960s, he identified a trend of progressively earlier age at menarche across cultures (1968). Since then, investigators have identified similar trends of earlier arrival of other markers of puberty, such as breast and pubic hair development (Herman-Giddens et al., 1997). These trends have diverged across race in the United States, with proportionately more African American girls experiencing earlier-onset puberty than white girls. The implications of these trends have ranged from debates over the threshold for premature puberty to investigations into factors that contribute to earlier-onset puberty (Kaplowitz & Oberfield, 1999).

Boys who enter puberty at an earlier age experience certain advantages, including higher self-esteem, greater popularity, and some advances in cognitive capabilities (King, 2002). These same boys may also be more likely to engage in risk-taking behavior, possibly because they often socialize with older boys (Steinberg & Morris, 2001). Girls, on the other hand, often have more problems associated with earlier entry into puberty, including lower self-esteem and elevated risk for anxiety, depression, and eating disorders. These girls are also more likely to engage in risk-taking behaviors, including earlier sexual intercourse.

Don't Blame It On Hormones

In the past, hormones were believed to be in a state of great flux, which presumably caused adolescents to be dramatic, erratic, intense, and risk-prone. Evidence suggests, however, that only minimal association exists between adolescent hormone levels and emotional/behavioral problems (Buchanan et al., 1992; King, 2002). Youth with higher levels of hormones do not appear to be at higher risk for emotional or behavioral problems (Dahl, 2004).

> ## Adolescence is a time of excitement, growth, and change.

Today, adolescent specialists view emotional intensity and sensation-seeking as normative behaviors of adolescence that are more broadly linked to pubertal maturation than to hormone levels. Pubertal stage rather than chronological age is linked to romantic and sexual pursuits, increased appetite, changes in sleep patterns, and risk for emotional disorders in girls. One group of investigators studying teen smoking and substance use found that increased age had no correlation with increased sensation-seeking or risky behavior (Martin et al., 2002). Instead, they determined that pubertal maturation was correlated with sensation-seeking in boys and girls, which, in turn, led to a greater likelihood of cigarette smoking and substance use.

Pubertal stage was clearly linked to difficulties that Derek began experiencing in school. He had been a solid student in 6th grade who scored in the average range and generally turned his homework in on time. He socialized with a group of same-age friends and was teased occasionally because he was skinnier and shorter than his peers. By 7th grade, however, he had begun his growth spurt. He was now a few inches taller and had developed facial hair. Although he appeared more confident, he also seemed more aggressive and was involved in several fights at school. He began to spend part of his time with a few 8th grade boys who were suspected of writing graffiti on a school wall.

A teacher who had a good relationship with Derek took him aside and spoke with him about the change in his behavior from 6th to 7th grade. Derek was able to talk about his own surprise at the changes, his wish for more respect, and his ambivalence about entering high school—he was worried about what teachers would expect of him. Derek and the teacher agreed to talk periodically, and the teacher arranged for Derek to meet with the school counselor.

The Adolescent Brain

Neuroscientists used to believe that by the time they reached puberty, youth had undergone the crucial transformations in brain development and circuitry. Data obtained through available technology supported this view, identifying similar brain structures in children and adults. The adolescent brain seemed entirely comparable to the adult brain.

This view of adolescent brain development has undergone a radical shift during the last decade, with the identification of ongoing brain changes throughout adolescence, such as synaptic pruning and myelination. People have the mature capacity to consistently control behavior in both low-stress and high-stress environments only after these neurobiological developments are complete. This maturation does not take place until the early 20s.

Synaptic pruning refers to the elimination of connections between neurons in the brain's cortex, or gray matter. In the 1990s, researchers determined that during adolescence, up to 30,000 synapses are eliminated each second (Bourgeois & Rakic, 1993; Rakic, Bourgeois, & Goldman-Rakic, 1994). The removal of these redundant synaptic links increases the computational ability of brain circuits, which, in turn, enhances a function intricately connected to risk taking: the capacity to regulate and rapidly stop activity. Myelination, which refers to the wrapping of glial cell membranes around the axon of neurons, results in increased speed of signal transmission along the axon (Luna & Sweeney, 2004). This facilitates more rapid and integrated communication among diverse brain regions.

Synaptic pruning and myelination, along with other neurobiological changes, facilitate enhanced cognitive capacity as well as behavioral control, also known as *executive function*. Executive function is the ability to interact in a self-directed, appropriate, organized, and purposeful manner. The prefrontal cortex plays a vital role in guiding executive function, which is also influenced by such areas of the brain as the hippocampus (which coordinates memory), the amygdala (which coordinates emotional processing), and the ventral striatum (which coordinates reward-processing). The prefrontal cortex is less mature, however, in young adolescents than in adults.

Given these three factors—an inability to completely regulate and refrain from certain activities, an absence of fully integrated communication among the various regions of the brain, and a less developed prefrontal cortex—it is not surprising that adolescents biologically do not have the same capacities as adults to inhibit their impulses in a timely manner.

Biology and Thrill-Seeking

By their mid-teens, adolescents appear to have achieved many decision-making abilities seen in adults (Steinberg

& Cauffman, 1996). In fact, studies have found that teens can identify the same degree of danger in risky activities that adults can—driving while intoxicated, for example (Cauffman, Steinberg, & Woolard, 2002). However, certain methodological flaws in studies of adolescents may have prevented investigators from accurately assessing adolescent risk taking (Steinberg, 2004). These flaws include evaluating teens individually rather than in the context of a group, within which most risk-taking behavior occurs; asking teens to evaluate theoretical situations, which may not sufficiently represent the challenges of actual situations; and evaluating teens in settings that reduce the influence of emotion or induce anxiety rather than generate the exhilaration associated with risk taking.

One result of these flaws may be that measures of adolescents' cognitive abilities—particularly their evaluation of risk—do not adequately reflect their actual cognitive and emotional processes in real time. Consequently, teens *appear* to have the cognitive capacities of adults yet continue to engage in more risky behaviors.

The emotional lives of adolescents also appear to shift during these years. Adolescents seek more intense emotional experiences than children and adults do. They appear to need higher degrees of stimulation to obtain the same experience of pleasure (Steinberg, 2004). Developments in an area of the brain called the limbic system may explain this shift in pursuit and experience of pleasure (Spear, 2000).

> Teenagers generally thrive in reasonable, supportive environments that have a predictable, enforced structure.

Ongoing cognitive development and emotional shifts result in a biologically based drive for thrill-seeking, which may account for adolescents' continued risk taking despite knowledge of the accompanying hazards. Some interventions attempt to reduce the potential for risky behavior through external means—laws and rules, for example—rather than placing sole emphasis on the practice of educating teens in risk assessment (Steinberg, 2004). Others have considered teens' ability to reason well in "cool" circumstances but their failure to do so when in "hot" situations that arouse the emotions. Providing adolescents with sufficient scaffolding, or a good balance of support and autonomy, may be particularly important (Dahl, 2004).

This kind of scaffolding would be especially effective with a student like Shauna. Shauna raised the concerns of school faculty soon after she started 9th grade. Her attendance, class participation, and assignment completion were erratic. She had also run away from home during the summer and received a warning for shoplifting. The school counselor learned that Shauna's parents had separated over the summer and that her mother was struggling to set limits in the absence of Shauna's father. The school counselor, several teachers, and the vice principal decided to meet with both of Shauna's parents.

Although tension between the parents was evident, both parents agreed that Shauna should come home immediately after school instead of going to the mall, which she had recently started to do. Both parents also felt strongly that she needed to regularly attend school and complete assignments. The parents arranged to meet with Shauna together to discuss their shared expectations for her. The parents and teachers agreed to stay in contact with one another regarding Shauna's attendance and homework. The group also decided that a home-based reward system might encourage Shauna's success at school. The reward system would involve outings to the mall and to friends' homes, with incrementally less adult supervision and more autonomy as she continued to succeed.

The Role of Educators

These new findings suggest some beneficial approaches that educators might follow to guide adolescents into healthy adulthood.

■ *Ensure that schools provide adolescents with vital support.* School bonding provides a protective influence for youth. The mentorship of a teacher can make the difference in a teen's course.

■ *Keep a long view.* Researchers have found that the benefits of successful interventions may disappear for a few years in adolescence to reappear in later adolescence (Masten, 2004). Other teens are late bloomers whose troubled earlier years are followed by success.

■ *Prioritize your concern.* The junior who has never been a problem and gets into trouble once is at a different level of risk than the 7th grader who has a long history of worrisome behaviors, such as fights, school truancy, mental illness, exposure to trauma, loss of important adult figures, or absence of stable supports. Act early for adolescents with long histories of risk taking.

■ *Remember that puberty is not the same for all teens.* Some adolescents enter puberty earlier than others, giving them a perceived social advantage as well as possible disadvantages. There may be a biological drive to risk taking in teens, which is expressed by individual teens at different ages.

■ *Remember that teens are not adults.* Having the scientific evidence to support the view that teens are not adults can be helpful to educators working with families, adolescents, or other professionals who may have unrealistic expectations for adolescents.

■ *Take advantage of adolescent passion.* Direct adolescents' enthusiasm toward productive ends. A teen's passion can become a bridge to learning about such topics as music theory, history, politics, race relations, or marketing.

■ *Reduce risk with firm structure.* Although teenagers dislike rules, they generally thrive in reasonable, supportive environments that have a predictable, enforced structure. For example, an authoritative stance in parenting—which reflects firmness coupled with caring—has repeatedly been found to be the most effective parenting strategy. Continue to maintain school rules and expectations, even when an adolescent continues to break the rules.

■ *Collaborate to solve problems.* Working with risk-taking adolescents can be demanding, taxing, and worrisome. Talk regularly with colleagues for support. Contact appropriate consultants when your concern grows. Teens who see teachers collaborate with other adults benefit from these healthy models of problem solving.

It's important for educators to keep in mind that up to 80 percent of adolescents have few or no major problems during this period (Dahl, 2004). Remembering that most adolescents do well can encourage the positive outlook that educators need to effectively work with youth during this exciting and challenging time in their lives.

References

Bourgeois, J-P., & Rakic, P. (1993). Changes of synaptic density in the primary visual cortex of the macaque monkey from fetal to adult stage. *Journal of Neuroscience, 13,* 2801-2820.

Buchanan, C. M., Eccles, J. S., & Becket, J. B. (1992). Are adolescents the victims of raging hormones? *Psychological Bulletin, 111,* 62-107.

Cauffman, E., Steinberg, L., & Woolard, J. (2002, April 13). *Age differences in capacities underlying competence to stand trial.* Presentation at the Biennial Meeting of the Society for Research for Adolescence, New Orleans, Louisiana.

Dahl, R. E. (2004). Adolescent brain development: A period of vulnerabilities and opportunities. *Annals of the New York Academy of Science, 1021,* 1-22.

Herman-Giddens, M. E., Slora, E. J., Wasserman, R. C., Bourdony, C.J., Bhapkar, M. V., Koch, G. G., et al. (1997). Secondary sexual characteristics and menses in young girls seen in office practice. *Pediatrics, 99,* 505-512.

Kaplowitz, P. B., & Oberfield, S. E. (1999). Reexamination of the age limit for defining when puberty is precocious in girls in the United States. *Pediatrics, 104,* 936-941.

King, R. A. (2002). Adolescence. In M. Lewis (Ed.), *Child and adolescent psychiatry* (pp. 332-342). Philadelphia: Lippincott Williams & Wilkins.

Luna, B., & Sweeney, J. A. (2004). The emergence of collaborative brain function: fMRI studies of the development of response inhibition. *Annals of the New York Academy of Science, 1021,* 296-309.

Martin, C. A., Kelly, T. H., Rayens, M. K., Brogli, B. R., Brenzel, A., Smith, W. J., et al. (2002). Sensation seeking, puberty, and nicotine, alcohol, and marijuana use in adolescence. *Journal of the American Academy of Child and Adolescent Psychiatry, 41,* 1495-1502.

Masten, A. S. (2004). Regulatory processes, risk, and resilience in adolescent development. *Annals of the New York Academy of Science, 1021,* 310-319.

Rakic, P., Bourgeois, J-P., & Goldman-Rakic, P. S. (1994). Synaptic development of the cerebral cortex. *Progress in Brain Research, 102,* 227-243.

Spear, P. (2000). The adolescent brain and age-related behavioral manifestations. *Neuroscience and Biobehavioral Reviews, 24,* 417-463.

Steinberg, L. (2004). Risk taking in adolescence: What changes, and why? *Annals of the New York Academy of Science, 1021,* 51-58.

Steinberg, L., & Cauffman, E. (1996). Maturity of judgment in adolescence. *Law and Human Behavior, 20,* 249-272.

Steinberg, L., & Morris, A. S. (2001). Adolescent development. *Annual Review of Psychology, 52,* 83-110.

Tanner, J. M. (1968). Early maturation in man. *Scientific American, 218,* 21-27.

Lisa F. Price, M.D., *is the Assistant Director of the School Psychiatry Program in the Department of Psychiatry at Massachusetts General Hospital, 55 Fruit St., YAW 6900, Boston, MA 02114. She is also an Instructor in Psychiatry at Harvard Medical School.*

Wearing Out Their Bodies?

As more kids train for sports like pros, they're suffering grown-up injuries

By Bill Hewitt; Reported by Lisa Ingrassia, in Malden; Anne Driscoll, in Lexington; Nancy Wilstach, in Birmingham; Sharon Harvey Rosenberg, in Miami; Steve Barnes, in Little Rock; Shannon Richardson, in Austin and Sara Libby, in Los Angeles

For as long as anyone can remember, 14-year-old Nick Mulcahy played baseball every chance he got. "These boys come home from school, drop their bags, and they're up at the baseball diamond until supper time," says his mother, Maureen, of Malden, Mass. Baseball is Nick's only organized sport, and he plays it all the time, sometimes three or four hours a day, which helped him become a star pitcher on his Little League and tournament leagues. Until, that is, earlier this year, when he developed alarming symptoms. In addition to pains, "my elbow started to click and lock. I couldn't move it," says Nick. Diagnosed with Little League elbow in both arms— essentially wear and tear from overuse in pitching *and* hitting—he had surgery on both arms and is out for most of the season. "It's so boring," he says, "just sitting on the bench."

Welcome to the little big leagues. At a time when the country is confronting an obesity epidemic among youth, there is a growing awareness of a very different problem: kids, some as young as 8 or 9, who are pushing themselves so hard in a variety of sports—or playing one sport year-round instead of just seasonally—that they end up with overuse injuries that were once the province of professional athletes. Ten years ago, for example, Dr. James R. Andrews, a sports surgeon in Birmingham, Ala., had not seen any pitchers under the age of 19 who needed

REALITY CHECK

Think your baseball phenom has what it takes to play in the majors? The odds are staggering.

9 MILLION: Approximate number of boys playing in organized leagues

9,700 Number of players on Division I college baseball teams

7,500 Players in the minor leagues

829 Players in the majors (29 percent of whom are foreign-born)

"Tommy John surgery," a procedure named after the former major leaguer in which a ruptured elbow ligament is replaced with a tendon from another part of the body. Last year he did 51 such operations on teens. "I shouldn't see any of those," says Dr. Andrews. "It is nearly completely preventable."

Youth baseball leagues generally set limits on how much kids can pitch in any given week to prevent overuse injuries. "The problem comes in, especially with younger players, with their participation in elite, travel-ball programs not affiliated with Little League," says Little League International spokesman Lance Van Auken, "where they have little or no oversight in how much a pitcher can be used." These days it is not uncommon for top players to play on two or even three teams, and to train every month of the year, which according to experts is the

HOW TO AVOID INJURIES

Experts offer advice on preventing overuse and keeping young athletes healthy

• "A kid needs at least three months off a year from any overhead-throwing-type sports," says Dr. James R. Andrews.

• Don't ignore discomfort. "Pain is an indication of injury or dysfunction," says Dr. Joseph Chorley, a pediatric sports medicine specialist at Texas Children's Hospital in Houston. "If there's pain, it should be taken care of."

• Parents need to take the lead in reining kids in, says Dr. Lyle Micheli, author of *The Sports Medicine Bible for Young Athletes*. "They sign them up, they drive them, they pay for it."

surest way to develop problems. Says Dr. Andrews: "The average kid we operated on had only the week of Thanksgiving and the week of Christmas off." Nick Mulcahy, for instance, limited his pitching to six innings a week. But for the past two years he has been playing a lot of baseball, including pitching and batting practice in the winter months, when he and his brothers would regularly go to a local indoor facility. Says his father, Steve: "Nicky's heart and soul is baseball."

Baseball pitchers are by no means the only athletes at risk. Some youth soccer players "will play six games in a weekend, three on Saturday and three on Sunday," says Dr. Jack

VanderSchilden, an orthopedic surgeon in Little Rock, shaking his head. "Six games, three on two days in a row! The pros couldn't tolerate that!" Maya Richard-Craven, 11, didn't subject herself to that sort of regimen, but she was playing and practicing with her soccer team an average of two times a week, as well as playing catcher in softball, when her knee began to pop out of place on her two years ago. Her mother, Leslie Richard, who is a pediatrician, was able to pop the knee back. Eventually the problem started to happen more frequently. The low point was being carried off the soccer field and taken to the emergency room, after which Maya was diagnosed with a condition in which the cartilage moves around more than it should. "This probably wouldn't have been a problem if she had not been so active," says Dr. Jennifer Weiss, who operated on Maya last September. After six months of physical therapy, Maya still experiences pain and swelling in the knee—and wonders how long it will be before she can resume normal workouts. "I'm not as good as I was before," she says, "because I'm so out of practice."

Then there is Sophie Dulberg of Lexington, Mass., who began gymnastics classes when she was 3. By 4 she was doing handstands, and in 2003 she was invited to join a competitive gymnastics team, which entailed training at least 10 to 12 hours a week. Today, at age 9, she can do 50 inverted sit-ups, hanging by her knees from a bar, and 64 push-ups. But she also had trouble walking without pain and running during recess. In April, after she complained about her heels hurting, she was diagnosed with a condition called Sever's disease, in which the growth plates of cartilage in the heel are damaged because of repeated pounding. With rest the condition can improve, but the chances of further repetitive injury are great if she continues to pursue the sport. "Ten or 15 years ago we never saw Sever's disease in young girls," says Sophie's physician, Dr. Lyle Micheli, director of the Division of Sports Medicine at Children's Hospital Boston. Sophie has voiced an interest, once she is healed, in continuing gymnastics. Her mother and father, though, are fairly sure they do not want her to become any more competitive. "The trade-off would be way too great," says her mother. "She's a social kid and that would really diminish any sort of social life."

"Six games, three on two days in a row! The pros couldn't tolerate that!"

—Little Rock sports physician
Dr. Jack Vanderschilden

More than a few sports medicine specialists lay much of the blame for the growing epidemic of injuries on overbearing parents, eager to see their budding star earn a college scholarship, or—better yet—make big bucks as a professional. "Everybody envisions their kid as the next Roger Clemens or the next Michael Jordan," says Dr. VanderSchilden. "But the reality is, if you look at the data, the likelihood of achieving that level is infinitesimally small" (see box). When Dr. Andrews first meets with the parents of his young patients, he asks them to write down all the championships, camps, private instruction and so forth that make up the athlete's résumé. "Then I walk out of the room," he says. "I give them about 15 minutes, and when I walk back in they've covered the board. They're proud of the kid's accomplishments. They don't see the relationship."

There is no question that many parents have high aspirations for their kids. Nick Mulcahy's mother, Maureen, for instance, only half-jokingly proclaims, "He's going to be in the starting lineup of the Red Sox one day." Steve Mulcahy acknowledges that he has done some soul searching since Nick needed surgery. "I would never do anything to hurt Nick. Maybe I was a part of the machine that pushed him a little too hard," says Steve. "I don't know." Sophie Dulberg's parents say they were unprepared for the competitive nature of organized kids' sports. Says her mother, Debi, a psychologist: "The people in gymnastics are very focused on commitment and responsibility. The culture has a life of its own."

But it's also true that the kids themselves often do the pushing. Corvin Lamb Jr., 13, is a track star in a Miami suburb who trains at least 10 hours a week and holds the national age-group record in the 400 meters. Last November he tore the anterior cruciate ligament—the ACL—in his knee in a football game, an injury rarely seen in kids. Since the surgery to repair the damage he has been cleared for light jogging but instead has started more aggressive workouts, to his parents' concern. "I cringed at first," says his father, Corvin Sr., a private school teacher and coach. "But once he's fixed something in his mind, he does exactly what he sets out to. He is very, very determined."

For Corvin Jr. his dedication is a natural outgrowth of his own lofty ambitions. "My big goal is to have a shoe named after me, like Michael Jordan or LeBron James," he says. "I want to be something in life." There is nothing wrong, of course, with aiming high. But as parents and physicians grapple with the injury epidemic, there is a newfound urgency to the old adage, slow and steady wins the race. "Some of these youngsters need to decide if they want to be all-stars as kids," says Dr. Andrews, "or all-stars when they grow up."

UNIT 3
Cognitive Development and Education

Unit Selections

Key Points to Consider

- Why does school violence occur and what can be done to prevent it?

- How does student health effect academic performance?

- How are advanced placement courses motivating students?

- How do middle schools provide a secure space for learning and personal meaning?

- Should Universities request depressed and suicidal students to drop out?

- How may college life be a poor environment for learning?

- How can the transition between public school and college be improved?

- Why do students cheat? How can schools prevent academic dishonesty?

Student Website
www.mhcls.com/online

Internet References
Further information regarding these websites may be found in this book's preface or online.

At-Risk Children and Youth
http://www.ncrel.org/sdrs/areas/at0cont.htm

Adolescence entails changes in cognitive capacities that are just as monumental as the biological changes. Whereas children tend to be more literal, more tied to reality and to the familiar—adolescents are more abstract, systematic, and logical. Adolescents can appreciate metaphors and sarcasm, they can easily think about things that do not exist, they can test abstract ideas against reality, and they can readily conceive of multiple possibilities. Many of these improvements in thinking ability contribute to conflicts with adults as adolescents become better able to argue a point or take a stand. They are better at planning out their case and anticipating counterarguments. They are also more likely to question the way things are because they now conceive of alternate possibilities.

The study of cognitive changes that occur in adolescence has largely been based on the work of the Swiss psychologist, Jean Piaget, and his colleague Barbel Inhelder. Piaget and Inhelder described the adolescent as reasoning at the formal operational stage. Children from the approximate ages of 7 to 11 years old were described as being in the "concrete operational" stage. Not all researchers agree with Piaget and Inhelder that changes in adolescent cognitive abilities represent true stage-related changes. They do, however, agree that adolescent thought is characteristically more logical, abstract, and hypothetical than that of children. Recognize, though, that having certain mental capacities does not mean that adolescents, or even adults for that matter, will always reason at their rational best!

Piaget's views on cognitive development have been very influential, particularly in the field of education. Awareness of the cognitive abilities and shortcomings of adolescents can make their behaviors more comprehensible to parents, teachers, counselors, and other professionals who work with them. Similarly, as Piaget suggested, schools need to take the developmental abilities and needs of adolescents into account in planning programs and designing curricula. In addition, Piaget's general philosophy was that learning must be active. Others in the field of education, however, caution that there are other important issues left unaddressed by Piaget. For example, the U.S. has an elevated school dropout rate, so we need to find alternatives for keeping the nation's youth in school.

Schools focus on individual students and on punishment. Only when schools take student concerns into account will schools become environments that stimulate attendance, interest, and harmony. School violence by disenchanted youth has peaked in the U.S. Schools need to promote a sense of belonging if disaffected and potentially violent students are to become members of the school community.

While developmentalists in the Piagetian tradition focus on the ways in which the thought processes of children and adolescents differ, other researchers have taken a different track—a psychometric approach. In this approach, the emphasis is on quantifying cognitive abilities such as verbal ability, mathematical ability, and general intelligence (IQ). The measurement of intelligence, as well as the very definition of intelligence, has been controversial for decades. A classic question is whether intelligence is best conceptualized as a general capacity that underlies many diverse abilities or as a set of specific abilities.

Traditional IQ tests focus on abilities that relate to success in school and ignore abilities such as those that tap creativity, mechanical aptitude, or practical intelligence.

The role of genetic versus environmental contributions to intelligence has also been controversial. At the turn of the century the predominant view was that intelligence was essentially inherited and was little influenced by experience. Today, the consensus is that an individual's intelligence is very much a product of both nature and nurture. An even greater controversy focuses on the role that heredity versus the environment plays in explaining racial, ethnic, and gender differences in performance on various cognitive tests such as IQ tests.

Adolescents clearly have larger vocabularies, more mathematical knowledge, better spatial ability, etc., than children. Their memories are better because they process information more efficiently and use memory strategies more effectively. Adolescents possess a greater general knowledge base than children, which enables adolescents to link new concepts to existing ideas. Stated another way, psychometric intelligence may well increase with age. On the other hand, because of comparisons to age peers, the relative performance of adolescents on aptitude tests remains fairly stable. A 9-year-old child's outstanding performance on an IQ test, for example, is fairly predictive that the same individual's IQ score at age 15 will be better than the score of most peers.

Performance on standardized tests, IQ or otherwise (e.g. achievement tests), is often used to place junior high and high school students in ability tracts, a practice that increasingly is questioned. Similarly, standardized test results compared across schools are being used to measure a school's educational effectiveness. These types of issues are addressed in the following set of articles.

The first selection discusses school violence. When students sense that they belong, schools become better learning environments with reduced anxiety. Katherine Bucher and M. Lee Manning point out that violence, bullying, sexual harassment, extortion, threats, and other forms of intimidation harm schools and students. The authors provide eight suggestions for making schools safer.

Beth Pateman explains that health programs in which teens learn how to have a healthy life-style raise academic achievement of students. More attention needs to be given to the overall health of adolescents including proper sleep and nutrition.

Jay Matthews presents evidence that high expectations in learning will improve self-esteem. The increase of students taking advanced placement (AP) tests are motivating both teachers and adolescents. Safer schools for students produce a better learning environment as pointed out by Linda Inlay. Some college students are involved in a life-style and environment of drinking and partying starting on Wednesday night. That is not conducive for learning, as pointed out by Steven Kotler.

Bill Hemmer reveals both strengths and weaknesses in improving rates of high school and college completion for low income and minority students. The next article examines cheating in high school and how it can be cured.

Sense of Belonging to School

Can Schools Make a Difference?

Xin Ma

There has been renewed public concern about students' sense of belonging to school (sense of school membership) following the recent waves of school violence in North America. Goodenow and Grady (1993) defined sense of belonging as the extent to which students feel personally accepted, respected, included, and supported in the school social environment. Maslow (1962) stated that the need of belonging has to be satisfied before other needs can be fulfilled. (Finn's (1989) identification-participation model indicates that unless students identify well with their schools (i.e., feel welcomed, respected, and valued), their education participation always will be limited. Applying the principles of affective psychology, Combs (1982) stated that successful student learning depends on four highly affective variables, one of which is the feeling of belonging or being cared for. In "The Discipline of Hope," M. Scherer (1998), editor of Educational Leadership, highlighted H. Kohl's (personal communication, 1998) emphasis on the critical importance of fostering a sense of belonging and love of learning in public education.

Students' sense of (or lack of) belonging to school has social consequences beyond recent tragedies of school violence. In a review of empirical studies on the growth and nature of juvenile gangs, Burnett and Walz (1994) concluded that gang-related problems increase when students do not have a sense of belonging to their school. A school district superintendent who interviewed gang members to determine their views about school reported that encouraging a sense of belonging to school was a major prevention and intervention strategy (Reep, 1996). In a phenomenological study in which Omizo, Omizo, and Honda (1997) interviewed boys about their gang membership, the authors revealed major themes such as sense of belonging, self-esteem, and protection.

Results of case studies indicate that sense of belonging is a direct cause of dropping out of high school (Fine, 1991). In an ethnographic study of culturally diverse adolescents identified as potential school dropouts, Schlosser (1992) reported that those whose teachers emphasized sense of belonging were more likely, compared with those whose teachers did not emphasize belonging, to ac-

cept their teachers' education values and to continue in school. On the basis of a review of an eclectic body of literature, Kagan (1990) developed a research model to determine whether treatment, behavior, perception, and cognition differ between students at risk of dropping out of high school and those not at risk. One major component of the model is that sense of belonging to school, which distinguishes students with and without risk, enhances commitment to schooling. Wang, Haertel, and Walberg (1998) described the roles of educators in promoting children's educational resilience (e.g., their demonstration of remarkable academic achievement despite conditions that put them at risk of academic failure such as family poverty, physical illness, parent divorce, substance abuse, and frequent relocation); sense of belonging was presented as an important ingredient in any educational program for children at risk of academic failure.

Sense of belonging to school appears essential to many educational processes and schooling outcomes. Goodenow (1991) investigated the relationship between students' sense of belonging in their classes and measures related to motivation, student effort, and academic achievement. Multiple regression analysis of 612 students in Grades 5 to 8 revealed that sense of belonging in a class was related to students' expectations of academic success, intrinsic interests in academic work, and course grades and to teachers' ratings of students' academic effort. A survey of 301 students in two multiethnic urban junior high schools with African American, European American, and Hispanic American students (each ethnic group comprising about one third of the participants) was designed to examine the correlation between sense of belonging and measures of motivation and achievement. Multiple regression analysis showed that even after controls for the impact of the immediate peer group's values, a student's sense of belonging still had a statistically significant impact on motivation as well as on engaged and persistent effort in difficult academic work (Goodenow & Grady, 1993). Gonzalez and Padilla (1997) identified high achievers and low achievers from among 2,169 Mexican American students in three high schools; multiple regression analysis showed that sense of belonging to school was the only statistically significant predictor of student academic grades.

Goff and Goddard (1999) studied the relationship between terminal core values and delinquency, substance use, and sexual behavior among 544 high school students. Results of analysis of variance indicated that students who valued self-respect, sense of belonging, and sense of accomplishment exhibited (statistically) significantly lower frequency of delinquent behavior and substance use. Romero and Roberts (1998) conducted a school-based survey in a large metropolitan area that included 3,071 students of African, European, Mexican, and Vietnamese descents; results of multiple regression analysis indicated that a stronger sense of belonging to one's racial-ethnic group was associated with more positive attitudes toward other racial-ethnic groups. Wendel, Hoke, and Joedel (1994) surveyed 70 outstanding middle school administrators and found from descriptive analyses that the ability of school administrators to create students' sense of belonging was essential for a successful school operation.

A student's sense of belonging to school develops in a school social environment. In a philosophical examination of issues related to sense of belonging, Edwards (1995) advocated that school administrators ensure that teachers must feel a sense of belonging to school so that they, in turn, can help their students feel a sense of belonging. In a position paper, Routt (1996) asserted that students perceive teachers who are attentive, respectful, and helpful as caring and concerned about their social and academic well being, which gives the students a sense of belonging and fosters their academic engagement. Kester (1994) conducted an action research (researchers and teachers collaborated on research design and process) to examine whether African American students in a multiage classroom with the same teacher for 3 years had a stronger connection to their school than students in other classrooms had. He reported that school structure and peer influence can interact to affect students' sense of belonging to school. Reviews of research literature suggest consistently that small high schools are in a better position than large schools to create a stronger sense of belonging (Cawelti, 1995; Cotton, 1996; Raywid, 1996). The researchers reported that attendance at small schools resulted in better student involvement, better interpersonal relationships, and easier management of individual and cooperative practices.

Using individual and focus-group interviews, Williams and Downing (1998) investigated the characteristics of classroom membership perceived by 51 middle school students from two school districts (one urban and one rural). Results of qualitative data analysis showed that having friends in class, interacting with peers, participating in class activities, and obtaining good grades indicated membership or sense of belonging. Children from four elementary schools participated in a survey study intended to improve their self-esteem through adult role-model intervention. One of the major descriptive data analyses indicated that a student's sense of belonging can be affected by the labels placed on the student (Greenberg, 1995).

Students' sense of belonging to school is a critical research topic in education because it constitutes a construct that is distinctly different from other constructs often discussed in education research, such as school climate and social support (Goodenow, 1991). Albert (1991) conceptualized sense of belonging in three Cs (connect, capable, and contribute). The first C emphasizes that students need to connect with one another by cooperative learning and with teachers by their greeting and encouraging the students. The second C emphasizes that teachers need to help students feel capable, by modified tasks and assignments that teachers design to provide students with successful learning experiences. The third C emphasizes that students need to contribute to their school by performing duties (e.g., being line leaders and lunch card collectors) that teachers assign to provide them with opportunities to feel valued.

Research Questions

There is widespread research evidence that sense of belonging to school is critical to the success of public education (see Scherer, 1998). A recent increase in the occurrences of serious school violence has put a heavier emphasis on educators to develop students' sense of belonging. The National School Safety Center reported that about one crime in every 6 (bullying, fighting, carrying weapons, and gang activities) occurs when school is in session (Kum-Walks, 1996). In contrast, empirical studies have lingered behind in advancing working knowledge for educators on students' sense of belonging. Most existing empirical studies have focused on documenting the educational benefit of a strong sense of belonging. There is a lack of empirical studies on the development of sense of belonging in a school social environment, particularly on what schools can do to shape and enhance students' sense of belonging. Specifically, little research evidence exists on how school context and climate affect students' sense of belonging. Unfortunately, most educators need adequate working knowledge in that aspect of sense of belonging. That aspect of school context and climate is also necessary to formulate any theories of students' sense of belonging to school. The present study is a direct response to that limitation.

Using survey data that describe students in Grades 6 and 8, I addressed the following three research questions:

1. Is there any variation in students' sense of belonging to school among students and schools in Grades 6 and 8? Specifically, to what extent are students or schools responsible for the variation in sense of belonging? Are schools equally effective (or successful) in developing students' sense of belonging (to

what extent do schools vary in affecting students' sense of belonging)?

2. If there is variation in sense of belonging among students, then what student characteristics are responsible for it? Specifically, are there individual differences related to gender, socioeconomic status (SES), native status, number of parents, number of siblings, academic achievement, self-esteem, and general health in students' sense of belonging in Grades 6 and 8?

3. If there is variation in sense of belonging among schools, then what school characteristics are responsible for it? Specifically, do students in schools with advantaged context (school size and school mean SES) have a better sense of belonging than do students in schools with disadvantaged context in Grades 6 and 8? Do students in schools with a positive climate (academic press, disciplinary climate, and parental involvement) have a better sense of belonging than do students in schools with a negative climate in Grades 6 and 8?

The two grade levels involved in this study were ideal for the examination of sense of belonging. Goodenow (1991) found that the beginning of secondary education is the most critical stage for the development of sense of belonging because students at this stage are in transition from childhood to adolescence (see also Eccles & Midgley, 1989).

Method

Setting and Data Sources

New Brunswick is the largest of Canada's three maritime provinces, located below Quebec and beside Maine. With an area about 73,440 kilometers in a roughly rectangular shape, the population of New Brunswick was about 757,000 people in 2000. The province is largely rural, and has a relatively homogenous population with few visible minorities. Most of the people live along the Atlantic Coast and in the St. John River valleys. About 33% of the population speaks French; New Brunswick is the only official bilingual province in Canada.

There are two provincially funded public education systems in New Brunswick. The Anglophone system has 12 school districts (English is the instructional language), and the Francophone system has 6 school districts (French is the instructional language). Both systems are governed by a parent-based structure, consisting of parent advisory councils at the school and district levels and two provincial boards (one Anglophone and one Francophone). Education is a provincial jurisdiction in Canada (i.e., provinces have total control of their education policies and practices). The Curriculum Development Branch in the provincial Department of Education sets goals and objectives of education. Specifically, administrators develop and implement curricula in all subject areas, recommend print and nonprint instructional resources, and suggest the purchase of equipment to support the prescribed curricula. Both school systems use the same provincial curricula but different languages for instruction.

Data used in the present study were collected in 1996 for the New Brunswick School Climate Study (NBSCS). All of the students in Grades 6 and 8 from the Anglophone school system participated in the NBSCS (6,883 Grade 6 students from 148 schools and 6,868 Grade 8 students from 92 schools). Therefore, the two data sets represent populations of students rather than samples of students. Students completed four achievement tests (mathematics, science, reading, and writing) and a student questionnaire.

The present study is a secondary data analysis in which I used the NBSCS database. Although the data were collected 7 years ago, they were suitable for this study because the NBSCS is the latest large-scale education survey available that contains comprehensive measures on students and their schools. In addition, there were no dramatic educational changes in the past 7 years in New Brunswick (e.g., curriculum and instruction remained largely the same). Therefore, the NBSCS data, although somewhat dated, can still be relevant for one to examine, for example, students' sense of belonging to school. At least, the present study can provide a historical profile for future senior high school students on their state of sense of belonging to school when they started middle school. This research also can offer useful information for investigations on students' sense of belonging that are now underway.

Measures

Students' sense of belonging to school was the outcome (dependent) variable. Explanatory (independent) variables were classified into student and school characteristics. Student characteristics included gender, SES, native status, number of parents, number of siblings, academic achievement, self-esteem, and general health. School characteristics were classified into school context variables, including size and mean SES; and school climate variables, including academic press, disciplinary climate, and parent involvement. Table 1 describes outcome, student-level, and school-level variables.

The NBSCS staff developed scales measuring sense of belonging, academic press, disciplinary climate, and parental involvement based on a theoretical schema on schooling process (see Willms, 1992). This schema contains constitutive definitions for these (and other) constructs and the operational guidance on the selection of measures for each construct. Other scales were borrowed directly from existing scales. The Self-Esteem subscale was taken from the Self-Description Questionnaire 1 (SDQ1; Marsh, 1992), and the General Health Scale was developed by the World Health Organization. I intended that these practices (developing scales on the basis of a

TABLE 1 Basic Statistics on the Anglophone and Francophone School Systems in New Brunswick

School system	Anglophone system	Francophone System
Student enrollment	86,555	38,387
Education staff	5,218	2,358
Support staff	2,539	1,280
Student-teacher ratio	16.5	
Average class size	23.4	
Graduation rate	0.86	
Dropout rate	0.03	

Note. Separate statistics were not available on student-teacher ratio, average class size, graduation rate, and dropout rate. Data source: New Brunswick Department of Education.

theoretical schema and borrowing scales from existing, popular, and well-documented scales) would reach an adequate match between constitutive and operational definitions. Researchers commonly used a 5-point scale to promote larger variance for statistical analysis.

At the student level, sense of belonging to school measured the extent to which students felt personally accepted, respected, included, and supported in the school social environment. Cronbach's alphas were .68 in Grade 6 and .73 in Grade 8. Gender was coded as 1= girls and 0 = boys, therefore, gender effects as reported later were female effects. In a similar logic, native status was coded as 1 = native and 0 = other; number of parents was coded as 1 = single parent and 0 = both parents. Self-esteem measured global attitudes toward self in academic and nonacademic areas. Cronbach's alphas were .87 in Grade 6 and .88 in Grade 8. The General Health Scale measured children's general physical and mental wellness. Cronbach's alphas were .77 in Grade 6 and .76 in Grade 8.

I used regular provincial achievement tests in mathematics, science, reading, and writing as academic achievement measures. A panel of curriculum specialists and experienced teachers developed the achievement tests on the basis of provincial curricula in the four school subjects. The reading test had 35 items in Grade 6 and 50 items in Grade 8; it measured reading comprehension of fiction and nonfiction passages. Two writing samples that were collected from each student in Grades 6 and 8 over a period of time were rated by a panel of teachers on a 6-point scale (unratable, weak, marginal, acceptable, competent, and superior). Student categorical writing scores were transformed to a continuous scale with a mean of 0 and a standard deviation of 1 (see Mosteller & Tukey, 1977). Mathematics and science achievement tests were administered to students in Grade 6 only. The mathematics test had 39 items that measured computation, concep-

tual understanding, and application in the areas of numeration, geometry, measurement, and data management. The science test had 33 items that measured knowledge and understanding of scientific concepts and processes. In the present study, the variable, academic achievement, was an average measure of academic achievement in Grades 6 and 8, respectively.

At the school level, school context variables included school size (in terms of student enrollment in Grades 6 and 8) and school mean SES (aggregated from student SES within each school). School climate variables included academic press, disciplinary climate, and parent involvement (aggregated from student responses within each school). Academic press measured the extent to which teachers and peers valued academic success and held high academic expectation (Cronbach's [alpha]s = .61 in Grade 6 and .65 in Grade 8); disciplinary climate measured the extent to which students complied with school rules of conduct (Cronbach's [alpha]s = .77 in Grades 6 and 8); and parent involvement measured the extent to which parents were involved in their children's education (Cronbach's [alpha]s = .77 in Grade 6 and .79 in Grade 8). For the purpose of data analysis, continuous variables at student and school levels were standardized (M = 0; SD = 1). There were a few dichotomous variables at the student level that were centered around their grand means.

"Reliability may be thought of as a special type of correlation that measures consistency of observations and scores" (Sax, 1997), and a correlation measure can be considered an effect-size index (see Cohen, 1988). These statistical properties allow one to evaluate roughly the adequacy in terms of reliability on scales used in the present study (see Table 1). The range of effect-size indices was between .61 and .88. According to Cohen, an effect-size index above .50 can be considered large in the behavioral sciences. Therefore, from the perspective of behavioral sciences, scales in this study appeared to be reliable.

Statistical Procedure

I used hierarchical linear modeling (HLM) techniques in which students were nested within schools for data analysis (see Bryk & Raudenbush, 1992). The use of HLM corresponded to the three research questions addressed previously in this study. HLM allowed me to partition the total variance in sense of belonging into within-school and between-school variances to address the first research question. Furthermore, HLM estimated student and school effects on sense of belonging simultaneously with adjustment for sampling and measurement errors to address the second and third research questions.

I developed two-level HLM models in which students were nested within schools. At the first (student) level, sense of belonging was regressed on gender, SES, native status, number of parents, number of siblings, academic achievement, self-esteem, and general health. The intercept of that regression represented an average measure of sense of belonging within each school, adjusted for student characteristics in that school. A slope of the regression associated with an explanatory variable represented the relationship between sense of belonging and the particular variable in that school. At the second (school) level, school average measures of sense of belonging were regressed on school context (school size and school mean SES) and climate (academic press, disciplinary climate, and parent involvement) variables. The slopes from the student-level model were fixed because my primary purpose in this study was to explain variation in sense of belonging among students and schools (see Thum & Bryk, 1997).

I performed the statistical procedure described in the preceding paragraphs for each grade level; specifically, I tested two HLM models. The null model contained only the outcome measure, without any explanatory variables at either the student or school level. The null model parti-tioned the total variance in sense of belonging into within-schools and between-schools components (for the first research question). The full model contained student-level and school-level variables that modeled within-school and between-school variations in sense of belonging (for the second and third research questions). With the results from Grades 6 and 8, I made a cross-sectional comparison to describe any pattern of change in students' sense of belonging.

Assumptions for the HLM models developed in this study were that (a) residuals at the student and school levels have a normal distribution with a population mean of zero and constant variance ($[\text{sigma}]^2$ at student level and [tau] at the school level) and (b) residuals at the school level are independent between schools. I examined those assumptions on the basis of the six-question procedure outlined in Snijders and Bosker (1999); no serious violation of HLM assumptions was detected. I removed a few extreme cases to improve the models (e.g., small schools with fewer than five students).

TABLE 2. **Descriptive Statistics for Outcome and Explanatory Variables at the Student and School Levels**

Variable	Grade 6		Grade 8	
	M	**SD**	**M**	**SD**
Sense of belonging (outcome variable)	3.76	0.81	3.79	0.79
Student characteristics (student-level explanatory variables)				
Gender (girls = 1, boys = 0)	0.49	0.50	0.55	0.83
Socioeconomic status (SES)	0.00	1.00	0.00	1.00
Native status (Native = 1, Others = 0)	0.01	0.10		
Number of parents (single parent = 1, both parents = 0)	0.14	0.34	0.16	0.37
Number of siblings	1.99	1.46	2.00	1.48
Academic achievement	0.00	1.00	0.00	1.00
Self-esteem	3.78	0.61	3.77	0.69
General health	4.06	0.68	4.1	0.65
School characteristics (school-level explanatory variables)				
School mean SES	0.00	1.00	0.00	1.00
School size	39.71	30.73	67.91	56.23
Academic press	3.72	0.16	3.58	0.15
Disciplinary climate	2.96	0.30	2.86	0.26
Parent involvement	2.27	0.17	1.90	0.12

Note. Calculations were based on 6,883 students from 148 schools in Grade 6 and 6,868 students from 92 schools in Grade 8. Native status was not available in Grade 8. SES and academic achievement were standardized variables at the student level. School mean SES was a standardized variable at the school level. Effect sizes were 0.04 for sense of belonging, 0.02 for self-esteem, 0.06 for general health, 0.90 for academic press, 0.36 for disciplinary climate, and 2.55 for parent involvement.

Results

Table 2 shows means and standard deviations of outcome and explanatory variables (at both student and school levels) in Grades 6 and 8. To compare the results between the two grade levels, I calculated average group standard deviation effect sizes for the major student-level and school-level variables (Abrami, Cholmsky, & Cordon, 2001). For a two-group comparison, an effect is small if half of its effect size is 0.10, medium if 0.25, and large if 0.40 (Cohen, 1988). At the student level, differences between the two grade levels in sense of belonging, self-esteem, and general health were all extremely small. At the school level, differences in academic press and parent involvement were large, whereas differences in disciplinary climate were small, between the two grade levels. The differences in school means were all in favor of Grade 6. Overall, school-level characteristics varied much more across the two grade levels than student-level characteristics.

Table 3 shows the proportion of variance in students' sense of belonging within and between schools. In Grades 6 and 8, about 96% of the variance in sense of belonging was attributable to the students. Although schools differed systematically in students' sense of belonging, they were responsible for only 4% of its variance (in both grades). I introduced student-level variables and school-level variables to explain the variations among students and schools.

Results of HLM models for students in Grades 6 and 8 are shown in Table 4. To illustrate the practical significance of an effect and to compare effects across the two grade levels, I needed a common metric. I used effect size (SD) unit in the present study, as advocated by Lee and Loeb (2000). In behavioral sciences, Rosenthal and Rosnow (1984) classified effect sizes more than 0.5 standard deviation as large, effect sizes between 0.3 and 0.5 standard deviation as moderate, and effect sizes less than 0.3 standard deviation as small.

Grade 6 girls demonstrated a more positive and statistically significant sense of belonging than did Grade 6 boys (effect size [ES] = 0.47 SD). According to Rosenthal and Rosnow (1984), that result was a practically moderate effect. Students with a lower level of academic achievement showed a more positive and statistically significant sense of belonging than did students with a higher level of academic achievement. However, with an effect size of 0.04 SD, the effect of academic achievement was practically small (or unimportant). Students with higher self-esteem reported a more positive and statistically significant sense of belonging than did students with lower self-esteem (ES = 0.72 SD, a practically large effect). Students with better general health demonstrated a more positive and statistically significant sense of belonging than did students with worse general health (ES = 0.44 SD, a practically moderate effect).

TABLE 3. Proportion of Variance in Sense of Belonging Within and Between Schools

Variable	Grade 6	Grade 8
Within schools	0.96	0.96
Between schools	0.04	0.04

The effect sizes were estimated with other variables in the statistically controlled model. In other words, each effect size represented a pure effect of its associated variable. The effect sizes were examined with other variables in the model being statistically controlled. In the case of students' sense of belonging in Grade 6, the cumulative effect of gender, self-esteem, and general health was highly significant, both statistically and practically. Therefore, student-level characteristics played a critical role in sense of belonging to school.

Grade 8 girls demonstrated a more positive statistically significant sense of belonging than did Grade 8 boys, but the effect size was much smaller than that in Grade 6 (0.11 SD vs. 0.47 SD, respectively). SES became a statistically significant predictor of students' sense of belonging (ES = 0.07 SD, a practically small effect). Students with a higher level of academic achievement showed a more positive statistically significant sense of belonging than did students with a lower level of academic achievement (ES = 0.06 SD, a practically small effect). Students with higher self-esteem showed a more positive statistically significant sense of belonging than did students with lower self-esteem (ES = 0.51 SD, a practically large effect). Students with better general health reported a more positive statistically significant sense of belonging than did students with worse general health (ES = 0.34 SD, a practically moderate effect). Finally, the cumulative effect of self-esteem and general health was significant both statistically and practically in Grade 8, indicating that student-level characteristics continued to play an important role in sense of belonging to school.

A comparison of effects between Grades 6 and 8 shows that gender differences (in favor of girls) in sense of belonging were practically moderate in Grade 6 but practically small in Grade 8. Effects of student's self-esteem were practically large on their sense of belonging in Grades 6 and 8. Students' general health showed a practically moderate effect on their sense of belonging in both Grades 6 and 8. Students' SES had no statistically significant effect on their sense of belonging in Grade 6, but a practically small effect in Grade 8. Self-esteem, gender, and general health were the most important predictors of sense of belonging in Grade 6, whereas self-esteem and general health were the most important predictors in Grade 8. Overall, as students progressed through junior high school, effects of student characteristics became smaller. This finding also could be observed from a comparison of cumulative effects between the two grade levels.

Although there were not many statistically significant predictors at the school level, the effects of statistically significant predictors at that level were practically large. In Grade 6, students in schools with higher academic press demonstrated a more positive statistically significant sense of belonging than did students in schools with lower academic press (ES = 6.26 SD, a practically large effect). In Grade 8, students in schools with a better disciplinary climate reported a more positive statistically significant sense of belonging than did students in schools with a worse disciplinary climate (ES = 5.70 SD, a practically large effect). Overall, school effects were not consistent in terms of statistically significant predictors of students' sense of belonging, but they were practically large across the two grade levels.

The bottom panel of Table 4 shows the proportion of variance accounted for at the student and school levels. The model explained 36% of the variance in sense of belonging among students in Grade 6 and 27% in Grade 8. The model accounted for 61% of the variance in sense of belonging among schools in Grade 6, and 65% in Grade 8. Although the percentages of variance explained were sufficient at the school level, those at the student level were low. That finding implied that other student-level characteristics were responsible for the majority of the variance in sense of belonging at the student level. A category of student-level characteristics was the interaction of a student with peers and teachers. Although the characteristics were not obtained, they might be important predictors of sense of belonging. Presumably, this interaction directly affects the extent to which the student feels accepted, respected, included, and supported in the school community.

Using cross-sectional data (at the middle school level), I highlighted the finding that discrepancies in student's sense of belonging to school were mainly within schools (between students) rather than between schools. I also attempted to explain differences among students and schools in sense of belonging with some student and school characteristics. As one of the most important findings in this study, I unveiled an empirical relationship between students' self-esteem and their sense of belonging. Self-esteem was the single most important predictor of sense of belonging, with fairly consistent effects across Grades 6 and 8.

The aforementioned finding implies that students' attitude toward themselves is transferable to their attitude toward school. Students who had a greater feeling of worthiness appeared to feel more comfortable in their schools than did those students who felt less worth. Beyond the data available in the present study, one may speculate that higher confidence in one's ability (e.g., academic, athletic, and social) may promote more active participation in school activities that often makes one feel that he or she is valued. However, low self-esteem, or doubt about one's ability, may alienate one from participation in school activities. Alienation may be the major reason for students' lack of sense of belonging to school. The rela-

TABLE 4. Hierarchical Linear Modeling Results of Student and School Effects on Sense of Belonging

Variable	Grade 6 Effect	Grade 6 SE	Grade 8 Effect	Grade 8 SE
Effects of student characteristics				
Gender	0.294 *	0.021	0.081 *	0.013
Socioeconomic status (SES)			0.046 *	0.011
Academic achievement	-0.023 *	0.011	0.044 *	0.011
Self-esteem	0.446 *	0.011	0.361 *	0.012
General health	0.274 *	0.011	0.243 *	0.011
Effects of school characteristics				
Academic press	0.094 *	0.016		
Disciplinary climate			0.075 *	0.019
Proportion of variance explained				
Within schools	0.36		0.27	
Between schools	0.61		0.65	

Note. SE = standard error. At the student level, Native status, number of parents, and number of siblings are not statistically significant in Grades 6 and 8. At the school level, school mean SES, school size, and parent involvement are not statistically significant in Grades 6 and 8.

* $p < .05$.

tionship between self-esteem and sense of belonging may be circular, with each enhancing the other.

The next important predictor of sense of belonging at the student level was general health. This finding seemed to convey a similar story about participation and alienation. Students with good health may have had more "capital" to participate in academic, athletic, and social activities in school than did students with poor health.

The theme of participation in school activities as it relates to students' sense of belonging to school was inferred in the present study not only by the most statistically significant predictors such as self-esteem and general health but also by predictors that were not statistically significant, including SES (practically unimportant in Grade 8 although statistically significant), native status, number of parents, and number of siblings. One may have noticed that these predictors all describe individual background characteristics and thus did not directly determine participation in school activities. Overall, perhaps the most important contribution of this study to the research literature is that it helps propose the research hypothesis that students' participation in school activities may be the key to their sense of belonging to school.

My findings also help dismiss some misperceptions that have long existed among the public. For example, many educators and administrators believe that native students are far more negative in their sense of belonging to school than are non-native students. In the present study, however, the predictor, native status, was not statistically significant. Therefore, if native students had a negative sense of belonging, then the problem appeared to be associated with their self-esteem and health status (which again brings the discussion to the issue of participation). Stated differently, once students' self-esteem and health status were taken into account, native students did not necessarily have more negative sense of belonging to school than did their non-native counterparts.

Similarly, the misperception exists that low-SES students tend to misunderstand the values of education; thus, they have a negative attitude toward school. In the present study, SES was not statistically significant in Grade 6 and was practically unimportant, although statistically significant, in Grade 8. In comparison with self-esteem and health status, SES was trivial in its effect on sense of belonging. In general, many misperceptions about sense of belonging's being associated with gender, SES, native status, number of parents, and number of siblings may well be dismissed in the presence of self-esteem and health status.

Because schools, in comparison with students, varied in a secondary way, it is perhaps not surprising that few school-level variables played important roles in explaining students' sense of belonging. Still, this study has shown some large school effects. In both Grades 6 and 8, school context variables (school size and school mean SES) were not statistically significant, whereas some school climate variables (academic press, disciplinary climate, and parent involvement) showed statistically significant effects. Therefore, school climate was more important than school context for students' sense of belonging to school. That finding highlights the fact that teachers can play a critical role in shaping students' sense of belonging because, unlike school context characteristics, school climate characteristics are usually under the direct control of school staff.

Another major finding at the school level was that school climate effects were not consistent in type (academic press was statistically significant in Grade 6; disciplinary climate was statistically significant in Grade 8) but were similar in magnitude. For the sixth graders, peers' and teachers' care for and concern about their academic wellness seemed to make them feel at home in school. One should understand that finding together with the one from the student level that showed a small effect of academic achievement on sense of belonging. Therefore, the academic achievement that students attain is not critical for their sense of belonging to school; what matters to their sense of belonging is the presence of caring peers and teachers, along with a lot of attention to their schoolwork and academic success. That conclusion adds to the research a "rare" finding that academic press has effects not only on students' cognitive wellness, such as

their academic success, but also on students' affective wellness, such as their sense of belonging.

For the eighth graders, however, the school disciplinary environment shaped their sense of belonging to school. An unsafe school is not a desirable place to be for most students. In this study, items descriptive of disciplinary climate were mostly about students' perceptions of disciplinary rules in school. Therefore, if students perceived school disciplinary rules as unfair, they developed a negative sense of belonging, even though their school disciplinary climate may not necessarily have been negative.

In sum, this study suggests (a) that students' sense of belonging to school is influenced more by their mental and physical conditions but less by their individual and family characteristics and (b) that students' sense of belonging to school is influenced by school climate characteristics rather than school context characteristics. Findings from the school level do indicate that teachers and administrators are in a powerful position to influence students' sense of belonging to school (the large school effect sizes suggest that schools can make a difference in students' sense of belonging to school). School climate that makes students feel that they are cared for, safe, and treated fairly is conducive to their developing a positive sense of belonging to school. Therefore, the practice of communal schools in which, among other things, interpersonal relationships are emphasized to create affective bonds among all school members (see Lee & Smith, 1995) may be instrumental in developing students' positive sense of belonging to school.

REFERENCES

Abrami, P. C., Cholmsky, R., & Cordon, R. (2001). Statistical analysis for the social sciences. Needham Heights, MA: Allyn & Bacon.

Albert, L. (1991). Cooperative discipline. Circle Pines, MN: American Guidance Service.

Bryk, A. S., & Raudenbush, S. W. (1992). Hierarchical linear models. Newbury Park, CA: Sage.

Burnett, G., & Walz, G. (1994). Gangs in the schools (Rep. No. EDO-CG-94-28). Greensboro, NC: ERIC Clearinghouse on Counseling and Student Services.

Cawelti, G. (1995). The missing focus of high school restructuring. School Administrator, 52(11), 12 16.

Cohen, J. (1988). Statistical power analysis for the behavioral sciences (2nd ed.). Hillsdale, NJ: Erlbaum.

Combs, A. (1982). Affective education or none at all. Educational Leadership, 39, 495–497.

Cotton, K. (1996). Affective and social benefits of small scale schooling (Rep. No. EDO-RC-96-5). Charleston, WV: ERIC Clearinghouse on Rural Education and Small Schools.

Eccles, J., & Midgley, C. (1989). Stage-environmental fit: Developmentally appropriate classrooms for young adolescents. In C. Ames & R. Ames (Eds.), Research on motivation in education: Goals and cognitions (pp. 215–286). San Diego, CA: Academic Press.

Edwards, D. (1995). The school counselor's role in helping teachers and students. Elementary School Guidance and Counseling, 29, 191–197.

Fine, M. (1991). Framing dropouts. Albany, NY: SUN Press.

Finn, J. (1989). Withdrawing from school. Review of Educational Research, 59, 117–142.

Goff, B. G., & Goddard, H. W. (1999). Terminal core values associated with adolescent problem behavior. Adolescence, 34, 47–60.

Gonzalez, R., & Padilla, A. M. (1997). The academic resilience of Mexican American high school students. Hispanic Journal of Behavioral Sciences, 19, 301–317.

Goodenow, C. (1991, April). The sense of belonging and its relationships to academic motivation among pre- and early adolescent students. Paper presented at the annual meeting of the American Educational Research Association, Chicago.

Goodenow, C., & Grady, K. (1993). The relationship of school belonging and friends' values to academic motivation among urban adolescent students. The Journal of Experimental Education, 62, 60–71.

Greenberg, R. N. (1995). Self-esteem enhancement through adult role-model intervention. Unpublished master's thesis, Saint Xavier University, Palatine, IL.

Kagan, D. (1990). How schools alienate students at risk: A model for examining proximal classroom variables. Educational Psychologist, 25, 105–125.

Kester, V. M. (1994). Factors that affect African American students' bonding to middle school. Elementary School Journal, 95, 63–73.

Kum-Walks, D. A. (1996). Responses to school violence by schools and students (Doctoral dissertation. Claremont Graduate University. 1996). Dissertation Abstracts International, 57, 4303A.

Lee, V. E., & Loeb, S. (2000). School size in Chicago elementary schools: Effects on teachers' attitudes and students' achievement. American Educational Research Journal, 37, 3–32.

Lee, V. E., & Smith, J. B. (1995). Effects of high school restructuring and size on early gains in achievement and engagement. Sociology of Education, 68, 241–270.

Marsh, H. W. (1992). Self Description Questionnaire (SDQ) I: A theoretical and empirical basis for the measurement of multiple dimensions of preadolescent self-concept. Macarthur, New South Wales, Australia: University of Western Sydney.

Maslow, A. (1962). Toward a psychology of belonging. Princeton, NJ: Van Nostrand.

Mosteller, F., & Tukey, J. W. (1977). Data analysis and regression. Reading, MA: Addison-Wesley.

Omizo, M. M., Omizo, S. A., & Honda, M. R. (1997). A phenomenological study with youth gang members: Results and implications for school counsellors. Professional School Counseling, 1, 39–42.

Raywid, M. A. (1996). Downsizing schools in big cities (Rep. No. EPO-UD-96-1). Columbia University, NY: ERIC Clearinghouse on Urban Education.

Reep, B. B. (1996). Lessons from the gang. School Administrator, 53(2), 26–29.

Romero, A. J., & Roberts, R. E. (1998). Perception of discrimination and ethnocultural variables in a diverse group of adolescents. Journal of Adolescence, 21, 641–656.

Rosenthal, R., & Rosnow, R. L. (1984). Essentials of behavioral research: Methods and data analysis. New York: McGraw-Hill.

Routt, M. L. (1996). Early experiences that foster connectedness. Dimensions of Early Childhood, 24, 17–21.

Sax, G. (1997). Principles of educational and psychological measurement and evaluation (4th ed.). Belmont, CA: Wadsworth.

Scherer, M. (1998). The discipline of hope: A conversation with Herb Kohl. Educational Leadership, 56(1), 8–13.

Schlosser, L. K. (1992). Teacher distance and student disengagement: School lives on the margin. Journal of Teacher Education. 43, 128–140.

Snijders, T. A. B., & Bosker, R. J. (1999). Multilevel analysis. Thousand Oaks, CA: Sage.

Thum, Y. M., & Bryk, A. S. (1997). Value-added productivity indicators: The Dallas system. In J. Millman (Ed.), Grading teachers, grading schools: Is student achievement a valid evaluation measure? (pp. 100–109). Thousand Oaks, CA: Corwin.

Wang, M. C., Haertel, G. D., & Walberg, H. J. (1998). Building educational resilience. Fastback, 43.

Wendel, F. C., Hoke, F. A., & Joekel, R. T. (1994). The search for success. Middle School Journal, 25(3), 48–50.

Williams, L. J., & Downing, J. E. (1998). Membership and belonging in inclusive classrooms: What do middle school students have to say? Journal of the Association for Persons With Severe Handicaps, 23, 98–110.

Willms, J. D. (1992). Monitoring school performance: A guide for educators. London: Falmer.

XIN MA is associate professor, Education Department, University of Alberta, Canada. His research interests include school effects, policy research, program evaluation, mathematics education, and statistical methods.

From Journal of Educational Research, Vol. 96, No. 6, July/August 2003. © 2003. Reprinted with permission of the Helen Dwight Reid Educational Foundation. Published by Heldref Publications, 1319 Eighteenth St., NW, Washington, DC 20036-1802.

Challenges and Suggestions for Safe Schools

Katherine T. Bucher; M. Lee Manning

In this article we look at challenges to safe schools and offer eight suggestions for ensuring the safety of students and educators. School violence includes unacceptable social behavior ranging from aggression that threatens or harms others (and the highly publicized acts of mass bloodshed) to bullying, threats (Hoang 2001), sexual harassment, gang violence, extortion, and other forms of intimidation (McEvoy 1999). It involves criminal acts in schools, inhibits development and learning, and harms the school's climate (Furlong and Morrison 2000). At least 10 percent of our nation's schools are unsafe (Walker and Eaton-Walker 2000). Also, the gravity of youth violence has increased in recent years. Although today's students may not be any more likely than yesterday's to experience violence, the violence they do experience more often results in serious injury (Kingery, Coggeshall, and Alford 1999). Confronted by increasing incidence of violent behavior in schools, educators are being asked to make schools safer (Sugai et al. 2000).

Many middle and secondary school students experience a variety of forms of violence—pushing, bullying, shoving, grabbing, slapping, verbal insults, and threats—that make their lives in school miserable. Of twelve students who stay home on any given day, one stays home due to fear (Harris 2000). Incidents of school violence are disturbing:

- Nearly 8 percent of students nationally reported having been threatened or injured with a weapon on school property during the prior twelve months (Leone et al. 2001).
- Slightly over 1 percent of students reported that they had been physically assaulted (Verdugo 1999).
- The odds that a student will be threatened or injured with a weapon in school are approximately one in fifteen, and the odds of getting into a physical fight are approximately one in eight (Reddy et al. 2001).
- Student surveys indicate that behaviors such as carrying a weapon at school are significantly more widespread than surveys of school administrators suggest (Doggeshall and Kingery 2001).
- Males reported much higher rates than females of weapon-carrying in schools (11 percent to 2.8 percent).
- Fourteen percent of students reported being in a physical fight at school during the past twelve months.
- Over 7 percent of students nationally reported having been threatened or injured with a weapon on school property during the past twelve months (Leone et al. 2000).

Suggestions for Promoting School Safety

National concern over school violence has led to federal, state, and local efforts to address the issue by creating new laws and policies, such as zero-tolerance, conducting targeted and random searches of students and their property, using metal detectors, and launching violence prevention education programs (Yell and Rozalski 2000). Educators should also consider the following eight suggestions for ensuring school safety.

Suggestion 1

Look for school conditions that might cause or contribute to school violence and aggression. For example, overcrowded or poorly supervised schools, and school communities with less tolerance for individual differences in abilities and attitudes have more aggressive and antisocial behavior (Furlong, Bates, and Smith 2001). Harris maintains that school authorities often condone "structural" violence, which results from an overemphasis on competition, the use of tracking which lowers self-esteem, and dictatorial administrators who make students resentful of authorities (Harris 2000). How adults perceive adolescents can also contribute to violence. In one study (Hedin, Hannes, and Saito 1985), two-thirds of the students believed that significant adults in their lives perceived them negatively.

Braaten (1999) also found that students believed that adults neither valued nor trusted them and did not treat them with respect. Other conditions that can lead to violence include insensitivity toward multicultural factors, student alienation, rejection of at-risk students by teachers and peers, and student anger and resentment at school routines and demands for conformity.

Suggestion 2

Make a commitment to civility and a positive school culture and climate. A safe school has a positive climate where people are trusted, respected, and involved. They work cooperatively; intolerance does not exist, nor are students harassed or threatened. Students feel that adults care for them as a group and as individuals. High expectations exist so that students are successful both academically and socially (Erb 2000). Some schools have unnecessarily harsh and punitive disciplinary practices that create a climate conducive to school violence (Hyman and Snook 2000). Educators can increase respect for authority by not disciplining students with peers present. Also, they can make punishments consistent and appropriate for the severity of the infractions (Kingery, Coggeshall, and Alford 1999).

A climate of emotional and verbal violence can be as damaging as physical violence. In fact, a lack of respect and constructive communication forms the foundation of violence and should be treated assertively (Plucker 2000). When educators focus on cognitive development and ignore affective domains, problems can result. Some students do not learn constructive and productive use of leisure time, to maintain a healthy lifestyle, or to practice personal hygiene (Scott 1998). Other students use violence to distinguish themselves from others and to express disgust toward mainstream school culture (Kostinsky, Bixler, and Kettl 2001).

Educators must teach young people how to behave and to address the sources of violence in their lives, and they must help them to recover from violence (Harris 2000). Students need to feel they belong to have opportunities to make real choices, to realize that effective communication can prevent violence, and to know the consequences of their actions (Plucker 2000). School uniforms can cultivate a sense of belonging and make it easy to distinguish between students and nonstudents (Schneider 2001a).

Educators can encourage civility by

1. focusing educational efforts on both cognitive and affective domains;
2. changing the school day from the traditional "periods" to a more flexible schedule;
3. providing times for students to socialize, eat a healthy lunch, and practice hygiene;
4. teaching students how to use their leisure time productively and acceptably;
5. providing age-appropriate discussions on drug abuse, sex, and violence;
6. structuring the school day to lessen emotional and physiological stress; and
7. teaching students how to think and act in restrooms, hallways, locker rooms, and lunchrooms (Scott 1998).

Suggestion 3

Take advantage of environmental design and technological innovations that contribute to students' and educators' safety. The physical school environment affects student behavior. In fact, violence occurs at predictable school locations—generally unsupervised ones (Astor, Meyer, and Behre 1999).

New schools should incorporate architectural designs that reduce the likelihood of school crime and vandalism and eliminate unnecessary student conflict due to overcrowding, inappropriate congregating, and brushing against one another in narrow school spaces. Existing schools can be improved by architectural retrofitting. In neither case does the school have to look and feel like a fortress (Walker and Eaton-Walker 2000).

In the wake of recent school shootings, an industry of school safety products has quickly developed (Reddy et al. 2001). Security-oriented measures and products include ID systems for students, staff, and visitors; cameras in key locations (e.g., behind shrubbery and walls that limit visibility); and metal detectors (Erb 2000). "Smart" cards have become a common means of access control. Issued to staff, they can instantly be canceled in case of card loss or theft. In addition, relatively inexpensive metal-detector wands can be used by security personnel or other staff to check for weapons. After hours or in controlled areas, alarms can detect intruders, signal emergency personnel for immediate help, and allow staff to use emergency "panic" buttons. Closed circuit television cameras can identify suspects after the fact. Unfortunately, although they can deter some criminal activity, cameras may be targeted by vandals (Schneider 2001b).

Uniformed police officers may make the school more secure, but they do little to make individual students feel safe (Dodd 2000). Still, police officers or school security managers trained in crime prevention through environmental design can examine a school's physical environment and recommend modifications to prevent or reduce violence (Hoang 2001). They can also work with students before violence occurs by coaching sports, serving as good listeners, and working with outside agencies to provide students with positive support instead of waiting for something bad to happen. Still, recent events have made clear that the presence of officers does not prevent all violence (Erb 2000).

Suggestion 4

Identify early warning signs of violence, while recognizing the dangers of student profiling. As concern about the safety of America's public schools increases, Furlong, Bates, and Smith (2001), referring mainly to school psychologists, indicated that school personnel have been asked to render professional judgments about potentially dangerous behaviors.

Undoubtedly, educators should know early warning signs—emotional and behavioral indicators that signal the potential for dangerous or violent behavior. However, educators must remember that, although such signs might indicate a problem, they do not necessarily pinpoint a violent student. Early warning signs of violence include social withdrawal, excessive feelings of isolation and being alone, excessive feelings of rejection, being a victim of violence, feeling picked on and persecuted, low school interest and poor academic performance, expression of violence in writings and drawings, uncontrolled anger, patterns of impulsive and chronic hitting and intimidating, a history of discipline problems, a history of violent and aggressive behavior, intolerance for differences and prejudicial attitudes, drug and alcohol use, affiliation with gangs, inappropriate access to firearms, and serious threats of violence (U.S. Department of Education 1998).

Unfortunately, educators often have difficulty identifying violence-prone students. Bender, Shubert, and McLaughlin (2001) used the term "invisible kids" to describe students generally unknown by many school personnel prior to incidents of violence. These quiet and shy students had not demonstrated overt problem behaviors in schools. Therefore, teachers were less likely to know them (Bender, Shubert, and McLaughlin 2001).

Educators can use profiling checklists to predict an individual student's potential for violent behaviors. However, while some people see student profiling as a promising tool, others perceive it as an ill-conceived response to school violence (Lumsden 2000). They believe that the use of profiles is inefficient and ineffective, carries considerable risk of false positives (e.g., many youths who demonstrate the profile are not violence risks), and has the potential to stigmatize students and deprive them of their civil liberties (Reddy et al. 2001).

Suggestion 5

Have written intervention plans for ensuring safety and for responding to violence. Walker and Eaton-Walker (2000) called for written school safety plans. Unfortunately, some administrators might be hesitant to draw up a written safety plan that could imply that the school is unsafe. Still, since the public knows schools' safety records, taking action is better than ignoring potential violence.

School intervention plans should be developed in cooperation with students, parents/guardians, and the community and school. The plans should include specific principles that research or expert experience shows contribute to success. The written prevention and response plan should contain

- descriptions of the early warning signs of potentially violent behavior and procedures for identifying dangerous students;

- descriptions of effective prevention practices that the school has undertaken to build responsive interventions;
- descriptions of intervention strategies that the school community can use to help students who are at risk of behavioral problems and more intensive, individualized interventions for students with severe behavioral problems or mental health needs; and
- a crisis intervention plan that includes immediate responses for imminent warning signs and violent behavior, as well as a contingency plan to be used in the aftermath of a tragedy (U.S. Department of Education 1998).

When planning a written safe schools plan, educators should consider three fundamental principles. First, the plan should be based on a public health model so that schools can systematically address the needs of all students, including those with academic, emotional, and behavioral problems. Second, approaches that emphasize punishment and control have been demonstrated to be ineffective. Third, effective, written, schoolwide prevention plans are comprehensive, involve a broad range of services and initiatives, and extend supports over a sufficient period of time (Leone et al. 2000).

Suggestion 6

Efforts to make schools safe should include collaborative relationships among administrators, teachers, students, parents, law enforcement officers, and various social service personnel (Stader 2000). Calling for "collaborative conversations," Dodd (2000) suggests that educators should view behavioral situations as problems to be resolved rather than actions to be punished and should ask disrupting students to help resolve problems. Such an approach will result in the student's being less likely to feel misunderstood or unfairly treated. To promote this collaboration with students, both administrators and educators can

- provide leadership toward promoting student responsibility for safer schools;
- coordinate student courts that are trained by local justice system experts;
- provide conflict resolution materials as well as appropriate training;
- develop a buddy system that assigns current students to newcomers to ease the transition;
- plan a school beautification campaign for the school and neighborhood using students as the work crew;
- provide a student tip line as an anonymous, nonthreatening way for students to report school crime (National School Safety Center 1999).

Suggestion 7

Build on zero-tolerance policies, but do not rely on them to solve all school problems. Zero-tolerance policies resulted from Congress's passing the Gun-Free Schools Act of 1994, which requires states to legislate zero-tolerance laws or risk losing federal funding (McAndrews 2001). Almost all schools have zero-tolerance policies for firearms (94 percent) and other weapons (91 percent). Eighty-seven percent of schools have zero-tolerance policies for alcohol, and 88 percent for drugs. Seventy-nine percent of schools have zero-tolerance policies for violence and tobacco (McAndrews 2001).

As school officials implement zero-tolerance policies, they must ensure that their approach is fundamentally fair and legally defensible (Essex 2000). Unfortunately, the development of zero tolerance has caused some administrators to treat all behaviors, minor and major, with equal severity. These increasingly broad interpretations of zero tolerance have resulted in a "near epidemic" (Skiba and Peterson 1999) of suspensions and expulsions for seemingly trivial reasons.

In light of litigation and controversy regarding zero tolerance, educators must keep several things in mind. First, zero tolerance should not be used solely to rid the school of troubled students. Second, administrators, teachers, parents, and community leaders should be involved in the formulation of zero-tolerance policies. Actual policies should guarantee students' constitutional rights. Zero-tolerance policies should not be seen as a "cure-all" (Essex 2000) for student misconduct. School officials should consider the student's history of behavior at school and the seriousness of the offense prior to determining punishment (Essex 2000).

Educators need to recognize that little evidence exists that zero tolerance actually makes schools safer. In fact, these policies might only give schools and communities a false sense of security (Skiba and Peterson 1999; Stader 2000). The policy has the potential to alienate students who are actually crying out for help through their negative behavior (Arman 2000).

Suggestion 8

Implement conflict resolution programs to help students see alternatives to violence. When schools develop conflict resolution programs, they create an environment that fosters the development of resiliency by helping students preserve relationships, showing youth how to control their own behavior, and offering a way to resolve conflicts peacefully. Students who learn negotiation and resolution procedures in school have more positive attitudes about conflict and are more likely to seek nonviolent remedies for conflicts in their lives. These results are even stronger when there is whole-school involvement in conflict resolution activities and academic integration of peace-making themes into school content (Harris 2000).

To develop a conflict resolution program, educators should

1. consider several conflict resolution approaches to determine the one that best meets students' and educators' needs;

2. never underestimate students' abilities and motivation to engage in conflict resolution;

3. maintain objectivity—let students know that decisions about causes and solutions have not already been reached;

4. be prepared to teach the purpose, goals, and steps of conflict resolution rather than assume students will know;

5. model how conflicts can be constructive and can lead to better understandings of others as well as oneself.

Conclusion

Educators have long dealt with behavior problems such as students' talking out of turn, goofing off, fighting, and bullying, however, educators in some schools struggle to deal with threats of violence and aggression. The safe schools movement represents an effort of educators, parents, and the community to provide students with safe havens in which to learn. Although far from exhaustive, these suggestions can help educators create a learning environment that is physically and psychologically safe for all students.

REFERENCES

Arman, J. F. 2000. In the wake of tragedy at Columbine High School. Professional School Counseling 3(3): 218-20.

Astor, R. A., H. A. Meyer, and W. J. Behre. 1999. Unowned places and times: Maps and interviews about violence in high schools. American Educational Research Journal 36(1): 3-42.

Bender, W. N., T. H. Shubert, and P. J. McLaughlin. 2001. Invisible kids: Preventing school violence by identifying kids in trouble. Intervention in School and Clinic 37(2): 105-11.

Braaten, S. 1999. Youth violence and aggression: "Why?" or, should we be asking, "Why not?" Preventing School Failure 44(1): 32-36.

Coggeshall, M. B., and P. M. Kingely. 2001. Cross-survey analysis of school violence and disorder. Psychology in the Schools 38(2): 117-26.

Dodd, A. W. 2000. Making schools safe for all students: Why schools need to teach more than the 3 R's. NASSP Bulletin 84(614): 25-31.

Erb, T. 2000. Interview with Gerald Bourgeois: Voice of experience on school safety. Middle School Journal 31(5): 5-11.

Essex, N. L. 2000. Zero tolerance approach to school violence: Is it going too far? American Secondary Education 29(2): 37-40.

Furlong, M. J., M. P. Bates, and D. C. Smith. 2001. Predicting school weapon possession: A secondary analysis of the youth risk behavior surveillance survey. Psychology in the Schools 38(2): 127-39.

Furlong, M. I., and G. Morrison. 2000. The school in school violence: Definitions and facts. Journal of Emotional and Behavioral Disorders 8(2): 71-99.

Harris, I. M. 2000. Peace-building responses to school violence. NASSP Bulletin 84(614): 5-24.

Hedin, D., K. Hannes, and R. Saito. 1985. Minnesota youth poll. Youth look at themselves and the world, Minneapolis: Center for Youth Development and Research, University of Minnesota.

Hoang, F. Q. 2001. Addressing school violence. The FBI Law Enforcement Bulletin 70(8): 18-27.

Hyman, I. A., and P. A. Snook. 2000. Dangerous schools and what you can do about them. Phi Delta Kappan 81(7): 488-93.

Kingery, P. M., M. B. Coggeshall, and A. A. Alford. 1999. Weapon carrying by youth. Education and Urban Society 31(3): 309-33

Kostinsky, S., E. O. Bixler, and P. A. Ketti. 2001. Threats of school violence in Pennsylvania after media coverage of the Columbine High School massacre: Examining the role of imitation. Archives of Pediatrics and Adolescent Medicine 155(9): 994-1008.

Leone, P. E., M. J. Mayer, K. Malmgren, and S. M. Meisel. 2000. School violence and disruption: Rhetoric, reality, and reasonable balance. Focus on Exceptional Children 33(1): 1-20.

----2001. School violence and disruption: Rhetoric, reality, and reasonable balance. Counseling and Human Development 33(8): 1-20.

Lumsden, L. 2000. Profiling students for violence. ERIC Digest 139. University of Oregon: College of Education.

McAndrews, T. 2001. Zero-tolerance policies. ERIC Digest 146. University of Oregon: College of Education.

McEvoy, A. 1999. The relevance of theory to the safe schools movement. Education and Urban Society 31(3): 275-85.

National School Safety Center. 1999. Working together to create safe schools. Westlake Village, CA National School Safety Center.

Plucker, J. A. 2000. Positive approaches to preventing school violence: Peace building in schools and communities. NASSP Bulletin 84(614): 1-4.

Reddy, M., R. Borum, J. Berglund, B. Vossekuil, R. Fein, and W. Modzeleski. 2001. Evaluating risk for targeted violence in schools: Comparing risk assessment, threat assessment, and other approaches. Psychology in the Schools 38(2): 157-72.

Schneider, T. 2001a. Safer schools through environmental design. ERIC Digest 144. University of Oregon: College of Education.

----. 2001b. Newer technologies for school security. ERIC Digest 145. University of Oregon: College of Education.

Scott, V. 1998. Breaking the cycle of incivility. High School Magazine 6(1): 4-7.

Skiba, R., and R. Peterson. 1999. The dark side of zero tolerance. Phi Delta Kappan 80(5): 372-76.

Stader, D. L. 2000. Preempting threats with sound school policy. NASSP Bulletin 84(617): 68-72.

Sugai, G., J. R. Sprague, R. H. Homer, and H. M. Walker. 2000. Preventing school violence: The use of office discipline referrals to assess and monitor school-wide discipline interventions. Journal of Emotional and Behavioral Disorders 8(2): 94-100.

U.S. Department of Education. 1998. Early warning timely response: A guide to safe schools. Washington, DC: U.S. Department of Education.

Verdugo, R. R. 1999. Safe schools: Theory, data, and practices. Education and Urban Society 31(3): 267-74.

Walker, H. M., and J. Eaton-Walker. 2000. Key questions about school safety: Critical issues and recommended solutions. NASSP Bulletin 84(614): 46-55.

Yell, M. L., and M. E. Rozalski. 2000. Searching for safe schools: Legal issues in the prevention of school violence. Journal of Emotional and Behavioral Disorders 8(3): 187-207.

Katherine T. Bucher and M. Lee Manning are professors in the Department of Curriculum and Instruction at Old Dominion University, in Norfolk, Virginia.

From *The Clearing House*, Vol. 76, No. 3, January/February 2003. © 2003. Reprinted with permission of the Helen Dwight Reid Educational Foundation. Published by Heldref Publications, 1319 Eighteenth St., NW, Washington, DC 20036-1802.

Healthier Students, Better Learners

*The Health Education Assessment Project helps teachers provide
the skills-based, standards-based health instruction that students need.*

By Beth Pateman

When we think back on health classes from our school days, many of us have only vague memories. We may recall some discussion of food groups, a film about puberty, or a lecture on dental hygiene conducted when the weather was too rainy to go outside for physical education. Few of us remember our K-12 health education experiences as being relevant to our lives outside the classroom.

Fortunately, that picture is changing. Asserting that "healthy students make better learners, and better learners make healthy communities," the Council of Chief State School Officers (CCSSO) and the Association of State and Territorial Health Officials (ASTHO) (2002) have summarized compelling research evidence that students' health significantly affects their school achievement. Even if their schools have the most outstanding academic curriculum and instruction, students who are ill or injured, hungry or depressed, abusing drugs or experiencing violence, are unlikely to learn as well as they should (Kolbe, 2002).

Effective health education programs have a vital role to play in enhancing students' health and thus in raising academic achievement. Kolbe's 2002 review of the research found that modern school health programs can improve students' health knowledge, attitudes, skills, and behaviors and enhance social and academic outcomes. How do these modern health programs differ from those that most of us remember from our school days? Thanks to growing knowledge about how to prevent unhealthy and unsafe behaviors among young people, today's exemplary health education combines *skills-based* and *standards-based* approaches.

Focus on Skills

The Centers for Disease Control and Prevention have identified six types of behavior that cause the most serious health problems in the United States among people over 5 years old: alcohol and other drug use, high-risk sexual behaviors, tobacco use, poor dietary choices, physical inactivity, and behaviors that result in intentional or unintentional injury. Stressing the importance of education efforts, the Centers state that

> these behaviors usually are established during youth; persist into adulthood; are interrelated; and are preventable. In addition to causing serious health problems, these behaviors contribute to many of the educational and social problems that confront the nation, including failure to complete high school, unemployment, and crime. (n.d.)

Effective health education programs have a vital role to play in enhancing students' health and thus in raising academic achievement.

In response to the Centers' focus on these major health-risk behaviors, education researchers have worked to identify educational approaches that positively affect health-related behaviors among young people. Many research studies have established the effectiveness of skills-based school health education in promoting healthy be-

Health Education Standards

- *Standard 1: Students will comprehend concepts related to health promotion and disease prevention.* For example, students will be able to identify what good health is, recognize health problems, and be aware of ways in which lifestyle, the environment, and public policies can promote health.
- *Standard 2: Students will demonstrate the ability to access valid health information and health-promoting products and services.* For example, students will be able to evaluate advertisements, options for health insurance and treatment, and food labels.
- *Standard 3: Students will demonstrate the ability to practice health-enhancing behaviors and reduce health risks.* For example, students will know how to identify responsible and harmful behaviors, develop strategies for good health, and manage stress.
- *Standard 4: Students will analyze the influence of culture, media, technology, and other factors on health.* For example, students will be able to describe and analyze how cultural background and messages from the media, technology, and friends influence health choices.
- *Standard 5: Students will demonstrate the ability to use interpersonal communication skills to enhance health.* For example, students will learn refusal and negotiation skills and conflict resolution strategies.
- *Standard 6: Students will demonstrate the ability to use goal-setting and decision-making skills to enhance health.* For example, students will set reasonable and attainable goals—such as losing a given amount of weight or increasing physical activity—and develop positive decision-making skills.
- *Standard 7: Students will demonstrate the ability to advocate for personal, family, and community health.* For example, students will identify community resources, accurately communicate health information and ideas, and work cooperatively to promote health.

Source: Joint Committee on National Health Education Standards. (1995).

havior and academic achievement (ASTHO & Society of State Directors of Health, Physical Education, and Recreation, 2002; Collins et al., 2002; Kirby, 2001). Lohrmann and Wooley (1998) determined that effective programs

- Focus on helping young people develop and practice personal and social skills, such as communication and decision making, to deal effectively with health-risk situations;
- Provide healthy alternatives to specific high-risk behaviors;
- Use interactive approaches that engage students;
- Are research-based and theory-driven;
- Address social and media influences on student behaviors;
- Strengthen individual and group norms that support healthy behavior;
- Are of sufficient duration to enable students to gain the knowledge and skills that they need; and
- Include teacher preparation and support.

New Standards for a Skills-Based Approach

In 1995, the American Cancer Society sponsored the development of national health education standards that use a skills-based approach to learning (Joint committee on National Health Education Standards, 1995). The standards, summarized below, advocate health literacy that enhances individuals' capacities to obtain, interpret, and understand basic health information and services and their competence to use such information and services in health-enhancing ways (Summerfield, 1995).

Together with the Centers for Disease Control and Prevention's priority health-risk behaviors, the national health education standards provide an important new framework for moving from an information-based school health curriculum to a skills-based curriculum. Skills-based health education engages students and provides a safe environment for students to practice working through health-risk situations that they are likely to encounter as adolescents.

An information-based approach to tobacco use prevention might require students to memorize facts about the health consequences of tobacco use, such as lung cancer, heart disease, and emphysema. In contrast, a skills-based approach ensures that students demonstrate the ability to locate valid information on the effects of tobacco use. Students learn and practice a variety of skills: For example, they use analysis to identify the influences of family, peers, and media on decisions about tobacco use and they use interpersonal communication skills to refuse tobacco use.

The skills-based approach outlined in the national health education standards helps students answer questions and address issues that are important in their lives. For example, young children need to learn how to make friends and deal with bullies. Older children need to practice a variety of strategies to resist pressures to engage in risky health behaviors while maintaining friendships. Early adolescents need to learn how to obtain reliable, straightforward information about the physical, emotional, and social changes of puberty. High school students need to learn to weigh their health-related decisions in terms of their life plans and goals. All students need to learn how to respond to stress, deal with strong feelings in health-enhancing ways, and build a reliable support group of peers and adults.

Sample Performance Task: Advocacy for Mental Health

Student Challenge

Your challenge is to select and examine a mental health problem, such as anxiety, depression, eating disorders, suicide ideation, bipolar disorder, or schizophrenia. Your tasks are to

• Locate and analyze valid information sources to determine the causes and symptoms of the problem.

• Explore treatment options and health-enhancing ways of managing the problem.

• Recommend helpful tips for talking with friends or family members who might be experiencing the problem.

• Provide a list of helpful community resources.

• Design a computer-generated brochure or presentation targeted to high school students that includes a summary of your information on causes, symptoms, and management/treatment; tips for talking with others; and a list of community resources.

Assessment Criteria for a Great Presentation

Your work will be assessed using the following criteria. You will be required to

• Provide accurate and in-depth information and draw conclusions about relationships between behaviors and health.

• Cite your information sources accurately and explain why your sources are appropriate.

• Provide specific recommendations for health-enhancing ways of managing stress and ways of talking with others about the problem.

• Demonstrate awareness of your target audience (high school students) and persuade others to make healthy choices.

Additional criteria may be determined by class members.

The Health Education Assessment Project

Standards-based health education requires a new approach to planning, assessment, and instruction. Although many educators are excited about the prospect of standards-based teaching in health education, they may lack a clear picture of what standards-based performance would look like in their classrooms. To address this need, the Council of Chief State School Officers' State Collaborative on Assessment and Student Standards initiated the Health Education Assessment Project in 1993 (see www.ccsso.org/scass).

The Health Education Assessment Project develops standards-based health resources through a collaborative process. Funding for the project comes from the Centers for Disease Control and Prevention and the membership fees of 24 state and local education agencies. During its first decade, the project has built a foundation for a health education assessment system, created an assessment framework, developed and tested a pool of assessment items, and provided professional development and supporting materials to help teachers implement the assessment system and framework.

A skills-based approach to tobacco use prevention ensures that students demonstrate the ability to locate valid information on the effects of tobacco use.

The project helps educators translate theory into practice. It provides educators with a wide range of assessment items developed in a variety of formats, including selected response, constructed response, and performance tasks (see the sample below). The project provides teacher and student rubrics for assessing performance and examples of student papers for scoring practice. Perhaps the greatest benefit to educators has been the hands-on professional development opportunities to practice aligning standards, assessment, and instruction for their own classrooms (CCSSO, 2003).

Classrooms in which students are evaluated by health education standards and criteria are substantially different from classrooms in which many teachers have taught and been taught. Teachers need hands-on preparation and experience with planning, implementing, and evaluating curriculum and instruction aligned with standards and assessment. The Health Education Assessment Project can improve the health of students by providing teachers with the tools they need to meet the important health needs of today's youth.

Beth Pateman is an associate professor at the Institute for Teacher Education, University of Hawaii at Manoa, Honolulu, HI 96822; (808) 956-3885; mpateman@hawaii.edu.

References

Association of State and Territorial Health Officials & Society of State Directors of Health, Physical Education, and Recreation. (2002). *Making the connection: Health and student achievement* (CDROM). Washington, DC: Authors.

Centers for Disease Control and Prevention, Division of Adolescent and School Health. (n.d.). *Health topics* [Online]. Available: www.cdc.gov/nccdphp/dash/risk.htm

Collins, J., Robin, L., Wooley, S., Fenley, D., Hunt, P., Taylor, J., Haber, D., & Kolbe, L. (2002). Programs that work: CDC's guide to effective programs that reduce health risk behavior of youth. *Journal of School Health, 72*(3), 93-99.

Council of Chief State School Officers. (2003). *Improving teaching and learning through the CCSSO-SCASS Health Education Assessment Project*. Washington, DC: Author.

Council of Chief State School Officers & Association of State and Territorial Health Officials. (2002). *Why support a coordinated approach to school health?* Washington, DC: Authors.

Joint Committee on National Health Education Standards. (1995). *National health education standards: Achieving health literacy.* Reston, VA: Association for the Advancement of Health Education.

Kirby, D. (2001). *Emerging answers: Research findings on programs to reduce teen pregnancy.* Washington, DC: The National Campaign to Prevent Teen Pregnancy.

Kolbe, L. J. (2002). Education reform and the goals of modern school health programs. *The State Education Standard, 3*(4), 4-11.

Lohrmann, D. K., & Wooley, S. F. (1998). Comprehensive school health education. In E. Marx & S. F. Wooley (Eds.), *Health is academic: A guide to coordinated school health programs* (pp. 43-66). New York: Teachers College Press.

Summerfield, L. M. (1995). *National standards for health education* (ERIC Digest No. ED 387 483). Washington, DC: ERIC Clearinghouse on Teaching and Teacher Education. Available: www.ericfacility.net/databases/ERIC_Digests/ed387483.html

The 100 Best High Schools in America

The surge in the number of students taking AP tests is changing life inside America's classrooms—and altering the rules of the college-admissions game. A look at a new set of winners for 2003.

BY JAY MATHEWS

IN THE 1970S, MIKE RILEY WAS A YOUNG CHICAGO TEACHER trying to save failing inner-city students. He found they blossomed if he simply sat them down each day after class and made sure they did their homework. "They went from F's to honor roll, and I realized that… they weren't dumb kids, just kids we hadn't connected to," he says. Riley learned that even the most apathetic students responded to a challenge—as long as they had the right support.

Today he is the superintendent of schools in Bellevue, Wash., a hilly and ethnically diverse Seattle suburb on the leading edge of a movement to take this lesson to the next level. Riley wants to make the hardest classes in U.S. high schools today—the college-level Advanced Placement (AP) or International Baccalaureate (IB) courses—mandatory for nearly all graduates. If he succeeds, he will help accelerate a transformation of American secondary education that has sparked intense debate among educators.

This month more than a million students in 14,000 high schools took 1,750,000 AP exams, a 10 percent increase over last year and twice the number of these college-level tests taken in 1996. That means that 245 more schools are eligible for the 2003 Challenge Index, which ranks 739 public schools according to the ratio of AP or IB tests taken by all students divided by the number of graduat-ing seniors. Schools that select more than half their students by exams or other academic criteria are not eligible, because they have few, if any, of the average students who need a boost from AP or IB. Some of these magnet schools achieve extraordinary results, partly because they get the best students. In the last index, in 2000, only 494 schools were included. (AP's younger, European-based counterpart, IB, is also on the rise, with 77,285 tests given in American schools this month.) The index uses AP and IB as a measure because schools that push these tests are most likely to stretch young minds—which should be the fundamental purpose of education.

AN ELITE REBELLION: Some private schools contend they can create a better curriculum and a few have dropped AP—although students can still take the tests

Some experts think AP is growing so fast and spreading so far it could eventually supplant the SAT and the ACT as America's most influential test. At Harvard—the dream school for many high-performing seniors—the dean of ad-

The Cream of THE CROP

Public schools are ranked according to a ratio devised by Jay Matthews: the number of Advanced Placement or International Baccalaureate tests taken by all students at a school in 2002 divided by the number of graduating seniors. For a list of every school scoring more than 1,000, see Newsweek.com.

	SCHOOL	RATIO
1	International Academy*–Bloomfield Hills, Mich.	6.323
2	Stanton College Prep*–Jacksonville, Fla.	5.639
3	Paxon*–Jacksonville, Fla.	4.668
4	Alabama School of Fine Arts–Birmingham, Ala.	4.567
5	Jericho–N.Y.	4.519
6	George Mason*–Falls Church, Va.	4.365
7	Myers Park*–Charlotte, N.C.	4.086
8	Science Academy of South Texas–Mercedes, Texas	4.024
9	H-B Woodlawn–Arlington, Va.	3.961
10	Los Angeles Center for Enriched Studies–Calif.	3.893
11	Manhasset–N.Y.	3.840
12	Wyoming–Cincinnati	3.782
13	Bellevue–Wash.	3.755
14	Highland Park–Dallas	3.693
15	Edgemont–Scarsdale, N.Y.	3.673
16	International–Bellevue, Wash.	3.643
17	Great Neck South–Great Neck, N.Y.	3.640
18	Newport–Bellevue, Wash.	3.625
19	Cold Spring Harbor–N.Y.	3.573
20	Mills University Studies–Little Rock, Ark.	3.564
21	Lincoln Park Academy*–Ft. Pierce, Fla.	3.521
22	W.T. Woodson*–Fairfax, Va.	3.448
23	Yorktown–Arlington, Va.	3.422
24	St. Petersburg*–Fla.	3.403
25	Brighton–Rochester, N.Y.	3.357
26	Great Neck North–Great Neck, N.Y.	3.298
27	Greeley–Chappaqua, N.Y.	3.240
28	Washington-Lee*–Arlington, Va	3.192
29	Wheatley–Old Westbury, N.Y.	3.146
30	Langley–McLean, Va.	3.144
31	Indian Hill–Cincinnati	3.100
32	Ft. Myers*–Fla.	3.075
33	Pittsford Mendon–Pittsford, N.Y.	3.053
34	Vandermeulen–Port Jefferson, N.Y.	3.040
35	Weston–Mass.	3.009
36	Westlake–Austin, Texas	3.004
37	Richard Montgomery*–Rockville, Md.	2.969
38	University Laboratory–Urbana, Ill.	2.932
39	Miami Palmetto-Miami, Fla.	2.914
40	Pittsford Sutherland–Pittsford, N.Y.	2.881
41	Lyndon B. Johnson–Austin, Texas	2.879
42	Enloe*–Raleigh, N.C.	2.879
43	Rye–N.Y.	2.878
44	Eastside*–Gainsville, Fla.	2.868
45	Walter Johnson–Bethesda, Md.	2.878
46	Westfield–Chantilly, Va.	2.848
47	La Jolla–Calif.	2.802
48	Providence–Charlotte, N.C.	2.800
49	Banneker–Washington, D.C.	2.796
50	Gunn–Palo Alto, Calif.	2.791
51	Hewlett–N.Y.	2.780
52	East Chapel Hill–Chapel Hill, N.C.	2.774
53	University–Irvine, Calif.	2,772
54	Atlantic Commuinty*–Delray Beach, Fla.	2.745
55	Robinson*–Fairfax, Va.	2.736
56	Wilson Magnet*–Rochester, N.Y.	2.735
57	Westwood*–Austin, Texas	2.709
58	Bernards–Bernardsville, N.J.	2.707
59	Miller Place–N.Y.	2.700
60	Syosset–N.Y.	2.699
61	Wootton–Rockville, Md.	2.699
62	South Side*–Rockville Centre, N.Y.	2.690
63	Millburn–N.J.	2.673
64	Kennedy–Bellmore, N.Y.	2.668
65	Harding Univ.*–Charlotte, N.C.	2.665
66	Steveson–Lincolnshire, Ill.	2.658
67	Foshay Learning Center–Los Angeles	2.651
68	Chagrin Falls–Ohio	2.625
69	Chantilly–Va.	2.620
70	East Hampton–N.Y.	2.598
71	North Shore–Glen Head, N.Y.	2.592
72	Buchholz–Gainsville, Fla.	2.573
73	Scarsdale–N.Y.	2.565
74	Churchill–Potomac, Md.	2.557
75	Torrey Pines–San Diego	2.541

continued on following page

The Cream of the Crop continued

76	Edina–Minn.	2.528
77	Roslyn–Roslyn Heights, N.Y.	2.505
78	Duxbury–Mass.	2.502
79	Mamaroneck–N.Y.	2.500
80	Bellaire*–Texas	2.493
81	Stonewall Jackson*–Manassas, Va.	2.489
82	Monta Vista–Cupertino, Calif.	2.470
83	Whitman–Bethesda, Md.	2.450
84	Ardsley–N.Y.	2.448
85	Lynbrook–San Jose, Calif.	2.442
86	Fairfax–Va.	2.436
87	Spurce Creek*–Port Orange, Fla.	2.435
88	Palos Verdes Peninsula–Rolling Hills Estates, Calif.	2.435
89	East Mecklenburg*–Charlotte, N.C.	2.434
90	Irondequoit–Rochester, N.Y.	2.432
91	Bronxville–N.Y.	2.429
92	Calhoun–Merrick, N.Y.	2.419
93	Troy*–Fullerton, Calif.	2.407
94	Sunny Hills*–Fullerton, Calif.	2.384
95	Oak Park–Calif.	2.382
96	Lewiston-Porter–Youngstown, N.Y.	2.367
97	North Hollywood–Los Angeles	2.349
98	Garden City–N.Y.	2.346
99	Sumner Academy*–Kansas City, Kans.	2.340
100	Croton-Harmon–Croton-on-Hudson, N.Y.	2.338

*GAVE IB TESTS. AP AND IB PARTICIPATION RATES ARE INDICATORS OF A SCHOOL'S EFFORTS TO GET STUDENTS TO EXCEL AND PREPARE FOR COLLEGE. SCHOOLS THAT CHOSE MORE THAN HLAF OF THEIR STUDENTS BY ENTRANCE EXAMINATIONS OR OTHER ACADEMIC QUALIFICATIONS WERE NOT CONSIDERED BECAUSE THEY HAVE VERY FEW OF THE AVERAGE STUDENTS THAT AP AND IB ARE USED TO HELP AND INSPIRE.

missions says AP is already a better predictor of college grades than the SAT. One reason could be that students get only one shot at the AP, unlike the SATs, which many retake several times in order to boost their scores. More important, AP tests a whole year of learning, while the SAT assesses a specific set of skills that many educators think have little relation to academic potential in college. College-admissions officers at many schools say that AP and IB have acquired the status of backstage passes at a rock concert. Selective universities begin to ask questions if they see that applicants have not taken the tests available at their high schools. Even freshmen and sophomores are crowding into AP courses once open only to juniors and seniors. At Miller Place High School on New York's Long Island, guidance director Joseph W. Connolly says 40

percent of this year's 10th graders took AP European history—an unheard-of proportion a decade ago.

Both AP and IB students answer lengthy free-response questions that are graded by actual human beings (AP also has multiple-choice questions). If their scores are high enough, students can earn college credit. They also get a taste of the higher-level exams they'll face on campus. Jordan Wish, a senior at Richard Montgomery High School in Rockville, Md., took two AP and four IB tests this month—25 hours of tests with not much time for sleep each night. "Right now I am not feeling so good," Wish said as he crammed in some last-minute studying for the difficult AP physics test. But he thinks the extra effort will be good preparation for Princeton, where he'll be a freshman this fall.

LEADING THE WAY: At the Science Academy of South Texas, many students from disadvantaged backgrounds learn to defy the odds

Proponents say AP and IB have exposed many average suburban teenagers to a level of instruction once reserved only for honor students and, even more significantly, have energized inner-city schools. From 1998 to 2002, AP participation by underrepresented minority students increased 77 percent and participation by low-income students increased 101 percent, while overall participation rose only 48 percent. But some administrators and university educators warn that pushing the programs too far and too quickly could dilute their benefits. A recent report by the National Research Council says AP and IB courses should delve more deeply into fewer topics. A few colleges have become more demanding as well. Last year Harvard announced that it would give advanced standing only to students who had the top AP grade, a 5, the equivalent of a college A, on four required AP tests. There are complaints that many of the new AP—students are failing the tests. And some high-school principals say that it is better for their more-ambitious students to take courses at local colleges rather than enroll in AP or IB. "There are many of us who would celebrate the exit of AP from high-school life," says Marilyn Colyar, assistant principal at San Marino High School in California. "I certainly believe in a rigorous curriculum for all students," she says, "but "a class can be challenging and relevant, AP or not."

THE CONTROVERSY OVER AP HAS BECOME PARTICULARLY intense in the private schools and affluent public schools that were the first to adopt the program in 1956, when it was little more than a way to keep high-performing seniors from getting bored. Andrew Meyers, head of the history department at the Ethical Culture Fieldston School in New York City, says he was not sympathetic three years ago when a student complained about being forced to stay on the AP superhighway without stopping to explore some intriguing side roads. But then, Meyers says, he realized that whenever a student in his AP American-history course asked a thoughtful question not quite on the topic, he often heard himself saying, "That's interesting... but we have to move on to the next era." Fieldston, Dalton, Exeter and a few other private schools have declared themselves AP-free zones. Instead of the AP history course he used to teach each spring, Meyers is offering one of his favorite electives, "Inventing Gotham," during which each student devises a historical tour of New York City. Similar electives are being offered at other schools shedding the AP label, although many of their students still take AP tests in order to impress colleges.

Many advocates of college-level courses say the prep schools are guilty of an elitist reaction to programs that are helping more and more average and below-average schools, as if AP and IB were last year's high fashions that had to be thrown out because similar clothes were being sold at Kmart. At the average high school, "the —kids would not get into elite colleges if they did not have AP courses," says Nicholas Lemann, author of "The Big Test," a history of the SAT, "but Fieldston knows that for socioeconomic reasons, their kids do not need AP to persuade those colleges to take them." Lemann and others fear that the rarefied complaints of privileged schools could slow the spread of AP and IB to poor districts where students need the challenge.

Some teachers have accused the College Board, which sponsors the AP, of promoting the program in order to collect the $80 test fees from all those students eager for an advantage in the college-admissions race. (IB is even more expensive, but schools usually pay the test fees.) Educators also bicker over the growing use of AP as a measure of school quality. NEWSWEEK's list of top high schools has been compared to U.S. News & World Report's annual "America's Best Colleges" list by educators who say such rankings distort the strengths of individual schools. The National Research Council report complained that the NEWSWEEK list had "taken on a life of its own," with high schools publishing their ratings and schools not making the list posting "disclaimers on their Web sites indicating why they are not there."

DESPITE THIS CRITICISM, THE MAJORITY OF EDUCATORS SAY they continue to support the growth of AP and IB. A recent straw-poll survey by the American School Board Journal found that 80 percent of readers wanted more of their students to take the college-level courses. And initial opposition often disappears if schools provide extra help for students who need it. Pat Hyland, principal of Mountain View (Calif.) High School, says she heard many worries when she opened her AP courses to all, but they soon

faded away. "We have added tutorial sessions and a variety of other measures to bolster the kids," she says.

Many communities have found that adding AP really turns a school around. Seven years ago, when Tim Berkey became principal of Perry High School in a rural area east of Cleveland, there were no AP or IB classes at all. He told teachers about the marked change in student attitude and achievement he had seen at his previous school, Adlai Stevenson in suburban Chicago, when the AP program was opened to everyone willing to work that hard. Five years ago Perry High started with 87 AP tests; this month it administered 214. "We believed in kids, held high expectations, provided them with the resources, tools and challenging opportunities, and then simply got out of their way," Berkey says.

Lemann, who thinks the SAT hinders educational improvement, says AP and IB have had the opposite effect— much to the surprise of many educators who are generally opposed to the spread of standardized tests. "It has become a wonderful and effective way to produce a massive upgrading of the high-school curriculum," Lemann says. "These were unintended consequences, but good unintended consequences."

The commitment to giving more high schoolers a useful dose of college exam-week trauma has turned an old elementary-school building in Bloomfield Hills, Mich., into an IB hothouse—and the top school on the 2003 NEWSWEEK list. Five hundred teenagers, picked by lottery from 13 local districts, have enrolled in the International Academy, while their neighborhood friends shy away from the workload. "I had no idea what I was getting myself into," says Bhavana Bhaya, a senior who took 30 hours of IB exams this month at the public school near Detroit, "but I am glad I am here." The effort paid off, says senior James Kurecka. He was afraid his 1270 SAT score and 27 ACT score would not have been enough to get into the University of Michigan's prestigious College of Engineering; he believes the IB label did the trick.

TAKING THE CHALLENGE: Admissions deans say that AP is a better predictor of college success than the SAT and that they look for students who've pushed themselves

Even students whose grades and test scores in high school were mediocre are more likely to graduate from college if they have had some challenging high-school — courses such as AP and IB, according to a 1999 study by U.S. Education Department researcher Clifford Adelman. That finding was particularly true for minorities. The Science Academy of South Texas, a public school that draws students from three rural counties in the Rio Grande Valley, has sent several migrant workers' children to high-tech colleges by exposing them to difficult AP assignments. Norma Flores, a senior, says she often started school late in the fall because her migrant-laborer family needed her in the cornfields. "I had to work twice as hard to catch up," she says. But next fall, fortified by college-level courses, she will study aerospace engineering at the University of Texas-Pan American campus in Edinburg.

Riley, the superintendent in Bellevue, says the criticism of AP and IB demonstrates how ubiquitous these programs have become, and how many previously ignored students are being helped. "Elitists will always try to find higher ground when it becomes apparent that others can scale their hill," he says. "While AP's standards, tests and curriculum have not changed, there are those who once thought the program was the gold standard but now see it as tarnished. What's the only, and I underscore only, thing that has changed? More kids are included." And like his students in Chicago nearly 30 years ago, he's betting that they will all thrive.

ALTERNATIVE SCHOOLS
Daring to Be Different
Reformers around the country have found new ways to motivate teens and they're inspiring others to break the mold

BY JAY MATHEWS

Tests aren't the only way to judge a high school. In the past decade, educators around the country have created dozens of intriguing models for reform. They include virtual high schools where all classes are online and "theme" schools based on environmental issues or the health-care profession. These schools tend to have "a strong identity shared by families and faculty alike," says Thomas Toch, writer-in-residence at the National Center on Education and the Economy and author of "High Schools on a Human Scale," published this month by Beacon Press. Some examples:

Urban Academy Laboratory High School, New York City: This public school of 120 students has made debate a teaching tool in every classroom. "What's your evidence?" could be the school motto; one of the most popular courses is officially titled "Are You Looking for an Argument?"

Despite drawing a typically urban mix of students, with many minorities and children of low-income parents, the school has a 3 percent dropout rate, while 95 percent of graduates go to college.

Christo Rey Jesuit High School, Chicago: Ninety-three percent of the 440 students at this Roman Catholic school come from low-income families, so Cristo Rey has found a novel way of financing private education that is now spreading to other cities. Per-student costs are $8,450, but the tuition is only $2,200. The rest of the money comes from students' own labor. Each of them puts in an eight-hour day, five days a month, in one of an assortment of banks, law firms and other private firms on Chicago's Loop, which pay $25,000 a year for each clerical job staffed by four rotating students. The work ethic pays off in other ways as well; 85 percent of graduates head for college.

Schools for Educational Evolution & Development (SEED) Public Charter School, Washington, D.C.: Drive past a small park in a low-income neighborhood of southeast Washington, and suddenly you find a brand-new prep school, resembling an old-line New England boarding school. The 230 students from mostly minority families live at the school all week in gleaming new dorms with computer connections, study halls and round-the-clock teachers. Two young management consultants came up with the idea, and it has created an atmosphere where distracted public-school children can finally focus on their studies.

Girard Academic Music Program, Philadelphia: This fifth-through-12th-grade school of 520 students in south Philadelphia draws mostly children from low-income families. Everyone studies music theory and "all of them can read and write their own music," says counselor Mae Pasquariello. Music lessons in every instrument (except piano) are free. There is also a strong emphasis on English, math, science and social science.

Marcus Garvey School, Los Angeles: A private school with 285 students, Marcus Garvey has a strong Afrocentric curriculum and scores that are often two years or more above grade level. It is in the Crenshaw district of South-Central Los Angeles, and some parents use the school to get their children up to the academic level of magnet programs in the public system.

Minnesota New Country School (MNCS), Henderson, Minn.: One of the first charter schools in the country, MNCS, located in a rural area 60 miles southwest of Minneapolis, proves that innovation isn't confined to cities. The school is run by a team of teachers (there's no principal) and students' work is project-based, says teacher Dean Lind, whose official title is "advisor." Students are required to make a 30-minute presentation in order to graduate. Topics for one recent senior class included "Building a Garden Pond," "History of Nursing" and "Theoretical Physics."

Safe Schools for the Roller Coaster Years

Structuring middle schools with adolescents' cognitive and psychological needs in mind creates a secure space for learning.

Linda Inlay

The "roller coaster years" is an apt descriptor of adolescence. One minute, a 7th grade girl is sweet and cooperative, and the next minute she's immersed in high drama because she doesn't like how she looks. A 6th grader no longer wants to hold her father's hand in public. An 8th grade boy, once a model student, is now more concerned about fitting in with the popular crowd.

As the director of River School, a small middle school in Napa, California, and a mother of two, I have encountered many behaviors like those described above. Changes taking place in adolescents' brains, even more than the obvious physical changes, are the catalyst for such dramatic ups and downs. To give adolescents a safe track to roll through these years undamaged, educators need to look at the emotional and psychological needs that come with this intense brain development. By attending to these needs, we can create safe schools that will enhance students' capacity to learn.

The Need to Experiment

Key parts of adolescents' brains develop at different rates. The brain's emotional centers surge into hyperdrive long before the "judgment seat"—the prefrontal cortex, which mitigates emotional ups and downs—has matured. In terms of their brains, adolescents are still more like children than young adults, although the appearance of physical maturity tricks us into thinking otherwise. It is not until age 25 that humans' prefrontal cortex matures and the capacity to make sound judgments is fully developed. Possibly this is why the highest car insurance premiums are charged to males under age 25.

During adolescence the brain's capacity to make connections nearly doubles, which encourages lots of experimentation between ages 11 and 25 (such as long hair in my generation and green hair today). During this time the brain is "hardwired," as the neural networks for certain tendencies and habits are established. After adolescence, the brain's capacity for connection returns to normal. The neural connections established during the teen years are kept intact and connections that were not used disappear. As Brownlee and colleagues put it,

> Teenagers are choosing what their brains are going to be good at—learning right from wrong, responsibility or impulsiveness, thinking or video games. (Brownlee, Hotinski, Pailthorp, Ragan, & Wong, 1999)

Creating a School That Supports Adolescents

The Need for Autonomy

Keeping in mind what I know of how the adolescent brain develops, I have structured the River School to help our students develop a sense of autonomy and responsibility as well as personal connectedness. In this stage, adolescents are trying on different personas to figure out "who they are." Analytical thinking also starts in adolescence and leads to questioning authority. Teenagers begin to separate emotionally from parents (no more hand-holding and lots of rolling of the eyes) and to develop their own unique identities—a crucial process in becoming psychologically healthy, independent adults.

When adolescent students feel safe to be themselves yet also connect to their peers, they are more grounded. This emotional safety provides a foundation that prevents narcissism on the one hand and reduces vulnerability to peer pressure on the other.

Rudolf Dreikurs (1971) wrote about the challenges of educating students during a period when social institutions were moving from a reliance on autocratic relationships to a focus on democratic relationships. I agree with Dreikurs that the old paradigm "Do as I say because I'm the adult" does not produce happy, responsible young people at home or in school. Nor does the permissive model, which produces what Shaw (2003) calls an epidemic of indulged children. When adults follow the autocratic model, children are passive; in the permissive paradigm, children have too much inappropriate power and become selfish and arrogant. Dreikurs offered another way to relate with young people: democratic parenting and democratic education in schools. This approach encourages adults and young people to treat each other with mutual respect and regard.

In keeping with this philosophy, teachers at River School provide a safe place where students can practice making good and poor choices within appropriate boundaries. Middle school students need the chance to make a lot of mistakes; that's part of the experimentation and limit-testing important to adolescence (Mackenzie, 2001). Child psychiatrist Jay Giedd has observed,

> I see kids who are cracking up because of the stress of the workload and because they see only one way to success, to getting a good job. They don't take many real risks because they are afraid. But maybe because of that, they have not learned to make their own decisions. That worries me. I think kids need to learn life's lessons.... They need to take risks, to make some mistakes. (quoted in Strauch, 2004)

In an environment that feels safe, mistakes can powerfully teach young people about choices and consequences, about freedom and responsibility. When students at our school lie about bad choices they have made, they invariably tell me they did so because they "didn't want to get in trouble." These students are willing to accept consequences for their mistakes, but they will lie if they fear having someone get angry at them. When human beings feel safe, they use their cerebral cortex rather than the "fight or flight" part of their brain, and they can better reflect on mistakes.

Instead of showing anger and disapproval when adolescents behave in undesirable ways, educators should guide teens to reflect on their behavior. Teenagers can then focus on themselves and the choices they made rather than worry about defending themselves against adult anger. At River School, teachers and student mentors lead students through the following reflective process, which trains

them to make better choices and accept responsibility for their mistakes:

■ Acknowledge your mistake instead of blaming, lying, or making excuses.

■ "Clean it up" with those involved.

■ Accept the consequence for the mistake.

■ Learn from your behavior so that you are less likely to make the mistake again.

■ Forgive yourself for the mistake and move on.

Richard DuFour talks about the "loose-tight" leadership style of principals in successful professional learning communities (DuFour & Eaker, 1998). The same leadership style can be applied to middle schools, with the school climate being "tight" in the sense of having clear expectations and consequences but "loose" in terms of allowing students to make appropriate choices.

As River School has become more democratic and respectful in relating with our students, we have found that some students' parents may be too autocratic while others may be too indulgent. Through parenting classes and conferences, we educate parents about the possibility of shifting more control to teenagers and letting teens learn from their mistakes through trial and error. A partnership of parents, teachers, and students has been very effective in helping students develop a strong sense of self and display personal and social responsibility.

The Need to Belong—Yet Be Yourself

Adolescents vacillate between two psychological needs—need for a sense of self and need for a sense of belonging (Adler, 1927/1992). Psychologist H. Scott Glenn (1989) believes that all human beings have three needs that help nurture both a sense of self and a sense of belonging: the need to be listened to, the need to be taken seriously, and the need to make a contribution.

At River School we attempt to fulfill these needs by organizing small listening groups, each composed of a teacher advisor and several students who meet regularly to share their concerns and successes. Students look forward to these sessions and often carry on even when the

teacher is absent. Besides providing a safe place to vent, listening groups encourage students to speak up for themselves, to think critically and develop opinions, and to engage more in their classes.

Listening groups encourage students to speak up for themselves, to think critically and develop opinions, and to engage more in their classes.

We also work hard to develop in students a sense of community and belonging through events that unite 6th, 7th, and 8th graders, such as "The Amazing Race" scavenger hunt in San Francisco. We team each 6th grade class with a group of 7th and 8th graders to form a "family" that meets at least once a month for community-building activities. Before we started this "family" program, many 6th graders were afraid of the 8th graders who tried to connect with them; the 8th graders felt rebuffed and gave up. Now the 6th grade students make friends with the older students and show more confidence, speaking up at school meetings, for example. We do not have a pecking order by grade level.

When our students feel emotionally safe, when they can walk down the halls unafraid of being teased, when they have people they can talk to about their concerns, and when adults nurture that climate of safety, students respond better to academic challenges.

The Need for Personal Meaning

We have learned over the years that unless curriculum is presented in ways that middle school students can connect with personally, they will forget what they have learned within a short time (National Middle Schools Association, 2002). For example, one teacher at River School helped students relate to the history of the American Revolutionary War by comparing the colonists' demands for autonomy and independence to adolescents' need to be heard and to have their rights considered by their parents.

Another way to help students connect to their learning is to have them develop their own questions to investigate within broad parameters set by the teachers. For example, when teachers at River School initiated a unit on cultures that have developed alongside rivers, they posed the overarching question, "How does geography affect culture and how do cultures affect geography?" Students then thought of subquestions that they were eager to investigate:

■ How does geography shape the religions and beliefs of a culture?

■ Does having less make people care more?

■ What comforts do people take for granted that make them less concerned about the earth?

We also help students at River School find meaning by tapping into their need to make a contribution. We encourage 8th graders in particular to contribute to creating a supportive student culture at the school by providing peer mediation, speaking at conferences, participating in a panel at a parenting class, hosting visitors, or mentoring struggling 6th graders. Our 6th and 7th graders act as ambassadors for the school, creating presentations (including one performed with music) to share at local elementary

schools. Such activities help students see that they matter at the school, lessen the attitude of entitlement and disdain that adolescents often display, and heighten their confidence and self-esteem.

When middle schoolers relate with adults and peers in mutually respectful ways, when they are not afraid to take intellectual risks, and when they are presented with a challenging and personally meaningful curriculum, they thrive academically and become engaged with their school community, laying the foundation for engagement in the larger community.

I witnessed the results of the culture of safety and engagement we foster at River School on one particular last day of school. After the last bell, the whole school lingered in the courtyard signing yearbooks, saying goodbye, hugging, and crying. Parents entering the courtyard were amazed at students' depth of caring and their uncharacteristic response to the start of summer. Whereas most adults remember middle school as one of the most uncomfortable and awkward passages in their lives, our students recall the River School fondly.

References

Adler, A. (1927/1992). *Understanding human nature.* Oxford, UK: One World Publications.

Brownlee, S., Hotinski, R., Pailthorp, B., Ragan, E., & Wong, K. (1999, Aug. 9). Inside the teen brain. *U.S. News and World Report.*

Dreikurs, R. (1971). *Character education and spiritual values in an anxious age.* New York: Alfred Adler Institute.

DuFour, R., & Eaker, R. (1998). *Professional learning communities at work.* Alexandria, VA: ASCD.

Glenn, H. S. (1989). *Raising self-reliant children in a self-indulgent age.* Rocklin, CA: Prima Publishing.

Mackenzie, R. (2001). *Setting limits for the strong-willed child.* Rocklin, CA: Prima Publishing.

National Middle Schools Association. (2002). *NMSA position statement on curriculum integration.* Available: www.nmsa.org/news/positionpapers/ integrativecurriculum.htm

Shaw, R. (2003). *Epidemic: The rot of American culture.* New York: HarperCollins.

Strauch, B. (2004). *The primal teen.* New York: Doubleday.

Linda Inlay is Director of the River School in Napa, California; 707-253-6813; linlay@nvusd.k12.ca.us.

From *Educational Leadership,* April 2005, pp. 41-43. Reprinted by permission of the Association for Supervision and Curriculum Development.

THE NEW COLLEGE DROPOUT

Universities ship emotionally troubled students back home.

Jason Feirman

WHILE MOST college freshmen spent May cramming for exams, Sue Schaller spent it as a cashier at a women's clothing store near her hometown of Arlington, Virginia.

Last fall, Schaller had been at New York University, earning A's and B's, when administrators told her to take a leave of absence. She had confided to a counselor that she felt depressed and, at times, suicidal. She was briefly hospitalized. Although Schaller was soon feeling better and her doctor even requested that she be allowed to stay, officials wouldn't budge. "I told the administrators that I wanted to be at NYU," Schaller says. "I loved my classes and my life at school."

Whether to force troubled students off campus is a quandary more colleges are struggling to handle, as the rate of serious emotional issues rises among college students. By many measures, psychological distress...including anxiety, depression, substance abuse and self-harm...is up dramatically among undergraduates. In a recent survey, more than 90 percent of college counseling centers reported seeing more students with serious mental health problems than in years past. Colleges face the difficult task of balancing the needs of distressed students with the responsibility to provide a safe learning environment for all.

But there's an elephant in the room: the threat of lawsuits. For New York University, it's a very big ele-phant. In the last 18 months, six NYU students have jumped to their deaths, although the school acknowledges only four as suicides. When Elizabeth Shin, a student at M.I.T., committed suicide in 2000, her family sued the university for $27 million, alleging the school failed to provide adequate care. Her family lost the case.

NYU's tactic may represent a new direction in campus mental health care. At Cornell University in New York, administrators say that forced medical leave is rare. However, that may be because students are given a "choice" by the school: six months of voluntary leave or 12 months of involuntary leave.

For some students, leaving campus can also mean leaving high-quality mental health care and university hospitals, which are traditionally key to helping troubled students get back on their feet. NYU spokesman John Beckman says the university considers whether students will be in therapy when making medical leave decisions.

Schaller says no one at NYU ever asked if she would be in counseling, or even if she had insurance to cover it. And, she says, the university hasn't contacted her since. Her parents' insurance plan has covered her therapy.

Some students say they might fare worse if kicked out of school. Harvard College senior Kristin Waller, who has dealt with depression since age 14, says she considers herself lucky that the university has not required her to take time off because she couldn't afford therapy and medication on her own. Throughout middle school and high school, her family was on welfare. At times, Waller says, she's felt "miserable" and suicidal in college, but she is now doing better.

Maggie Olona, director of the student counseling service at Texas A&M University, admits that college administrators know families aren't always supportive, either financially or emotionally. But that doesn't mean colleges must fill the void. "Even if home is not a supportive place, it's the responsible place," she says. Of the one or two Texas A&M students placed on leave each year, most return to school within 12 months and are more successful than before, Olona says. Administrators at NYU and other universities echo these sentiments. Colleges usually require a physician or therapist to certify a student for return.

Some colleges have another strategy: The University of Illinois at Urbana-Champaign mandates counseling for suicidal students. Student[s] must attend four therapy sessions following a suicide threat or attempt. Paul Joffe, director of the suicide prevention program, says the university's suicide rate has been cut in half since the program began in the 1980s. Of the 2,000 students who have gone through the sessions, only one has been asked to take leave. The student returned and graduated.

From *Psychology Today*, May/June 2005, pp. 38. Copyright © 2005 by Sussex Publishers, Inc. Reprinted by permission.

THE PERILS OF HIGHER EDUCATION

Can't remember the difference between declensions and derivatives? Blame college. The undergrad life is a blast, but it may lead you to forget everything you learn.

Steven Kotler

WE GO TO COLLEGE TO LEARN, TO SOAK UP a dazzling array of information intended to prepare us for adult life. But college is not simply a data dump; it is also the end of parental supervision. For many students, that translates into four years of late nights, pizza banquets and boozy week ends that start on Wednesday. And while we know that bad habits are detrimental to cognition in general—think drunk driving—new studies show that the undergrad urges to eat, drink and be merry have devastating effects on learning and memory. It turns out that the exact place we go to get an education may in fact be one of the worst possible environments in which to retain anything we've learned.

DUDE, I HAVEN'T SLEPT IN THREE DAYS!

Normal human beings spend one-third of their lives asleep, but today's college students aren't normal. A recent survey of undergraduates and medical students at Stanford University found 80 percent of them qualified as sleep-deprived, and a poll taken by the National Sleep Foundation found that most young adults get only 6.8 hours a night.

All-night cramfests may seem to be the only option when the end of the semester looms, but in fact getting sleep—and a full dose of it—might be a better way to ace exams. Sleep is crucial to declarative memory, the hard, factual kind that helps us remember which year World War I began, or what room the French Lit class is in. It's also essential for procedural memory, the "know-how" memory we use when learning to drive a car or write a five-paragraph essay. "Practice makes perfect," says Harvard Medical School psychologist Matt Walker, "but having a night's rest after practicing might make you even better."

Walker taught 100 people to bang out a series of nonsense sequences on a keyboard—a standard procedural memory task. When asked to replay the sequence 12 hours later, they hadn't improved. But when one group of subjects was allowed to sleep overnight before being retested, their speed and accuracy im-proved by 20 to 30 percent. "It was bizarre," says Walker. "We were seeing people's skills improve just by sleeping."

For procedural memory, the deep slow-wave stages of sleep were the most important for improvement—particularly during the last two hours of the night. Declarative memory, by contrast, gets processed during the slow-wave stages that come in the first two hours of sleep. "This means that memory requires a full eight hours of sleep," says Walker. He also found that if someone goes without sleep for 24 hours after acquiring a new skill, a week later they will have lost it completely. So college students who pull all-nighters during exam week might do fine on their tests but may not remember any of the material by next semester.

Walker believes that the common practice of back-loading semesters with a blizzard of papers and exams needs a rethink. "Educators are just encouraging sleeplessness," says Walker. "This is just not an effective way to force information into the brain."

WHO'S UP FOR PIZZA?

Walk into any college cafeteria and you'll find a smorgasbord of French fries, greasy pizza, burgers, potato chips and the like. On top of that, McDonald's, Burger King, Wendy's and other fast-food chains have been gobbling up campus real estate in recent years. With hectic schedules and skinny budgets, students find fast food an easy alternative. A recent Tufts University survey found that 50 percent of students eat too much fat, and 70 to 80 percent eat too much saturated fat.

But students who fuel their studies with fast food have something more serious than the "freshman 15" to worry about: They may literally be eating themselves stupid. Researchers have known since the late 1980s that bad eating habits contribute to the kind of cognitive decline found in diseases like Alzheimer's. Since then, they've been trying to find out exactly how a bad diet might be hard on the brain. Ann-Charlotte Granholm, director of the Center for Aging at the Medical University of South Carolina, has recently focused on trans fat, widely used in fast-food cooking because it extends the shelf life of foods. Trans fat is made by bubbling hydrogen through unsaturated fat, with copper or zinc added to speed the chemical reaction along. These metals are frequently found in the brains of people with Alzheimer's, which sparked Granholm's concern.

To investigate, she fed one group of rats a diet high in trans fat and compared them with another group fed a diet that was just as greasy but low in trans fat. Six weeks later, she tested the animals in a water maze, the rodent equivalent of a final exam in organic chemistry. "The trans-fat group made many more errors," says Granholm, especially when she used more difficult mazes.

When she examined the rats' brains, she found that trans-fat eaters had fewer proteins critical to healthy neurological function. She also saw inflammation in and around the hippocampus, the part of the brain responsible for learning and memory. "It was alarming," says Granholm. "These are the exact types of changes we normally see at the onset of Alzheimer's, but we saw them after six weeks," even though the rats were still young.

Students who fuel their studies with fast food have something serious to worry about: They may literally be eating themselves stupid.

Her work corresponds to a broader inquiry conducted by Veerendra Kumar Madala Halagaapa and Mark Mattson of the National Institute on Aging. The researchers fed four groups of mice different diets—normal, high-fat, high-sugar and high-fat/high-sugar. Each diet had the same caloric value, so that one group of mice wouldn't end up heavier. Four months later, the mice on the high-fat diets performed significantly worse than the other groups on a water maze test.

The researchers then exposed the animals to a neurotoxin that targets the hippocampus, to assess whether a high-fat diet made the mice less able to cope with brain damage. Back in the maze, all the animals performed worse than before, but the mice who had eaten the high-fat diets were most seriously compromised. "Based on our work," says Mattson, "we'd predict that people who eat high-fat diets and high-fat/high-sugar diets are not only damaging their ability to learn and remember new information, but also putting themselves at much greater risk for all sorts of neurodegenerative disorders like Alzheimer's."

WELCOME TO MARGARITAVILLE STATE UNIVERSITY

It's widely recognized that heavy drinking doesn't exactly boost your intellect. But most people figure that their booze-induced foolishness wears off once the hangover is gone. Instead, it turns out that even limited stints of overindulgence may have long-term effects.

Less than 20 years ago, researchers began to realize that the adult brain wasn't just a static lump of cells. They found that stem cells in the brain are constantly churning out new neurons, particularly in the hippocampus. Alcoholism researchers, in turn, began to wonder if chronic alcoholics' memory problems had something to do with nerve cell birth and growth.

In 2000, Kimberly Nixon and Fulton Crews at the University of North Carolina's Bowles Center for Alcohol Studies subjected lab rats to four days of heavy alcohol intoxication. They gave the rats a week to shake off their hangovers, then tested them on and off during the next month in a water maze. "We didn't find anything at first," says Nixon. But on the 19th day, the rats who had been on the binge performed much worse. In 19 days, the cells born during the binge had grown to maturity—and clearly, the neurons born during the boozy period didn't work properly once they reached maturity. "[The timing] was almost too perfect," says Nixon.

While normal rats generated about 2,500 new brain cells in three weeks, the drinking rats produced only 1,400. A month later, the sober rats had lost about half of those new cells through normal die-off. But all of the new cells died in the brains of the binge drinkers. "This was startling," says Nixon. "It was the first time anyone had found that alcohol not only inhibits the birth of new cells but also inhibits the ones that survive." In further study, they found that a week's abstinence produced a twofold burst of neurogenesis, and a month off the sauce brought cognitive function back to normal.

What does this have to do with a weekend keg party? A number of recent studies show that college students consume far more alcohol than anyone previously suspected. Forty-four percent of today's collegiates drink enough to be classified as binge drinkers, according to a nationwide survey of 10,000 students done at Harvard University. The amount of alcohol consumed by Nixon's binging rats far exceeded intake at a typical keg party—but other research shows that the effects of alcohol work on a sliding scale. Students who follow a weekend of heavy drinking with a week of heavy studying might not forget everything they learn. They just may struggle come test time.

CAN I BUM A SMOKE?

If this ledger of campus menaces worries you, here's something you really won't like: Smoking cigarettes may actually have some cognitive benefits, thanks to the power of nicotine. The chemical improves mental focus, as scientists have known since the 1950s. Nicotine also aids concentration in people who have ADHD and may protect against Alzheimer's disease. Back in 2000, a nicotine-like drug under development by the pharmaceutical company Astra Arcus USA was shown to restore the ability to learn and remember in rats with brain lesions similar to those found in Alzheimer's patients. More recently Granholm, the scientist investigating trans fats and memory, found that nicotine enhances spatial memory in healthy rats. Other researchers have found that nicotine also boosts both emotional memory (the kind that helps us *not* put our hands back in the fire after we've been burned) and auditory memory.

There's a catch: Other studies show that nicotine encourages state-dependent learning. The idea is that if, for example, you study in blue sweats, it helps to take the exam in blue sweats. In other words, what you learn while smoking is best recalled while smoking. Since lighting up in an exam room might cause problems, cigarettes probably aren't the key to getting on the dean's list.

Nonetheless, while the number of cigarette smokers continues to drop nationwide, college students are still lighting up: As many as 30 percent smoke during their years of higher education. The smoking rate for young adults between the ages of 18 and 24 has actually risen in the past decade.

All this news makes you wonder how anyone's ever managed to get an education. Or what would happen to GPAs at a vegetarian university with a 10 P.M. curfew. But you might not need to go to such extremes. While Granholm agrees that the excesses of college can be "a perfect example of what you shouldn't do to yourself if you are trying to learn," she doesn't recommend abstinence. "Moderation," she counsels, "just like in everything else. Moderation is the key to collegiate success."

STEVEN KOTLER, *based in Los Angeles, has written for* The New York Times Magazine, National Geographic, Details, Wired and Outside.

Studies Reveal Strengths, Weaknesses

Improving Rates of High School Graduation and College Completion for Low-Income and Minority Students

Bill Hemmer

An in-depth analysis of high school and college graduation data shows that only one in three eighth graders in 1988 earned an Associate's degree 12 years later.

At the same time, a new national study of public perceptions of our education system shows that most Americans recognize that a college degree is critical for economic success, yet most people also believe that our education system, particularly high schools, is failing to prepare young people for higher education.

The Boston-based Jobs for the Future (JFF) today released the two reports, conducted for JFF by the Parthenon Group and Lake Snell Perry & Associates (LSPA), at "Double the Numbers," a national conference focused on improving the rates of college success for youth who are underrepresented in postsecondary education. More than 400 education leaders, public officials, and policymakers are participating in this conference, which is exploring ways to "plug the leaks" in the so-called education pipeline and improve the high school-to-college transition rates, especially for lower-income and minority youth.

According to the national public opinion survey, Americans are aware of the barriers to success that students encounter in high school and college, yet many people also underestimate the challenges that young people—including lower-income and minority youth—face in attempting to earn a college degree. The results show near universal agreement that the high number of students who fail to graduate from high school and complete a college degree is a major problem for the national economy.

"The United States faces the daunting task of improving a major pipeline that is seriously limited," said Hilary Pennington, CEO of Jobs for the Future. "This pipeline is not in a foreign nation. It is our education system, which wastes human potential at an alarming rate."

At a news event in Washington, DC, Pennington and other experts called on states and the federal government to take a number of steps to improve high school graduation, college enrollment, and completion rates, especially for low-income, minority students.

Based on the reports, JFF issued recommendations for federal and state policies that would "double the numbers" of young people who complete college or earn another postsecondary credential:

- Align expectation, curricula, and assessments with those of postsecondary institutions.
- Provide all students with opportunities and support to take and succeed in advanced courses.
- Connect students to the world beyond the high school walls by internships, community service, and work experience.
- Set up data systems that track students over time and hold postsecondary and secondary institutions accountable for how well they help students complete a recognized postsecondary credential by age 26.
- Eliminate boundaries between high school and college. For example, early college high schools, middle college high schools, and dropout recovery programs at community colleges permit students to accelerate their route to higher education and earn college credit at the same time.
- Offer incentives that reward secondary and postsecondary institutions when students successfully progress to and through college.

"The nation can no longer focus on high school reform as a standalone endeavor and regularly ignore as many as half of the young people who drop out of the education system before earning high school and college degrees," says Pennington. "And we're spending millions of dollars and substantial political capital building high school exit exams that ignore the next part of the pipeline: how to ensure that students gain the credentials and the education required for career jobs and college-level studies."

The research by the Parthenon Group examined the return that states and the nation would gain on investments designed to increase the number of students attending college. Doubling the numbers offers potential economic, as well as social and civic benefits. Economic benefits include increased tax revenues; social and civic benefits include reduction in unemployment and increased voter participation rates.

The JFF/LSPA opinion survey shows that Americans are optimistic about many of the initiatives already in use nationwide to prepare all students for high school and college success: for example, smaller high schools, need-based aid, and scholarship programs. According to the poll, Americans believe cost is the most important impediment faced by students—especially from lower-income families—in the pursuit of a college degree.

The Gates Millennium Scholars (GMS)—supported by the Bill & Melinda Gates Foundation and administered by the United Negro College Fund—is an example of a scholarship program that helps qualified minority youth attend the higher education institution of their choice. Early analysis of the program shows that GMS scholarship recipients are more likely than non-recipients to attend and stay in a four-year or private college.

"Qualified students, regardless of the race, ethnicity, or financial background, should not have to trim their ambitions and be denied the opportunity to attend college," said Tom Vander Ark, executive director of education at the Bill & Melinda Gates Foundation. "Gates Millennium Scholars are showing that when financial and other barriers are removed, students from the most challenging backgrounds can achieve, attend college, and prepare to become leaders in a range of professions and our communities."

But cost is not the only obstacle, the poll says. A majority of Americans believes that high schools need to do more to prepare students for college. They want to see better high school teachers in the classroom. Moreover, they feel it is important for guidance counselors to do more to help students understand the value of college

and to help them choose and apply to colleges that are right for them.

According to the JFF/Parthenon Group research, the barriers to college entrance and success are especially great for low-income families and other underrepresented youth, including minorities and immigrants who are learning English. For example, only 19 percent of lower-income families complete an Associate's degree or higher, compared to 76 percent of high-income families.

All states have room for improvement in overall degree attainment. However, the nature of the problem varies across states, driving the need for tailored solution sets to address state-specific challenges along the higher education pipeline. The emphasis in some states might be focused on high school graduation rates, while others might address post-secondary access and attainment issues.

According to the report, if the United States is to address anticipated shortages of 12 million highly skilled workers by 2020, we must radically change how we educate and support low-income students and minority students, who comprise the fastest-growing segments of the youth population. This requires transforming how we prepare young people for college, breaking down the barriers that separate schools and postsecondary education, and developing new incentives for individuals to attend college and for institutions to enroll and retain students.

The public opinion study found near universal agreement that the high number of students who fail to go from high school to complete a college degree is a major problem facing the nation. Moreover, most people appreciate that this problem threatens not only the economic well-being of students who leave school without a college (or even a high school) degree but also the potential of the U.S. economy as a whole.

References

National partners in the "Double the Numbers" conference include the Bill & Melinda Gates Foundation, Carnegie Corporation of New York, the Ford Foundation, and the W.K. Kellogg Foundation.

The national public opinion survey of 1,010 Americans age 18 and older was conducted by Lake Snell Perry & Associates in September through October 5, 2003. It included oversamples of African Americans and Hispanics. Altogether, 639 non-Hispanic whites, 161 non-Hispanic African Americans, and 171 Hispanics were surveyed. For results based on total sample, oversampled groups were weighted to reflect their true representative proportion.

The New Cheating Epidemic

More (and younger) kids are taking the easy way out to get good grades in school. Even worse, parents are actually helping students get away with it. Redbook reports on this troubling trend— and tells you how to keep your children honest.

Anne Marie Chaker

While grading essays, Eileen Theim, a teacher in Bethesda, Maryland, came across some lines in a seventh grader's assignment that sounded suspiciously eloquent. After a quick search online, Theim found the phrase in question—a professional writer's web-site. When Theim confronted the student about the stolen lines, "the student said, 'Oh, OK,' as if she didn't know it was wrong," Theim recalls. Asked to redo the essay, the student chose to merely cut the lines she'd lifted and resubmit it.

If you think that this student was the exception and that most kids wouldn't dream of cheating on schoolwork, you're in for a surprise. Recent studies show that the majority of students cheat. In a survey by the Josephson Institute of Ethics, 74 percent of high schoolers say they've cheated on an exam at least once; this is up 13 percent from a decade ago. And 59 percent of middle schoolers admit to the same crime, according to a study conducted at Rutgers University in New Jersey. Even younger kids are cheating, according to one teacher's experiment in Rigby, Idaho: When the teacher, Sharon Jones, asked second and fifth graders to grade their own tests, all but three kids cheated to get the reward she'd promised high scores: a candy bar.

Making matters worse is that teachers and parents are allowing— even helping—kids to cheat, seeing it as the only way for them to survive and stay sane in these high-stakes, fast-paced times. Under more pressure to keep test scores up than ever, schools are sometimes abandoning their ethics to meet their goals. And parents, pained at the sight of their kids in tears or up late slaving over homework, are increasingly willing to finish those assignments themselves.

But what, exactly, is driving so many students, at such early ages, to cheat? And why are adults—their alleged role models—letting them get away with this deceit? Redbook reveals this disturbing trend and how you can encourage your kids to stay honest.

New High-Tech Hicks

We're all familiar with the usual ways kids cheat, from crib sheets written on sneakers to coughing codes between classmates. But these days, cheating has gone high tech. Pagers can transmit test answers without telltale whispers; websites such as school sucks.com hawk custom-written term papers on any topic. Ken Rodoff, a high school teacher in Springfield, Pennsylvania, was recently introduced to the powers of a laser printer when he uncovered a student's thumbnail-size crib sheet, printed in a font just large enough to read. "I have to admit it, it was impressive," he says. Though he failed that student, he doubts he's spotting every cheat sheet. "They're so small," he says.

These tech-savvy scams make it easier than ever for students to slide phony work by teachers, who are often unaware that cheating is going on—or just don't care. "Ninety-eight percent of cheaters don't get caught, and only half of those caught are punished," estimates Michael Josephson, president of the Josephson Institute, a Marina del Rey, California, research institute.

Sadly, it's the honest students who sometimes get the short end of the stick. "Once, an eleventh grader arrived at my after-school book club crying," says one school librarian. "She said that earlier that week, students in her history class had gotten a hold of their exam before they had to take it." But the girl had refused to look at it, and her grade ended up being lower than those of the cheaters. Even so, she refused to rat out her peers. The girl's teacher felt that little could be done, since she couldn't tell who'd cheated. "Here was a girl who was trying to do the right thing," says the librarian. But she was paddling against the current, which allowed others to thrive while she faltered.

Students in Crisis

Why are so many kids becoming cheaters? Largely because the pressure they're under to succeed is more intense than ever—

and hits them as early as primary school. "These days getting on the honor roll or into elite secondary schools is increasingly difficult. I've seen third graders with private tutors," says John Dacey, Ph.D., an author of Your Anxious Child. Plus, the growing importance of extracurricular activities as a way to stand out to admissions boards is forcing students to spread themselves thin. Combine all this with the fact that young kids often lack the judgment or self-control to enable them to do the right thing, and some are bound to take the easy way out by copying their neighbors' test answers. "Kids are starving for some free time," says Dacey. "They'll do what it takes to get some hours to themselves."

One reason this pressure to excel starts early is standardized tests, now taken as often as once a year starting in kindergarten in some states, says Kevin Welner, a director of the Education and the Public Interest Center at the University of Colorado in Boulder. Kids who don't perform well may be held back, shuttled into less advanced curricula, or denied entrance into selective middle and high schools.

For Maria Vidal de Haymes, 40, this emphasis on standardized tests rather than on a school's curriculum convinced her to pull her seventh-grade son out of a Chicago public school at the end of the term and enroll him in a private school. "The better public high schools in this area pretty much only accept kids who score above the 95th percentile on the Iowa Test of Basic Skills [a standardized test]," she says. "These tests are demoralizing for kids, especially when their friends make it into good high schools and they don't. Parents with seventh and eighth graders are all panicking."

And as if high-stakes tests didn't produce enough anxiety, kids are doing nearly twice as much homework as they did 20 years ago, according to a study by the University of Michigan in Ann Arbor. Given these time constraints, Dianna Ewton, 40, empathized when her ninth-grade daughter confessed that she's copied friends' homework. "I gave her hell, but I can see why she did it," she says. "Her field hockey practice lasts until 5:30, and she also volunteers at the YMCA, babysits, and plays flute in the school band." Copying, she concludes, is her daughter's attempt to make ends meet.

School for Scandal

Perhaps most shocking, teachers themselves are cheating as well. Last October teachers and principals in 14 Chicago-area elementary schools were investigated for helping students answer questions on the Iowa tests, which are mandatory for students in the third, sixth, and eighth grades. So far, a substitute teacher and teacher's aide have been dismissed. What's more, some teachers claimed that their supervisors had told them to cheat on the tests to jack up the scores; one teacher claimed she'd lost her job after refusing to do it.

What drove these schools into such shady territory? A fear that low standardized test scores will have dire consequences for the school itself. "Last year alone, three Chicago schools were shut down as a result of their students' overall performance on the

test," says the Chicago Teachers Union President Deborah Lynch. And President Bush's January 2001 signing of the No Child Left Behind Act ratchets up the pressure even more, requiring annual standardized testing of all students in third through eighth grade. High poverty schools that get federal funding and don't show an adequate yearly progress five years in a row face a state-government takeover. "This doesn't give schools much time at all to improve," says Melanie Mitchell, assistant director of the Keenan Institute for Ethics at Duke University. "I wouldn't be surprised if it tempts some schools to cheat."

Parents Who Help too Much

With the stakes so high, even parents don't always play fair when it comes to their child's education. While most adults wouldn't approve of kids' copying each other's homework, more than one in five parents say they've done part of a child's homework assignment themselves, according to a study by Public Agenda, a research firm in New York.

AnneLise Wilhelmsen, 41, of Los Alamitos, California, freely admits she's had a hand in doing her fourth-grade son's homework. In particular, she recalls watching her 9-year-old son struggle to complete a geography assignment. When she realized he couldn't get it done in time, she lent a hand. "Strictly speaking, this may have been cheating, but it was the right decision for this boy on this specific day," she says. "It [excessive homework] cuts into family time. It cuts into our children's opportunity to be children."

Etta Kralovec, an author of The End of Homework: How Homework Disrupts Families, Overburdens Children and Limits Learning, doesn't blame parents for helping so much. "Parents don't want to, but they also don't want their child to get bad grades or to have a meltdown trying to get everything done," she says. Another reason some parents do homework is so that they can spend more quality time with their kids. "We're increasingly protective of family time," Kralovec says. So much so, in fact, that at one school in Piscataway, New Jersey, parents staged protests decrying the amount of homework their kids received. The school now has "homework caps" limiting the amount of homework teachers can assign.

While schools often justify heavy homework loads by claiming that they boost standardized-test scores, this doesn't hold true for elementary school students, says Harris Cooper, professor of educational psychology at the University of Missouri in Columbia. "Younger kids don't have the cognitive skills or the attention span to benefit from long periods of study," Cooper explains. Some experts even say it's detrimental to young kids, who get frustrated and lose interest in subjects they once adored.

Why Cheating Goes Unpunished

Teachers say some forms of cheating are easier to spot than others. For instance, spotting homework that's benefited from a parent's "help" is a no-brainer. Some parents make it even more obvious by turning in assignments in their own handwriting. But calling parents on their rule-bending is often more trouble than it's worth. One New York middle school teacher says she argues with parents over grades on homework they've helped with "on a weekly basis." "They'll demand that I change the grade from a C to an A," she says. "I usually say, 'You get an A, but your kid gets a C.'" But more often than not, this teacher's principal recommends that she inflate the grade, and she does. "I'm an untenured teacher," she points out. "What else am I supposed to do?"

Christine Pelton, a former tenth-grade biology teacher at Piper High School in Kansas, knows all too well the consequences of standing up to irate parents. In December 2001, she found out that 28 of her students had cut and pasted essays off websites. She gave those students zeros, causing many to fail the course. A parental uproar ensued. "I got phone calls in the middle of the night from people cursing," she says. After the superintendent and the school board forced her to pass the students, she resigned in disgust. The superintendent and some board members have since left the district. "But I got a lot of respect from students," she says. "They said they were glad someone had finally stood up to the students who cheated."

How to Cheat-Proof Your Child

While containing such widespread cheating may seem daunting, parents can do so in various ways, starting in their own homes. Even before kids head off to kindergarten, you should have a talk with them, telling them that cheating is wrong and won't be tolerated (for tips on this topic, refer to "How to Talk to Your Child About Cheating").

But since even honest kids will be tempted to cheat if everyone else is getting away with it, parents also have to push for school-wide reform. The best place to do this is at a school board meeting. "Parents often make the mistake of approaching teachers," says Kralovec. But, surprisingly, teachers won't be able to do much; only principals and school boards have the power to put an end to rampant cheating, through changes in school policy (to find out when your local school board meets, inquire at the school principal's office).

What kinds of policies should parents request? For starters, ask that the board prohibit teachers from giving the same test to students in different periods of the same class, or from year to year. This measure will keep students from passing tests around to their peers who may be taking them later. You can also request that teachers keep a close eye on students during tests.

But teaching students to behave ethically on their own is a far more important and challenging goal for schools, says Don Mc-Cabe, founder of the Center for Academic Integrity. To this end, parents can ask the school board to write and enforce an honor code delineating what constitutes cheating and how students will be penalized if caught doing so. Having clear guidelines that are explained to students regularly goes a long way toward keeping students in line. Students and parents should receive a copy of this code at the beginning of every school year; after big

tests, students should sign a waiver stating that they haven't cheated and are aware of the consequences if they do. These regular reminders will also discourage cheating.

Heavy homework loads may also be part of the problem. To keep your kids from feeling so pressed for time that they copy pals' assignments, ask the school board to make some homework nongraded (especially for younger kids) and to establish homework caps. Ron Bolandi, a school superintendent in Tewksbury, New Jersey, has implemented these policies, and while it's too early to tell how they will affect the incidence of cheating, Bolandi knows one thing for sure: "Students love it," he says. "They say now they can stop staying up until 3 a.m. doing homework and have a life."

How to Talk to Your Child About Cheating

Acknoweldge the pressure he's under. Lecturing your child about cheating by simply saying "Don't do it" will create a you-versus-him dynamic that will likely cause him to stop listening to you. Instead say, "I know you're incredibly busy and stressed about school, and that it must be tempting to cheat. But it's still not right." This lets him know you're on his side without conveying that cheating's OK.

Don't say "You'll get caught." Too many kids get away with cheating for you to be able to convince your child that this is true. Instead appeal to his sense of morality by asking him, "How would you feel if someone cheated off you in your favorite class—and got the better grade?" It'll be much harder for him to cheat if he visualizes what it's like to be in the victim's shoes, says Caroline Watts, a psychologist at Children's Hospital in Boston.

Reassure him that grades don't matter that much. Kids often think that their getting high marks means more to you than their doing the right thing. Emphasize that this isn't the case by saying, "I'd be much, much more disappointed in you if you cheated than if you failed a test."

Is Your Child Cheating?

4 ways to find out if your kid earned his grades the honest way.

1. Even if you swear your child isn't cheating, it's good to check in with him regularly to establish that you're monitoring his work to see what he's learned. If you know that your child had a big exam, for example, ask him. "So what were some of the questions on that test you took today?" If he can't remember any, it may mean he copied off someone else, filling in the answers without really reading the questions.

2. Look in on your child frequently while he's doing homework, asking him if he needs any help. If he never has questions, is reluctant to … show you what he's working on, or refuses to work in the same room with you, it may suggest he's doing something you wouldn't approve of, such as exchanging answers with his friends.

3. Ask to see his resources—books, encyclopedias, etc.—for written assignments. If he can't provide them, it may mean he has pasted his essay off the Web or gotten it from someone else.

4. Read his written assignments. If a word he uses seems too sophisticated for someone his age, ask him to define it. If he can't explain it—or the overall point of his essay, for that matter—it may spell trouble.

Once You Know the Score

If your child fails three or more of these measures, there's a very good chance he's cheating. What then? While alerting his teacher and making your child face the consequences at school may seem the right things to do, Michael Josephson of the Josephson Institute usually recommends against this plan. "It may destroy any trust your child has in you," points out Josephson. "The important issue is that the child should be punished at home in a way that conveys that this is not acceptable." You should also address the underlying situation that led your child to cheat. If, for example, he's spread too thin by all his activities, suggest cutting a few of the less important ones so he'll have time to finish his schoolwork without cutting corners.

UNIT 4

Identity and Social-Emotional Development

Unit Selections

Key Points to Consider

- How can adults improve the emotional development of teens?

- What is emotional intelligence and how can it be fostered in the classroom?

- Can body image effect self-esteem and career choices?

- How important is sufficient sleep on the emotional stability of teens?

Student Website

www.mhcls.com/online

Internet References

Further information regarding these websites may be found in this book's preface or online.

ADOL: Adolescence Directory On-Line
http://education.indiana.edu/cas/adol/adol.html

American Academy of Child and Adolescent Psychiatry
http://www.aacap.org/

Each age period is associated with developmental tasks. A major aspect of psychosocial development for adolescents is the formation of a coherent personal identity. Erik Erikson referred to this as the adolescent identity crisis. Identity formation is a normative event, but it represents a turning point in human development that has consequences for later psychosocial skills.

Children's identities often represent an identification with parents and significant others. Adolescents reflect on their identity and come to some sense of who they are and who they are not. Identity formation involves an examination of personal likes and dislikes; political, religious, and moral values; occupational interests, as well as gender roles and sexual behaviors. Adolescents must also form an integrated sense of their own personality across the various roles they engage in (e.g., son or daughter, student, boyfriend or girlfriend, part-time worker, etc.).

To aid in the identity formation process, Erikson advocated that adolescents be given a license to explore alternative roles and values. He believed that such a moratorium period would allow

adolescents to make commitments that reflect true personal choices. James Marcia elaborated on Erikson's ideas about identity formation. He described four identity statuses that depend on the degree of exploration an adolescent engages in and whether the adolescent makes choices or commitments to certain paths. Adolescents who are actively searching and evaluating options are said to be in a moratorium, as Erikson described. An identity-achieved status eventually is expected to follow this moratorium period. Other adolescents adopt values and life roles without experiencing a period of questioning. These adolescents are called identity-foreclosed as they essentially conform to parental expectations for themselves. Conformity to parents is not automatically a sign of identity foreclosure, however. Identity-achieved individuals often make choices that fit parental values and expectations but they do so only after some self-reflection. As a result, they are more invested in their choices and more self-confident. Finally, Marcia describes some adolescents as identity-diffused. These adolescents have not undergone a period of questioning and exploration, nor have they made clear ideological, occupational, or personal commitments. Identity-diffusion is expected in early adolescents, but it is seen as developmentally immature in college-age adolescents.

Erikson also proposed some differences in male and female identity development. Females were presumed to delay full identity development until the formation of an intimate relationship (that is, marriage). Interpersonal issues were seen as more paramount in female identity development with the occupational domain being more relevant for male identity development. Recent research indicates that there are fewer gender differences in identity development than may have been true of earlier generations when Erikson did his work (1950s). Modern psychologist Carol Gilligan maintains that moral decision making is another area of gender differences. She argues that females' moral values and moral judgments reflect more concern for interpersonal relationships and for caring about others. Males, she says, have a legalistic outlook that is less compassionate and more focused on the abstract application of rules. Unfortunately, Gilligan's ideas have not been fully tested to date.

An area that has received recent attention is how identity development may differ for minority individuals. In addition to ideological, occupational, sexual, and interpersonal commitments, ethnicity is a salient component that must be integrated into a person's identity. Adolescents may or may not identify with their respective ethnic group, but instead may reject their own ethnicity. Jean Phinney has articulated several phases characteristic of ethnic identity development. Similar to identity foreclosure, some minority adolescents adopt the values of the dominant culture and possess an unexamined ethnic identity. Others are in moratorium and are wrestling with conflicts between the dominant culture and their own culture. Finally, adolescents with an achieved ethnic identity feel an emotional attachment to their ethnic group and come to some resolution integrating ethnic group values with the dominant culture's values.

Whether you are male or female, minority or majority, identity issues have implications of emotional health, self-concept, and self-esteem. Adolescents' self-concepts become more and more abstract as they begin to think of themselves in terms of personality traits. They compare themselves to others in order to evaluate their own characteristics and abilities. They often construct an ideal self that is difficult to live up to. The abstract nature of their self-concept means that self-evaluation is more removed from concrete, observable behaviors and, thus, subject to distortion. Adolescents just like Rosa who are struggling with identity issues are also likely to undergo fluctuations in their self-concept as they explore alternative roles, values, and personalities.

Another important aspect of identity is self-esteem, which reflects how good one feels about oneself. The essential question is, "Am I okay?" Self-esteem is at a low point in early adolescence relative to other age periods. In adolescence, more dimensions contribute to self-esteem than is the case in childhood. Global self-esteem measures are often less informative, because adolescents' self-esteem varies in different domains (e.g., physical attractiveness, peer acceptance, academic competence, and athletic competence). Research by Susan Harter and her colleagues indicates that feeling good about one's physical appearance is the number one predictor of overall self-esteem in adolescents. Pubertal changes heighten concern about body image and appearance. Females compared to males are even more concerned about their looks and are much more likely to have a negative body image. Contrary to most expectations, recent studies show that self-esteem in African Americans is comparable to that of Caucasian Americans. Little work on self-esteem has been done in other minority populations.

The articles in this unit elaborate on the theme of identity and social-emotional development. The power of adult empathy is emphasized in Ernest Mendes' article. The social-emotional problems in school create a need to teach the skills of emotional intelligence in the classroom as explained by Linda and Nick Elksnin.

Social-emotional development is influenced by many factors. Paul Rudnick reports on a mother's story of her struggle with an unattractive daughter. A teen's emotional stability and development is greatly influenced by proper health habits. The consequences of insufficient sleep are explored in the last article of this unit.

What Empathy Can Do

Students respond to us because we care—and because they like us.

By Ernest Mendes

With pursed lips and a furrowed brow, Julie strode into my second-period social studies class. She sat down, slammed her books on the desk, and said, "I hate this class!" I stood at my podium, reviewing my notes for the next period. On hearing her remark, I looked up and saw that Julie was not happy. I took a deep breath and walked slowly toward her. I squatted down next to her desk.

"Julie, you're really upset. What's wrong?" I asked.

"It's not fair. I hate this!" She paused. I waited. "We had a stupid pop quiz in math last period. I didn't have time to study last night because we had to pick my grandma up from the airport and got home late."

I acknowledged her frustration, took another deep breath, and said,

> Julie, just hang in there today. Do whatever you can. It's tough to have that happen first thing in the morning.

I walked back to my podium. By now, most of the sophomore students had arrived.

As class began, I noticed that Julie sat dazed at her desk. After about 15 minutes, she opened her notebook and began to participate in class. When the bell rang, she left without a word, which wasn't unusual for her; she rarely spoke when she entered my class and never made eye contact.

The next day, Julie was the first to arrive in class once again. As she passed by my podium, she smiled at me, her eyes bright, and said exuberantly, "Good morning, Mr. Mendes."

"Good morning, Julie," I replied.

"So, what are we going to do today?" she asked. I gave her a thumbnail sketch. When class began, she actively participated. When class was over, she passed by me and said enthusiastically, "Have a good day, Mr. Mendes." The next day—and every day thereafter—she greeted me, participated in class, and

left with a goodbye. She raised her grade from a C to an A that semester.

What happened here? Am I suggesting that my empathetic response during a brief conversation influenced her behavior that dramatically? Dozens of variables were present in Julie's life during that time. I know from my 23 years of teaching, however, that Julie's change was not an exception, but rather the rule. Every student with whom I consciously made an effort to establish a rapport or a caring relationship demonstrated dramatic changes in behavior, effort, and performance.

Positive responses create an emotional bank account that can absorb relational difficulties that occur along the way.

Students do respond just because we care—and because they like us. Some educators want students simply to respect rather than like their teachers. But earning the respect of students is not enough. Students must perceive that we care, and even that we like them deep down, as people. As it turns out, they will work harder for someone they like than for someone they simply respect. And in our professional adult capacity, we can maintain both friendship-like qualities and our leadership role.

Having rapport means that two people are alike physiologically, emotionally, or cognitively, even if the similarity is temporary. Knowing students' interests and concerns is one sure way to build rapport. Being physically on the same level when talking with students—matching their rate of speech and their tone when it is positive—can help build rapport. Using students' names during lectures and acknowledging all responses in some way during class discussions are also part of building rapport.

What does it take to build rapport? The teacher needs a genuine desire to build a connection with students and strategies for reframing experiences so that they elicit a student's interest rather than frustration.

Nurture and Structure

Moustakas (1994) asks student teachers to draw from personal experience to create a profile of an effective relationship with a caring adult and then work to replicate this relationship with their students. Students feel special, for example, when the teacher affirms their interests and needs and makes suggestions rather than impositions. Psychologist Carl Rogers (1951) described the ideal therapeutic relationship as one in which the therapist is genuine and nonjudgmental, providing unconditional positive regard. Teachers can develop these characteristics of a good therapist to create healthy teacher-student relationships.

Developing caring relationships does not negate the need for limits and structure in the classroom. Students need both structure and nurture, and the ways in which the teacher responds to these needs in the classroom are crucial. Caring teachers succeed in managing their classrooms effectively, including maintaining discipline, solving problems, and setting expectations, limits, and rewards (Gootman, 1997). Caring classrooms are home to warm, supportive, stable relationships and to the social and ethical dimensions of learning (Lewis, Schapps, & Watson, 1996).

Emotional Intelligence

Self-awareness and self-management are crucial elements of emotional intelligence. Self-awareness entails identifying your own emotional state—knowing when you feel frustrated, for example, and why. Self-awareness includes being able to distinguish between your own feelings and those of others.

Self-management is the ability to manage your emotions and use them to move toward a desired outcome. Self-managing behavior might include taking some deep breaths or calming yourself with internal suggestions, such as "Relax" or "I can handle this." Once you have achieved self-control, it is easier to listen and respond to others with *I-messages*, stating how the other person's statement is affecting you.

> **Earning the respect of students is not enough. Students must perceive that we care, and even that we like them deep down, as people.**

When we are aware and in control of our own emotions, we also need to be aware of other people's emotions so that we can make appropriate choices about how and what we communicate. Training and coaching can help develop this skill in reading between the lines.

In a study that measured the emotional intelligence of 49 high school teachers, I found that a teacher's ability to accurately identify emotions was directly related to the number of years that the teacher had taught (Mendes, 2002). This finding is consistent with other research on emotional intelligence (Mayer, Caruso, & Salovey, 2000). Classroom teachers must possess these competencies if they are to succeed with students.

Choosing Empathy

Sometimes empathy can serve multiple purposes. For example, viewing a situation empathetically can lead to a calmer internal state, which can influence the response of the teacher. In the case of Julie, I thought about how awful it is to feel that angry and almost out of control. That insight influenced my behavior. In addition, my observation allowed me to perceive Julie's upset state. This ability to read and identify emotions works together with self-management and leads to the optimal timing of responses.

In the classroom, we might be excited about a great activity for our students. But if a student is having a bad day, how do we respond? Do we perceive the student as apathetic and as having a negative attitude? Do we stick to our behavioral management plan and give the student a warning, soon to be followed by a set of consequences?

How do we discern, in the moment, what state the student is in and what course of action would be best? It's not always an easy task. The observation skills required to make these quick daily decisions are part of empathy.

The Adolescent Brain

Every time I read about neuroscientists' findings about developmental stages, I am amazed that adolescents can function in a classroom at all. The adolescent's brain is undergoing a state of reorganization, and the frontal lobe region, which is crucial in controlling impulses and making healthy decisions, has not finished developing (Giedd et al., 1999). Further, uncontrollable temper outbursts and violence may be due to mini-seizures in the temporal lobes (Amen, 1998). When making important decisions, the amygdala, an emotional trigger, gets activated more frequently in an adolescent brain than in an adult brain. Hormones magnify the intensity of moods and behavior (Amen, 1998). A bad family situation, for example, may be wreaking havoc inside the student's head.

These difficulties are not excuses for student performance and behavior, but they represent some of the factors that play into the observable behavior you see every day. When I remember these mitigating factors, I feel more empathy.

How to Build Relationships

- Acknowledge all responses and questions.
- Mention students' names, skills, ideas, and knowledge in your presentations—without mentioning weaknesses or confidential information.
- Use self-disclosure when appropriate. Be a real person.
- Use responses beginning with "I agree," "I appreciate," and "I respect."
- Ask students about their interests. Collect an information card at the beginning of the year and have students update it regularly. Pay attention to students' nonverbal responses and make adjustments as you capture their interest or hit neutral ground.
- Build on what you hear from students by sharing stories, interests, and worries.
- Display empathy with individuals and with classes by communicating what you think their needs or feelings might be.
- Listen actively. Match students' expressions and conveyed moods. Paraphrase their message, when appropriate. Know your students' world and go there first to open the relationship door.

Opening the Relationship Door

Gottman describes people's attempts to make connections with others as *bidding* (Gottman & DeClaire, 2001). We make numerous attempts at interpersonal connections throughout the day, in all of our relationships, and people can respond to our bidding in one of three ways: toward the bid, away from it, or against it.

For example, if a person in your proximity commented on the warm weather, and you asked him to pass the newspaper, you would be moving *away* from response. If instead you agreed that a heat wave is in the making, you would be moving *toward* the attempted bid for connection. You would be making an *against* response if you replied, "What are you, the weather man?" Relationships that include many *toward* responses are more durable than those with many *away* and *against* responses. Positive responses create an emotional bank account that can absorb relational difficulties that occur along the way.

Bidding takes verbal and nonverbal forms. Depending on the relationship, a glance, a touch, or a verbal "hey" may be appropriate. When a student asks a question that is out of context and unrelated to the classroom discussion, we have choices: We can ignore it; acknowledge it and suggest another time to address it; or make a sarcastic response. Every response is either making a deposit to or a withdrawal from our relationship account. When an individual, either in a group or one-on-one, risks sharing an idea or thought with you, you have an opportunity to deposit or withdraw. Which will you choose?

> Students need both structure and nurture, and the ways in which the teacher responds to these needs in the classroom are crucial.

We may need to practice making clear, recognizable bids to others. When we do not clearly communicate with students, they may misinterpret our intention. For example, an after-class conversation regarding a student's behavior may start out harshly and set the conversation on a downward spiral:

> Jessie, knock it off. I'm tired of your wisecracks in class. You're being a smart aleck, and you're going to be sorry if you don't stop.

Instead, the teacher should ask the student what's going on:

> You didn't seem your usual self today in class.

The student explains. The teacher uses self-control:

> When you said, "This class is stupid," I became defensive and felt angry because I thought you were attacking me in front of the class. I want to know where that comment came from.

The student explains. The teacher responds:

> In the future, if you're angry with me or at something else, I want you to take out a piece of paper and write me a note describing your feelings and why you feel that way. Then you can share it with me later. How does that sound?

The student comments. The teacher finishes:

> OK, I'll talk with you more tomorrow.

This dialogue is only one of the typical, ongoing bidding scenarios we face daily. How we bid and respond to bids has a cumulative effect.

To open the relationship door, teachers need to understand their students' world. To build relationships in the classroom, teachers need to know their students, their own strengths and limitations, and how to connect with students by demonstrating genuine interest in them.

References

Amen, D. G. (1998). *Change your brain, change your life.* New York: Random House.

Giedd, J. N., Blumenthal, J., Jeffries, N. O., Castellanos, F. X., Liu, H., Zijdenbos, A., Paus, T., Evans, A. C., & Rapoport, J. L. (1999). Brain development during childhood and adolescence. *Nature Neurosciences*, 2(10), 861-863.

Gootman, M. (1997). *The caring teacher's guide to discipline: Helping young students learn self-control, responsibility, and respect.* Thousand Oaks, CA: Corwin.

Gottman, J., & DeClaire, J. (2001). *The relationship cure*. New York: Crown Publishers.

Lewis, C., Schapps, E., & Watson, M. (1996). The caring classroom's academic edge. *Educational Leadership*, 54(1), 16-21.

Mayer, J., Caruso, D., & Salovey, P. (2000). Emotional intelligence meets traditional standards for an intelligence. *Intelligence, 27*(4), 267-298.

Mendes, E.J. (2002). *The relationship between emotional intelligence and occupational burnout in secondary school teachers*. Ann Arbor, MI: ProQuest Information and Learning Company.

Moustakas, C. (1994). *Phenomenological research methods*. Thousand Oaks, CA: Sage.

Rogers, C. (1951). *Client-centered therapy: Its current practice, implications, and theory*. Boston: Houghton Mifflin.

Ernest Mendes is an education consultant and President of Mendes Training and Consulting, 374 E. H St., Ste. A, PMB-314, Chula Vista, CA 91910; erniemendes@cox.net; www.erniemendes.com.

Fostering Social-Emotional Learning in the Classroom

Linda K. Elksnin; Nick Elksnin

Teachers face enormous challenges meeting both the academic and social-emotional needs of learners in their classrooms. In this article we discuss ways in which teachers can promote social-emotional learning. First, we discuss the construct of emotional intelligence and how it can be improved through social-emotional learning. We then review strategies teachers can use to improve learners' emotional, social, and interpersonal problem solving skills.

It is estimated that between 15 and 22 percent of U.S. youth have social-emotional difficulties warranting intervention (Cohen, 2001; Mogno & Rosenblitt, 2001). Students at risk for school failure are particularly vulnerable for social-emotional problems. For example, 75 percent of students with learning disabilities (LD) exhibit social skills deficits (Kavale & Forness, 1996), and the U.S. Department of Education (1996) reported that 29 percent of adolescents with disabilities require social skills instruction beyond high school.

Regular education classrooms include ever-increasing numbers of at-risk students. For example, special education students receive most, if not all, of their education in regular education classrooms (U.S. Department of Education, 2001). It is clear that teachers face enormous challenges meeting learners' academic and social-emotional needs. In this article we discuss ways in which teachers can promote social-emotional learning in their classrooms. First we discuss the construct of emotional intelligence and how it can be improved through social-emotional learning. We then review strategies teachers can use to improve learners' emotional, social, and interpersonal problem solving skills.

Emotional Intelligence and Social-Emotional Learning

The term emotional intelligence was first used in 1990 by Salovey and Mayer, who offer this definition:

Emotional intelligence involves the ability to perceive accurately, appraise, and express emotion; the ability to access and/or generate feelings when they facilitate thought; the ability to understand emotion and emotional knowledge; and the ability to regulate emotions to promote emotional and intellectual growth (Mayer & Salovey, 1997).

Goleman (1995) popularized the construct of emotional intelligence in his book, Emotional Intelligence: Why It Can

Matter More Than IQ. The term EQ, or emotional quotient, was coined by Bar-On (1997) to differentiate emotional intelligence from cognitive intelligence, which is measured by intelligence tests. EQ is thought to be comprised of five domains (Goleman, 1995; Mayer & Salovey, 1997):

- knowing ones' emotions
- managing one's emotions
- motivating oneself
- recognizing emotions of others
- effectively using social skills when interacting with others

Less genetically determined than IQ, emotional intelligence can be taught by teachers and parents. Even more encouraging is that EQ skills overlap, creating a "spillover" effect: Teaching one skill improves other EQ skills. Social-emotional learning (or social-emotional education) involves using procedures and methods to promote EQ.

Within two years after publication of Goleman's book, more than 700 school districts implemented social emotional learning (SEL) programs designed to teach students social-emotional skills (Ratnesar, 1997). SEL programs focus on emotional awareness, social skills, and interpersonal problem solving (Cohen, 2001). In the sections that follow, we discuss ways in which teachers can foster social-emotional learning in their classrooms.

Emotional Awareness

The ability to perceive and understand emotions develops with age. Children as young as three can identify sadness, happiness, and fear using nonverbal cues such as facial expression, gestures, and voice tone (Nabuzoka & Smith, 1995). At this age they begin to understand causes of feelings. However, children who are at risk for school failure may only acquire these skills through direct instruction (Gumpel & Wilson,

1996; Most & Greenbank, 2000). In addition, many children (and some adults) may require help in understanding subtle shifts in emotion represented by family groupings as identified by Bodine and Crawford (1999):

> *Anger: Fury, outrage, resentment,*
> *wrath, exasperation, indignation,*
> *vexation, acrimony, animosity,*
> *annoyance, irritability, hostility*
> *Sadness: Grief, sorrow, cheerlessness,*
> *gloom, melancholy, self-pity,*
> *Loneliness, dejection, despair (p. 82)*

Understanding one's own emotions is prerequisite to self control and anger management (Bodine & Crawford, 1999). Understanding the emotions of others is essential if learners are to read social situations accurately and respond to them appropriately. Without emotional understanding, students will misread the behaviors of others. Teachers can help learners increase their emotional understanding by teaching nonverbal communication skills and by becoming emotion coaches.

Nonverbal Communication Skills

Most (i.e., 93%) of emotional meaning is conveyed without words: Fifty-five percent through facial expressions, body posture, and gestures, and thirty-eight percent through tone of voice (Mehrabian, 1968). In order to understand one's emotions and the emotions of others, learners must have adequate nonverbal communication skills. Nowicki and Duke (1992) and Duke, Nowicki, and Martin (1996) identified six areas of nonverbal communication: paralanguage, facial expressions, postures and gestures, interpersonal distance (space) and touch, rhythm and time, and objectics. Instructional goals are for learners to recognize nonverbal messages of others and to effectively express themselves nonverbally. Teachers can reach these goals by using activities described in Table 1.

Paralanguage. Paralanguage is comprised of nonword sounds that convey meaning. Examples include tone of voice, rate of speech, emphasis and variation in speech, and nonverbal sound patterns such as "mmmmmmmm." Learners need to understand how voice tone conveys emotion. In order to avoid cognitive conflict voice tone and words must match. Similarly, learners need to recognize that speech rate conveys emotion. They also should be aware of their own speech rate and be able to adjust it to meet listeners' needs. Emphasis and variation in speech conveys and changes meaning. The sentence "I didn't say you stole the car," takes on different meanings depending on which word is emphasized:

> **I** *didn't say you stole the car.*
> *I **didn't** say you stole the car.*
> *I didn't say **you** stole the car.*
> *I didn't say you **stole** the car.*
> *I didn't say you stole the **car**.*

Table 1

Activities for Teaching Nonverbal Communication Skills

Area of Nonverbal Communication	Activity
Paralanguage	
Tone of Voice	Identify emotions when teacher reads sentence using different voice tones.
	Read a script when given different situations surrounding different emotions.
Nonverbal Sound Patterns	Use different types of paralanguage to express feelings.
Rate of Speech	Match rate with emotions such as happy, angry, sad.
	Tape voice and count number of words spoken per minute; compare with others.
Facial Expressions	Demonstrate "resting face."
	Make facial expressions to convey different emotions.
	Identify emotions conveyed by people in public, on TV, and in magazines.
Postures and Gestures	Assemble a dictionary of gestures/postures conveying specific emotions.
	Demonstrate postures under formal/informal situations.
Interpersonal Distance and Touch	Identify types of conversations that should/should not occur in each spatial zone.
	Discuss feelings when personal space is invaded.
	Demonstrate a touch for an emotion when role playing.
Rhythm and Time	Estimate length of time to complete activities.
	Keep track of number of times late or on time.
	Describe examples of public and private time.
Objectics	Develop dress codes for specific situations and use magazine pictures to illustrate.
	Describe image conveyed by dress when observing people in public.
	Develop dictionary of "in" styles.

Facial Expressions. People are expected to look at other's faces during conversation, and learners may need to be taught to engage in eye contact. Ability to read facial expressions is related to understanding that the face includes three zones: forehead and eyes, nose and cheeks, and mouth. Awareness of facial zones and the resting face (a person's unconscious facial expression) can be taught directly.

Postures and Gestures. Learners must learn to interpret postures and gestures and to use them appropriately. For example, the teacher may regard a student as bored and disinterested by how that student sits in class.

Interpersonal Distance (Space) and Touch. Hall (1966) identified four spatial zones among Americans: intimate zone (i.e., nearly touching to 18 inches away), personal zone (i.e., 18 inches to 4 feet away), social zone (i.e., 4 to 12 feet away), and public zone (i.e., 12 feet and more). Learners need to be taught about these zones as violating a zone may result in a serious faux pas. Learners who respect classmates' personal space are more accepted by peers and are less apt to get into difficulty when working with others. Learners also need to know about mental space that holds private topics. Learning to read people to determine if they feel that their mental space has been invaded is a useful skill. Finally, students also must learn what constitutes appropriate and inappropriate touching.

Rhythm and Time. Some principles of rhythm and time students need to understand and practice include being in sync with others, managing time, arriving on time, and knowing the difference between private and public time. Students need to be able to read messages conveyed through others' use of time (e.g., being made to wait in the doctor's office) and have their use of time match the intended message (e.g., spending time with friends means you care about them). Many learners need direct instruction in how to estimate and manage time.

Objectics. Objectics includes style of dress and hair, use of jewelry and cosmetics, and personal hygiene that allow learners to fit in with a group. Learners need to understand the difference between image (self perception) and impression (other's perception of an individual). Objectics are particularly important for young adolescents, whose desire to fit in is overpowering. Teachers and parents should not pretend to understand preadolescent and adolescent fashion rules, but should rely instead on observing children in school and magazines, at the mall, and on TV. Students may need to be taught how to dress to convey their desired image and how to dress for different situations.

Emotion Coaching

Once learners acquire adequate nonverbal communication skills, emotional understanding can be further improved through use of emotion coaching, a technique developed by John Gottman (1997). Teachers and parents acting as emotion coaches can use a five-step process to provide guidance about emotions. Parents and teachers first need to be aware of the learner's emotion. Gottman recommends that adults put the child's situation into an adult context. For example, how we feel when our boss dresses us down during a staff meeting is similar to how a child feels when a teacher reprimands the child in front

of the class. Step Two involves recognizing uncomfortable emotions as teaching opportunities and discussing feelings rather than punishing or criticizing. Emotions are validated rather than evaluated during Step Three. Step Four involves helping the learner label his emotion. The skills learned during nonverbal communication lessons will help learners use words to label how they feel. The final step involves helping the learner solve the problem that led to the feeling. Problem solving is discussed in detail elsewhere in this article.

Social Skills

Adequate interpersonal skills are an important component of emotional intelligence. Types of social skills include interpersonal behaviors needed to make and keep friends, such as joining in and giving compliments; peer-related social skills valued by classmates, such as sharing and working cooperatively; teacher-pleasing social skills related to academic success, such as listening and following directions; self-related behaviors, such as following through and dealing with stress; communication skills such as attending to the speaker and conversational turn taking; and assertiveness skills (Elksnin & Elksnin, 1998). Learners demonstrate two types of social skills problems: acquisition problems and performance problems.

Acquisition Problems

An acquisition problem occurs when a learner lacks specific social skills. Each social skill must be taught directly. Teachers can prepare to teach a social skill by providing the learner with a definition of the skill, the steps required to perform the skill, a rationale for learning the skill, situations in which to use the skill, role play situations in which to practice the skill, and social rules that govern skill use (see Elksnin & Elksnin, 1995).

Social skills are taught during role playing. The teacher first performs each skill step while talking out loud to model cognitive decisions. The teacher then guides the learner through the skill while providing specific, informative feedback to improve performance. Finally, the teacher provides opportunities for the learner to independently practice the skill. Many social skills curricula are available. A well-developed social skills program provides a taxonomy of social skills, along with analyses of skills steps.

Performance Problems

Performance problems occur when the learner knows how to perform the skill yet fails to do so. Causes of performance problems include failure to determine when to use a skill or failure to receive adequate reinforcement for skill use. In the first case, coincidental teaching can be used to encourage students to practice skills. In the second case, classmates can be recruited to praise the learner for using the skill.

Coincidental teaching. Coincidental teaching involves teaching social skills as situations occur in the natural environment (Schulze, Rule, & Innocenti, 1989). Teachers can use coincidental teaching in their classrooms and teach parents to use it at home. The first step is to identify social skills to target during the day and situations that call for skill use. For example, the teacher may identify "sharing" as the target skill and cooperative groups and free play as situations likely to require sharing. After situations are identified, the teacher determines times during the day that are supportive of coincidental teaching. For example, while the teacher is actively monitoring cooperative learning groups may not be the best time to coincidentally teach social skills. Once appropriate situations and times are identified, the teacher looks for opportunities for learners to use the skill, prompts learners to use the skill, and praises learners following skill use. Teaching parents to coincidentally teach provides students with even more practice opportunities (Elksnin & Elksnin, 2000).

Peer reinforcement. Often learners who perform social skills fail to receive reinforcement from classmates. These learners may even be punished for past mistakes (Scott & Nelson, 1998). In these situations, teachers must recruit peer support. Two examples of peer-mediated interventions illustrate the power of the peer group to enhance social skills performance. The first example is positive peer reporting, which involves reinforcing peers with tokens when they publicly praise appropriate social behavior. Jones, Young, and Friman (2000) taught peers to give positive feedback to socially rejected, delinquent adolescents by looking at the learner, smiling, stating a positive thing the learner did or said, and verbally praising the learner. Steps were posted on class bulletin boards as reminders. Peer acceptance of rejected learners improved and the number of positive statements made by their peers increased. In a second study, elementary-aged learners were taught how to recognize socially appropriate behavior (Skinner, Cashwell, & Skinner, 2000). They then were asked to "tootle," or tell the teacher when peers behaved in a socially appropriate manner, rather than "tattle," or tell the teacher when peers did or said something inappropriate. Socially appropriate behavior of students in this fourth-grade classroom increased substantially.

Problem Solving

In addition to possessing adequate social skills, emotionally intelligent learners are effective social problem solvers (Salvin & Madden, 2001). Problem solving can and should be taught, and it is important for teachers to model problem solving by "thinking out loud." Learners can be taught to problem solve using this sequence (D'Zurilla & Goldfried, 1971):

1. Define the problem.
2. Generate possible solutions.
3. Select a solution.
4. Predict outcomes if solution is implemented.
5. Select an alternative solution if predicted outcome is not positive.
6. Evaluate outcome after solution is implemented.
7. Decide what to do in a similar situation.

The FIG TESPN Routine and Social Skill Autopsies are two approaches that incorporate these steps that are especially useful in the classroom.

FIG TESPN Routine. Elias, Tobias, and Friedlander (1999) developed the FIG TESPN Routine as a process parents and children can use to solve social problems. Teachers also can use this routine. The eight steps of FIG TESPN include

1. Feelings cue me to thoughtful action.
2. I have a problem.
3. Goal gives me a guide.
4. Think of things I can do.
5. Envision outcomes.
6. Select my best solution.
7. Plan the procedure, anticipate pitfalls, practice, and pursue it.
8. Notice what happened, and now what?

During Step One, learners are taught that bad feelings signal a problem that needs to be solved. Learners are taught that problems cannot be solved effectively without labeling the emotion or the bad feeling. The teacher can use many of the strategies discussed earlier to increase emotional understanding. Step Two emphasizes that the learner "owns" the problem. He may not have caused the problem, but it is his responsibility to solve it. During this step, learners also learn that actions, not feelings, solve problems. Step Three focuses on goal setting to direct actions and reduce stress. Learners generate possible solutions during Step Four. Learners are taught that every action has consequences during Step Five. Based on predicted outcomes learners select a solution to the problem during Step Six. The original problem is revisited at this point. Step Seven emphasizes that problems are likely to occur when implementing any plan. By anticipating problems before implementing a plan, learners are less likely to become discouraged. During the final step of FIG TESPN, learners self-evaluate and are taught that not all plans will be successful. Several curricula that focus on interpersonal problem solving also are available.

Social Skill Autopsies. Lavoie (1994) recommends using social skill autopsies after the learner experiences a negative (or positive) social outcome. Autopsies involve analyzing the events surrounding a social outcome by asking the learner what she did, what happened when she did it, and what she will do in a similar situation based upon the positive or negative direction of the outcome. Autopsies should only be conducted privately and only after the learner has dealt with her emotions. For this reason, they can be used as part of the emotion coaching process. The obvious advantage of social skill autopsies is that they can be used any time and any place. If school personnel and parents "autopsy" social behavior, learners will become more skillful interpersonal problem solvers.

Conclusion

Emotional intelligence may be as important as, or even more important than, cognitive intelligence. Many learners, particularly those at risk for school failure, do not possess the social-emotional skills needed to be emotionally intelligent. However, these skills can and should be taught. In this article we reviewed ways in which teachers can improve learners' emotional understanding, social skills, and interpersonal problem-solving ability. Social-emotional learning enables learners to effectively "understand, process, manage, and express the social and emotional aspects of [their] lives" (Cohen, 2001).

References

Bar-On, R. (1997). BarOn Emotional Quotient Inventory, user's manual. Toronto, ON: MultiHealth Systems, Inc.

Bodine, R. J., & Crawford, D. K. (1999). Developing emotional intelligence. Champaign, IL: Research Press.

Camp, B. W., & Bash, M. A. S. (1985a). Think aloud, grades 1-2. Champaign, IL: Research Press.

Camp, B. W., & Bash, M. A. S. (1985b). Think aloud, grades 3-4. Champaign, IL: Research Press.

Camp, B. W., & Bash, M. A. S. (1985c). Think aloud, grades 5-6. Champaign, IL: Research Press.

Cartledge, G., & Kleefeld, J. (1991). Taking part. Circle Pines, MN: American Guidance Service.

Cartledge, G., & Kleefeld, J. (1994). Working together. Circle Pines, MN: American Guidance Service.

Cohen, J. (Ed.). (2001). Caring classrooms/intelligent schools: The social emotional education of young children. NY: Teachers College Press.

Coombs-Richardson, R., Evans, E. T., & Meisgeier, C. H. (1996a). Connecting with others, K-2. Champaign, IL: Research Press.

Coombs-Richardson, R., Evans, E. T., & Meisgeier, C. H. (1996b). Connecting with others, 3-5. Champaign, IL: Research Press.

Coombs-Richardson, R., Evans, E. T., & Meisgeier, C. H. (1996c). Connecting with others, 6-8. Champaign, IL: Research Press.

Duke, M. P., Nowicki, S., Jr., & Martin, E. A. (1996). Teaching your child the language of social success. Atlanta, GA: Peachtree.

Dygdon, J. (1993). CLASSIC. Brandon, VT: Clinical Psychology Publishing Company.

D'Zurilla, T. J., & Goldfried, M. R. (1971). Problem solving and behavior modification. Journal of Abnormal Psychology, 78(1), 107-126.

Elias, M. J., Tobias, S. E., & Friedlander, B. S. (1999). Emotionally intelligent parenting. New York: Harmony Books.

Elksnin, L. K., & Elksnin, N. (1995). Assessment and instruction of social skills. San Diego: Singular.

Elksnin, L. K., & Elksnin, N. (1998). Teaching social skills to students with learning and behavior problems. Intervention in School and Clinic, 33, 131-140.

Elksnin, L. K., & Elksnin, N. (2000). Teaching parents to teach their children to be prosocial. Intervention in School and Clinic, 36, 27-35.

Goldstein, A. P. (1997). The PREPARE curriculum. Champaign, IL: Research Press.

Goldstein, A. P., & McGinnis, E. (1997). Skill-streaming the adolescent. Champaign, IL: Research Press.

Goleman, D. L. (1995). Emotional intelligence: Why it can matter more than IQ. New York: Bantam Books.

Gottman, J. (1997). Raising an emotionally intelligent child. New York: Simon & Schuster.

Gumpel, T., & Wilson, M. (1996). Application of a Rasch analysis to the examination of the perception of facial affect among persons with mental retardation. Research in Developmental Disabilities, 17(2), 161-171.

Hall, E. (1966). The hidden dimension. New York: Doubleday.

Hazel, J. S., Schumaker, J. B., Sherman, J. A., & Sheldon, J. (1996). ASSET. Champaign, IL: Research Press.

Jones, K. M., Young, M. M., & Friman, P. C. (2000). Increasing peer praise of socially rejected delinquent youth: Effects on cooperation and acceptance. School Psychology Review, 15, 30-39.

Lavoie, R. (Producer). (1994). Learning disabilities and social skills with Richard Lavoie: Last one picked ... first one picked on. Washington, DC: WETA.

Kavale, K. A., & Forness, S. R. (1996). Social skills deficits and learning disabilities: A meta-analysis. Journal of Learning Disabilities, 29, 226-237.

Mannix, D. (1993). Social skills activities for special children. West Nyack, NY: Center for Applied Research in Education.

Mayer, J. D., & Salovey, P. (1997). What is emotional intelligence? In P. Salovey & D. J. Sluyter (Eds.), Emotional development and emotional intelligence: Educational implications (pp. 3-31). New York: Basic Books.

McGinnis, E., & Goldstein, A. R. (1997). Skill-streaming the elementary school child. Champaign, IL: Research Press.

McGinnis, E., & Goldstein, A. P. (2003). Skill-streaming in early childhood. Champaign, IL: Research Press.

Mehrabian, A. (1968). Communication without words. Psychology Today, 24, 52-55.

Most, T., & Greenbank, A. (2000). Auditory, visual, and auditory-visual perception of emotions by adolescents with and without learning disabilities, and their relationship to social skills. Learning Disabilities Research & Practice, 15, 171-178.

Mugno, D., & Rosenblitt, D. (2001). Helping emotionally vulnerable children: Moving toward an empathic orientation in the classroom. In J. Cohen (Ed.), Caring classrooms/intelligent schools: The social emotional education of young children (pp. 59-76). NY: Teachers College Press.

Nabuzoka, D., & Smith, K. (1995). Identification of expressions of emotions by children with and without learning disabilities. Learning Disabilities Research & & Practice, 10, 91-101.

Nowicki, S., Jr., & Duke, M. P. (1992). helping the child who doesn't fit in. Atlanta, GA: Peachtree.

Ratnesar, R. (1997, September). Teaching feelings 101. Time, XXX, 62.

Salovey, P., & Mayer, J. D. (1990). Emotional intelligence. Imagination, Cognition, & Personality, 9, 185-211.

Salovey, P., & Sluyter, D. J. (Eds.). (1997). Emotional development and emotional intelligence: Educational implications. New York: Basic Books.

Schulze, K. A., Rule, S., & Innocenti, M. S. (1989). Coincidental teaching: Parents promoting social skills at home. Teaching Exceptional Children, 21, 24-27.

Scott, T. M., & Nelson, C. M. (1998). Confusion and failure in facilitating generalized social responding in the school setting: Sometimes 2 + 2 = 5. Behavioral Disorders, 23(4), 264-275.

Skinner, C. H., Cashwell, T. H., & Skinner, A. L. (2000). Increasing tottling: Effects of a peer-monitored group contingency program on students' reports of peers' prosocial behaviors. Psychology in the Schools, 37, 263-270.

Slavin, R. E., & Madden, N. A.(2001). One million children: Success for all. Thousand Oaks, CA: Corwin.

Shure, M. B. (2001a). I can problem solve, elementary. Champaign, IL: Research Press.

Shure, M. B. (2001b). I can problem solve, kindergarten. Champaign, IL: Research Press.

Shure, M. B. (2001c). I can problem solve, preschool. Champaign, IL: Research Press.

Stephens, T. M. (1992). Social skills in the classroom (2nd ed.). Odessa, FL: Psychological Assessment Resources.

U.S. Department of Education (1996). Eighteenth annual report to Congress on the implementation of The Individuals with Disabilities Education Act. Washington, DC: Author.

U.S. Department of Education (2001). Twenty-third annual report to Congress on the Implementation of the Individuals with Disabilities Education Act. Washington, DC: Author.

Waksman, S., & Waksman, D. D. (1998). Waksman social skills curriculum. Austin, TX: PRO-ED.

From *Education*, Vol. 124, No. 1, Fall 2003. © 2003 by Project Innovation, Inc. Reprinted with permission.

A MOTHER'S STORY

Paul Rudnick

…Parents would certainly deny it, but Canadian researchers have made a startling assertion: parents take better care of pretty children than they do ugly ones.

—*The Times.*

Until I saw the article in the *Times*, I'd felt so utterly alone. Was I the only one? The sole parent on earth who knew the anguish, the heart-shattering despair of—All right, I'll just say it, right out loud. I am the mother of an ugly child. She's not deformed or handicapped or odd; she's unattractive.

Even during my pregnancy, I'd had my suspicions. I remember peering at the ultrasound screen as my obstetrician told me, "Look, it's a brand-new life," and all I could say was "Fine, but why are we watching the Discovery Channel?" And then, after I gave birth, a nurse placed something on my chest and cooed, "Here's your little miracle," and I glanced down, bewildered, and asked, "Who ordered the veal scaloppine?"

For the next few years, when guests would drop by, I'd pretend that Lisa, as we'd named her, was a Duraflame log. As she grew older, I referred to her as our new cocker spaniel, although no one really believed this, because, of course, cocker spaniels are adorable. I did, however, begin to read to Lisa, and the titles included "The Four Little Pigs" and "The Little Engine That Settled."

When Lisa turned five, I was faced with an agonizing decision: where could we send her to school? Shockingly, there are no facilities in this country specifically designed for the education of ugly children, except for a few fringe programs dedicated to computers. So we were eventually forced to send her to school in England, where she was extremely popular. But I remained torn—she was an American child, and sooner or later, at least on vacations, she'd have to return home. The solution became obvious: a large box. I'd have the headmistress simply FedEx Lisa to our address, although whenever the package arrived there'd always be that terrible moment when my heart leaped, because I'd think, Someone's sent me a gift! Perhaps it's a fully outfitted wicker picnic basket, or a case of champagne! But then I'd hear that sound—the breathing.

I tried to be a generous, loving parent; whenever Lisa clawed at her paper bag I'd murmur, "Oh, but sweetheart, it's from Hermes." Still, there were those mornings when she'd want to leave the house in just jeans and a T-shirt, so I'd improvise. I'd say, "When we're in the park, let's play a wonderful game. Let's pretend that I'm a beautiful princess and you're a bench." And if strangers stared at us and asked, "Why are you sitting on that poor child and enjoying your lunch?," I'd defend Lisa, proudly declaring, "She's not poor!"

Our favorite holiday was, naturally, Halloween. I'd get all gussied up as a lovely ballerina, and Lisa would be my pancreas. We also liked to take long autumn drives through the countryside, to see the leaves change; whenever I'd spot a particularly vibrant red maple or a blaze of yellow, I'd cry, "Look!," and pause to listen for her delighted knock from the trunk. Malls and other public spaces could still be a challenge, but this was handily solved when I learned to play the concertina and bought Lisa a little felt hat and lederhosen. Still, perhaps it was Lisa's older sister, Renee, who suffered the most. Renee was stunningly gorgeous, and she always felt the most profound tenderness for the sibling she called her little brother. As a lesson in compassion, I'd say, "Who does Mummy love the most?," and Renee and Lisa would giddily shriek, "Me! Me!" And then I'd ask, "And who does Mummy pity?"

Despite all of this joy, this infinite maternal concern, I always knew that a dreaded era loomed: puberty. How could I make Lisa understand that, although she was a brilliant, vivacious young lady and the balm of my soul, dating would be impossible, even underwater? But then I hit upon a remedy. For Lisa's first formal dance, I arranged for her to be escorted by Bobo, an adolescent male grizzly bear. "It's just like Noah's ark!" I trilled, as I snapped their photo; Lisa was a bit apprehensive at first, until I pointed out that the arrangement was for only one night, and that they would both be muzzled. I'm pleased to report that the evening was a huge success, thanks to a few open garbage cans, a dab of lard behind Lisa's ear, and the fact that no one will ever know that I slipped Bobo five hundred dollars and got him drunk.

Blessedly, today Lisa is well over thirty and happily married to Jorge, our houseboy, who now has his green card, a Chelsea duplex, and one of Lisa's kidneys. And just the other day Lisa said to me, "Mom, it's really inner beauty that counts, isn't it? Isn't that what life's all about?" I took her face in my hands and I replied, "Yes, of course it is, my darling." And I smiled, because, thankfully, it's true—ugly kids will believe anything.

The Consequences of Insufficient Sleep for Adolescents

Links Between Sleep and Emotional Regulation

Any review of adolescent lifestyles in our society will reveal more than a dozen forces converging to push the sleep/arousal balance away from sleep and toward ever-higher arousal. What harm could there be in trying to push back a little toward valuing sleep? The potential benefits, according to Dr. Dahl, seem enormous.

BY RONALD E. DAHL

ADOLESCENTS often "get by" with relatively little sleep, but it may be far less than they need. The observations of many parents, educators, and clinicians are in close agreement with a wealth of scientific data about the growing frequency of this worrisome pattern of behavior. As discussed in other articles in this special section, there has been recent progress in understanding many of the factors that contribute to adolescent sleep loss, including the role of early school starting times and the role of various biological and social influences on adolescents' self-selected bedtimes.

The increasing evidence that teenagers seem to be getting less sleep leads inevitably to the pragmatic question "How much sleep do adolescents really need?" Unfortunately, the medical/scientific answer to this question seems tautological. Sufficient sleep is defined as "the amount necessary to permit optimal daytime functioning."

As impractical as that answer may appear, there are two important reasons for such a definition. First, sleep requirements can be remarkably different across individuals. Second, at a physiological level, sleep and waking states are closely intertwined aspects of a larger system of arousal regulation. (Sleep researchers often use the Chinese symbol of yin/yang to designate the interrelationship of sleep/wake states.)

At the center of this discussion is a critical and pragmatic point: any evaluation of the sleep habits of adolescents must include a careful consideration of the *waking consequences* of sleep loss. The question becomes, in essence, "What are the daytime signs of diminished functioning that indicate insufficient sleep?" While there is a shortage of well-controlled re-

search studies that seek to answer this question, this article focuses on the convergence of evidence suggesting that *changes in mood and motivation are among the most important effects of sleep loss*. Thus an important place to begin looking for evidence of insufficient sleep among adolescents is in the area of emotional or behavioral difficulties.

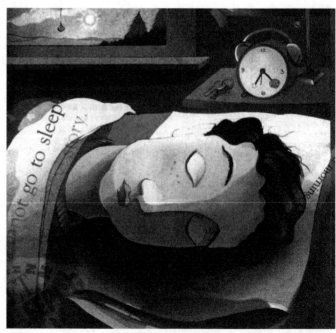

Illustration by Brenda Grannan

There is no shortage of epidemiological and clinical studies documenting recent increases in the rates of many psychiatric disorders among adolescents. Certainly many complex factors are likely to have contributed to the emotional and behavioral problems of teenagers, but the possible link to adolescent sleep patterns bears some scrutiny. There is clear evidence that sleep loss *can* lead to the development or exacerbation of behavioral and emotional problems.[1] The key question is "How great is the contribution of sleep deprivation to these problems?" The magnitude of this link remains an open question that can only be answered through careful empirical research.

In the meantime, these issues have enormous ramifications for the fields of medicine and education with regard both to the physical and mental health of adolescents and to detriments to effective learning and social development. Many policy decisions will be influenced by our understanding and interpretation of the importance of sleep in these areas.

In this article I provide an overview of current scientific and clinical information regarding the consequences of insufficient sleep in adolescents. I pay particular attention to links between sleep and emotional regulation. The following is a brief outline of the main points to be presented:

1. *Sleepiness.* This is the most direct consequence of adolescent sleep loss, and it manifests itself most significantly in difficulty getting up on time for school and in falling asleep in school. These problems can further contribute to conflicts with parents and teachers and to poor self-esteem. Sleepiness is also associated with a strong tendency toward brief mental lapses (or microsleeps) that greatly increase the risk of motor vehicle and other kinds of accidents.

2. *Tiredness.* This is a symptom of sleep loss and includes changes in motivation—particularly difficulty initiating behaviors related to long-term or abstract goals and decreased persistence in working toward goals.

3. *Mood, attention, and behavior.* Sleep loss can have negative effects on the control of mood, attention, and behavior. Irritability, moodiness, and low tolerance for frustration are the most frequently described symptoms in sleep-deprived adolescents. However, in some situations, sleepy teenagers are more likely to appear silly, impulsive, or sad.

4. *Impact of emotional and behavioral problems.* Emotional arousal and distress can cause both difficulty falling asleep and sleep disruptions. Behavioral problems and family chaos can contribute to even later bedtimes and to sleep schedules that are ever more incompatible with school schedules.

5. *Bi-directional effects.* There are bi-directional effects between sleep and behavioral/emotional problems. It can be difficult at times to identify the causal links. For example, a depressed adolescent with severe sleep problems may be showing sleep disturbances that stem from depression or mood problems that stem from sleep disruption. Sleep loss can also contribute to a negative spiral or vicious cycle of deterioration. That is, sleep loss can have a negative effect on mood and behavior, which leads to subsequent emotional/behavioral difficulties that further interfere with sleep. This produces a sequence of negative effects in both domains. In some clinical cases, such negative spirals appear to be a pathway to withdrawal from school or serious psychiatric problems.

The Need for Sleep: An Overview

Before discussing the specific consequences of insufficient sleep in adolescents, it is necessary to begin with a general overview on what sleep is and why it is necessary at all.

Sleep is *not* simply rest. Mere rest does not create the restorative state of having slept. (Anyone who doubts this should try the following experiment tonight: spend eight hours resting in bed, with eyes closed, body relaxed, mind floating, in a deeply tranquil state, but without ever going to sleep; then keep track of your mood and performance tomorrow.) The fundamental difference between sleep and a deeply relaxed wakefulness is that sleep involves dropping into a state with a relative *loss of awareness of and responsiveness to the external world.* This state of unresponsiveness appears to be necessary for the restorative processes that occur during sleep to take place.

Furthermore, sleep itself is an *active* process. Sleep involves dynamically changing patterns and progressive stages, with some brain regions showing a great deal of activity in some sleep stages. Moreover, there are several aspects of sleep necessary for full restoration, including the continuity, timing, and patterning of different stages of sleep, as well as the timing of the sleep in relation to other biological rhythms.

For example, if subjects are permitted a full night's sleep but are awakened every 15 minutes for brief periods, on the following day they will report tiredness, fatigue, and emotional changes similar to having obtained insufficient amounts of sleep. Similarly, if subjects are permitted as much sleep as they need but are selectively deprived of one sleep stage—such as REM (rapid eye movement) sleep or delta sleep—they also report daytime consequences. And, as anyone who has experienced jet lag can attest, sleep that occurs at the wrong circadian phase is often fragmented and inefficient at restoration.

Sleep is not some biological luxury. Sleep is essential for basic survival, occurring in every species of living creature that has ever been studied. Animals deprived of sleep die. (Experiments with rats show that they can survive without sleep for about as long as they can survive without food.) Yet the specific function of sleep—*why* it is necessary for survival—remains a scientific mystery and the focus of a great deal of investigation.

Within this scientific mystery, however, are two important clues that are relevant to discussions of sleep and adolescent health. First, sleep seems to be particularly important during periods of brain maturation. (Across species, maturing individuals sleep more than fully mature individuals.) Second, sleep is naturally restricted to times and places that feel safe. Most species have evolved mechanisms to ensure that sleep is limited to such safe places as burrows and nests and to times of relative safety from predators. In humans, there is a similar tendency for safe feelings to promote sleep while feelings of threat or stress tend to inhibit sleep.

These links between sleep and stress are an important source of sleep disruption among adolescents. A key point can be best illustrated by a brief consideration of the evolutionary underpinnings of these biological links between sleep and emotion. For most of early human history, large nocturnal-hunting carnivores surrounded our ancestors, who had no access to physically safe sleep sites. (Humans cannot sleep in trees or on cliff edges, because we lose all muscle tone during REM sleep.) In the human ancestral environment, the main protection against predators was a close-knit social group. The human brain evolved under conditions that made this sense of social belonging and social connectedness the basis for feelings of relative safety. Natural tendencies in the human brain continue to reflect these links, so that fears of social rejection can evoke powerful feelings of threat and so lead to sleep disruption, while feelings of love, caring, and social connection create a feeling of safety and so promote sleep.

Finally, it is important to consider the ways in which the sleep and vigilance systems change during adolescent development. The maturation of humans during puberty includes physical and mental changes in preparation for taking on adult roles (with increased demands for threat appraisal and response). Changes in the vigilance system include a greater capacity for sleep disruptions from social stresses, including fears, anxieties, and emotional arousal.[2] Thus adolescent sleep systems appear to become more vulnerable to stress at a time when social turmoil and difficulties are often increasing.

Consequences of Insufficient Sleep in Adolescents

There is a surprising lack of controlled studies examining the effects of sleep deprivation or insufficient sleep among adolescents. However, there is extensive circumstantial evidence, clinical evidence, and research in adults that is relevant to these questions. While there is a general convergence of these findings, one important caveat is that we need a greater number of direct investigations. A second note of caution is that we lack information about *long-term* or *chronic* effects of insufficient sleep, since the limited data available have addressed only the immediate and short-term effects of sleep loss.

In brief, there are four main effects of acute sleep loss: 1) sleepiness, 2) motivational aspects of tiredness, 3) emotional changes, and 4) alterations in attention and performance. Before discussing each of these briefly, I wish to stress one general principle that applies across categories: the influence of *effort*. That is, the effects of sleep deprivation can be offset or even overridden for *short* periods of time by increased effort (or by increasing the external motivation to perform through rewards or punishments). The good news here is that most capabilities can be maintained over a short interval if necessary, while the bad news is that everything is harder to do. In some ways this is the cardinal feature of sleep deprivation: it takes increased effort to perform the same cognitive, emotional, or physical tasks.

1. *Sleepiness.* The most obvious and direct effect of inadequate sleep is a feeling of sleepiness. Sleepiness is most problematic during periods of low stimulation, such as in the classroom, when reading or driving, or when doing repetitive

activities. Highly stimulating activities—particularly those involving physical activity or emotional arousal—can often mask moderate levels of sleepiness. Thus many sleep- deprived adolescents report that they can stay out very late at night and not feel tired, whereas if they were to lie quietly reading a book, they would fall asleep in minutes.

Another important aspect of sleepiness is the tendency toward brief mental lapses or micro-sleeps. Often, an individual is not even aware of these short gaps in awareness and responsiveness. However, such a lapse in the midst of driving, operating machinery, or doing anything else that requires vigilance can have dire consequences.

Several indirect consequences of sleepiness are also worth mentioning. These include adolescent conflicts with parents and teachers that arise from the difficulty of getting up in the morning or the ease of falling asleep in class; increased use of stimulants (particularly caffeine and nicotine); and synergistic effects with alcohol (the impairments from a combination of alcohol and sleepiness appear to be more than additive, resulting in a deadly combination of influences).

2. *Tiredness.* A separate symptom of sleep loss that can be defined as a feeling of fatigue or decreased motivation is tiredness. Tiredness makes it difficult to initiate (and persist at) certain types of behavior (especially tasks deemed boring or tedious). The effects of tiredness are less apparent when performing tasks that are naturally engaging, exciting, or threatening—perhaps because it is easier to recruit extra effort to offset tiredness. Conversely, the effects of tiredness are more pronounced for tasks that require motivation to be derived from abstract goals or consequences (e.g., reading or studying uninteresting material in order to increase the chances of attaining some future reward).

Tedious tasks without the imminent prospect of reward (or fear of immediate consequences) are much more difficult to initiate and complete when one has been deprived of sleep. Similarly, tasks that require planning, strategy, or a complex sequence of steps to complete are more difficult when one is tired. This general category of tasks (requiring motivation linked to abstract goals, delayed rewards/consequences, planning, strategy, and so on) involves abstract processing areas in the front of the brain (regions of the prefrontal cortex) that appear to be particularly sensitive to sleep deprivation.[3] The potential relevance of these types of motivational changes to educational goals and processes seems obvious.

3. *Emotional changes.* The emotional changes that are secondary effects of sleep loss are very important but very complex. There are at least three factors that make this a complicated area for investigators: 1) the emotional effects of sleep deprivation appear to be highly variable across individuals and across situations, 2) emotion and emotional regulation are very hard to measure accurately, and 3) there are bi-directional interactions between mood and sleep disturbances (this third aspect was noted above and will be addressed separately below).

One of the main sources of information in this area comes from clinical descriptions of children and adolescents with various sorts of sleep disorders or transient sleep disruptions. There are also a few studies (including ongoing research in our laboratory) that obtain measures of emotion before, during, and after a single night of sleep deprivation, and then again following a recovery sleep.

The major theme across these studies is evidence suggesting *mood lability*. Not only does there appear to be greater variability in emotional states following sleep loss, but there also appears to be less control over emotional responses in many adolescents. For example, if faced with a frustrating task, a sleep-deprived teenager is more likely to become angry or aggressive. Yet, in response to something humorous, the same subject might act more silly or inane. Several adolescents reported increased crying reactions during sad scenes in videotaped movies when they were sleep-deprived. Many subjects reported increased irritability, impatience, and low tolerance for frustration when asked to perform tedious computer tasks. In general, these findings often looked like a decrease in inhibition or conscious control over emotions following sleep loss. It is also important to point out that some subjects seemed to show no measurable changes in any emotion when sleep-deprived.

These results are quite preliminary, include a high degree of variability across individuals, and will require replication with larger samples to establish statistical significance. However, these findings fit very well within a general pattern of similar observations regarding *effortful control*. That is, the primary emotional changes following sleep loss suggest a decrease in the ability to control, inhibit, or modify emotional responses to bring them into line with long-term goals, social rules, or other learned principles. Effortful control over emotion involves regions of the prefrontal cortex of the brain that are similar to those discussed previously with regard to abstract goals.

Changes in emotional regulation that result in decreased control following sleep loss could have serious consequences in terms of many high-risk behaviors among adolescents. The inability to control emotional responses could influence aggression, sexual behavior, the use of alcohol and drugs, and risky driving. Clearly, additional research will be needed to better delineate these complex but important issues relevant to adolescent health.

4. *Changes in attention and performance.* Following sleep loss, changes in attention and performance also represent a complex area of investigation in children and adolescents. There are three main points. First, sleep loss is associated with brief mental lapses in attention during simple tasks that can be partially offset by increased effort or motivation. Second, sleep deprivation can sometimes mimic or exacerbate symptoms of ADHD (attention deficit/hyperactivity disorder), including distractibility, impulsivity, and difficulty with effortful control of attention. Third, there is also emerging evidence that sleep deprivation has marked influences on the ability to perform complex tasks or tasks that require attention in two or more areas at the same time.

While the first point about brief mental lapses has already been addressed, the latter two points warrant some discussion. A potential link between ADHD symptoms and sleep deprivation has received considerable discussion from several investigators.[4] Both ADHD and sleep deprivation are associated with

difficulty with self-control of behavior, attention, and impulses. Both ADHD and the daytime symptoms of sleep deprivation will often respond to stimulant medication. Furthermore, ADHD symptoms are more frequent in children with sleep disorders, and there has been some reported improvement in ADHD symptoms in children following treatment of sleep problems. Finally, other studies have reported increased rates of sleep complaints and disorders in children diagnosed with ADHD. This is a very complex area, and disentangling the connections and relative contributions across these domains will require additional careful studies.

One pragmatic recommendation, however, is quite simple. For any child or adolescent who exhibits symptoms of ADHD, the importance of a good night's sleep and a regular sleep/wake schedule should be emphasized to avoid the consequences of sleep loss that could exacerbate symptoms.

One of the most interesting areas of study is evidence that some types of complex tasks may be particularly sensitive to the effects of sleep deprivation. James Horne has presented extensive evidence showing that dual tasks and tasks that require creative or flexible thinking are sensitive to sleep loss.[5] (These tasks all require abstract processing in areas of the prefrontal cortex.) Our own research group has generated similar findings in its examination of dual tasks following sleep deprivation in adolescents and young adults. For example, students with one night of sleep deprivation exhibited no significant changes in performance on a difficult computer task and showed no effect on postural balance. However, when the students performed both tasks simultaneously, sleep deprivation had a marked effect on balance.[6] In recent pilot studies we have also found the same pattern of results in adolescents performing cognitive and emotional tasks. Performance at either task could be maintained following sleep deprivation—but not both.

On one hand, detriments in performing a dual task (like controlling thoughts and feelings at the same time) might sound like an esoteric or subtle effect of sleep deprivation; on the other hand, it is important to point out that fluency in such dual tasks is the foundation of social competence. These are the daily challenges that must be balanced in the everyday life of adolescents: thinking and solving problems while navigating the emotional reactions of complex social situations, using self-control over impulses and emotions while pursuing goals, experiencing anger yet weighing the long-term consequences of actions. If further research substantiates the marked effects of insufficient sleep on these types of complex tasks in adolescents, then we should have significant concerns about the importance of sleep patterns in the normal development of social competence.

Sleep and Emotional Disorders in Adolescents

It is essential to underscore the complex intersection between sleep regulation and behavioral and emotional problems in adolescents. Clearly, there are two-way interactions between these systems. The regulation and timing of sleep can be altered by behavioral or emotional disorders, while cognitive, behavioral, and emotional control during daytime hours can be influenced by the way adolescents sleep. Furthermore, daytime activities, changes in the environment, and stressful events can have profound transient effects on sleeping patterns in the absence of any clear-cut psychopathology. In addition, medications used to treat psychiatric disorders often affect sleep, and sleep loss can exacerbate mood and behavioral symptoms.

Perhaps the best-studied example of such interactions is the relationship between sleep and depression. Subjective sleep complaints are very common in children and adolescents who have been diagnosed with Major Depressive Disorder (MDD). Symptoms include insomnia (75% of cases) and hypersomnia (25%). Hypersomnia difficulties are reported more frequently after puberty. Insomnia symptoms usually include difficulty falling asleep and a subjective sense of not having slept deeply all night.

Recently, clinicians and researchers have seen increasing numbers of adolescents with overlapping phase delay disorders or other sleep/wake schedule disorders associated with depression. Depressed adolescents frequently have difficulty falling asleep, are unable to get up or refuse to go to school, sleep until late in the day, complain of extreme daytime fatigue, and, over time, shift to increasingly more delayed sleep/wake schedules. Likewise, surveys reveal that adolescents who get less than 6¾ hours of sleep each school night or report more than a two-hour difference between school night and weekend bedtimes have a higher level of complaints of depressed mood than adolescents who get more sleep or who sleep on more regular sleep/wake schedules.

Clinicians who are experienced with these problems have pointed out that in many cases it is difficult to differentiate decreased motivation, school refusal/anxiety, delayed circadian phase, attention difficulties, and depressive symptomatology. Clearly, both sleep patterns and behavioral symptoms must be carefully assessed in an effort to prevent the problems, diagnose them accurately, and plan successful treatment.

There is also evidence of changes in the sleeping electroencephalograms (EEGs) of depressed adolescents, including increased time to fall asleep and altered patterns of REM sleep. Furthermore, changes in EEG measures of sleep predicted an increased recurrence of depressive episodes during longitudinal follow-ups in early adulthood.[7]

In some cases, treatment of sleep complaints and problems—including regularizing the sleep/wake schedule, cognitive behavioral therapy for insomnia, and short-term treatment with medication for severe insomnia—can have a positive impact on depressive symptoms.[8] On the other hand, effective treatment of depression can also be a critical aspect of improving sleep.

Negative Spirals?

As I described above, one area of concern with regard to the interconnections between sleep and emotional disturbances is

the potential for a progressive sequence or spiral of negative effects. Insufficient sleep can amplify emotional difficulties, which can then produce further sources of distress and increased disruption of sleep. The reason for this concern arises more from clinical experience than from any controlled studies, and so the concern is perhaps best illustrated by describing a case.

Jay had a history of poor sleep habits (e.g., bedtimes past midnight, erratic sleep/wake schedule) beginning in about seventh grade. In ninth grade the problems became worse as he struggled to get to sleep at night (usually falling asleep at 1 a.m.) and to wake up in the morning and then had problems with distractibility and behavior at school. He also reported some symptoms of depression, including loss of interest in some activities, daytime fatigue, and worsening performance at school. His symptoms improved transiently in the summer, when he slept from 3 a.m. until noon.

In 10th grade Jay began attending a high school that started at 7:30 a.m., which required him to wake up at 6 a.m. to meet the school bus at 6:30 a.m. He had a very difficult time getting up for school at that hour because his average bedtime was 2 a.m. He made several attempts to go to bed earlier but found himself unable to fall asleep. He was never able to follow through in a way that would permit him to establish an earlier pattern of bedtime, and he quickly reverted to his 3 a.m.-to-noon sleep schedule on all weekends and holidays. Jay sometimes stayed up working at his computer or watching television—he says this was because he hated the feeling of lying in bed trying unsuccessfully to fall asleep. Before long, he was regularly missing school or arriving late and falling asleep in class.

Jay, who had at one time been identified as a gifted student, was failing most of his classes and appeared increasingly lethargic, subdued, and uninterested in school. His school counselor referred him to a mental health clinic. Over the course of several months, he was diagnosed as having depression with some ADHD symptoms (e.g., difficulty finishing tasks, distractibility). Trials of antidepressants and stimulant medication resulted in small transient improvements in some symptoms, but Jay was never able to reestablish good sleep patterns that were compatible with his school schedule. Eventually he withdrew from school, became increasingly depressed and withdrawn, and was hospitalized after a serious suicide attempt.

At the time of hospitalization, Jay had severe chronic insomnia and a major depressive disorder. Despite multiple interventions, these problems persisted. He showed very little motivation to return to school and appeared to have chronic depressive symptoms. At discharge his long-term prognosis was not promising.

In a case such as Jay's, it is impossible to disentangle the relative contributions of the sleep and mood dysregulations. While no general conclusions can be drawn from this single case, it does illustrate the complexity of these interactions and the importance of obtaining a better understanding in these areas.

Policy Decisions for Today and Direction for the Future

Frequently in this article I have cautioned readers about the need for additional research to improve our understanding of the complex issues arising from the consequences of insufficient sleep among adolescents. Our current knowledge is preliminary and based on a paucity of controlled data. Furthermore, we are probably at an equally early stage in our understanding of the behavioral and emotional problems of adolescents.

Nonetheless, behavioral and emotional difficulties are currently the largest source of morbidity and mortality among adolescents. While it is possible that sleep loss makes only a minuscule contribution to adolescents' problems with emotional regulation, it is extremely likely that it plays some role. It is also quite possible that insufficient sleep plays a significant role in leading up to some of these problems in a vulnerable set of individuals.

Identifying vulnerability to sleep loss may represent an important future direction for research, since there appear to be such large individual differences in the effects of acute sleep loss. Such vulnerability could be related to a tendency to need more sleep, to being a "night owl," or to a biological vulnerability toward emotional disorders.

Clearly, more research is needed to help inform policy makers, whose decisions will further affect adolescent sleep patterns. Cost-benefit analyses regarding the relative importance of sleep will require more precise quantification in these areas. In the meantime, one might make a reasonable case that the odds are heavily in favor of sleep as an increasingly important health concern among adolescents.

To reiterate the main point with which I began, adequate sleep is defined as the amount necessary for optimal daytime functioning. It appears that the potentially fragile underpinnings of adolescent social competence (controlling thoughts and feelings at the same time) may be most sensitive to the effects of inadequate sleep. Any review of adolescent lifestyles in our society will reveal more than a dozen forces converging to push the sleep/arousal balance away from sleep and toward ever-higher arousal. What harm could there be in trying to push back a little toward valuing sleep? The potential benefits seem enormous.

Notes

1. Ronald E. Dahl, "The Regulation of Sleep and Arousal: Development and Psychopathology," *Development and Psychopathology*, vol. 8, 1996, pp. 3-27.
2. Ronald E. Dahl et al., "Sleep Onset Abnormalities in Depressed Adolescents," *Biological Psychiatry*, vol. 39, 1996, pp. 400-410.
3. James A. Horne, "Human Sleep, Sleep Loss, and Behaviour Implications for the Prefrontal Cortex and Psychiatric Disorder," *British Journal of Psychiatry*, vol. 162, 1993, pp. 413-19.
4. Ronald D. Chervin et al., "Symptoms of Sleep Disorders, Inattention, and Hyperactivity in Children," *Sleep*, vol. 20, 1997, pp. 1185-92.
5. Horne, op. cit.
6. Abigail Schlesinger, Mark S. Redfern, Ronald E. Dahl, and J. Richard Jennings, "Postural Control, Attention and Sleep Deprivation," *Neuroreport*, vol. 9, 1998, pp. 49-52.
7. Uma Rao et al., "The Relationship Between Longitudinal Clinical Course and Sleep and Cortisol Changes in Adolescent Depression," *Biological Psychiatry*, vol. 40, 1996, pp. 474-84.
8. Ronald E. Dahl, "Child and Adolescent Sleep Disorders," in idem, ed., *Child and Adolescent Psychiatric Clinics of North America: Sleep Disorder* (Philadelphia: W. B. Saunders, 1996).

RONALD E. DAHL, M.D., is an associate professor of psychiatry and pediatrics at the University of Pittsburgh Medical Center, Pittsburgh, Pa.

From *Phi Delta Kappan*, January 1999, pp. 354-359. © 1999 by Phi Delta Kappan International. Reprinted by permission of the publisher and author.

UNIT 5
Family Relationships

Unit Selections

Key Points to Consider

- Do support groups help parents of teens who are out of control?

- Why are today's youth so busy and distressed? What can families do about it?

- What effect may over-protective parents have on their teens?

- What are some preventative measures that may help decrease the impact of domestic violence?

- Does inter-parental violence have an effect on the emotional stability of teens?

- Who causes the extreme pressure and stress in teen sports?

Student Website

www.mhcls.com/online

Internet References

Further information regarding these websites may be found in this book's preface or online.

CYFERNET: Cooperative Extension System's Children, Youth, and Family Information Service
   http://www.cyfernet.org/

Help for Parents of Teenagers
   http://www.bygpub.com/parents/

Stepfamily Association of America
   http://www.stepfam.org

In order to understand the influence of a family on its members, the family needs to be viewed as a system. This means that parents do not simply shape their child; rather, each part of the family influences the other parts. For example, just as parents influence their children's behavior, children not only influence their parents' behavior, but their parents' relationship with each other. A child who complies with parental rules may put less stress on the parents than a child who is consistently in trouble. The compliant child's parents may argue less with each other over issues like discipline. Similarly, the parents' marital relationship influences how each parent interacts with the children. Parents whose marriage is stressed may have less patience with the children or may be less available to their children. This means that factors affecting one part of the system have implications for the rest of the system.

We can describe adolescents as changing in three major areas: biology, cognition, and social skills. As adolescents enter puberty, parents see their children become sexually mature individuals. How parents react to this may be influenced by a variety of factors, including the parents' view of their own development. Parents who see their own attractiveness or health or sexuality decline may react to their child's development very differently than do parents who have a more positive view of themselves.

Adolescents' cognitive development may also distress their relationship with their parents. As adolescents become more cognitively sophisticated, they frequently become more questioning of parental rules. Although the adolescent's demand for reasons underlying parental judgments may reflect newly developed cognitive skills—a positive development from an intellectual perspective—it may increase conflicts with parents. Parents who expect their rules to be obeyed without question may be more upset by their child's arguments than parents who expect to discuss rules and rule violation.

Concurrent with these physical and cognitive changes, adolescents also undergo social changes. These include increased demands for autonomy and independence. Parents whose children were docile and compliant prior to adolescence may feel their authority threatened by these changes. Parents may find it more difficult to discipline children than before. This may be especially problematic for families who had difficulty controlling their children earlier in childhood.

Although families may be viewed as a system, there is no one form that this system takes on. In the 1950s the ideal form of the family system was a breadwinner father, a homemaker mother, and "Leave it to Beaver" type children. Today families take many different forms. About 50 percent of American adolescents will live in single-parent families for some period. This rate is higher for African Americans. About 75 percent of women with school-age children are employed outside the home. About 21 percent of American children live in blended families, with stepsiblings and a stepparent. It is clear that there is no "typical" family. Does this mean that the family plays a less significant role in the life of the adolescent? The research indicates no. The family is still among the most important influences on an adolescent. How well adolescents resist peer pressure, how successful they are developing an identity, and what they strive for in the future all seem predominantly influenced by the family. The first article by Stephanie Dunnewind addresses the need for support groups that some parents of teens have. A network of support eases problems for parents and out-of-control teens. On the other hand there are many teens who strive to please parents, teachers, and peers. The second article explains that some teens go too far in pleasing everyone and become overloaded and overscheduled. There is still another group of parents who are overprotective of children and produce adolescents who become depressed as explained by Hara Estroff Marano.

Two articles deal with the topic of domestic violence and maritally violent homes. The emotional effect on adolescents can be devastating. The final article addresses the pressure some parents put on adolescent athletes.

Support Network Eases Problems for Parents of Out-of-Control Teens

BY STEPHANIE DUNNEWIND

Five of them were there when the businesswoman had to speak to the judge at her daughter's court sentencing for drug use. They were there when she called at 1 a.m. for help. And they were there, every two weeks, at a restaurant to support her in her struggles.

"This group saved my marriage, it saved me and it really saved my daughter," said the Seattle businesswoman, who asked not to be identified. "My daughter humbled me and brought me to my knees. Through this group, I was able to stand up again."

The Changes Parent Support Network in Seattle offers support groups for parents with out-of-control teenagers—kids who do drugs, cut school, run away, shoplift, steal or hit family members. Besides the weekly groups, members are encouraged to form smaller "teams" whose members provide more personalized counsel.

"Parents feel so hopeless," said Detective Jennifer Baldwin of the Redmond (Wash.) Police Department, who spoke to the group and serves on its board of directors. "They feel like there's nowhere to go."

Baldwin garnered lots of nods—and some tears—when she prefaced a speech to the group by quoting her pastor. "He said that when you have a baby, your heart leaves your body and becomes them, walking around out there."

These parents' hearts aren't just walking around. They're drugged out on crystal meth, arrested for choking their mother, threatening suicide, lying for money to buy drugs, hanging out with prostitutes, stealing checks.

It's easy for parents of young children, or those with grown children who made it through adolescence unscathed, to brush off these parents' pain by figuring the kids turned out that way because the parents messed up somehow.

Listen at a Changes support group for just a few minutes, however, and it's overwhelmingly obvious that while no parent will claim to be perfect, none are heartless. They're heartbroken.

"They helped me through the worst time in my life," said one mother.

The group acknowledges parents' anguish in wondering where a daughter is when she stays out all night. It acknowl-edges the difficulty of refusing to bail a son out of jail and the embarrassment of asking for a restraining order against one's own child.

But Changes doesn't focus on the past. Instead, it emphasizes learning how to live with the present and alter the future.

"They don't just sit and share stories back and forth," Baldwin said. "It's about developing new ideas of what to do when things go sideways."

The group's philosophy is this: "We can control only ourselves and our home," said Changes Executive Director Terri Suzuki. "We make small changes in our own behavior and the child responds to those changes. But we can't control our child."

The 20-year-old group incorporated as a nonprofit in 1996. The Seattle group and one in Redmond, which splintered off last spring, draw 30 or more people each week, while smaller groups operate in three other Washington locations—Des Moines, Kent and Bremerton.

Changes is the first place many parents feel safe to talk about how terrible home life is.

"At work, someone will talk about how their son was accepted to Harvard, and another will say, 'Mine's going to Yale,' " said Suzuki, who was awakened at 6 one morning by police after her then-teenage daughter stole a cab ride. "You can't just say, 'Mine's going to jail.' "

When parents attend their first meeting, they always think their story is the worst, said the Seattle businesswoman. "But you soon realize yours is nothing. This group gets you off the pity party."

Most parents have one or two children besides their "star" child, so named because that child's name carries an asterisk next to it on the parent's nametag at group meetings. That's the child who brought them—usually in desperation—to the group, but parents are quick to point out that they also have a son in law school, say, or a daughter who is a teacher.

Even after their children have moved out, many parents stay to counsel new members who are going through what they did.

"Parents can learn so much from other parents who are not professionals but who have been through the fire themselves," said Roland Tam Sing, a therapist with Family Reconciliation

Services, a Washington state program that helps troubled families. "For new parents, meeting veteran parents who have seen their kids through a crisis can help them realize there is a light at the end of the tunnel."

As part of the program, parents make a stand, or a long-term goal, and then set weekly steps to gradually achieve it.

At a recent meeting, parents went around the room sharing their goals (no "try" allowed): "I will not give in to my kid's demands." "I will not allow my children to take advantage of me." "I will not parent my adult children."

One mother said her week's aim was to find a way to connect with her son. After promising not to "ACE" (advise, criticize or explain to) her teenager, "it's just silence," she said. "It's kind of sad—if I'm not ACEing my kid, I'm not talking to him."

Another mom's stand—"I will let my child experience the consequences of his behavior"—translated into her weekly step of not nagging her son about his upcoming probation meeting. She would drive him there if he asked, but she wasn't going to set it up for him.

"We hold kids responsible for what they do, while society wants to hold parents responsible," said Suzuki.

In a crisis situation, most parents react and then consider better options, Suzuki said. Thus the group's motto: Think. Plan. Act.

Much of that planning happens not in the larger group meetings, but in five- to eight-member teams. Some teams stay in contact by e-mail, while others meet in person or talk by phone.

When one woman's son stole a car and drove to California, the police wanted her to come down and get him. She called her team members, who supported her decision to hold her son accountable for his actions.

For Suzuki, accountability meant setting a curfew for her daughter, who would stay out all night. If her daughter wasn't home when expected, Suzuki called the police to report her as a runaway.

While the teams offer support, they also hold members to their promises. "Your biggest work happens in your team," said Virginia Day, the group's representative.

Her team threatened to drop her if she and her husband didn't stop blaming each other for their son's problems. "That's what it took," Day said.

She asks team members to read letters before she sends them to her son, who is in a school for troubled teens in Mexico.

Members who attend court hearings help by taking notes to make sure the parent remembers all the key points. "The parent in that situation is so emotional it's easy to forget what goes on," Suzuki said.

When she met with her daughter's principal, eight members of her support team showed up. She would drive her daughter to school but her daughter sneaked out.

"I was doing everything I could to keep her in school, but I knew they wanted to blame me for it," she said.

She believes her team's presence helped demonstrate her commitment to the principal.

"There was a huge change in attitude," she said. "It was now, 'How do we work to solve this?'"

From *Seattle Times*, January 21, 2003. © 2003 by Knight Ridder/Tribune News Service. Reprinted with permission of Tribune Media Services Reprints.

Learning To Chill: Overloaded at school and overscheduled at home, stressed-out kids— with their parents' blessing—are saying 'Enough!'

Susan Schindehette

Last year, not long after entering Peterson Middle School as an accelerated sixth grader, Wendy Gregg hit the wall. "If you were late or your homework was incomplete, you got a gold note, and three gold notes was detention," says the formerly perfectionist 11-year-old from Sunnyvale, Calif. "I had seen detention in movies, but I didn't know what it was. I thought only weirdos got it, or people who smoked."

Wendy never actually did time herself, but despite three hours a night of homework, she soon saw her usual A's replaced by B minuses. "I felt pretty stupid," she says, recalling how mortified she was at being assigned to write about why she had fallen off the honor roll. She began to break out in cold sweats and often had stomachaches. In her class photo, says principal Bob Runyon, "Wendy was the only one not looking at the camera. She was staring off to the side."

In January, when Wendy's "scary feelings" were diagnosed as anxiety attacks, her parents—Jenny, 37, a homemaker, and Bill, 41, an aerospace engineer—did a major rethink. "My husband and I decided to pull her out of the pressure cooker," says Jenny. The Greggs took Wendy out of Peterson and homeschooled her for a semester. They reprioritized, making more time for her piano lessons, basketball and I Love Lucy videos. Says her mother: "We reclaimed a lot of her time."

Last month a buoyant Wendy returned to Peterson as a seventh grader in a standard curriculum. Whenever she starts to tense up, she pulls out the "stress kit" that she made in her local Girl Scout troop—a white paper bag painted with a lake and stocked with Silly Putty (for squeezing out tension), notes from friends, an origami bird and her favorite blue nail polish. "Last year I would have been scared," she says of returning to school. "This time I was so excited I couldn't stop smiling."

Wendy's story is hardly unique. From Portland to Peoria, experts say, plenty of kids are nearing meltdown from stress. The evidence is obvious: third graders hauling 25-lb. book bags to class; 12-year-olds juggling their soccer schedules on PalmPilots; a growing number of teens teaming up with $200-an-hour business consultants to teach them CEO-style time-management skills.

According to studies by such groups as the Centers for Disease Control and the American Institute of Stress, nearly half of kids report stress symptoms from headaches to short tempers; children as young as 9 are now experiencing anxiety attacks; and from 1980 to 1997 the number of 10-to-14-year-olds who committed suicide increased 109 percent. In an era when 40 percent of school districts have eliminated recess and 21 percent of teens rate a lack of time with their parents as a top concern, children risk becoming what a paper by the Harvard University admissions office recently termed "dazed survivors of some bewildering lifelong boot camp."

The source of the trouble is easy to track: anxiety-ridden moms and dads. Determined to get their children into increasingly competitive colleges and a tight job market down the road, today's parents are demanding more academic rigor (and thus more homework), even in grade school. To further beef up future resumes—and, often, to keep the kids occupied while both parents hold down jobs—they're also cramming after-school hours with extracurricular activities. The upshot, says Dr. Alvin Rosenfeld, a New York City psychiatrist and author, is that "parenting has become the most competitive sport in America. "Adds Georgia Witkin, assistant professor of clinical psychology at Mount Sinai School of Medicine: "It's as if an epidemic is spreading from us to them."

How To Help Your Kid Cope

If your child seems unduly worried or scared, is day-dreaming too much or having trouble sleeping because of academic pressure and overscheduling, says Georgia Witkin, director of the Stress Program at Mount Sinai School of Medicine in New York City, try the following:

- Establish regular mealtimes and bedtimes. Predictability helps reduce kids 'stress.
- Schedule unstructured play periods. If neither parent can be home, hire a responsible teen as an overseer.
- As a role model, make sure your kids see you relaxing with a book or listening to music—not just paying bills and cleaning house.
- Plan stress-reducing family time with your children, whether it's a picnic, outdoor games or just a round of Monopoly.
- If your kids are overwhelmed by homework, don't be afraid to let teachers and school administrators know.

The good news is that some families—and organizations—have begun to fight back. Last September, for instance, the Girl Scouts introduced a Stress Less badge, awarded so far to more than 60,000 8-to-11-year-old girls (including Wendy Gregg). The entire town of Ridgewood, N.J., encouraged its citizens to clear their calendars for a "Ready, Set, Relax!" family night last spring. In Austin 6-to-12-year-olds can enroll in a program that teaches them painting, dancing and acting—without the pressure to achieve that often accompanies such extracurriculars. "Once in a while we get a call from a parent saying they want their child to be in a 'real 'production, like Oliver! or Annie," says Jeanne Henry, the city's cultural arts education supervisor. "We explain that if the kids come here after school and feel like doing nothing, that's okay. They can do nothing."

Public schools are joining the stress-busting movement as well—and not only in affluent communities. When teachers in San Francisco noticed in 1997 that students were stressed out, they started teaching yoga. Today Cathy Klein, 30, offers it to her second graders at the inner-city Daniel Webster Elementary School. "Yoga calms me," says 6-year-old Filoi Sevatase, a regular at the twice-weekly, 20-minute sessions. "I like doing it when I'm mad or sad, like when my sister hits me or makes me cry." That relaxation technique is also on the curriculum in Atlanta preschools, where 4-year-olds learn to center themselves with the help of a Copee Bear hand puppet. Reports program director Gloria Elder: "Ninety-five percent of their teachers say it helps."

But the biggest push comes from parents like Bill Doherty, 57, a social sciences professor and father of two who lives in Roseville, Minn. In 1999, when he began noticing "6-year-olds with daily planners," Doherty helped launch Putting Family First, a local organization dedicated to reclaiming family time. One of the group's first seal-of-approval certificates went to the conference-winning Wayzata High School football team coached by Brad Anderson, 38. The team has long refused to bench players when they skip practice for family obligations. Josh Rounds, 18, a senior middle linebacker, says that when he missed the first week of practice because of a family vacation, "it was no problem. I got right back into football when I came home."

Anderson says his own family has experienced scheduling overload firsthand. "As a parent you want to provide opportunities for your kids—gymnastics, swimming, church choir, Brownies, piano lessons. But my wife and I had to sit down with our PalmPilots to figure out how we were going to get them from one thing to another." Instead the couple decided to pare back, limiting their two girls to no more than two after-school activities each. Now, he says, "the kids 'favorite thing is family night—playing a game of Battleship together or going to an outdoor concert."

In the nearby town of Plymouth, the Peterschmidt family came to a similar decision three years ago, when they almost lost themselves in a blur of frenetic activity. "I can't bear to look at the calendar from that year. It was crazy," says mother Margaret, 45, who goes by the nickname Bugs. "Every night we'd say, 'What's next? 'before running to get Max to his church group or Betsy to soccer." Max, 14, who is just starting ninth grade at Wayzata High, also shudders at the memory: "Trumpet, Scouts, violin, advanced math, church youth group, recreational soccer. And I was depressed because I felt like I had no time to do anything at all." Adds Betsy, now 11, who was equally overscheduled: "I needed a break."

The kids weren't alone in feeling stressed out. In the fall of 1999 a chronically tired Bugs went to the doctor, who found that she had walking pneumonia. During a week of mandatory bed rest, she recalls, "my kids gave me all kinds of stress-relieving gifts—an aromatherapy candle, a little fountain for the kitchen counter. It was a clear message."

One that she and her husband, Eric, 47, a marketing director for Honeywell, finally heeded. Today, after curtailing their schedules, the Peterschmidts are enjoying a newfound tranquility. "Life is so much better now," says Bugs. "But it's like finding religion or quitting smoking: You don't realize how good you feel until you've done it." These days dinner's on the table at 6:15—no phone calls allowed. Family members talk to one another. The kids roast marshmallows and play flashlight tag—"like tag but with light," Betsy explains. "And it's in the dark, so it's much funner."

Each week, Max has a violin lesson, while Betsy takes piano from a teacher who comes to the house. "We don't have huge blowups like we used to," says Bugs. As for Peterschmidt pere: "When I come home from work," marvels Eric, "the first thing my son says is, 'Dad, how was your day?' Isn't that neat?"

A NATION OF WIMPS

Parents are going to ludicrous lengths to take the lumps and bumps out of life for their children. However well-intentioned, parental hyerconcern and microscrutiny have the net effect of making kids more fragile. That may be why the young are breaking down in record numbers.

BY HARA ESTROFF MARANO

MAYBE IT'S THE CYCLIST IN THE PARK, TRIM UNDER his sleek metallic blue helmet, cruising along the dirt path … at three miles an hour. On his tricycle.

Or perhaps it's today's playground, all-rubber-cushioned surface where kids used to skin their knees. And … wait a minute … those aren't little kids playing. Their mommies—and especially their daddies—are in there with them, coplaying or play-by-play coaching. Few take it half-easy on the perimeter benches, as parents used to do, letting the kids figure things out for themselves.

Then there are the sanitizing gels, with which over a third of parents now send their kids to school, according to a recent survey. Presumably, parents now worry that school bathrooms are not good enough for their children.

Consider the teacher new to an upscale suburban town. Shuffling through the sheaf of reports certifying the educational "accommodations" he was required to make for many of his history students, he was struck by the exhaustive, well-written—and obviously costly—one on behalf of a girl who was already proving among the most competent of his ninth-graders. "She's somewhat neurotic," he confides, "but she is bright, organized and conscientious—the type who'd get to school to turn in a paper on time, even if she were dying of stomach flu." He finally found the disability he was to make allowances for: difficulty with Gestalt thinking. The 13-year-old "couldn't see the big picture." That cleverly devised defect (what 13-year-old can construct the big picture?) would allow her to take all her tests untimed, especially the big one at the end of the rainbow, the collegeworthy SAT.

Behold the wholly sanitized childhood, without skinned knees or the occasional C in history. "Kids need to feel badly sometimes," says child psychologist David Elkind, professor at Tufts University. "We learn through experience and we learn through bad experiences. Through failure we learn how to cope."

Messing up, however, even in the playground, is wildly out of style. Although error and experimentation are the true mothers of success, parents are taking pains to remove failure from the equation.

"Life is planned out for us," says Elise Kramer, a Cornell University junior "But we don't know what to want." As Elkind puts it, "Parents and schools are no longer geared toward child development, they're geared to academic achievement."

No one doubts that there are significant economic forces pushing parents to invest so heavily in their children's outcome from an early age. But taking all the discomfort, disappointment and even the play out of development, especially while increasing pressure for success, turns out to be misguided by just about 180 degrees. With few challenges all their own, kids are unable to forge their creative adaptations to the normal vicissitudes of life. That not only makes them risk averse, it makes them psychologically fragile, riddled with anxiety. In the process they're robbed of identity, meaning and a sense of accomplishment, to say nothing of a shot at real happiness. Forget, too, about perseverance, not simply a moral virtue but a necessary life skill. These turn out to be the spreading psychic fault lines of 21st century youth. Whether we want to or not, we're on our way to creating a nation of wimps.

THE FRAGILITY FACTOR

College, it seems, is where the fragility factor is now making its greatest mark. It's where intellectual and developmental tracks converge as the emotional training wheels come off. By all accounts, psychological distress is rampant on college campuses. It takes a variety of forms, including anxiety and depression—which are increasingly regarded as two faces of the same coin—binge drinking and substance abuse, self-mutilation and other forms of disconnection. The mental state of students is now so precarious for so many that, says Steven Hyman, provost of Harvard University and former director of the National Institute of Mental Health, "it is interfering with the core mission of the university."

OVERPARENTING CAN CREATE LIFELONG VULNERABILITY TO ANXIETY AND DEPRESSION.

The severity of student mental health problems has been rising since 1988, according to an annual survey of counseling center directors. Through 1996, the most common problems raised by students were relationship issues. That is developmentally appropriate, reports Sherry Benton, assistant director of counseling at Kansas State University. But in 1996, anxiety overtook relationship concerns and has remained the major problem. The University of Michigan Depression Center, the nation's first, estimates that 15 percent of college students nationwide are suffering from that disorder alone.

Relationship problems haven't gone away; their nature has dramatically shifted and the severity escalated. Colleges report ever more cases of obsessive pursuit, otherwise known as stalking, leading to violence, even death. Anorexia or bulimia in florid or subclinical form now afflicts 40 percent of women at some time in their college career. Eleven weeks into a semester, reports psychologist Russ Federman, head of counseling at the University of Virginia, "all appointment slots are filled. But the students don't stop coming."

Drinking, too, has changed. Once a means of social lubrication, it has acquired a darker, more desperate nature. Campuses nationwide are reporting record increases in binge drinking over the past decade, with students often stuporous in class, if they get there at all. Psychologist Paul E. Joffe, chair of the suicide prevention team at the University of Illinois at Urbana-Champaign, contends that at bottom binge-drinking is a quest for authenticity and intensity of experience. It gives young people something all their own to talk about, and sharing stories about the path to passing out is a primary purpose. It's an inverted world in which drinking to oblivion is the way to feel connected and alive.

"There is a ritual every university administrator has come to fear," reports John Portmann, professor of religious studies at the University of Virginia. "Every fall, parents drop off their well-groomed freshmen and within two or three days many have consumed a dangerous amount of alcohol and placed themselves in harm's way. These kids have been controlled for so long, they just go crazy."

Heavy drinking has also become the quickest and easiest way to gain acceptance, says psychologist Bernardo J. Carducci, professor at Indiana University Southeast and founder of its Shyness Research Institute. "Much of collegiate social activity is centered on alcohol consumption because it's an anxiety reducer and demands no social skills," he says. "Plus it provides an instant identity; it lets people know that you are willing to belong."

WELCOME TO THE HOTHOUSE

Talk to a college president or administrator and you're almost certainly bound to hear tales of the parents who call at 2 a.m. to protest Branden's C in economics because it's going to damage his shot at grad school.

Shortly after psychologist Robert Epstein announced to his university students that he expected them to work hard and would hold them to high standards, he heard from a parent—on official judicial stationery—asking how he could dare mistreat the young. Epstein, former editor in chief of *Psychology Today*, eventually filed a complaint with the California commission on judicial misconduct, and the judge was censured for abusing his office—but not before he created havoc in the psychology department at the University of California San Diego.

Enter: grade inflation. When he took over as president of Harvard in July 2001, Lawrence Summers publicly ridiculed the value of honors after discovering that 94 percent of the college's seniors were graduating with them. Safer to lower the bar than raise the discomfort level. Grade inflation is the institutional response to parental anxiety about school demands on children, contends social historian Peter Stearns of George Mason University. As such, it is a pure index of emotional over-investment in a child's success. And it rests on a notion of juvenile frailty—"the assumption that children are easily bruised and need explicit uplift," Stearns argues in his book, *Anxious Parenting: A History of Modern Childrearing in America*.

Parental protectionism may reach its most comic excesses in college, but it doesn't begin there. Primary schools and high schools are arguably just as guilty of grade inflation. But if you're searching for someone to blame, consider Dr. Seuss. "Parents have told their kids from day one that there's no end to what they are capable of doing," says Virginia's Portmann. "They read them the Dr. Seuss book *Oh, the Places You'll Go!* and create bumper stickers telling the world their child is an honor student. American parents today expect their children to be perfect—the smartest, fastest, most charming people in the universe. And if they can't get the children to prove it on their own, they'll turn to doctors to make their kids into the people that parents want to believe their kids are."

What they're really doing, he stresses, is "showing kids how to work the system for their own benefit."

And subjecting them to intense scrutiny. "I wish my parents had some hobby other than me," one young patient told David Anderegg, a child psychologist in Lenox, Massachusetts, and professor of psychology at Bennington College. Anderegg finds that anxious parents are hyperattentive to their kids, reactive to every blip of their child's day, eager to solve every problem for their child—and believe that's good parenting. "If you have an infant and the baby has gas, burping the baby is being a good parent. But when you have a 10-year-old who has metaphoric gas, you don't have to burp him. You have to let him sit with it, try to figure out what to do about it. He then learns to tolerate moderate amounts of difficulty, and it's not the end of the world."

ARRIVEDERCI, PLAYTIME

In the hothouse that child raising has become, play is all but dead. Over 40,000 U.S. schools no longer have recess. And what play there is has been corrupted. The organized sports many kids participate in are managed by adults; difficulties that arise are not worked out by kids but adjudicated by adult referees.

"So many toys now are designed by and for adults," says Tufts' Elkind. When kids do engage in their own kind of play parents become alarmed. Anderegg points to kids exercising time-honored curiosity by playing doctor. "It's normal for children to have curiosity about other children's genitals," he says. "But when they do, most parents I know are totally freaked out. They wonder what's wrong."

Kids are having a hard time even playing neighborhood pickup games because they've never done it, observes Barbara Carlson, president and cofounder of Putting Families First. "They've been told by their coaches where on the field to stand, told by their parents what color socks to wear, told by the referees who's won and what's fair. Kids are losing leadership skills."

A lot has been written about the commercialization of children's play but not the side effects, says Elkind. "Children aren't getting any benefits out of play as they once did." From the beginning play helps children learn how to control themselves, how to interact with others. Contrary to the widely held belief that only intellectual activities build a sharp brain, it's in play that cognitive agility really develops. Studies of children and adults around the world demonstrate that social engagement actually improves intellectual skills. It fosters decision-making, memory and thinking, speed of mental processing. This shouldn't come as a surprise. After all, the human mind is believed to have evolved to deal with social problems.

THE ETERNAL UMBILICUS

It's bad enough that today's children are raised in a psychological hothouse where they are overmonitored and oversheltered. But that hothouse no longer has geographical or temporal boundaries. For that you can thank the cell phone. Even in college—or per-

A DANGEROUS NEW REMEDY FOR ANXIETY

Of all the disorders now afflicting young people, perhaps most puzzling is self-injury—deliberate cutting, cigarette-burning or other repetitive mutilation of body tissue. No one knows whether it's a sudden epidemic or has been rising gradually, but there appears to be an absolute increase in occurrence: "It has now reached critical mass and is on all our radar screens," says Russ Federman, director of counseling at the University of Virginia.

It's highly disturbing for a student to walk into a dorm room and find her roommate meticulously slicing her thighs with a shard of glass or a razor. But it may be the emblematic activity of the psychically shielded and overly fragile. People "do it to feel better. It's an impulsive act done to regulate mood," observes Armando Favazza, author of *Bodies Under Siege: Self Mutilation in Psychiatry and Culture.*

It's basically a very effective "home remedy" for anxiety, states Chicago psychiatrist Arthur Neilsen, who teaches at Northwestern University. People who deliberately hurt themselves—twice as many women as men—report "it's like popping a balloon." There's an immediate release of tension. It also serves an important defense—distraction—stresses Federman. "In the midst of emotional turmoil, physical pain helps people disconnect from the turmoil." But the effect is very short-lived.

Self-harm reflects young people's inability to find something that makes them feel fully alive. Earlier generations sought meaning in movements of social change or intellectual engagement inside and outside the classroom. "But young people are not speaking up or asking questions in the classroom," reports John Portmann, professor of religious studies at the University of Virginia and author of *Bad for Us: The Lure of Self-Harm.* It may be that cutting *is* their form of protest. So constrained and stressed by expectations, so invaded by parental control, they have no room to turn—except against themselves. —*HEM*

haps especially at college—students are typically in contact with their parents several times a day, reporting every flicker of experience. One long-distance call overheard on a recent cross-campus walk: "Hi, Mom. I just got an ice-cream cone; can you believe they put sprinkles on the bottom as well as on top?"

"Kids are constantly talking to parents," laments Cornell student Kramer, which makes them perpetually homesick. Of course, they're not telling the folks everything, notes Portmann. "They're not calling their parents to say, 'I really went wild last Friday at the frat house and now I might have chlamydia. Should I go to the student health center?'"

The perpetual access to parents infantilizes the young, keeping them in a permanent state of dependency. Whenever the slightest difficulty arises, "they're constantly referring to their parents for guidance," reports Kramer. They're not learning how to manage for themselves.

Think of the cell phone as the eternal umbilicus. One of the ways we grow up is by internalizing an image of Mom and Dad and the values and advice they imparted over the early years. Then, whenever we find ourselves faced with uncertainty or difficulty, we call on that internalized image. We become, in a way, all the wise adults we've had the privilege to know. "But cell phones keep kids from figuring out what to do," says Anderegg. "They've never internalized any images; all they've internalized is 'call Mom or Dad.'"

Some psychologists think we have yet to recognize the full impact of the cell phone on child development, because its use is so new. Although there are far too many variables to establish clear causes and effects, Indiana's Carducci believes that reliance on cell phones undermines the young by destroying the ability to plan ahead. "The first thing students do when they walk out the door of my classroom is flip open the cell phone. Ninety-five percent of the conversations go like this: 'I just got out of class; I'll see you in the library in five minutes.' Absent the phone, you'd have to make arrangements ahead of time; you'd have to think ahead."

Herein lies another possible pathway to depression. The ability to plan resides in the prefrontal cortex (PFC), the executive branch of the brain. The PFC is a critical part of the self-regulation system, and it's deeply implicated in depression, a disorder increasingly seen as caused or maintained by unregulated thought patterns—lack of intellectual rigor, if you will. Cognitive therapy owes its very effectiveness to the systematic application of critical thinking to emotional reactions. Further, it's in the setting of goals and progress in working toward them, however mundane they are, that positive feelings are generated. From such everyday activity, resistance to depression is born.

What's more, cell phones—along with the instant availability of cash and almost any consumer good your heart desires—promote fragility by weakening self-regulation. "You get used to things happening right away," says Carducci. You not only want the pizza now, you generalize that expectation to other domains, like friendship and intimate relationships. You become frustrated and impatient easily. You become unwilling to work out problems. And so relationships fail—perhaps the single most powerful experience leading to depression.

FROM SCRUTINY TO ANXIETY . . . AND BEYOND

The 1990s witnessed a landmark reversal in the traditional patterns of psychopathology. While rates of depression rise with advancing age among people over 40, they're now increasing fastest among children, striking more children at younger and younger ages.

PARENTS NEED TO GIVE KIDS— AND THEMSELVES—A BREAK BY LOOSENING THEIR INVASIVE CONTROL: SOONER OR LATER, MOST KIDS WILL BE FORCED TO CONFRONT THEIR OWN MEDIOCRITY.

In his now-famous studies of how children's temperaments play out, Harvard psychologist Jerome Kagan has shown unequivocally that what creates anxious children is parents hovering and protecting them from stressful experiences. About 20 percent of babies are born with a high-strung temperament. They can be spotted even in the womb; they have fast heartbeats. Their nervous systems are innately programmed to be overexcitable in response to stimulation, constantly sending out false alarms about what is dangerous.

As infants and children this group experiences stress in situations most kids find unthreatening, and they may go through childhood and even adulthood fearful of unfamiliar people and events, withdrawn and shy. At school age they become cautious, quiet and introverted. Left to their own devices they grow up shrinking from social encounters. They lack confidence around others. They're easily influenced by others. They are sitting ducks for bullies. And they are on the path to depression.

TEENS USE IRONY AND DETACHMENT TO "HIDE IN PLAIN SIGHT." THEY JUST DON'T WANT TO BE EXPOSED TO ANY MORE SCRUTINY.

While their innate reactivity seems to destine all these children for later anxiety disorders, things didn't turn out that way. Between a touchy temperament in infancy and persistence of anxiety stand two highly significant things: parents. Kagan found to his surprise that the development of anxiety was scarcely inevitable despite apparent genetic programming. At age 2, none of the overexcitable infants wound up fearful if their parents backed off from hovering and allowed the children to find some comfortable level of accommodation to the world on their own. Those parents who overprotected their children—directly observed by conducting interviews in the home—brought out the worst in them.

A small percentage of children seem almost invulnerable to anxiety from the start. But the overwhelming majority of kids are somewhere in between. For them, overparenting can program the nervous system to create lifelong vulnerability to anxiety and depression.

There is in these studies a lesson for all parents. Those who allow their kids to find a way to deal with life's day-to-day stresses by themselves are helping them develop resilience and coping strategies. "Children need to be gently encouraged to take risks and learn that nothing terrible happens," says Michael Liebowitz, clinical professor of psychiatry at Columbia University and head of the Anxiety Disorders Clinic at New York State Psychiatric Institute. "They need gradual exposure to find that the world is not dangerous. Having overprotective parents is a risk factor for anxiety disorders because children do not have opportunities to master their innate shyness and become more comfortable in the world." They never learn to dampen the pathways from perception to alarm reaction.

Hothouse parenting undermines children in other ways, too, says Anderegg. Being examined all the time makes children extremely self-conscious. As a result they get less communicative; scrutiny teaches them to bury their real feelings deeply. And most of all, self-consciousness removes the safety to be experimental and playful. "If every drawing is going to end up on your parents' refrigerator, you're not free to fool around, to goof up or make mistakes," says Anderegg.

Parental hovering is why so many teenagers are so ironic, he notes. It's a kind of detachment, "a way of hiding in plain sight. They just don't want to be exposed to any more scrutiny."

Parents are always so concerned about children having high self-esteem, he adds. "But when you cheat on their behalf to get them ahead of other children"—by pursuing accommodations and recommendations—"you just completely corrode their sense of self. They feel 'I couldn't do this on my own.' It robs them of their own sense of efficacy." A child comes to think, "if I need every advantage I can get, then perhaps there is really something wrong with me." A slam dunk for depression.

Virginia's Portmann feels the effects are even more pernicious; they weaken the whole fabric of society. He sees young people becoming weaker right before his eyes, more responsive to the herd, too eager to fit in—less assertive in the classroom, unwilling to disagree with their peers, afraid to question authority, more willing to conform to the expectations of those on the next rung of power above them.

UN-ADVICE FOR PARENTS

CHILL OUT! IF YOU'RE NOT HAVING FUN, YOU MAY BE PUSHING YOUR KIDS TOO HARD.

- Never invest more in an outcome than your child does.
- Allow children of all ages time for free play. It's a natural way to learn regulation, social skills and cognitive skills.
- Be reasonable about what is dangerous and what is not. Some risk-taking is healthy,
- Don't overreact to every bad grade or negative encounter your child has. Sometimes discomfort is the appropriate response to a situation—and a stimulus to self-improvement,
- Don't be too willing to slap a disease label on your child at the first sign of a problem; instead, spend some time helping your child learn how to deal with the problem.
- Peers are important, but young people also need to spend time socializing with adults in order to know how to *be* adults.
- Modify your expectations about child-raising in light of your child's temperament; the same actions don't work with everyone.
- Recognize that there are many paths to success. Allow your children latitude— even to take a year off before starting college.
- Don't manipulate the academic system on behalf of your child; it makes kids guilty and doubtful of their own ability,
- Remember that the goal of child-rearing is to raise an independent adult. Encourage your children to think for themselves, to disagree (respectfully) with authority, even to incur the critical gaze of their peers.

ENDLESS ADOLESCENCE

The end result of cheating childhood is to extend it forever. Despite all the parental pressure, and probably because of it, kids are pushing back—in their own way. They're taking longer to grow up.

Adulthood no longer begins when adolescence ends, according to a recent report by University of Pennsylvania sociologist Frank E Furstenberg and colleagues. There is, instead, a growing no-man's-land of postadolescence from 20 to 30, which they dub "early adulthood." Those in it look like adults but "haven't become fully adult yet—traditionally defined as finishing school, landing a job with benefits, marrying and parenting—because they are not ready or perhaps not permitted to do so." Using the classic benchmarks of adulthood, 65 percent of males had reached adulthood by the age of 30 in 1960. By contrast, in 2000, only 31 percent had. Among women, 77 percent met the benchmarks of adulthood by age 30 in 1960. By 2000, the number had fallen to 46 percent.

BOOM BOOM BOOMERANG

Take away play from the front end of development and it finds a way onto the back end. A steady march of success through regimented childhood arranged and monitored by parents creates young adults who need time to explore themselves. "They often need a period in college or afterward to legitimately experiment—to be children," says historian Stearns. "There's decent historical evidence to suggest that societies that allow kids a few years of latitude and even moderate [rebellion] end up with healthier kids than societies that pretend such impulses don't exist."

Marriage is one benchmark of adulthood, but its antecedents extend well into childhood. "The precursor to marriage is dating, and the precursor to dating is playing," says Carducci. The less time children spend in free play, the less socially competent they'll be as adults. It's in play that we learn give and take, the fundamental rhythm of all relationships. We learn how to read the feelings of others and how to negotiate conflicts. Taking the play out of childhood, he says. Is bound to create a developmental lag, and he sees it clearly in the social patterns of today's adolescents and young adults, who hang around in groups that are more typical of childhood. Not to be forgotten: The backdrop of continued high levels of divorce confuses kids already too fragile to take the huge risk of commitment.

JUST WHOSE SHARK TANK IS IT ANYWAY?

The stressful world of cutthroat competition that parents see their kids facing may not even exist. Or it exists, but more in their mind than in reality—not quite a fiction, more like a distorting mirror. "Parents perceive the world as a terribly competitive place," observes Anderegg. "And many of them project that onto their children when they're the ones who live or work in a competitive environment. They then imagine that their children must be swimming in a big shark tank, too."

"It's hard to know what the world is going to look like 10 years from now," says Elkind. "How best do you prepare kids for that? Parents think that earlier is better. That's a natural intuition, but it happens to be wrong."

What if parents have micromanaged their kids' lives because they've hitched their measurement of success to a single event whose value to life and paycheck they have frantically overestimated? No one denies the Ivy League offers excellent learning experiences, but most educators know that some of the best programs exist at schools that don't top the *U.S. News and World Report* list, and that with the right attitude—a willingness to be engaged by new ideas—it's possible to get a meaningful education almost anywhere. Further, argues historian Stearns, there are ample openings for students at an array of colleges, "We have a competitive frenzy that frankly involves parents more than it involves kids themselves," he observes, both as a father of eight and teacher of many. "Kids are more ambivalent about the college race than are parents."

Yet the very process of application to select colleges undermines both the goal of education and the inherent strengths of young people, "It makes kids sneaky," says Anderegg. Bending rules and calling in favors to give one's kid a competitive edge is morally corrosive.

Like Stearns, he is alarmed that parents, pursuing disability diagnoses so that children can take untimed SATs, actually encourage kids to think of themselves as sickly and fragile. Colleges no longer know when SATs are untimed—but the kids know. "The kids know when you're cheating on their behalf," says Anderegg, "and it makes them feel terribly guilty. Sometimes they arrange to fail to right the scales. And when you cheat on their behalf, you completely undermine their sense of self-esteem. They feel they didn't earn it on their own."

In buying their children accommodations to assuage their own anxiety, parents are actually locking their kids into fragility. Says the suburban teacher: "Exams are a fact of life. They are anxiety-producing. The kids never learn how to cope with anxiety."

PUTTING WORRY IN ITS PLACE

Children, however, are not the only ones who are harmed by hyperconcern. Vigilance is enormously taxing—and it's taken all the fun out of parenting. "Parenting has in some measurable ways become less enjoyable than it used to be," says Stearns. "I find parents less willing to indulge their children's sense of time. So they either force feed them or do things for them."

Parents need to abandon the idea of perfection and give up some of the invasive control they've maintained over their children. The goal of parenting, Portmann reminds, is to raise an independent human being. Sooner or later, he says, most

kids will be forced to confront their own mediocrity. Parents may find it easier to give up some control if they recognize they have exaggerated many of the dangers of childhood—although they have steadfastly ignored others, namely the removal of recess from schools and the ubiquity of video games that encourage aggression.

THERE ARE KIDS WORTH WORRYING ABOUT—KIDS IN POVERTY.

The childhood we've introduced to our children is very different from that in past eras, Epstein stresses. Children no longer work at young ages. They stay in school for longer periods of time and spend more time exclusively in the company of peers. Children are far less integrated into adult society than they used to be at every step of the way. We've introduced laws that give children many rights and protections—although we have allowed media and marketers to have free access.

In changing the nature of childhood, Stearns argues, we've introduced a tendency to assume that children can't handle difficult situations. "Middle-class parents especially assume that if kids start getting into difficulty they need to rush in and do it for them, rather than let them flounder a bit and learn from it. I don't mean we should abandon them," he says, "but give them more credit for figuring things out." And recognize that parents themselves have created many of the stresses and anxieties children are suffering from, without giving them tools to manage them.

While the adults are at it, they need to remember that one of the goals of higher education is to help young people develop the capacity to think for themselves.

Although we're well on our way to making kids more fragile, no one thinks that kids and young adults are fundamentally more flawed than in previous generations. Maybe many will "recover" from diagnoses too liberally slapped on to them. In his own studies of 14 skills he has identified as essential for adulthood in American culture, from love to leadership, Epstein has found that "although teens don't necessary behave in a competent way, they have the potential to be every bit as competent and as incompetent as adults."

Parental anxiety has its place. But the way things now stand, it's not being applied wisely. We're paying too much attention to too few kids—and in the end, the wrong kids. As with the girl whose parents bought her the Gestalt-defect diagnosis, resources are being expended for kids who don't need them.

There are kids who are worth worrying about—kids in poverty, stresses Anderegg. "We focus so much on our own children," says Elkind, "It's time to begin caring about all children."

Prevention of Domestic Violence During Adolescence

David A. Wolfe, Ph.D., and Peter G. Jaffe, Ph.D.

Some days it seems that little progress has been made in addressing the fundamental causes and consequences of domestic violence and its effects on children. The problem seems as serious as ever, and the major underlying causes, such as abuse of power, inequality, and modeling of violence in the home, have remained largely unchanged over the past three decades. The government response has been to manage adult domestic violence, which involves providing services on an individual basis only when absolutely necessary. Crisis management is a necessary part of the response to adult domestic violence, but more proactive strategies of prevention are also strongly needed.

The news is not all bad; in fact, encouraging progress has been made in less than two decades. Scientific, professional, and activist groups have played a prominent role in recognizing the links between domestic violence and child adjustment problems, among other issues. A growing interest by researchers and clinicians in the field of domestic violence has made it possible to establish a scientific foundation for implementing prevention and treatment initiatives and public policy to end domestic violence. The field is in the process of finding alternatives to violence that can be activated in each community in a manner that stimulates interest, informs choices, and promotes action to decrease violence and abuse in the lives of children, youth, and families.

In this article, key issues in the prevention of domestic violence are reviewed. Included are discussions of the goals of prevention programs and theories of the causality of domestic violence and abuse. Next, prevention efforts designed to address the needs of children and adults are viewed through a developmental, or life-span, lens. Critical issues for prevention programs are described for adolescents. Finally, research and policy implications are explored for violence prevention endeavors in a number of settings, from homes, schools, and neighborhoods to courts and the culture at large.

Emerging Goals of Prevention Efforts

Emerging changes in public policy, legislation, and service delivery illustrate a commitment to finding ways to reduce the prevalence and harmful effects of adult domestic violence. Still, strategies that address the issue at a broader level need to be developed and evaluated. Such strategies must take into account the many factors that influence the likelihood of adult domestic violence and those that promote nonviolence. There are established precedents for such an approach, such as public health campaigns to eliminate health risks among adolescents and health promotion campaigns to encourage healthy (low-risk) behaviors among segments of the population (Hamilton & Bhatti, 1996; Sherman et al., 1998). These approaches, adopted primarily for known health issues, hold considerable promise for behavioral issues as well because they recognize that change occurs through finding positive ways to communicate messages about healthy families and relationships.

One way to envision the goal of prevention is to promote attitudes and behaviors that are incompatible with violence and abuse, and that encourage the formation of healthy, nonviolent relationships. The implications of this paradigm are significant and far reaching if attention and resources are primarily focused on the occurrence of undesirable behavior, such as identified acts of violence, prevention efforts are usually directed toward identification, control, and punishment. However, if the goal of prevention is the promotion of healthy, nonviolent relationships, attention and resources are more likely to be directed toward establishing and building trust, respecting others' thoughts and expressions, and encouraging and supporting growth in relationships. This perspective implies a different list of intervention and educational possibilities, such as school-based curricula, neighborhood-based health and social services, and family-based child and health care.

Theories of Causality

The prevention of domestic violence at first glance seems impeded by a lack of theoretical consensus as to its fundamental causes. However, the foundation of prevention programs might include several important principles:

- Domestic violence has been ignored as a major health, criminal, and social problem until recently and remains poorly understood among the general population.

- Domestic violence is a complex problem that cannot be understood by a single variable. Explanations require a multifaceted approach that recognizes individual behavior within a familial and cultural context (Dutton, 1995).

- The significance of childhood trauma, including witnessing adult domestic violence, is common to all theories even though there is disagreement as to the processes involved. In general, these processes include learning maladaptive behaviors through modeling and reinforcement by people in the child's family, neighborhood, and cultural environment (Emery & Laumann-Billings, 1998). In turn, prevention efforts may include efforts to prevent children from ever experiencing such trauma as well as community readiness to respond as soon as possible to children in violent homes.

- As long as domestic violence is seen as acceptable behavior or tolerated by silence through public attitudes, institutions, and the media, there is little chance of changing individual behavior. In other words, the prevention of domestic violence is everyone's business and is each human services provider's responsibility.

Although far from realized, domestic violence prevention efforts have begun to organize around the principle of building on strengths and developing protective factors in an effort to deter violence and abuse. Learning to relate to others, especially intimates, in a respectful, nonviolent manner is a crucial foundation for building effective prevention strategies for related forms of violence and abuse between partners.

Prevention Efforts

Because violence in intimate relationships is deeply rooted in early family experiences and in broader cultural and social influences, deciding where to focus prevention efforts for greatest impact is a critical starting point. In principle, prevention efforts should involve every aspect of social ecology. Societal, community, and neighborhood forces; schools and peer groups; family processes; and individual strengths and weaknesses have all been linked to adult domestic violence. Therefore, all of these influences play a role in the prevention of violence and care should be taken to ensure that the interventions are appropriate and beneficial. The following discussion will focus exclusively on interventions aimed at adolescents (for discussion of the other age groups, see Wolfe & Jaffe, 2001).

Adolescence is a time of important cognitive and social development, during which teenagers learn to think more rationally and become capable of thinking hypo-

thetically. At the same time, they must develop and use effective decision-making skills involving complex interpersonal relationships, including an awareness of possible risks and considerations of future consequences and balancing their own interests with those of their peers, family members, and dating partners. Conformity to parental opinions gradually decreases, and the tendency to be swayed by peers increases until late adolescence. By mid-adolescence, romantic partners increase in their importance as social support providers (Furman & Buhrmester, 1992). Thus, early to mid-adolescence offers a unique opportunity for learning healthy ways to form intimate relationships, and teenagers are often keen to explore this unfamiliar territory.

Youth, especially those who grew up experiencing violence in their homes, profit from education and skills that promote healthy relationships and provide useful alternatives to violence and abuse. Clear messages about personal responsibility and boundaries, delivered in a blame-free manner, are generally acceptable to this age group, whereas lectures and warnings are less helpful. By offering youth the opportunities to explore the richness and rewards of relationships, they become eager to learn about choices and responsibilities. The initiation phase of social dating is a prime opportunity to become aware of the ways in which violent and abusive behavior toward intimate partners may occur, often without purpose or intention. This premise holds true not only for individuals from violent and abusive family backgrounds where negative experiences were prominent but also for other adolescents (Gray & Foshee, 1997).

A discussion of choice and responsibility for one's own behavior and how abusiveness has different consequences and meanings for young men and women is a critical step in enhancing youth awareness and recognition of dating violence (Gray & Foshee, 1997). Moreover, facilitating discussions about the meaning of violent dynamics, violent acts, and woman abuse simultaneously raises awareness of these issues and provides an opportunity to deal directly with issues of blame, responsibility, and victim-victimizer dynamics within the context of teenage dating relationships. Programs delivered universally through the high school often involve activities aimed at increasing awareness and dispelling myths about relationship violence. These activities can include: a) school auditorium presentations involving videotapes, plays, or a survivor's speech; b) classroom discussions facilitated by teachers and community professionals involved in domestic violence intervention, such as shelter staff or law enforcement personnel; c) detailed lesson plans, programs, and curricula that encourage students to examine those attitudes and behaviors that promote or tolerate violence (these exercises serve as an introduction to nonviolent alternatives in relationships); and d) peer counseling and peer support groups to assist students in developing empowerment initiatives.

The prevention of domestic violence is everyone's business and is each human services provider's responsibility.

Community-based programs for the prevention of relationship violence have goals similar to those of school-based programs, although they are intended for a more selective population, such as teenagers who are at greater risk of dating violence because of their early childhood experiences or similar risk factors. One example is the Youth Relationships Project (Wolfe et al., 2003), which was developed to help youth understand the critical importance of the abuse of power and control in relationship violence and relate these to their own social and dating relationships. The Youth Relationships Project involves adolescents referred from active caseloads of child protective service agencies who experienced violence and abuse in their families. They are informed of the program by their child protection caseworker, counselor, or other community agent. The program has an emphasis on building healthy, nonviolent relationships rather than attending treatment per se (which adolescents generally resist). Because the Youth Relationships Project is a secondary prevention program, participation does not require evidence of dating violence. Through group discussion and exercises, the youth learn how to select appropriate alternatives to abuse and violence with dating partners. This strategy builds on current strengths and identifies negative relationship factors at a time when teenagers are motivated to learn about intimate relationships.

Efforts to provide youth with such positive educational and cultural experiences in which power is understood, not abused, are very recent, and program evaluations are incomplete. Early findings, however, show that youth are responsive to such information, especially if they are involved in its design and delivery. Six dating violence prevention programs designed for high school teenagers have included evaluation components (Wekerle & Wolfe, 1999). Each program addressed specific skills and knowledge that oppose the use of violent and abusive behavior toward intimate partners. Positive changes were found across the studies in violence-related attitudes and knowledge as well as self-reported perpetration of dating violence. Although preliminary, such efforts indicate that adolescents are receptive to these learning opportunities.

Policy and Research Implications

Regardless of their attractiveness, prevention and health promotion efforts have not been popular strategies among professionals or the general public for addressing the problem of domestic violence. Prevention entails environmental and cultural explanations in addition to individual ones for causes of violence and necessitates a strong commitment to large-scale, proactive intervention using public resources rather than individually focused, private interests. Furthermore, prevention requires social and political action directed at achieving fundamental change. Nevertheless, we owe it to children, young people, and families to consider building other bridges that promote competency and adaptive behavior in an effort not only to prevent something unwanted but also to bolster potential and growth for individuals and society.

Although there is a paucity of evaluative data, there is general agreement that children and adolescents, especially those growing up in violent homes, are an important prevention focus. The following major prevention strategies and research issues stand out:

- Based on the collective wisdom of family court judges, child protection agencies, and domestic violence programs, there is a need to expand existing collaborative efforts by child protection and domestic violence agencies and staff to a more comprehensive primary prevention program (National Council of Juvenile and Family Court Judges, 1998).

- There is a growing recognition that crime prevention needs to focus on homes and communities to the extent that both are recognized as risk factors in violent behavior. Many children are exposed to violence not only in their homes but also in their neighborhoods and schools, which means there is a need for extensive collaboration among service systems. Thus, initial efforts may have to target high-risk neighborhoods and communities rather than assessing one client (potential victim) at a time (Earls, 1998).

- Primary prevention programs should be available in all schools and be developed as partnerships among students, teachers, parents, and community agents who have knowledge and expertise about domestic violence. For adolescents, the programs need to be relevant to their interests, such as dating violence, and actively involve counseling, such as peer support and peer models. A major challenge for the domestic violence field involves better collaboration with the more general crime prevention strategies that are being actively promoted in U.S. schools. There are overlapping strategies (e.g., clearly naming the problem), and domestic violence is often an underlying issue and concern for children. Although many parents and teachers are worried about violence in general, most children are more likely to witness and experience violence among people they know and trust. Therefore, the domestic violence issues are more relevant for them.

- Programs need to be planned according to both individual and institutional readiness for change. For example, boys and men may become defensive in discussions on violence against women and underlying issues of inequality until they have a better appreciation of the broader problems of violence in society. Therefore, programs have to acknowledge the stepping stones from awareness of a problem to a deeper understanding and ultimately an ongoing commitment for social change (for further discussion see Jaffe, Wolfe, Crooks, Hughes, & Baker, 2004).

In the prevention of adult domestic violence, a clear commitment is needed from all levels of government to address these issues comprehensively, with the goal of establishing a consistent, coordinated, and integrated approach for each community. Given the extensive nature of domestic violence and its accompanying human suffering, this commitment to prevention cannot be postponed.

David A. Wolfe, Ph.D., is with the Department of Psychiatry, Centre for Addiction and Mental Health, University of Toronto. Peter G. Jaffe, Ph.D., is with the Center for Children and Families in the Justice System, London Family Court Clinic, and is an Adjunct Professor in the Departments of Psychiatry and Psychology of the University of Western Ontario.
This article is adapted from David A. Wolfe and Peter G. Jaffe (2001). Prevention of domestic violence: Emerging initiatives. In S.A. Graham-Bermann & J.L. Edleson (Ed,.), Domestic Violence in the Lives of Children: The Future of Research, Intervention, and Social Policy (pp. 283-298). Washington DC: American Psychological Association. It appears here with permission from The Future of Children, a publication of the David and Lucile Packard Foundation.

References

Dutton, D.G. (1995). *The Domestic Assault of Women: Psychological and Criminal Justice Perspectives.* Vancouver, B.C., Canada: University of British Columbia Press.

Earls, F. (1998, September). *Linking Community Factors and Individual Development* [Research preview] (NIJ 170603). Washington DC: U.S. Department of Justice, National Institute of Justice.

Emery, R.E., & Laumann-Billings, L. (1998). An overview of the nature, causes, and consequences of abusive family relationships: Toward differentiating maltreatment and violence. *American Psychologist, 53,* 121–135.

Furman, W., & Buhrmester, D. (1992). Age and sex differences in perceptions of networks of personal relationships. *Child Development, 63,* 103–115.

Gray, H.M., & Foshee, V. (1997). Adolescent dating violence: Differences between one-sided and mutually violent profiles. *Journal of Interpersonal Violence, 12,* 126–141.

Hamilton, N., & Bhatti, T. (1996). *Population Health Promotion: An Integrated Model of Population Health and Health Promotion.* Ottawa, Ontario: Health Canada.

Jaffe, P., Wolfe, D.A., Crooks, C., Hughes, R., & Baker, L. (2004). The Fourth R: Developing healthy relationships through school-based interventions. In P. Jaffe, L. Baker, & A. Cunningham (Eds.), *Protecting Children From Domestic Violence: Strategies for Community Intervention* (pp. 200–218). New York: Guilford.

National Council of Juvenile and Family Court Judges. (1998). *Family Violence: Emerging Programs for Battered Mothers and Their Children.* Reno, NY: Author.

Sherman, L.W., Gottfredson, D.C, MacKenzie, D.L., Eck, J., Reuter, P., & Bushway, S.D. (1998, July). *Preventing Crime: What Works, What Doesn't, What's Promising* [Research in brief I (NIJ 171676)]. Washington DC: U.S. Department of Justice, National Institute of Justice.

Wekerle, C, & Wolfe, D.A. (1999). Dating violence in mid-adolescence: Theory, significance, and emerging prevention initiatives. *Clinical Psychology Review, 19,* 435–456.

Wolfe, D.A., & Jaffe, P.D. (2001). Prevention of domestic violence: Emerging initiatives. In S.A. Graham-Bermann & J.L. Edleson (Eds.), *Domestic Violence in the Lives of Children: The Future of Research, Intervention, and Social Policy* (pp. 283–298). Washington DC: American Psychological Association.

Wolfe, D.A., Wekerle, C, Scott, K., Straatman, A., Grasley, C, & Reitzel-Jaffe, D. (2003). Dating violence prevention with at-risk youth: A controlled outcome evaluation. *Journal of Consulting and Clinical Psychology, 71,* 279–291.

Adolescents From Maritally Violent Homes

Maura O'Keefe, Ph.D., and Shirley Lebovics, M.S.W., L.C.S.W

Dad was always really mean. He blamed us whenever anything went wrong at home. He would hit all of us when he was mad, but Mom got most of it. He drank, but hit her when he was sober too. Once he beat her so badly, she could barely get up. We thought he might have killed her. Billy [Susan's brother, age 14] often tried to stop him, but it didn't help. It only made Dad hit Billy too. I tried to stay out of it. I wish I'd been tougher and done something, but I just couldn't get up the nerve.

—from Susan, age 13

It is estimated that between 3.3 million and 10 million children in the U.S. witness physical violence between their parents each year (Straus, 1991). The types of interparental violence children observe may range from overhearing some form of violent behavior from their bedrooms, to seeing severe acts of violence such as beatings, chokings, or assaults with guns and knives. In many cases, these children observe repeated acts of violence perpetrated by multiple partners throughout their childhood.

Although the high number of children witnessing wife-battering is not a new phenomenon, it is only within the past two decades that these effects have been documented. The extant research has focused on the impact of husband to wife violence on children, however, children may also witness wife to husband violence, although it is likely to be less severe (Archer, 2002). Moreover, although research findings indicate that both the prevalence and dynamics of violence in gay and lesbian relationships are similar to that in heterosexual couples (Renzetti & Wiley, 1996), there are no studies investigating the impact on children who may witness this violence. It is likely, however, that the effects are the same. Adverse effects of witnessing domestic or interparental violence have been found in a number of domains of child functioning including cognitive, social, emotional, and behavioral. Both clinical case reports and empirical studies indicate that children who witness violence between parents exhibit a high frequency of externalizing behavior problems (such as aggression, noncompliance, and delinquency), internalizing behavior problems (such as depression, anxiety, and somatic complaints), and symptoms mirroring post-traumatic stress disorder (Edelson, 1999; Graham-Bermann & Levendosky, 1998). On measures of social competence, such as participation in social activities, children who witnessed domestic violence scored significantly below their peers (Fantuzzo et al., 1991). Other problems noted among these children include deficits in problem solving; low self-esteem; lack of empathy; and school adjustment difficulties such as poor academic performance, difficulties in concentration, and school phobia (Edelson, 1999). Further, children growing up in violent homes learn that violence is an appropriate and acceptable means of resolving conflict in intimate relationships, a lesson that may have both short and long-term consequences (Rossman, 2001).

The vast majority of studies documenting the effects of witnessing interparental violence on children's functioning have sampled youth who are between preschool and puberty and who reside with their mothers at battered women's shelters. However, less is known about adolescents exposed to interparental violence. This lack of information may be partly due to the fact that adolescents often do not to stay with their mothers at shelters. Also, many shelters do not allow adolescent males to stay with their mothers, making it even less likely that they will be included in the research. Further, adolescents, by virtue of their age, physical size, and greater independence, may be viewed as less in need of protection and therefore perhaps less deserving of concern.

> *Children growing up in violent homes learn that violence is an appropriate and acceptable means of resolving conflict in intimate relationships.*

The little that is known about the effects of interparental violence on adolescents indicates that adolescent witnesses of domestic violence have higher rates of aggression compared to those from nonviolent homes (McCloskey & Lichter, 2003). They are also more likely to have a fatalistic view of the future and are at increased risk for such problems such as delinquency, school truancy, early sexual activity, substance abuse, and suicide (Herrera & McCloskey, 2001; O'Keefe, 1996; Spaccarelli, Coatsworth & Bowden, 1995). Further, there is considerable empirical support for the intergenerational transmission of violence hypothesis—the notion that children from violent families carry violent and violence-tolerance roles to their adult intimate relationships. Numerous studies have found that witnessing interparental violence places individuals (particularly males) at high risk for perpetrating as well as being the recipient of violence, not only in their dating relationships, but in their marriages as well (O'Keefe, 1997; Reitzel-Jaffe & Wolfe, 2001).

Clearly, the critical nature of the consequences of exposure to interparental violence on adolescents' adjustment underscores the need for accurate assessment of interparental violence as well as for effective prevention, intervention, and treatment. The goal of this article is to discuss common reactions by adolescents who witness interparental violence and some of the ways in which exposure to this violence may impede adolescent development. These findings are based on a review of the literature as well as the authors' clinical experience and research.

Adolescent's Reactions to Interparental Violence

Adolescents vary in their feelings, defense mechanisms, and strategies they employ to cope with the trauma of growing up in a violent home. Common reactions to witnessing violence may include feelings of shame, rage, fear, and anxiety. The consequences of the violence, however, may be far-reaching and reverberate throughout many areas of the adolescent's life, including school performance, social relationships, personal safety, self-esteem, and future stability.

Shame

Domestic violence is a family secret. Last night's fight is not discussed openly among family members and must never be mentioned outside the family. Adolescents carry these secrets and are often burdened by the responsibility of censoring any remarks about their parents' relationship.

Because adolescents are self conscious about both their physical and social appearance; anything that calls attention to themselves as different from peers may be experienced as embarrassing or as a threat to their self-esteem. A home life which includes a father who batters and a mother who shows the physical and emotional consequences of being battered may be a source of great shame. The adolescent may be reluctant to invite friends home due to fear of exposure. The need for secrecy may lead to social isolation at a time when acceptance and support from peers is especially essential to social development.

Fear and Anxiety

The general climate in homes where domestic violence occurs is often one of apprehension, tension, and a feeling of "walking on eggshells," as evidenced in the case studies of both Jimmy and Lenny. The family is frequently in a state of disequilibrium, never knowing when the next violent incident may occur. Adolescents may fear being the next target of attack or doing something that will provoke their fathers to attack their mothers. Some adolescents may become paralyzed with feelings of anxiety that may not only permeate the family atmosphere, but affect other areas of their lives, such as their ability to cope with normative stresses or plan future education or career goals.

Traumatic-Reactions

Adolescents may develop symptoms of post-traumatic stress disorder (PTSD) as a result of observing repeated or severe interparental violence. This is not surprising; seeing one's mother being beaten can be a terrifying event at any age. PTSD symptoms identified in children of battered women include a re-experiencing or preoccupation with the traumatic event (such as nightmares or distressing recollections of the violence); increased arousal symptoms (such as somatic complaints, sleep disturbances, fears, and temper outbursts); and avoidance or psychic numbing (Graham-Bermann & Levendosky, 1998; McCloskey & Walker, 2000). These symptoms are also found in adolescents and may manifest in ways that are more difficult to discern, particularly if chronic. For example, running away from home or delinquency may disguise underlying PTSD symptoms (Jaffe et al., 1990). Because disclosure of family violence is unlikely, there may be little opportunity for resolution of the trauma.

Alliances With the Batterer

It is not uncommon for children of battered women to develop an alliance with the batterer. Some may blame their mothers for the tension at home and feel angry at them for provoking the abuse. This alliance with the father against the mother may even manifest itself in assaults directed at the mother. These assaults often begin during adolescence, when the child becomes physically stronger than his or her mother.

> *It is not uncommon for children of battered women to develop an alliance with the batterer.*

A factor that may account for the adolescent's alliance with the batterer is fear. In any fearful situation, a paradoxical attachment and unconscious collusion may develop between victim and aggressor. This phenomenon is a process wherein a child may unconsciously identify with the perpetrator as a means of warding off danger. This defense mechanism is never fully effective; even when a strong alliance exists with the father, it is usually accompanied by underlying feelings of ambivalence, confusion, or guilt.

Parentification

Adolescents who have grown up in maritally violent homes may feel responsible for maintaining safety and peace in the home. They may assume a parental role, defending their mothers from their fathers' abuse or providing younger siblings with support and reassurance, particularly during violent episodes (Jaffe et al., 1990).

One of the tasks that adolescents face is individuation from the family system. Due to the dysfunctional nature of a violent family system, however, this becomes a difficult if not impossible task for adolescents. The parentified adolescent may be concerned about who will take care of the family if he or she leaves. The assumption of a parental role frequently precludes the youth from having his or her own dependency needs met and may interfere with the development of a healthy sense of self, as well as the achievement of independence from parents.

Aggression

The relationship between witnessing interparental violence and acting aggressively has been substantiated by a number of empirical studies. Research also indicates that violent youth are more likely than nonviolent youth to have witnessed or been victims of violence in their homes (Kratcoski, 1985; Yexley, Borowsky, & Ireland, 2002). Modeling has been proposed as one means by which aggression develops (Bandura, 1973). Children from violent homes learn to imitate both the physical expression of anger and the types of problem-solving strategies evidenced by their parents, and thus develop aggressive behaviors and poor conflict resolution skills of their own. Physical aggression is often first directed at siblings and peers, and later used in their own families of procreation (Cornell & Gelles, 1982).

Rage

Like their mothers, adolescents from maritally violent homes may be the recipients of physical, sexual, and emotional abuse. A child growing up in such an abusive home may initially use denial to cope with his or her strong feelings. As the years progress and the violence increases, the feelings of pain and anger may increase in intensity to the point where they cannot be denied effectively. The adolescent may then become overwhelmed by anger and rage.

Since adolescents have a strong need to feel a sense of control over their surroundings, they may experience a deep sense of rage not only about the violence, but about their powerlessness to remedy the situation. They may also feel rage at their mothers for tolerating the abuse or staying in the marriage. Like their mothers, they may harbor fantasies and wishes that their father would somehow disappear or die. One 13-year-old boy who was residing at a battered women's shelter with his mother reported that after a particularly violent incident, he and his mother bought rat poison, ground it up, and served it to the batterer in his dinner.

Depression

Adolescents from violent homes are at high risk for depression and suicidal behavior (O'Keefe, 1996; Yexley, Borowsky, & Ireland, 2002). Many possible factors contribute to this. The adolescent's experience of interparental violence as a traumatic, uncontrollable, and pervasive stressor may lead to feelings of helplessness, apathy, and despair. Second, chronic or severe battering may result in the mother's psychological unavailability, lack of nurturance, or diminished parenting ability, that leaves the child or adolescent vulnerable to depression (Levendosky & Graham-Bermann, 2000). Third, the adolescent may experience the loss of the idealized and wished-for family, as well as the real loss of one parent, should a divorce take place.

Characteristic symptoms associated with depression in adolescents may include a loss of interest in activities, sluggishness, inability to concentrate, and/or changes in sleeping and eating patterns. He or she may be unable to set goals, achieve them, or feel a sense of satisfaction when they are achieved. Depression in the adolescent may also be manifested by displays of anger, as it is often the underlying emotion in the adolescent's acting out behaviors (Mishne, 1986).

Runaways

As children move into adolescence, they may become increasingly unwilling to live with the violence. Some may seek relief by running away from home. One study reported that witnessing interparental violence was an important predictor of runaway behaviors among adolescent females (Elze et a1., 1996). Another study found that adolescent males in residential placement facilities who had witnessed interparental violence were more likely to have run away from home than were males who had not witnessed such violence (Carlson, 1990). Although their unwillingness to live in an unhealthy situation may be viewed as a sign of strength, adolescent runaways are extremely vulnerable to other dangers, such as drug abuse, rape, pregnancy, and sexually transmitted diseases (Booth & Zhang, 1997; Greene, Ennett, & Ringwalt, 1997).

Delinquency

As children from violent homes move into adolescence, they may begin to engage in behaviors serious enough to come to the attention of the juvenile justice authorities. These behaviors may include substance abuse, truancy, gang involvement, assaults, robbery, use of weapons, setting fires, or other illegal activity (Herrenkohl et a1., 2000). Considering the lack of positive role models, it is not surprising to find the adolescent rebelling against authority figures.

Case Study: Jimmy

Jimmy, age 13, attended 8th grade at the local public school. He was the oldest of three children in an intact family. His sisters were ages 9 and 7. Jimmy's father worked as an accountant and his mother worked as a nurse. Jimmy was referred for treatment by his teacher due to a long-standing history of defiant behavior. His grades included C's and D's and had worsened considerably since 7th grade. Jimmy's acting out involved lying, stealing from peers, and extreme rudeness to all of his teachers. He would often disrupt the classroom with various pranks or by disturbing other students.

Jimmy was described by his teachers as socially isolated and unpopular due to his aggressive behavior. He spent most of his time alone. His mood was usually sullen and angry. He was also reported to "pick fights" with classmates which led to physical violence and injuries on the schoolyard. These led the principal to suspend Jimmy on two occasions.

During the intake session with Jimmy and his parents, marital tension was noticeable. His father was dominating and voiced loud, harsh statements about how Jimmy's behavior was not to be tolerated. He was openly critical of both Jimmy and Jimmy's mother. He blamed his wife for Jimmy's misbehavior because she was "too easy on him." Jimmy's mother appeared noticeably uncomfortable with her husband's manner and accusations, but said little.

Attempts by the clinician to address any difficulties between the parents were met with resistance by Jimmy's father. He insisted he was paying for therapy only to "get Jimmy to shape up…" He refused to participate in future sessions and made no ongoing contact with the therapist. Jimmy's mother assumed responsibility for bringing Jimmy in and occasionally discussed her difficulties disciplining Jimmy at home.

Jimmy formed a positive relationship with the therapist, who was a male in his mid-thirties. Jimmy eventually referred to the terrible shouting matches at home. However, Jimmy voiced high regard for his father and defended his angry outbursts. He continually made excuses for his father, referring to how hard his father worked to support the family, and all the bad breaks he had in life.

Jimmy's love and admiration for his father were the few emotions he voiced with any conviction. He idolized his father, despite his father's physical and verbal abuse of the entire family. Jimmy said little about his feelings about his mother, but regarded her as lazy and as a "bad wife." He blamed his mother for the fights that went on at home, stating she always provoked his father. He wished his parents would divorce so that he could live with his father.

Researchers have identified numerous family factors consistently associated with delinquency, including child physical abuse, interparental conflict, inconsistent and inappropriate discipline, maternal depression, and criminal behavior of parents (Herrenkohl et al., 2000). Many of these factors are also present in families in which domestic violence occurs. One researcher noted that violently delinquent adolescents almost always have another violent member in their family (Kratcoski, 1985).

Dating Violence

There are several unique aspects of adolescence that may make teenagers particularly vulnerable to dating violence. Because they are generally inexperienced in relationships, adolescents may have difficulty managing the complexity of feelings and conflicts that arise in intimate relationships. They may romanticize these relationships and interpret jealousy, possessiveness, and abuse as signs of love. Additionally, peer pressure may require that the adolescent have a boyfriend or girlfriend; the fear of being different or violating peer norms can create enormous stress and rigid conformity to gender role stereotypes. Finally, due to their struggle for independence or conflicts with parents, many adolescents may not ask for any help from adults to cope with conflict or frightening experiences in their dating relationships (Jackson, 2002).

Dating violence has been called a training ground for marital violence and is a link between witnessing violence in one's family of origin and using it in one's family of procreation (Jorgensen, 1986). Further, adolescents, particularly males, from violent homes have been found to be at increased risk for inflicting violence in dating relationships (O'Keefe, 1997). It has been postulated that the intergenerational transmission of violence may be the result of modeling aggressive parental behaviors, learning aggression as a coping or problem solving strategy, and increased frustration and sensitivity to power imbalances as a result of growing up in a coercive, conflictual, and low-warmth family environment (Langhinrichsen-Rohling & Neidig, 1995).

It should also be noted that whereas witnessing interparental violence may influence the later use of violence in dating relationships, it does not fully explain it. Other factors, such as being the victim of parental abuse, low socioeconomic status, poor self-esteem, acceptance of violence in dating relationships, exposure to violence in one's community, and having friends in violent relationships have been found to differentiate adolescents who inflicted violence in dating relationships from those who did not (Arriaga & Foshee, 2004; Malik, Sorenson, & Aneshensel, 1997; O'Keefe, 1998).

Vulnerability and Protective Factors

Not all children who grow up in maritally violent homes are behaviorally disturbed, nor do all become involved in abusive relationships in adolescence or adulthood. As-

Case Study: Lenny

Lenny, age 16, was one of four sons of a Spanish-speaking mother who was separated from her husband. Lenny's siblings were ages 13, 6, and 4. After 17 years of a severely abusive marriage, Lenny's mother left home and sought safety at a local shelter with her two younger children. Since adolescents were not admitted there, Lenny and his 13-year-old brother were placed at a crisis youth shelter. Services between the two sites were coordinated so that family sessions were possible.

Lenny was a soft-spoken, sensitive, and gentle young man. He was engaging, likeable, and communicated well. He maintained a realistic and mature view of people and the world. He never engaged in the power struggles with authority that were typical of many other adolescents at the shelter.

During the intake interview, Lenny relayed examples of the wife abuse he had witnessed. His father would reportedly not only beat his mother, but force her to dress like a prostitute. He would rarely allow her out of the house or to spend time with her family. The threats to harm or even kill his wife were frequently heard by all the children.

Lenny's role at home was that of a parentified child. He took pride in being the protector and caregiver to his mother and siblings. He was consistently focused on offering them reassurance, assistance, or affection. His adoration and high degree of concern for his mother was quite pronounced. One example was his attempt to hide the knife his father used when making threats.

Lenny's protective and caring manner was apparent at the shelter as well. He was often seen holding and kissing his younger brothers. During one incident in which another teenager argued with Lenny's brother, Lenny immediately ran to his brother's defense in an attempt to "rescue" him. He also enjoyed serving as the interpreter for his mother during family counseling sessions.

During another incident at the shelter, Lenny heard screaming from a resident and immediately jumped to offer assistance to staff. He mentioned in session that whenever he would hear conflict he would respond "automatically." He felt a sense of duty to be helpful by mediating.

In subsequent sessions with his counselor Lenny stated that he loved his father, but felt that his father was "really messed up." He voiced dismay that his mother didn't have the "husband she really deserved." Lenny also expressed his pervasive fear of his father, which did not abate during his shelter stay. He was concerned that despite the protection of the shelter, his father would eventually find and kill them.

sessing for the presence of both risk and protective factors is important in understanding the unique effects of violence exposure on child adjustment and for explaining why some children from violent homes appear to function well, while other children exhibit severe behavioral and emotional problems.

With regard to risk factors, child physical and sexual abuse are two forms of maltreatment that frequently co-exist in families with domestic violence (Edelson, 1999). In addition, there may be a multitude of other risk factors present including parental alcohol and drug use, high levels of verbal conflict, poverty, parental psychiatric disorders, and child neglect (Wolfe, 1997). It is likely that the combined effects of these stressors are cumulative; that is, those who experience multiple stressors are likely to have more behavioral problems.

Research also indicates that a high proportion of children from violent homes appear to be quite resilient (Hughes, Graham-Bermann, & Gruber, 2001). Factors associated with resiliency which mitigate the deleterious effects of exposure to interparental violence include: a positive child temperament (low emotionality and high sociability), positive feelings of self-worth, school competence, a positive relationship with the mother, and perceived social support (Levendosky, Huth-Bocks, & Semel, 2002; O'Keefe, 1994). Future research should explore these and other factors that may mediate or moderate the effects of exposure to interparental violence on child and adolescent adjustment.

Summary

The clinical and research literature confirm that witnessing interparental violence has numerous negative consequences for children's functioning. The vast majority of research has focused on preschool and school-age children, largely because younger children are more likely to stay with their mothers at battered women shelters and are thus more available as research participants. The emerging literature on adolescents demonstrates that growing up in maritally violent homes places them at high risk for social, emotional, and behavioral problems both in the short and long-term. In fact, adolescents may be a particularly vulnerable population since they may have witnessed interparental violence throughout their childhoods and the changes associated with this life stage may further add to their vulnerability. It is important for clinicians working with adolescents from violent homes to understand adolescents' reactions to the violence and ways in which exposure to interparental violence may impede their development. Clearly, intervention programs need to be developed which focus on helping adolescents heal from the trauma of witnessing violence as well as helping them develop skills for building healthy relationships.

Maura O'Keefe, M.S.W., Ph.D., is an Associate Professor at the USC School of Social Work. She has extensive clinical experience working with battered women and their children. Her research projects have included such topics as post-traumatic stress disorder in battered women, children of battered women, and battered women in prison. She is also interested in cross-cultural research and has conducted workshops on domestic violence in Hong Kong, Thailand, and Korea.

Shirley Lebovics, M.S.W., L.C.S.W., is a graduate of the USC School of Social Work. She is a full-time private practitioner with a specialty in domestic violence.

This article is adapted and updated from Maura O'Keefe and Shirley Lebovics (1998). Intervention and Treatment Strategies with Adolescents from Maritally Violent Homes. In A.R. Roberts (Ed.), Battered Women and Their Families: Intervention Strategies and Treatment Programs, 2nd Edition. New York: Springer Publishing. Used with permission from Springer Publishing Company, Inc., New York 10036.

References

Arriaga, X.B., & Foshee, V.A. (2004). Adolescent dating violence: Do adolescents follow in their friends: or their parents' footsteps? *Journal of Interpersonal Violence, 19*(2), 162-184.

Archer, J. (2002). Sex differences in physically aggressive acts between heterosexual partners: A meta-analytic review. *Aggression and Violent Behavior, 7,* 213-351.

Bandura, A. (1973). *Aggression: A Social Learning Analysis.* Englewood Cliffs, NJ: Prentice Hall.

Booth, R., & Zhang, Y. (1997). Conduct disorder and HIV risk behaviors among runaway and homeless adolescents. *Drug and Alcohol Dependence, 48,* 69-76.

Carlson, B.E. (1990). Adolescent observers of marital violence. *Journal of Family Violence, 5,* 285-299.

Cornell, C.P., & Gelles, R.J. (1982). Adolescent to parent violence. The *Urban and Social Change Review, 15,* 8-14.

Elze, D., Stiffman, A.R., & Dore, P. (1996). Family Violence as a Predictor of Runaway Behavior Among Adolescent Females. Paper presented at the First National Conference on Children Exposed to Family Violence, Austin, TX.

Edelson, J. (1999). Children's witnessing of adult domestic violence. *Journal of Interpersonal Violence, 14*(8),526-534.

Fantuzw, J.W., DePaola, L.M., Lambert, L., Martino, T., Anderson, G., & Sutton, S. (1991). Effects of interparental violence on the psychological adjustment and competencies of young children. *Journal of Consulting & Clinical Psychology, 59,* 258-265.

Graham-Bermann, S.A., & Levendosky, A.A. (1998). Traumatic stress symptoms in children of battered women. *Journal of Family Violence, 14,* 111-128.

Greene, J.M., Ennett, S.T., & Ringwalt, C.L. (1997). Substance use among runaway youths and homeless youths in three national samples. *American Journal of Public Health, 87,* 229-235.

Herrenkohl, T.I., Maguin, E., Hill, K.G., Hawkins, J.D., Abbott, R.D., & Catalano, R.F. (2000). Developmental risk factors for youth violence. *Journal of Adolescent Health, 26,* 176-186.

Herrera, V.M., & McCloskey, L.A. (2001). Gender differences in the risk for delinquency among youth exposed to family violence. *Child Abuse & Neglect, 25,* 1,037-1,051.

Hughes, H.M., Graham-Bermann, S.A., & Gruber, G. (2001). Resilience in children exposed to domestic violence. In S.A. Graham-Bermann & J.L. Edelson (Eds.), *Domestic Violence in the Lives of Children: The Future of Research, Intervention and Social Policy,* (pp. 67-91). Washington DC: American Psychological Association.

Jackson, S. (2002). Abuse in dating relationships: Young people's accounts of disclosure, non disclosure, help-seeking and prevention education. *New Zealand Journal of Psychology, 31*(2),79-89.

Jaffe, P., Wolfe, D., & Wilson, S.K. (1990). *Children of Battered Women.* Newbury Park, CA: Sage.

Jorgensen, S.R. (1986). *Marriage and the Family: Development and Change.* New York: MacMillan.

Kratcoski, P.C. (1985). Youth violence directed toward significant others. *Journal of Adolescence, 8,* 145-157.

Langhinrichsen-Rohling, I., & Neidig, P. (1995). Violent backgrounds of economically disadvantaged youth. Risk factors for perpetrating violence? *Journal of Family Violence, 19,* 243-261.

Levendosky, A.A., & Graham-Bermann, S.A. (2000). Behavioral observations of parenting in battered women. *Journal of Family Psychology, 14*(1), 80-94.

Levendosky, A.A., Huth-Bocks, A., & Semel, M.A. (2002). Adolescent peer relationships and mental health functioning in families with domestic violence. *Journal of Clinical and Child and Adolescent Psychology, 31*(3), 206-218.

Malik, S., Sorenson, S.B., & Aneshensel, C.S. (1997). Community and dating violence among adolescents: perpetation and victimization. *Journal of Adolescent Health, 21*(5),291-302.

McCloskey, L.A., & Lichter, E.L. (2003). The contribution of marital violence to adolescent aggression across different relationships. *Journal of Interpersonal Violence, 18*(4), 390-412.

McCloskey, L.A., & Walker, M. (2000). Posttraumatic stress in children exposed to family violence and single-event trauma. *Journal of the American Academy of Child & Adolescent Psychiatry, 39*(1), 108-115.

Mishne, I.M. (1986). *Clinical Work with Adolescents.* New York: The Free Press.

O'Keefe, M. (1994). Adjustment of children from maritally violent homes. *Families in Society, 75,* 403-415.

O'Keefe, M. (1996). The differential effects of family violence on adolescent adjustment. *Child and Adolescent Social Work Journal, 13,* 51-68.

O'Keefe, M. (1997). Predictors of dating violence among high school students. *Journal of Interpersonal Violence, 12,* 546-568.

O'Keefe, M. (1998). Factors mediating the link between witnessing interparental violence and dating violence. *Journal of Family Violence, 13*(1), 39-57.

Reitzel-Jaffe, D., & Wolfe, D.A. (2001). Predictors of relationship abuse among young men. *Journal of Interpersonal Violence, 16,* 99-115.

Renzetti, C., & Wiley, C. (1996). *Violence in Gay and Lesbian Domestic Partnerships.* Newbury Park, CA: Sage.

Rossman, B.B. (2001). Longer term effects of children's exposure to domestic violence. In S.A. Graham-Bermann & J.L. Edelson (Eds.), *Domestic Violence in the Lives of Children: The Future of Research, Intervention and Social Policy,* (pp. 35-67). Washington, DC: American Psychological Association.

Spaccarelli, S., Coatsworth, I.D., & Bowden, D.S. (1995). Exposure to serious family violence among incarcerated boys: Its association with violent offending and potential mediating variables. *Violence & Victims, 10*(3), 163-182.

Straus, M.A. (1991). *Children as Witness to Marital Violence: A Risk Factor for Life-Long Problems Among a Nationally Representative Sample of American Men and Women.* Paper presented at the Ross Roundtable titled "Children and Violence," Washington DC.

Wolfe, D.A. (1997). Children exposed to marital violence. In O.W. Barnett, C.L. Miller-Perrin, & R.D. Perrin (Eds.), *Family Violence Across the Lifespan* (pp. 136-157). Thousand Oaks, CA: Sage.

Yexley, M., Borowsky, I., & Ireland, M. (2002). Correlation between different experiences of intrafamilial physical violence and violent adolescent behavior. *Journal of Interpersonal Violence, 17*(7), 707-720.

As seen in *Prevention Researcher,* February 2005, pp. 3-7, originally from *Battered Women and Their Families,* 2e, 1998. Copyright © 1998 and 2005 by Springer Publishing Company, Inc., New York 10036. Adapted by permission.

Who's Killing Kids' Sports?

David Oliver Relin

Two years ago, when he was still in high school, pro basketball prospect LeBron James inked an endorsement contract with Nike worth between $90 million and $100 million. Five days later, the $1 million contract Nike offered to Maryland soccer prodigy Freddy Adu seemed almost ordinary, except for one detail—Freddy was just 13 years old.

In the summer of 2003, Jeret Adair, a 15-year-old pitcher from Atlanta, started 64 games with his elite traveling baseball team—more than most pro players pitch in an entire season. After the ligament in his elbow snapped, he had to undergo reconstructive surgery, a process once reserved for aging professional pitchers. In 2004, his doctor, James Andrews, performed similar surgery on 50 other high school pitchers.

Last March, Valerie Yianacopolus of Wakefield, Mass., was sentenced to one year of probation, including 50 hours of community service, and ordered to watch a sportsmanship video after she was found guilty of assaulting an 11-year-old boy who was cheering for the opposing team at her son's Little League game.

And in June, according to state police, Mark Downs, the coach of a youth T-ball team near Uniontown, Pa., allegedly offered one of his players $25 to throw a baseball at the head of a 9-year-old disabled teammate so the injured boy wouldn't be able to play in an upcoming game. League rules mandate that every healthy child play at least three innings. "The coach was very competitive," said State Trooper Thomas B. Broadwater. "He wanted to win."

A Sports Culture Run Amok

Across the country, millions of children are being chewed up and spit out by a sports culture run amok. With pro scouts haunting the nation's playgrounds in search of the next LeBron or Freddy, parents and coaches are conspiring to run youth-sports leagues like incubators for future professional athletes. Prepubescent athletes are experimenting with performance-enhancing drugs. Doctors are reporting sharp spikes in injuries caused by year-round specialization in a single sport at an early age. And all too often, the simple pleasure of playing sports is being buried beneath cutthroat competition.

"If I had to sum up the crisis in kids' sports," says J. Duke Albanese, Maine's former commissioner of education, "I'd do it in one word—adults."

Some adults, Albanese says, are pushing children toward unrealistic goals like college sports scholarships and pro contracts. According to National Collegiate Athletic Association (NCAA) statistics, fewer than 2% of high school athletes will ever receive a college athletic scholarship. Only one in 13,000 high school athletes will ever receive a paycheck from a professional team.

"There is a terrible imbalance between the needs kids have and the needs of the adults running their sports programs," says Dr. Bruce Svare, director of the National Institute for Sports Reform. "Above all, kids need to have fun. Instead, adults are providing unrealistic expectations and crushing pressure."

> ## "If I had to sum up the crisis in kids' sports, I'd do it in one word—adults."
> —J. Duke Albanese, Sports Done Right

As a result, Svare says, at a time when an epidemic of obesity is plaguing the nation's youth, 70% of America's children are abandoning organized sports by age 13. "The only way to reverse this crisis," Svare argues, "is to fundamentally rethink the way America's kids play organized sports."

Is Change Possible?

Many communities *are* trying to change the way they approach children's sports. Florida's Jupiter-Tequesta Athletic Association, facing a rash of violent behavior by sports parents, now requires them to take an online course on how to behave at their children's athletic events. School officials in Connecticut, concerned about the toll of too much focus on a single sport, instituted a statewide ban on students playing on a private travel team during the same season they play their sport in high school.

But no reform effort is more aggressive than that of the state of Maine, where educators, student athletes and others have teamed up to launch a counterrevolution called Sports Done Right. Led by J. Duke Albanese and Robert Cobb, dean of the University of Maine's College of Education, and funded by a federal grant secured by U.S. Sen. Susan M. Collins, the project aims to radically remake Maine's youth-sports culture and provide a model that the rest of America might emulate.

The Maine Challenge

Their first step is a sweeping campaign to dial down the kind of competition that leads many kids to drop out of sports at an early age. "I was a high school football coach—I know how badly communities want their teams to win," Albanese says. "We're not saying there's anything wrong with competition. We're saying what's appropriate at the varsity level is out of bounds in grade school and middle school. That's a time to encourage as many children as possible to play. Period."

To do that, the Sports Done Right team held statewide summit meetings before producing an action plan. It chose 12 school districts as the program's pilot sites, but so many other districts clamored to participate that it is now under way in dozens more.

The program has identified core principles that it insists must be present in a healthy sports environment for kids, including good sportsmanship, discouragement of early specialization and the assurance that teams below the varsity level make it their mission to develop the skills of every child on every team, to promote a lifelong involvement with sports.

Sports Done Right's second task is to attack the two problems it says are most responsible for the crisis in kids' sports—the behavior of parents and coaches.

Problem #1: Out-of-Control Adults

The behavior of adults has been at the center of the debate about reforming kids' sports ever since 2002, when Thomas Junta of Reading, Mass., was convicted of beating Michael Costin

to death during an argument at their sons' youth hockey practice. "I've watched adult civility in youth sports spiral downward since the early 1990s," says Doug Abrams, a law professor at the University of Missouri, who has tracked media reports of out-of-control sports parents for more than a decade. "At one time, adults who acted like lunatics were shunned as outcasts. But today, they are too often tolerated."

The nearly 100 Maine students PARADE interviewed recited a litany of incidents involving adults behaving badly, including examples of their own parents being removed from sporting events by police. Nate Chantrill, 17—a shot-putter and discus thrower at Edward Little High School in Auburn and a varsity football player—volunteers to coach a coed fifth-grade football team. "One game, a parent flipped out that we didn't start his daughter," Chantrill recalls. "He was screaming, using bad language and saying she's the best player out there. Parents take this stuff way too seriously. Fifth-grade football is not the Super Bowl. It's a place for your kid to learn some skills and have fun. One parent can ruin it for all the kids."

That's why each Sports Done Right district is holding training sessions to define out-of-bounds behavior at sporting events and requiring the parents of every student who plays to sign a compact promising to abide by higher standards of sportsmanship.

Problem #2: Poor Coaching

Dan Campbell, who has coached Edward Little's track team to two state championships, says he sees too many of his peers pressing to win at all costs and neglecting their primary responsibility—to educate and inspire children. "One coach can destroy a kid for a lifetime," he says. "I've seen it over and over."

"I was at an AAU basketball game where the ref gave the coach a technical and threw him out of the game," says Doug Joerss, who was starting center on Cony High

---

How To Be a Good Sports Parent

Fixing the crisis in kids' sports begins at home. Here are some tips from Sports Done Right to get parents started:

- **Encourage your child,** regardless of his or her degree of success or level of skill.
- **Ensure a balance** in your student athlete's life, encouraging participation in multiple sports and activities while placing academics first.
- **Emphasize enjoyment,** development of skills and team play as the cornerstones of your child's early sports experiences while reserving serious competition for the varsity level.
- **Leave coaching to coaches** and avoid placing too much pressure on your youngster about playing time and performance.
- **Be realistic** about your child's future in sports, recognizing that only a select few earn a college scholarship, compete in the Olympics or sign a professional contract.
- **Be there** when your child looks to the sidelines for a positive role model.

School's basketball team. "Then the coach swung at the ref. The kids ended up on the floor, getting into a huge brawl. You look up to coaches. Kids think, 'If it's OK for them to do it, it's OK for me to do it.'"

A campaign to improve the quality of coaching is at the center of Sports Done Right. "The most powerful mentors kids have are coaches," J. Duke Albanese says. "Coaches don't even realize the extent of their influence." He disparages the national trend to offer coaches salary incentives based on their won-lost records. Instead, Sports Done Right recommends compensation based on their level of training. And each pilot school district is encouraged to send coaches to continuing-education classes in subjects like leadership and child psychology.

Exporting Good Sense

Educators in 30 states have requested more information from

Sports Done Right. "We think a small place like Maine is a perfect place to get kids' sports culture under control," says Albanese. "And if we can do that, maybe we can export the good sense Maine is famous for to the rest of the country."

An example of that good sense recently occurred at a Sports Done Right pilot site. "An influential parent, a guy who volunteers to coach sixth-grade basketball, wanted the kids divided into an A and a B team, so he could coach just the elite kids," says Stephen Rogers, the principal of Lyman Moore Middle School. "I said we weren't going to separate the kids and discourage half of them. We were going to encourage all of our interested kids to play."

"But we won't win the championship," the parent complained.

"I don't really care," Rogers replied. "We're not talking about the Celtics. We're talking about sixth-graders."

UNIT 6

Peers and Contemporary Culture

Unit Selections

Key Points to Consider

- What behaviors are considered to be "risk-taking" behaviors? What can be done to help reduce these problems?

- What factors influence teen drinking? How does drinking relate to teen mortality?

- Does media exposure to terrorism influence teens' emotional distress?

Student Website

www.mhcls.com/online

Internet References

Further information regarding these websites may be found in this book's preface or online.

Higher Education Center for Alcohol and Other Drug Prevention
http://www.edc.org/hec/

Justice Information Center (NCJRS): Drug Policy Information
http://www.ncjrs.org/drgswww.html

National Clearinghouse for Alcohol and Drug Information
http://www.health.org/

Adolescents are without a doubt more peer-oriented than any other age group. But it is simplistic to assume that peer influence is always negative and that it outweighs parental influence. Research demonstrates that the nature of the parent-child relationship is consistently the best predictor of adolescent psychological health and well-being. Adolescents who have poor relationships with their parents are precisely the adolescents who are most susceptible to negative peer influences. Poor parent-adolescent relationships are not the norm during the pubertal years, but, rather, conflicted relationships more likely represent a continuation of poor family relationships from childhood.

Research also indicates that most adolescents feel close to and respect their parents. Most adolescents share their parents' values, especially when it comes to moral, religious, political, and educational values. The school the adolescent attends, the kind of neighborhood the parents live in, whether the parents attend religious services, and what parents do for a living all influence their children. Parental choices such as these have a definite impact on their children for the network of friends they select.

Several factors have contributed to the misconception that adolescents reject their parents in favor of peers. First, peers play a greater role in the adolescent's day-to-day activities, style of dress, and musical tastes than do parents. Second, parents often confuse the adolescent's struggle for autonomy with rebellion. G. Stanley Hall's views of adolescence as a biologically necessary time of "storm and stress" contributed to this confusion as well. Similarly, Anna Freud, arguing from her father's psychoanalytic tradition and her own experience with troubled adolescents, maintained that the adolescent-parent relationship is highly laden with conflicts causing adolescents to turn to their peers. According to Anna Freud, such conflicts ensure a successful resolution of the Oedipus/Electra complex. This model of intense parent-adolescent conflict has not been empirically supported and can be detrimental if parents fail to seek help because they believe intense conflict is "normal" during adolescence.

Another myth about peer influence during adolescence is that it is primarily negative. As Thomas Berndt discusses in his research, peer influence is mutual and has both positive and negative effects. Peer pressure is rarely coercive, as is popularly envisaged. It is a more subtle process where adolescents influence their friends and the friends influence them. Just as adults do, adolescents choose friends who already have similar interests, attitudes, and beliefs.

Until recently, researchers paid little attention to the positive effects of peers on adolescent development. Among other things, friends help adolescents develop role-taking and social skills, conquer the imaginary audience referred to in the last unit, and act as social supports in stressful situations. Although they decry peer pressure as an influence on their children, no thinking parents would want their son or daughter to be a social outcast without friends.

Another misconception about peer relations is that teen culture is a unified culture with a single way of thinking and acting. A visit to any secondary school today will reveal the variety of teen cultures that exist. The formation of peer groups and adolescent crowds is partly a function of a school structure and school activities. As in past decades, one can find jocks, populars, brains, delinquents, and nerds. One would also encounter members of today's grunge and body-piercing crowds. Media attention is often drawn toward bizarre or antisocial groups further contributing to the myth that peer influence is primarily negative.

Music is very much a part of youth culture, although there is no universal type of music liked by all adolescents. One way adolescents have always tried to differentiate themselves from adults has been though music. On the other hand, today, adults are concerned that music, movies, and television have gone too far in the quest for ever-more shocking and explicit sexual and violent content. Widespread and easy access to the Internet has also compounded concerns about the types of material today's adolescents are exposed to.

In addition to school and leisure activities like sports, today adolescents spend considerable time in the part-time work force. Work has usually been seen as a positive influence on adolescent development. Society points to the positive outcomes of developing responsibility and punctuality, knowledge of the working world, and appreciating the value of money. Research does corroborate the existence of the positive effects of work, but adolescents have been spending an increasing number of hours in the work force. Recent studies find that adolescents who work over 20 hours per week are more involved in drug use and delinquent activity, have more psychological and physical complaints, and perform more poorly in school. Although there may be a tendency for adolescents who are predisposed toward such behaviors to be disengaged from school and, therefore, work more in the first place, longitudinal data suggest that working exacerbates these tendencies.

The first article in this unit discusses risk-taking behavior among adolescents that sometimes results in risky business. The author provides the readers with teaching techniques to help the teacher work with these teens.

The next two articles are on the topic of adolescent use of alcohol. The influences of peers, family, school, and religion is explored. All of these influences are of major importance. Alcohol use among adolescents is a growing problem. The last article speaks of emotional distress associated with media exposure to terrorism.

Risky Business: Exploring Adolescent Risk-Taking Behavior

Tammy Jordan Wyatt, Fred L. Peterson

Ongoing behavioral research has documented the growing prevalence of adolescent health risk behaviors, such as tobacco use, sexual activity, alcohol and other substance use, nutritional behavior, physical inactivity, and intentional injury.[1] Newer youth risk behaviors, such as pathological gambling, are emerging as threats to public health.[2] Risk, risk taking, and risk behavior are important and relevant topics for exploring in health education classes. The goal of health educators, teachers, administrators, and parents alike should be to encourage youth to engage in constructive risk-taking behavior rather than alternative destructive behavior.

Risk has been defined as any action where the opportunity exists for success as well as some possibility for failure.[3] Risk taking can be defined as the participation in potentially health-compromising activities with little understanding of, or in spite of an understanding of, the potential negative consequences. The behavior is volitional, has an uncertain outcome (either positive or negative), and results from an interplay between the biopsychosocial processes of adolescence and the environment.[4] Risk taking is essential for positive growth and maturation. Risk taking may come in many forms such as physical, social, emotional, psychological, and financial. The challenge is to channel youth risk taking into positive, health-enhancing experiences and to provide realistic alternative options to destructive behavior. Constructive risk taking is an essential tool in the life of an adolescent. It allows for discovery and establishment of one's identity. Constructive risk taking is health enhancing in nature and may result in positive outcomes. Constructive risk-taking behavior includes activities that fulfill the need for thrill seeking that are healthy and legal. Examples of constructive risk taking include outdoor physical activities such as wilderness hiking and camping, swimming, bicycling, riding a motorcycle, or rock climbing; volunteer community service that is spiritually uplifting but also challenging such as working at an urban homeless shelter; and choosing to serve in a leadership role as an officer in an extracurricular organization. Risk taking only becomes destructive or negative when the risks are dangerous. Positive risks, often referred to as challenges, can turn negative risks in a more health-enhancing direction or prevent them from ever occurring. However, a key to enhancing involvement in constructive risk taking is the ability for young people to assess risks throughout one's lifetime. Youth need guidance, support, and opportunities to explore their values and attitudes regarding the risk-taking activities that they may face on a daily basis. Helping an adolescent understand and define his or her own risk taking is critical to risk assessment. Questions adolescents should ask themselves regarding various risk-taking activities include the following: What are the potential negative risks? What are the potential benefits? Do the benefits outweigh the dangers? Does this activity put others or me in danger? Is there a safe and enjoyable way to engage in this activity[5]

Lesson Objectives

Following completion of Risky Business, students will be able to

1. Understand the concepts of risk, risk behavior, and risk taking.
2. Review different risk behaviors and rank order them according to importance.
3. Identify positive alternative risk behaviors to the risk behaviors portrayed.
4. Engage in risk-assessment thinking skills.

National Health Education Standards

1. Students will demonstrate the ability to practice health-enhancing behaviors and reduce health risks.
2. Students will demonstrate the ability to use interpersonal communication skills to enhance health.
3. Students will demonstrate the ability to use goal-setting and decision-making skills to enhance health.[6]

After introducing and providing concrete examples of the concepts of risk, risk behavior, and risk taking, the instructor will begin the Risky Business learning activity.

Materials and Resources

Each student will need a plain sheet of 8.5 × 11-inch paper cut into 12 equal pieces of any shape and a pen/pencil.

Grade Level/Subject Area

This lesson may be used with middle school, high school, and/or college-aged students. The technique can be modified to fit the age and maturity level of different groups. For example, some characters and definitions may be omitted or modified for age appropriateness. Total time needed to facilitate the activity will vary with the age of the audience. The activity requires about 30-45 minutes to complete.

Activity and Strategies

Inform students that no talking, discussion, or remarks will be allowed during the initial stage of the activity. Provide each student a plain sheet of 8.5 × 11-inch paper. Instruct students to tear the paper into 12 equal pieces of any shape. Inform students that "I will state a character name and ask that you print that name on one piece of paper. I will then give you a definition, which is related to the character. Put the character name on the paper and the definition in your head. Don't worry; the definitions will be easy to remember. I will then state a second character name and its definition. Place that name only on the second piece of paper and keep its definition in your head. We will continue this process until all 12 characters have been identified and defined." Figure 1 lists the character names used in this activity as well as the definitions of each character. While stating each character name, it may prove beneficial to write the name on a chalkboard or dry erase board so students see the name as they hear it. Once all 12 characters and definitions have been stated, repeat them to refresh each student's memory of the various definitions.

Part 1: Individual Rankings

Instruct students to rank each character from most important to least important. Once each character has been ranked, have the students list them on paper from 1 to 12. Again, with 1 being most important and 12 being least important. Students will ask what is meant by most and least important. State that they should decide what most and least important means to them.

Part 2: Small Group Rankings

Once students have their own ranking, divide the class into groups of 4-5. Using only discussion (not voting), have each group come up with a consensus or group ranking. This should take approximately 15 minutes. Tell each group that a spokesperson for their group will present to the class their rankings as well as their reasons for those rankings of most to least important. Each group should be given approximately 5-10 minutes to present group rankings and reasons for those rankings. Each group should be able to justify the rankings based on discussions that occurred in the group process as well as the manner in which the rankings were made. Similarly, each group should state its definition of most and least important. While each group discusses the group rankings, place them in order on the chalk/dry erase board, allowing the class to compare the rankings of each small group.

Figure 1
List of Activity Characters and Definitions

Character	Definition
Safer Sex	14-year-old is sexually active and uses condoms correctly and consistently 100% of time.
Hetero	College freshman engages in unprotected sex with multiple partners of opposite gender.
Fight	High school basketball player injures teammate in physical fight after a game.
Thin	Eighth-grade student uses starvation and exercise as a means of weight control.
Blunt	16-year-old smokes 1-2 marijuana joints on weekends.
Drive	High school senior rides in car with classmate who has been drinking alcohol.
Cut	Middle school student engages in self-mutilation (cutting) to ease pain and depression.
Scream	Seventh-grade student regularly verbally abuses classmates.
Homo	High school student engages in oral sex with same-sex partners but uses barrier methods 100% of the time.
Binge	College student regularly binge drinks on weekends with friends.
Goth	15-year-old wears black clothing, is obsessed with death, and has multiple tattoos and body piercings.
Feel	Middle school student is overweight and eats excessively large amounts of food when feeling sad or depressed.

Part 3: Large Group Discussion

After the groups have presented their rankings, return the class to their individual seats for a class discussion. Figure 2 contains questions designed to summarize and bring closure to this activity. Comparisons of the small group rankings and definitions of most and least important should be discussed. Elaboration into the differences among group rankings and definitions should occur, noting that differences in definitions are analogous to differences in opinion, ideas, etc. Encourage students to discuss any problems that occurred during the group process regarding coming to a consensus. Elaboration on teamwork and group dynamics may be necessary.

Within the large group setting, ask students to visualize each character. Repeating the definitions of each may be necessary. Ask each student to state the gender of each character. Note that each definition is purposely written in a non–gender specific manner. It is here that prejudices or biases may emerge. Ask students to elaborate on any perceptions, prejudices, and biases that may have influenced the rankings.

Figure 2
Activity Discussion Questions

- How did you proceed to rank these characters?
- How did you define "most important" and "least important"?
- Did you have any problems coming to a consensus regarding the rankings?
- What gender are each of these characters?
- We each have perceptions, prejudices, and biases. How did these interfere with the communication within your group?
- Risk assessment questions for each character's behavior
  What are the potential negative risks?
  What are the potential benefits?
  Do the benefits outweigh the dangers?
  Does this activity put others or myself in danger?
  Is there a way to engage in this activity that is enjoyable and safe?
  What positive alternative behaviors might you suggest for replacing the risk behaviors exhibited by the characters?

Finally, use the following questions to conduct a risk assessment for each character: What are the potential negative risks to this behavior? What are the potential benefits? Do the benefits outweigh the dangers? Does this activity put others or myself at risk? Is there a safe and enjoyable way to engage in this activity? What are alternative constructive risk-taking activities for each of the 12

characters that would provide the same physiological, psychosocial, and emotional outcomes?

Although this activity can be completed in 1 class period, it may be useful to continue the discussion of risk, risk behavior, and risk taking in a follow-up period to reinforce concepts and facilitate understanding of the role of risk taking in one's life.

References

1. Centers for Disease Control and Prevention. Surveillance summaries, May 21, 2004. *MMWR.* 2004;53(SS-2):1-29.
2. Dickson L, Derevensky JL, Gupta R. The prevention of youth gambling problems: a conceptual model. *J Gambl Stud.* 2002;18(2):97-160.
3. Peterson F. The nuts and bolts of adolescent risk-taking behavior: a primer for Texas school health professionals. *Tex Sch Health Brief.* 2002; April:6-8.
4. Irwin CE, Jr., Millstein SG. Biopsychosocial correlates of risk-taking behaviors during adolescence. Can the physician intervene? *J Adolesc Health Care.* 1986;7(suppl 6):82S-96S.
5. Ponton L. *The Romance of Risk—Why Teenagers Do the Things They Do.* New York, NY: Basic Books; 1997.
6. The Joint Committee on National Health Education Standards. *National Health Education Standards: Achieving Health Literacy.* Atlanta, Ga: American Cancer Society; 1995.

Tammy Jordan Wyatt, PhD, *Assistant Professor, (tammy.wyatt@utsa.edu), Health Education, Department of Health and Kinesiology, University of Texas at San Antonio, 6900 North Loop 1604 West, San Antonio, TX 78249; and* **Fred L. Peterson, PhD,** *Associate Professor, (fpeterson@ mail.utexas.edu), Child, Adolescent, and School Health, Department of Kinesiology and Health Education, University of Texas at Austin, Bellmont Hall 222, 2100 San Jacinto Blvd, Austin, TX 78712.*

Family, Religious, School, and Peer Influences on Adolescent Alcohol Use

W. Alex Mason, Ph.D., and Michael Windle, Ph.D.

The family plays a primary socializing role in the lives of boys and girls. The quality of relationships within the family is a particularly important element in the development of adolescent behaviors. A great deal of research demonstrates that family interactions characterized by parental nurturance, warmth, and social support reduce adolescents' risk for involvement in a variety of problem behaviors, including alcohol use and abuse. Of course there are other important socializing influences during adolescence. Peer relationships, in particular, become more influential during this developmental period, and peers can have a potent impact on the alcohol use of teens. The influence of the school is important as well. An individual's response to the socializing influence of the school has important consequences for the development of problem behaviors in adolescence. Attitudes and behaviors that reflect low commitment to school (e.g., academic failure, dislike for school, low educational aspirations) can increase the likelihood that an adolescent will initiate and maintain the use of alcohol. Also, investigators have recognized increasingly that religion can have an impact on the attitudes and behaviors of youth. A sense of religious commitment and sentiment (often referred to more generally as religiosity) is associated with decreased risk for alcohol use among adolescents.

Few studies of adolescent alcohol use have examined simultaneously the complex relationships that exist among family, religious, school, and peer influences. Toward this end, one goal of this study was to develop a better understanding of the ways in which the family affects alcohol use among youth. In addition to direct effects, the family may have indirect effects on adolescent alcohol use through the secondary socializing influences of peers, school, and religion. For example, boys and girls who have close and supportive relationships within the family may tend to associate with non-drinking peers, which may decrease their risk for alcohol use. Whether the effect is direct or indirect, it is evident that family relationships influence adolescent alcohol use. However, it is also likely that alcohol use among youth affects (i.e., diminishes) the quality of family interactions. Drinking may also result in increased association with alcohol-using peers, as well as decreased academic performance and religiosity. A second goal of this study was to examine possible feedback or reciprocal effects of adolescent alcohol use on the family and on the socializing influences of peers, school, and religion.

Method

We analyzed longitudinal survey data collected from 840 mid-adolescent boys (n = 443) and girls (n = 397) attending a large, suburban (non-parochial) school district in western New York. Beginning in the fall of the 1988-1989 academic year, data were collected using a four-wave design with 6-month intervals between surveys. The average age at the first wave of data collection was 15.5 years. The sample was predominantly white (98.5%) and middle class, and the majority (74%) of participants were Catholic. Adolescents provided information about their own alcohol use, as well as about the alcohol use of their close friends. The surveys also included a self-report measure of family social support and questions regarding school performance (i.e., grade point average) and religiosity (i.e., importance of religion and frequency of church attendance). The content of the surveys varied somewhat at each of the four waves of data collection. In this study, family social support was measured at Times 1 and 3, and all other variables were measured at Times 2 and 4. We tested the plausibility of a model that hypothesized that family social support would be related to later adolescent alcohol use both directly and indirectly, through the peer, school, and religion variables (first aim of the study). The model also hypothesized that adolescent alcohol use would be related, in turn, to later family social support, as well as to later religiosity, peer alcohol use, and school grades (second aim of the study).

Results

Results showed that the hypothesized model was plausible. Figure 3.1 presents a diagram of the statistically significant paths. The coefficients reported in the figure are standardized and can range from –1.0 to 1.0. Values close to –1.0

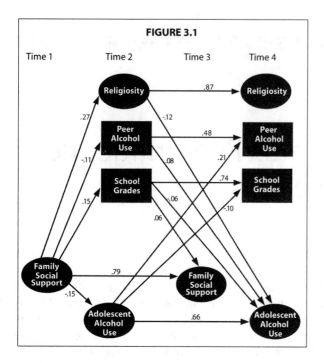

FIGURE 3.1

indicate a strong negative relationship between variables, values close to 1.0 indicate a strong positive relationship; and values close to zero indicate a weak or nonexistent relationship. As the figure illustrates, family social support measured at Time 1 was associated positively with religiosity and school grades at Time 2, and negatively with peer and adolescent alcohol use at Time 2. The associations among these variables were moderate in strength.

Each of the Time 2 variables was associated, in turn, with self-reported adolescent alcohol use at Time 4. The significant positive path leading from Time 2 to Time 4 adolescent alcohol use indicates that alcohol use was relatively stable over time; an adolescent who reported a high level of alcohol use at Time 2 tended to report a high level of alcohol use at Time 4, relative to other adolescents in the study. Among the remaining Time 2 variables, religiosity was the strongest predictor of Time 4 alcohol use. The negative value of this path estimate indicates that a high level of religiosity was associated with less alcohol use over time. Better school grades at Time 2 were associated also with less alcohol use at Time 4. Having close friends who drink alcohol was associated with more alcohol use over time.

Family interactions characterized by parental nurturance, warmth, and social support reduce adolescents' risk for involvement in a variety of problem behaviors, including alcohol use and abuse.

Adolescents who reported a high level of family social support at Time 1 also tended to report a high level of family social support at Time 3. School grades measured at Time 2 were associated with family social support measured at Time 3. More specifically, better school grades predicted an increase in family social support; however, this was not a strong relationship.

We also examined the effects of alcohol use measured at Time 2 on religiosity, school grades, and peer alcohol use measured at Time 4. Alcohol use at Time 2 predicted an increase in association with peers who use alcohol and a decrease in school grades over time. Contrary to expectations, adolescent alcohol use measured at Time 2 was not associated with a reduction in religiosity at Time 4, nor was it associated with a reduction in family social support at Time 3.

Discussion

This study demonstrates that the family, the school, religion, and peers play prominent roles in the alcohol use of adolescent boys and girls. The influence of the family was both direct and indirect. We found that perceived family social support at Time 1 had a direct, negative association with adolescent alcohol use at Time 2. Family social support predicted lower levels of alcohol use among the participants over time. In addition, family social support at Time 1 indirectly predicted reduced adolescent alcohol use at Time 4 through the religion, school, and peer variables.

The family, the school, religion, and peers play prominent roles in the alcohol use of adolescent boys and girls.

Interestingly, religion was especially important in the link between family social support and adolescent alcohol use. Boys and girls who reported having emotionally close and supportive families were more likely to be religiously committed over time than youth from less supportive families. Furthermore, religiosity was associated with reductions in adolescent alcohol use. These findings indicate that the family provides an important social context for the development of adolescent religiosity and that religious commitment, in turn, reduces risk for alcohol use among teens.

Findings indicated also that family socialization is related to adolescent alcohol use, in part, through a process of peer selection. We found that family social support was directly and negatively related to peer alcohol use. Mid-adolescent boys and girls from supportive families tended to associate with non-alcohol-using peers. In turn, such associations reduced alcohol use during late adolescence. In addition to the effects of peer alcohol use on adolescent alcohol use, we found that drinking was positively related to association with alcohol-using peers. This finding indicates that peer and adolescent alcohol use may be related reciprocally: teens who drink alcohol tend to increase their associations with peers who drink, which, in turn, tends to increase their own alcohol use.

The measure of school grades also played an important role in linking family social support with adolescent alcohol use. A high level of perceived family social support was associated over time with self-reports of better grades; in turn, better grades were associated with reduced alcohol consumption. In addition to the effects of school grades on adolescent drinking, we found that alcohol use was associated with lower school grades over time. Taken together, these findings suggest a process in which low school performance increases risk for alcohol use which, in turn, decreases school performance.

It is important to note that participants in this study were predominantly white, middle class, and Catholic. Thus, additional studies are needed to determine whether or not the current findings generalize to adolescents of varying racial and ethnic backgrounds, as well as to boys and girls affiliated with other religions traditions. Nevertheless, this study contributes to the literature by examining the complex relationships that exist among family, religious, school, and peer influences on adolescent alcohol use. The findings have implications for the development of effective preventive interventions by suggesting that programs should be multifaceted and targeted at multiple domains of influence in adolescents' lives. In this regard, family-based programs that incorporate intervention components focused on peers and schools may offer the most promise. Such programs would benefit as well from a consideration of the value that many adolescents and their families place on religion and spirituality. As a whole, the findings of this study illustrate the importance of moving beyond the mere identification of risk and protective factors for adolescent alcohol use to a deeper understanding of the processes or mechanisms through which such factors have their effects.

W. Alex Mason, Ph.D., is with the Social Development Research Group at the University of Washington. *Michael Windle, Ph.D.,* is professor of Psychology at the University of Alabama at Birmingham. This study was supported by National Institute of Alcohol Abuse and Alcoholism Grant No. R37-AA0786l awarded to Michael Windle.

This article is condensed, with permission, from W.A. Mason and M. Windle (2001). Family, religious, school, and peer influences on adolescent alcohol use: A longitudinal study. Journal of Studies on Alcohol, 62,44-53. Copyright by Alcohol Research Documentation, Inc. Rutgers Center of Alcohol Studies, Piscataway, NJ 08854.

Alcohol Use Among Adolescents

Michael Windle, Ph.D.

Adolescent alcohol use is statistically normative behavior in the United States. By their senior year of high school, the vast majority of adolescents have drunk alcohol at some point in their lifetime, with a substantial subset of adolescents drinking at high levels and experiencing a range of serious alcohol-related problems. On the basis of national survey data, the occurrence of a heavy drinking episode (i.e., having five or more drinks on a single occasion) was reported by about 25% of tenth graders and 30% of twelfth graders, and the average age of alcohol use initiation (or first drink) has decreased from 17.8 years in 1987 to 15.9 years in 1996. Alcohol use among teens has been associated with the three most common forms of adolescent mortality: accidental deaths (such as fatal automobile or boat crashes), homicides, and suicides. On average, eight adolescents a day in the U.S. die in alcohol-related automobile crashes, and nine out of ten teenage automobile accidents involve the use of alcohol. With a national school sample, suicide attempts were 3 to 4 times more likely among heavy drinking adolescents relative to abstainers.

In addition, alcohol use among adolescents is significantly associated with a range of other health-compromising behaviors. Higher levels of alcohol use are associated with more frequent, often unprotected, sexual activity among adolescents, which poses increased risk for teen pregnancy and sexually transmitted diseases, including potentially life-threatening diseases such as HIV. An earlier onset of alcohol use and higher levels of use among adolescents have also been associated with poorer academic functioning and higher rates of school dropout.

Adolescent Alcohol-Related Behaviors

The systematic, large-scale study of adolescent alcohol-related behaviors (for example alcohol use, alcohol problems, binge drinking episodes) is, historically and scientifically speaking, a relatively recent phenomenon. Among the most long-standing and well-known U.S. national studies of adolescent substance use (including alcohol use) is the Monitoring the Future Studies (MFS), which were initiated circa 1975 to provide national surveillance data on adolescent substance use practices. The MFS has provided annual national surveys of adolescent substance use practices and associated attitudes about various features of substance use (such as perceived harmfulness, perceived avail-

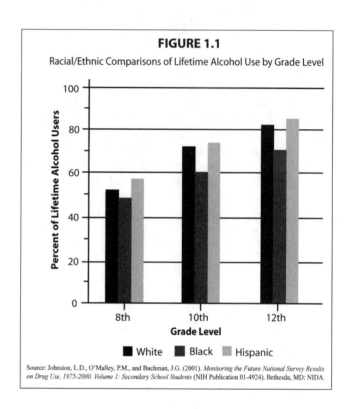

FIGURE 1.1

Racial/Ethnic Comparisons of Lifetime Alcohol Use by Grade Level

Source: Johnston, L.D., O'Malley, P.M., and Bachman, J.G. (2001). *Monitoring the Future National Survey Results on Drug Use, 1975-2000. Volume 1: Secondary School Students* (NIH Publication 01-4924). Bethesda, MD: NIDA.

ability). Over approximately the first 20 years of the MFS, the annual survey samples consisted solely of high school seniors. In recent years, the MFS has expanded to include eighth and tenth graders; this is important because of historical trends in substance use that indicate an earlier age of onset for substance use among children.

The following presentation of epidemiological findings about adolescent alcohol use are based largely on the MFS; findings from other regional or local studies are used to substantiate other significant considerations.

The data provided in Figure 1.1 indicates that the prevalence of using alcohol increases across grade levels for three racial/ethnic groups. However, it is important to note that by eighth grade over 50% of these children report having consumed an alcoholic beverage. Racial/ethnic group differences indicate a particularly high prevalence of lifetime alcohol use among Hispanic children. Similar to findings in previous studies, black adolescents have the lowest rate of lifetime alcohol use. Research findings from earlier MFS cohorts and from other epidemiological studies have also indicated very high (if not the highest) prevalence of lifetime alcohol use among Native American children and adolescents, as well as quite low rates among Asian-Americans. Parenthetically, it should be recognized that drinking practices among adolescents (and adults) may vary considerably for subgroups (for example, for different Native American tribes, for Mexican-Americans versus Puerto Ricans) within the broad racial/ethnic groups used to present these data.

In addition to lifetime use of alcohol, another useful index of trends in adolescent drinking references heavy or binge drinking episodes. Binge drinking refers to the consumption of five or more drinks in a single setting over the last two weeks. In contrast to lifetime alcohol use, the binge drinking index is designed to assess potentially problematic drinking that may contribute to current problems (for example poorer school performance) and may be prognostic of longer term difficulties. The data presented in Figure 1.2 indicates both high rates of binge drinking and increases across grade levels. Differences are also indicated for the three racial/ethnic groups. Hispanic adolescents had substantially higher rates of binge drinking than whites or blacks among eighth graders. Black adolescents had the lowest prevalence of binge drinking across all three grade levels, substantially lower than their white and Hispanic counterparts. White adolescents had the greatest increases in the prevalence of binge drinking across grade levels.

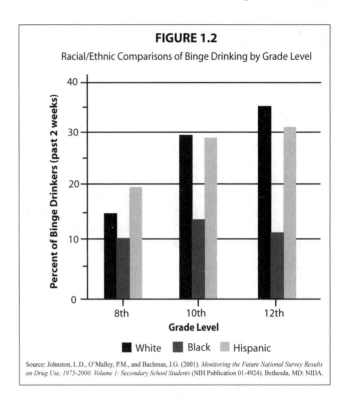

FIGURE 1.2

Racial/Ethnic Comparisons of Binge Drinking by Grade Level

Source: Johnston, L.D., O'Malley, P.M., and Bachman, J.G. (2001). *Monitoring the Future National Survey Results on Drug Use, 1975-2000. Volume 1: Secondary School Students* (NIH Publication 01-4924). Bethesda, MD: NIDA.

> ### *Alcohol use among teens has been associated with the three most common forms of adolescent mortality.*

While there is variability across grade levels and racial/ethnic groups, the prevalence of binge drinking among adolescents, considered collectively, is quite high.

Gender provides yet another potential source of variation among adolescent drinking practices. It has been proposed that historical shifts toward more gender equality in work and family roles among adults may be contributing to a convergence in drinking practices among male and female adolescents. If lifetime use is evaluated, there are few gender differences in alcohol use (80.9% of males vs. 79.5% of females report lifetime use). However, for more serious indicators of alcohol use, such as binge drinking and daily alcohol use, boys have a significantly higher prevalence than girls (36.7% of males report binge drinking compared to 23.5% of females and 4.7% of males report daily drinking vs. 1.1 % of females). These findings are consistent with other studies in supporting the inference that boys are more likely than girls to engage in more serious levels of alcohol use (i.e., more frequently and at higher quantities) and to have more alcohol-related problems.

These epidemiological findings provide a broad picture of the drinking practices of adolescents. It is evident that the vast majority of adolescents consume alcohol at some time during adolescence, with a substantial number also engaging in binge drinking episodes. The study of more extensive alcohol prob-lems among adolescents is a relatively recent phenomena, but the current data highlight high rates of such problems among adolescents. These alcohol problems are of concern because of their potential compromising influences on both current and future health functioning.

Adolescent Alcohol Disorders

As the preceding information demonstrates, data on adolescent alcohol use practices has increased substantially over the past 25 years or so. However, these national and regional survey studies have not included data on the number of adolescents meeting formal clinical diagnostic criteria for alcohol disorders. The available evidence, based on a few recent community studies, suggests that between 3% and 32% of adolescents meet lifetime criteria for an alcohol disorder.

In one study, 3-4% of adolescents between the ages of 14-16 years had an alcohol disorder. However, the prevalence of alcohol disorders of adolescents between the ages of 17-20 years was 8.9% for girls and 20.3% for boys. In another study, 32.4% of 386 older adolescents, mostly seniors in high school, had a lifetime alcohol disorder. Boys (37.6%) were more highly represented than girls (26.8%) with regard to the prevalence of an alcohol disorder. With a community sample of 3,021 adolescents and young adults in Munich, Germany, 25.1 % of men and 7.0% of women had an alcohol disorder. Furthermore, the occurrence of alcohol disorders indicated low rates at age 13-14 years, with a rapid increase to a peak at 15-17 years, followed by a gradual decrease from 18-24 years. Cultural differences between the U.S. and Germany may contribute to this somewhat earlier onset of heavier alcohol involvement by German youth.

Nevertheless, it is evident that the prevalence of alcohol disorders among adolescents is sufficiently high to merit increased concern and responsiveness from those concerned with the health and welfare of our youth.

Summary

Scientific studies of alcohol use among adolescents over the past 30 years or so have indicated high rates of usage as well as an earlier age of onset for alcohol use. More recent surveys have also indicated high rates of binge drinking and the manifestation of multiple alcohol problems. Although based on a limited number of local community studies, it has been estimated that between 3% and 32% of adolescents meet lifetime criteria for an alcohol disorder. These data clearly indicate the need for increased intervention efforts that target the initiation, escalation, and maintenance of alcohol use, as well as the treatment of alcohol disorders during adolescence.

Michael Windle, Ph.D., *is professor of Psychology and director of the Center for the Advancement of Youth Health at the University of Alabama at Birmingham. This research was supported by Grant No. K37-AA07861 awarded to Michael Windle from the National Institute on Alcohol Abuse and Alcoholism.*

This article is adapted from M. Windle (1999). Alcohol Use Among Adolescents. *Sage Publications. It appears here with permission from the publisher, all rights reserved.*

As seen in *Prevention Researcher,* September 2002, pp. 1, 3, condensed from *Alcohol Use Among Adolescents,* 1999. Copyright © 2002 by Sage Publications. Reprinted by permission. www.sagepub.com

Terrorism, the Media, and Distress in Youth

By Rose L. Pfefferbaum, Ph.D., M.P.H., Robin H. Gurwitch, Ph.D., Madeline J. Robertson, J.D., M.D., Edward N. Brandt, Jr., M.D., Ph.D., and Betty Pfefferbaum, M.D., J.D.

The 1995 bombing of the Alfred P. Murrah Federal Building in Oklahoma City ushered in a new focus in childhood trauma that accompanies disaster. Prior research in the United States in this area had primarily addressed natural disasters and man-made incidents with relatively few casualties such as school shootings. Because children were widely believed a target in the Oklahoma City bombing—19 died in the day care center in the building—concern about the welfare of youth, in general, was heightened. Since a goal of terrorism is to create fear and intimidation in the broader society, monitoring the reactions and recovery of the extended community was also important. Furthermore, since media coverage may influence reactions to a traumatic event, studies following the Oklahoma City bombing examined the relationship between exposure to media coverage and emotional reactions of youth in the community. The results of these studies suggest prevention and intervention strategies with respect to the media and its impact on victims and the public.

Most studies of youth in Oklahoma City used post-traumatic stress reactions as the primary outcome measure. Post-traumatic stress disorder (PTSD) includes three clusters of symptoms that develop in response to an extreme traumatic stressor: persistent intrusive re-experiencing of the stressor, persistent avoidance of reminders of the event and numbing of general responsiveness, and persistent symptoms of arousal. According to the American Psychiatric Association (APA), the trauma can be experienced directly or indirectly. Physical presence at a disaster site, such as the scene of a terrorist attack, constitutes exposure. Witnessing and/or close relationship to victims are also recognized as exposure, but other potential mechanisms of indirect exposure are not specifically addressed. Exposure to intensive media coverage of a horrific event, for example, is not included as a form of exposure in APA diagnostic criteria for PTSD. Nonetheless, extended exposure to media coverage may result in heightened anxiety and worries about safety and security. Concerns about reoccurrence may also increase if exposure to the coverage becomes a focal point of daily activity. Although individuals are unlikely to meet criteria for a diagnostic disorder, the resulting distress can interfere with normal functioning and may be cause for concern.

Findings in Oklahoma City middle and high school students seven weeks after the bombing revealed a small but significant relationship between bombing-related television viewing and post-traumatic stress reactions. This sample did not include youth physically present at the bomb site, and most students in the study who knew direct victims were not closely related to them. One might expect different results in youth who were directly exposed. In any case, this work has important implications with respect to the response of youth to media coverage of terrorist events.

The relationship between media exposure and emotional reactions to the Oklahoma City bombing was explored in another sample of indirectly exposed middle school students residing 100 miles from Oklahoma City. This study was completed two years after the bombing, just as the federal trial of Timothy McVeigh was beginning. The study found a small but significant association between enduring post-traumatic stress reactions and both print and broadcast media exposure, Print exposure, in fact, was more strongly associated with post-traumatic stress than broadcast exposure, but this may reflect uneven distribution of broadcast exposure since most students in the study were highly exposed to broadcast coverage while there was a wider variation in the amount of print exposure across the sample, It is possible, however, that the findings reflect true differences in the effects of print and broadcast exposure. In some instances at least, print exposure may require intentional effort reflecting greater interest and perhaps greater distress. Those with more intense reactions to the incident may have actively sought print coverage. These findings suggest the importance of monitoring all forms of media coverage rather than limiting concern to television.

Although individuals are unlikely to meet criteria for a diagnostic disorder, the resulting distress can interfere with normal functioning and may be cause for concern.

The relationship between post-traumatic stress reactions and media exposure in the sample of middle school youth residing 100 miles from Oklahoma City was contingent upon their psychological reactions to media coverage. Thus, one is advised to monitor reactions to coverage as well as amount and content of

Table 2
Steps in Media-Related Trauma Intervention

- **Observe and assess media exposure even in those not directly exposed to traumatic event**
- **Take a media history**
  - Address all forms of media coverage (not just television)
  - Ascertain amount and type of media exposure especially relative to established patterns
  - Determine extent to which media exposure is deliberate as opposed to passive
  - Identify when media exposure occurs (e.g., in the morning, after school, at bedtime)
  - Ascertain whether media exposure occurs alone, with adults, or with peers
  - Evaluate content
  - Assess reactions to coverage including behavioral as well as emotional states
  - Determine impact on functioning at home, in school, and in other settings
- **Discuss traumatic events and media coverage**
  - Address reactions and concerns
  - Clarify misperceptions
- **Assist in processing emotions related to media coverage**
  - Explore feelings aroused by images and/or words
  - Validate feelings expressed
  - Observe and reflect, but do not reinforce hostile feelings
  - Encourage journaling and drawing as methods for expressing and processing feelings
- **Reassure about safety**
  - Listen to concerns
  - Identify activities and precautions to enhance safety
  - Avoid making false or misleading assurances
- **Suggest and practice coping strategies**
  - Redirect to other activities
  - Share relaxation exercises
  - Teach thought-stopping techniques
  - Explore cognitive restructuring
  - Designate focused time for media exposure
- **Limit media exposure to highly traumatic events and reminders**
- **Assist parents**
  - Teach about reactions to traumatic events
  - Allow adults to process their thoughts and feelings about the events and coverage
  - Discuss how adult conversations and distress related to media coverage can adversely impact youth
  - Provide permission for adults to limit media coverage
  - Provide guidelines for television viewing
  - Provide guidelines for discussing media coverage of events

exposure without necessarily assuming that media exposure is responsible for adverse reactions. Youth with increased arousal, for example, may seek media coverage to obtain information or to maintain the heightened state of arousal. Therefore, it is important to discuss with youth their reactions to traumatic events and to media coverage of those events, to listen to and reassure them about safety without misleading them, to assist them in processing emotions, and to redirect them to other activities as warranted. See Table 2 for a summary of interventions.

There may be developmental differences in children's responses to media exposure. Much younger children do not have the same cognitive abilities as older children and adolescents and may process images differently. Preschool children viewing repeated newscasts of the World Trade Center being attacked and then falling, for example, may have believed that each replay represented a different building being destroyed, Adolescents would understand the reality of thousands killed in the terrorist attacks while younger children would not have the cognitive schema to understand the importance of these numbers or the irreversibility of death. Furthermore, media coverage of disasters presents actual events that are novel and that carry information different from the usual fictional and non-fictional violence youth are routinely exposed to in their television viewing. In young children, the relationship between exposure to a traumatic event and reaction to it may be complicated by a child's difficulty distinguishing fictional and non-fictional events.

Recent studies suggest that the effects of media coverage may differ depending on various aspects of exposure. Jennifer Ahern and colleagues, for example, found an association between the frequency of viewing certain images and both PTSD and depression in adults directly involved in or affected by the September 11, 2001, attacks but not in study participants who lacked this tie to the attacks. For victims directly exposed through physical presence, media reminders of an event may rekindle arousal associated with the event. For those less directly exposed, media coverage itself may be the trigger for initial arousal and later, repeated media viewing may be retraumatizing.

Studies emerging since the September 11, 2001, attacks have examined the content of television coverage as well as the amount of viewing. Ahern and colleagues, for example, found a trend between increased frequency of viewing certain images, such as people falling or jumping from the building, and the prevalence of PTSD and depression using their measures. Frequency of viewing the image of the building collapsing was not associated with either PTSD or depression.

It is important to remember that the relationship between media exposure and both acute and later reactions does not establish cause and effect. While it is tempting to assume that media exposure leads to adverse outcomes, this conclusion ignores other plausible explanations. The relationship between acute reactions and media exposure may also suggest that youth who are aroused are drawn to the information provided by the media and/or that information seeking itself is a coping strategy for some. It is possible that other factors are responsible for the link between media exposure and these emotional states as well.

The findings of these Oklahoma City and September 11 studies have implications for prevention and intervention. While these studies did not address a number of important issues such as if and how information was processed with others, it would seem prudent that exposure to media coverage of terrorist events be limited and monitored by parents. The pervasiveness of the media in Western society and the potential for passive exposure, especially in youth, suggest the importance of a proactive approach on the part of professionals who should routinely take a media history, especially following major events such as terrorist attacks, even in those not directly exposed. Such a history would include amount and type of exposure, changes in amount and type of exposure relative to established patterns, assessment of content, extent to which exposure is deliberate and focused as opposed to passive, when exposure occurs, whether others are present when exposure occurs and relationship to those others, as well as emotional and behavioral changes associated with exposure.

Youth may turn to the media when experiencing heightened arousal and/or as a method for managing distress, providing parents and professionals with excellent opportunities for prevention and intervention with them by eliciting and addressing concerns, clarifying misconceptions and misattributions, and suggesting and practicing coping strategies. Youth who do not want to discuss an event should not be forced to do so. Rather, they should understand that the topic is acceptable for discussion at the time or in the future.

In assisting adolescents as they process emotions related to media coverage, it is helpful to explore how images and words make them feel and to validate expressed feelings. Reflect but do not reinforce hostile reactions, such as extreme hatred and strong desire for revenge, since such feelings do not aid healing and may impair functioning. Intervention is warranted if one expects these negative feelings to result in angry or hurtful action against others.

Parents may benefit from educational materials in the form of age-appropriate guidelines for television viewing and for discussing media coverage with their children. They also may need to discuss their own thoughts and feelings about events and media coverage. Teaching parents about normal reactions to traumatic events may enable them to identify adverse reactions more quickly.

While the media are often criticized, they do have a vital role in information sharing in the aftermath of terrorist incidents. In fact, at times of crisis, most adults in our society quite naturally turn to the news media to obtain information. Moreover, a free press goes to the heart of who we are as a nation. Nonetheless, given that terrorists seek opportunities to transmit their messages and to instill fear and intimidation, and given that media coverage of terrorist events may lead to adverse consequences for youth, parents and professionals will want to be attentive to the exposure and reactions of youth to media coverage of horrific events. As professionals learn more about the relationship between media exposure to trauma and distress reactions in youth, we will be better able to develop and refine guidelines for parents and the media.

Rose L. Pfefferbaum, Ph.D., M.P.H., is director of the Terrorism and Disaster Preparedness Center, Phoenix College, Phoenix, Arizona. **Robin H. Gurwitch, Ph.D.,** *is associate professor in the Department of Pediatrics, University of Oklahoma Health Sciences Center, Oklahoma City, Oklahoma.* **Madeline J. Robertson, J.D., M.D.,** *is associate professor and* **Edward N. Brandt, Jr., M.D., Ph.D.,** *is Regents Professor, in Health Administration and Policy, College of Public Health, University of Oklahoma Health Sciences Center.* **Betty Pfefferbaum, M.D., J.D.,** *is professor and chairman of the Department of Psychiatry and Behavioral Sciences, University of Oklahoma Health Sciences Center.*

Acknowledgment: Supported under Award Number MIPT106-113-2000-020 from the Oklahoma City National Memorial Institute for the Prevention of Terrorism and the Office of Justice Programs, National Institute of Justice, Department of Justice. Points of view in this document are those of the authors and do not necessarily represent the official position of the Oklahoma City National Memorial Institute for the Prevention of Terrorism or the Department of Justice. Also supported by grants from the Commonwealth Fund, the Presbyterian Health Foundation, and the Open Society Institute's Project on Death in America.

UNIT 7
Teenage Sexuality

Unit Selections

Key Points to Consider

- What should be taught in sex education classes in public schools?

- Should congress give more financial support to abstinence-only sex education?

- What is your view of the abstinence movement?

- How may living together before marriage have a negative effect on mate selection?

Student Website

www.mhcls.com/online

Internet References

Further information regarding these websites may be found in this book's preface or online.

American Sexual Behavior
http://www.norc.uchicago.edu/online/sex.pdf

CDC National AIDS Clearinghouse
http://www.cdcnpin.org/

Welcome to AboutHealth
http://www.abouthealth.com/

Like other aspects of psychological development, sexuality is not an entirely new issue that surfaces for the first time during adolescents. Children are known to be curious about their bodies at a very early age. And of course, sexual interest and development continues after adolescence. Most would argue that adolescence is a fundamentally important time for the development of sexuality.

During adolescence there is an increase in the sex drive as a result of hormonal changes. During puberty individuals become capable of sexual reproduction. Individuals also develop the secondary sex characteristics that serve as a basis for sexual attraction and as dramatic indicators that the young person is no longer physically a child.

The nature and extent of adolescent sexuality clearly have changed in recent years. Several different patterns of sexual behavior characterize contemporary adolescents. Many of the patterns include engagement in sexual behaviors that place the young person at risk of experiencing health, psychological, and social problems.

In much of American culture, the link between marriage and sexual activity has practically disappeared. This means that there is no particular age for sanctioning the initiation of sexual activity. Largely as a result of such changes, sexual activity is initiated at earlier ages than in the past, by increasing proportions of adolescents.

Attitudes toward sex became more liberal from the late 1960s through the 1970s. The changed attitude, which was generally more liberal, has had a major impact on several major implications for youth's attitude today toward sex. First, there has been a greater openness in our society in sexual matters. Both the printed page and media openly discuss such topics as abortion, rape, and sexual abuse. Just a generation ago such topics were not discussed as openly as they are today. The natural conse-

quence is that youth today, who have been brought up in this atmosphere, are much more open and often feel more comfortable discussing sexual issues openly and honestly with both peers and adults. A second attitude change is that more adults and teens than a generation ago consider sexual intercourse outside of marriage as acceptable. No longer do many consider legal marriage as a required sanction for sex. Many believe that sex is acceptable within a "relationship," and some youth have adopted the liberal attitude that casual sex or sex for primarily personal pleasure whether or not a relationship exists is acceptable.

Many adolescents are initiating sexual intercourse at an earlier age than in the previous generation. Gender attitudes continue to demonstrate a difference in belief systems. Young women are much more likely than men to desire a strong relationship or even marriage before engaging in sexual intercourse.

Many of the problems associated with teenage sexual activity have increased with more teens' sexual involvement. American teenagers have one of the highest rates of premarital pregnancies in the world. Although more teenagers are now using contraceptives than in the past there is still a large number who use no method of birth control or fail to use it properly. Legal abortion is an option that has become increasingly available even though it continues to be highly controversial. Because youth often delay making a decision to abort the baby, more complications persist. In addition, mental agony and guilt accompany making such a major decision.

Increased sexual activity also corresponds to a rise in sexually transmitted diseases. The most common among youth are gonorrhea, chlamydia, and herpes. Although some of the sexually transmitted diseases (STD) may continue in the body for the rest of their life and effect reproduction, the AIDS disease often results in an early, painful death. In an attempt to prevent a nationwide epidemic, educational programs teaching about sex, diseases, and how to prevent the spread of these are taught around the country. Although not accepted by many, abstinence is the only true method to prevent sexually transmitted diseases.

Sexual abuse of and violence toward youth is all too common in America. Many adolescent girls experience unwanted sexual activities by dates and boyfriends. These experiences have a profound impact on behavior and development of young people. Sexual abuse is often linked to problems such as binge drinking and suicidal idealism. The true prevalence of rape is further complicated by the fact that most rapes are committed by someone known to the teenage victim, rather than a stranger who jumps out of "nowhere." These "date rapes," as they are sometimes la-beled, are much less likely to be reported to authorities than those in which the woman is assaulted.

A major problem today is that a majority of youth continue to get most of their education and information about sex from the least reliable source, their peers. Informal sex education usually begins in the home when the child is young, but many homes give little instruction about sex to their preteen or teen—a time when they need good solid information. Two articles in this section address whether Congress should or should not fund absti-nence-only sex education. A third article deals with what should be told to teenagers about sex. One article discusses a growing number of youth who are choosing abstinence. And finally is an article addressing the common practice of living together.

What to Tell the Kids about Sex

KAY S. HYMOWITZ

SEX education has been the Middle East of the culture wars and one of the longest-running, most rancorous battlegrounds of American social policy. For nearly 40 years, conservatives—many of them, though by no means all, observant Catholics and fundamentalist Christians—have been battling the increasing presence in the public schools of a permissive strain of sex education that came to be known as "comprehensive sexuality education." Unlike sex-ed programs from the first half of the twentieth century that had frowned on teen sex, comprehensive sexuality education affected a morally neutral or even positive stance toward adolescent sexual activity, supporting what was usually described as teenagers' "autonomous decision making," and promoting their use of contraception.

The spread of comprehensive sexuality education in the schools coincided with a steep rise in teen sexual activity. The number of teen girls who had had sex went from 29 percent in 1970 to 55 percent in 1990. Fourteen percent of sexually active teens had had four or more partners in 1971; by 1988, that number had increased to 34 percent. But though sex educators had sought to encourage teens to practice what they called "responsible decision making," their efforts did not seem to be paying off. Throughout the 1970s and 1980s American teenagers were not just having more sex; they were getting pregnant—and at rates that far surpassed those in other industrialized countries. Between 1972 and 1990, there was a 23 percent increase in the rate of teen pregnancy, and there was a similar increase between 1975 and 1990 in births to teen mothers.

The culture war

Thus it is hardly surprising that the new sex ed became a rallying point for the populist uprising that eventually gave rise to Reagan Democrats, the school-choice movement, and other grassroots groups chafing at the social upheavals of the sixties. Traditionalist parents opposed to sex education were often the working- and middle-class mothers of school-aged children. Sex educators, on the other hand, had influential friends in Washington and New York, including Planned Parenthood, the Sexuality Information and Education Council of the United States (SIECUS), and leading professional groups like the American Medical Association. While the federal government never directly funded comprehensive sexuality-education programs, over the years it did provide numerous funding streams, such as that from the Centers for Disease Control's (CDC) Division of Adolescent and School Health (DASH), that were often used to support them.

True, in the early years of the Reagan administration, traditionalists had one notable success in Washington when Congress passed the Adolescent Family Life Act (AFLA), earmarking $11 million for programs to "promote chastity and self-discipline." But "the chastity bill," as it came to be called, became bogged down in the courts when opponents charged that it violated the separation of church and state, and it remained a marginal cause and the subject of much eye-rolling among health professionals. At any rate, by the time AFLA was passed, 94 percent of school districts saw "informed decision making" as the major goal of sex education according to a 1981 study by the Alan Guttmacher Institute, and for years after that, comprehensive sex education, though often sanitized for middle-class communities, was the national norm.

Today, the reign of comprehensive sex ed appears to be faltering. This is largely due to Title V, a junior provision of the Personal Responsibility and Work Opportunity Reconciliation Act (PRWORA), the landmark 1996 welfare-reform bill. Title V put substantial money behind what is now known as "abstinence education"—that is, teaching children to abstain from sexual intercourse. States could receive $50 million a year for five years in the form of a block grant as long as they matched three dollars for every four from the federal government. In 2000, Congress added another abstinence initiative called Special Projects of Regional and National Significance (SPRANS). Today, the federal government earmarks over $100 million annually for abstinence education. But despite close analysis by researchers and journalists on the legislation and its impact on welfare mothers and their children, in the seven years since Congress passed welfare reform, Title V's rationale and legacy remain somewhat clouded.

A broad coalition

Critics and supporters of Title V can agree on one thing: At the time it was passed, it was a profoundly radical initiative. The architects of Title V believed that they were challenging not just the sex-ed establishment but American society overall. In a paper written for the American Enterprise Institute, Ron Haskins and Carol Statuto Bevan, congressional aides closely involved in writing Title V, conceded that "both the practices and standards in many communities across the country clash with the standard required by the law." And this, they wrote, "is precisely the point.... [T]he explicit goal of abstinence education programs is to change both behavior and community standards for the good of the country." Determined to avoid the fate of AFLA, whose language had been broad enough to sneak through some programs that were all but indistinguishable from those run by sexuality educators, the authors of Title V introduced a strict eight-point definition of abstinence education. These were "education or motivational programs" that had as their "exclusive purpose teaching the social, psychological and health gains from abstaining from sexual activity." Abstinence from sexual activity outside marriage, the definition also required, is "the expected standard for all school-age children." The bill allowed some flexibility—funded projects could not be inconsistent with any part of the definition but they didn't have to emphasize each part equally—but Title V was unusually specific, as well as unusually radical.

Yet much as abstinence education was promoted by social and religious conservatives determined to overthrow the liberal, nonjudgmental approach to sex ed, it also benefited from the reluctant backing of moderates frustrated with the status quo and the policies supporting it. Many Title V supporters saw a direct connection between welfare reform and sex-education reform; both could contribute to the battle against out-of-wedlock births tied to government dependency. PRWORA allows states to use a number of strategies intended to discourage out-of-wedlock births, such as a family cap and an end of direct payments to teen mothers; abstinence education was partly intended to be another weapon in that arsenal. Title V's eight-point definition of abstinence education includes several points whose purpose is to plant the ideal of childrearing inside marriage in young minds and to promote the idea that "bearing children out of wedlock is likely to have harmful consequences for the child, the child's parents, and society."

Moderates who eventually got behind abstinence education were also troubled by continuing high rates of teen pregnancy. True, by the early nineties, a decline in teen sexual activity, pregnancy, and abortion began, trends that continue to this day. According to the CDC's Youth Risk Behavior Survey, in 1991, 54.1 percent of high school students reported having sex; by 2001 that number was 45 percent. Those reporting multiple (more than four) partners declined from 18.7 percent to 14.2 percent. Pregnancy rates declined too—the CDC just announced that teen-birth rates decreased by another 5 percent in 2002, for a cumulative 28 percent decline since 1990. However, according to a 2001 study by the Alan Guttmacher Institute, even after the declines of the last decade, teen-birth, pregnancy, and abortion rates in the United States remain considerably higher than those in France, Sweden, Canada, and Great Britain. Moreover, American girls are more likely to start having sex before age 15 and to have multiple partners than their counterparts in those countries. In the United States, a full 25 percent of high school seniors have already had four or more partners, a much rarer phenomenon in the contrasting countries.

What also made the 1990s decline in teen pregnancy and sexual activity look less impressive was the growing incidence of sexually transmitted diseases. When most parents of today's teenagers were their age, the only widely reported sexually transmitted diseases in the United States were syphilis and gonorrhea. By the last decade of the century, common STDs grew to encompass over 20 kinds of infections. They include not just the one everyone knows, HIV-AIDS, but other viral diseases that can be asymptomatic and that while not fatal, are difficult, and in some cases impossible, to cure. While condom use among teenagers increased—in 2001, 57.9 percent of teens who had had sex reported using a condom in the three months prior to the survey, up from 46.2 percent in 1991—teenagers were still contracting three million STDs every year, far exceeding rates in other industrialized countries.

Everyone for abstinence?

Within a short time after Title V was passed into law, it began to seem that the idea of abstinence for teenagers wasn't so radical anymore. Just about everyone connected to the business of sex education had taken to embracing the word abstinence—to the point of meaninglessness and much terminological confusion. A mere decade ago, abstinence was something of a laughingstock at places like the CDC and state departments of health. These days it is hard to find a state authority, sex-ed program, or organization, including Planned Parenthood, that doesn't promote "teaching abstinence." In using the term, educators sometimes mean they tell teens that abstaining from sex is one option to consider, much as comprehensive sex educators do. By "teaching abstinence," others mean they strongly encourage teens not to have sex, but still offer them information about how to use contraception. Both of these approaches fall under the now commonplace rubric "abstinence plus."

"Abstinence only" educators, on the other hand, teach abstinence as the only acceptable choice and discuss contraception almost entirely in terms of its failure to protect kids from pregnancy and STDs. To make matters more complicated, some abstinence supporters reject the "abstinence only" label as an overly narrow description of their goals and prefer "authentic abstinence." Meanwhile, the National Campaign Against Teen Pregnancy, the most prominent, middle-of-the-road organization in the business, has begun to promote an "abstinence first" message, apparently in order to clarify the ambiguity of "abstinence plus." Significantly, "abstinence only" programs are the only ones eligible for Title V money.

These skirmishes over terminology highlight the fact that even as American opinion leaders have grown more comfortable with the abstinence message, the handshake agreement about "teaching abstinence" only papers over a bitter, ongoing culture war. Not surprisingly, money and jobs, as well as ideology, are at stake.

For all the recent success of the abstinence forces, comprehensive sexuality education remains deeply embedded in the public-health infrastructure. While the number of schools teaching "abstinence only" has clearly grown, they are still in the minority: According to a recent article in Family Planning Perspectives, in 1988, 2 percent of school districts reported teaching abstinence as the sole way to prevent pregnancy whereas by 1999, 23 percent reported doing so. The liberal SIECUS receives money from the CDC to train teachers of curricula on HIV and AIDS that are indistinguishable from comprehensive sex-ed programs. A host of organizations including SIECUS, Planned Parenthood, the National Abortion Rights Action League, various AIDS and gay-rights organizations, as well as the National Association of County and City Health Officials, have begun a campaign entitled NoNewMoney.org to stop the federal government from putting any more funds behind abstinence education.

Meanwhile, teacher unions often balk at abstinence curricula. The New Jersey Education Association has opposed a legislative proposal to "stress abstinence." The National Education Association (NEA) suggests that members in "abstinence only" districts "lobby for those funds to be used in after-school community programs so schools can be free to teach a more comprehensive program." In 2001, the NEA and 34 national organizations including Planned Parenthood, Advocates for Youth, and the ACLU, put out a joint statement declaring abstinence education "ineffective, unnecessary, and dangerous" as well as a form of "censorship" and an "affront [to the] principles of church state separation." A number of states, including California, Oregon, Missouri, and Alabama have introduced "medically accurate" laws on the books that abstinence supporters claim are backhanded attempts to sabotage their programs.

An emotional appeal

What is it these programs actually teach? The most common accusation against them is that they are crude, didactic efforts to get kids to "just say no." Whatever truth this generalization may have held years ago, it does not hold up to careful scrutiny today. For one thing, today's abstinence programs are extremely varied. Title V funds over 700 programs. The Abstinence Education Clearinghouse, a resource organization founded 8 years ago, has 1,300 paid affiliates and includes 74 curricula in their directory, up from 49 just 2 years ago. The early curricula funded by AFLA tended to be created with conservative middle-American communities in mind. Today, many programs—like Title V itself—are targeting lower-income kids. Some programs are aimed at preteens, some late teens, others even in their twenties. Some are community-based, others are school-based. Of those that are school-based, some are one or two sessions, others much longer. Some involve peer mentoring, some adult mentoring, some parental education. Community-based programs might use ad campaigns or cul-

tural events or both. Some programs heavily emphasize delaying sex until marriage; others seem to be aiming to get kids to delay sex at least until they leave high school. Some programs get specific about what sexual behavior is permissible—one talks about avoiding the "underwear zone," another about going no further than holding hands and kissing—and some avoid these details altogether.

Still, today's abstinence programs share a few standard features. The first and most obvious is that they teach, as the Title V definition puts it, that "sexual activity outside the context of marriage is likely to have harmful psychological and physical effects." They aim to impress youngsters with the costs of ignoring the message, much the way drug or alcohol programs do, emphasizing the risk of pregnancy and sexually transmitted diseases. One widely used activity is a graphic slide show of the effects of STDs produced by the Medical Institute for Sexual Health in Austin, Texas. The gruesome slides of genital warts and herpes sores are reminiscent of pictures of diseased lungs shown in antismoking classes. Abstinence educators strongly emphasize—critics accuse them of actually lying about—the failure rate of condoms in protecting against pregnancy and STDs. Where comprehensive sex-ed programs promote safe sex and risk reduction—"Reducing the Risk" is the name of one well-known comprehensive program—abstinence programs are intent on risk elimination.

When critics charge abstinence education with being "fear based," they are overstating things; the newer abstinence curricula spend a relatively short amount of time on this sort of material. But there is no question that some of the warnings against sex tend toward the melodramatic. Abstinence educators are partial to stories of young people who have suffered heartbreak and misery after having sex with an unfaithful or diseased partner. In one of the more extreme examples of cautionary advice, "No Second Chance," a video sometimes shown in abstinence classes that has raised a lot of eyebrows in the media, a student asks a nurse, "What if I want to have sex before I get married?" "Well, I guess you have to be prepared to die. And you'll probably take with you your spouse and one or more of your children."

Most abstinence proponents believe premarital sex is genuinely destructive of young people's emotional and physical well-being, but some of them also cite several tactical reasons for their sensationalism. For one thing, they argue that kids should be scared. Early pregnancy does ruin lives; STDs can as well. It's not enough for kids to know how AIDS is transmitted, they argue; they need to dread the disease. For another, it makes sense to appeal to an age group partial to horror movies and gross-out reality shows—according to Health and Human Services, most programs are addressed to 9 to 14 year olds—through their emotions as well as their reason.

In fact, abstinence proponents believe that emphasizing the emotions surrounding sex sets them apart from the comprehensive sex-ed camp. They argue that comprehensive sex education gives the impression that sexual intercourse is a relatively straightforward physical transaction that simply requires the proper hygienic accessories. Abstinence proponents start with the assumption that sex elicits powerful crosscurrents of feeling that teenagers are unable to manage. Some cite new brain research showing that in adolescents the frontal lobes, the seat of judgment and self-control, are still undeveloped. They also believe that teens are not only incapable of mature, fully committed relationships but that teens have yet even to learn what such relationships are made of.

Character counts

There is much more to these programs than an appeal to the emotions. In the later-model abstinence programs, delaying sex is treated as part of a broader effort to adopt a mindful, take-charge attitude toward life. Curricula usually incorporate goal-setting exercises; some of the more intensive also include character education. The tag line on the cover of the "Game Plan" workbook, part of a curriculum for middle schoolers sponsored by the basketball star A.C. Green from one of the oldest abstinence organizations, the Illinois-based Project Reality, says, "Everybody has one lifetime to develop your Game Plan." The booklet asks students to write down answers to questions like "What are some of your goals for the future?" "What will it take for you to reach these goals?" The workbook also tries to anticipate some of the temptations that lure kids away from their "game plan." "Describe some activities that could make it difficult for you to accomplish your goals," it asks. One section tells students to "think about how much time you spend each day on … TV, radio/CD's, the Internet," and asks them to analyze media messages and consider "whether those messages will help them achieve their goals."

Character education reinforces these sorts of activities. As Operation Keepsake, a Cleveland area program, puts it, the point is "to develop strong character qualities for healthy relationships to endure." Character education is also supposed to promote the autonomy that would help kids resist the unhealthy influence of a powerful peer group and glamorous media. "It's OK to stand against the crowd," Operation Keepsake urges its students. Some programs also add community-service requirements to their character component, such as reading to the elderly at nursing homes.

A Washington D.C.-based program called Best Friends, a highly regarded intervention project created by Elayne Bennett, also emphasizes character development. Bennett developed her program after working with at-risk girls and being struck by how depression and the sense of helplessness often led to sexual activity as well as drug and alcohol use. Bennett was determined to instill in drifting young women a sense of their own efficacy, or what is called in more therapeutic circles "empowerment." Best Friends' Washington D.C. program is used in schools with a large number of high-risk girls, the vast majority of them African-American. Looking at pregnancy rates of the 14 and 15 year olds in her targeted population, Bennett concluded that she had to begin her program at age 11 when "[girls'] attitudes are still forming."

What is unique about Bennett's approach is that instead of softening children's allegiance to the peer group, she tries to turn it into a force for individual improvement. "The best kind of friend is one who encourages you to be a better person," is one of the program's core messages. The girls in a selected class are designated "Best Friends" who meet at least once a month with a teacher, and once a week in a special fitness class, as well as at events like fashion shows, cultural activities, and recognition ceremonies. Once or twice a year there is a motivational speaker, a married woman with a successful career from the surrounding community who tells her life story, including how she met and married her husband, a narrative that Bennett says the girls particularly relish. The program also relies a good deal on mentoring. Each girl has a teacher-mentor from her school with whom she meets 30 to 40 minutes per week when she can complain about trouble with another teacher or talk about problems at home or with friends. Best Friends Foundation now licenses programs in 25 cities, reaching a total of 6,000 girls, and has recently started a Best Men program for boys.

Changing hearts and minds

The most common objection to abstinence education has always been that it turns its back on reality. Kids are going to have sex no matter what you tell them, and the best thing to do is to teach them how to be mature and responsible about it, the argument runs. What evidence do we have that it is possible to teach kids to abstain from sex?

One thing we can say with some certainty is that it is possible to change kids' attitudes on the subject. Mathematica Research, which was awarded a federal grant to examine the problem, is conducting the most rigorous study to date of abstinence education, examining 11 diverse programs each involving 400 to 700 subjects. Mathematica began following its subjects several years ago when the children's average age was 12 and one-half and will continue to do so until they are 16 or 17, so the organization will not have its final results until 2005. But its 2002 interim report confirms that teenagers are open to the abstinence message when teachers are clear about their message and appear committed to kids' well-being. "Youth tend to respond especially positively to programs where the staff are unambiguously committed to abstinence until marriage," the researchers write, "and when the program incorporates the broader goal of youth development." This change in attitude is not likely with less thorough curricula, which kids often view as "just another class."

Indeed, though it's not clear how much abstinence programs can claim credit for the decline in teen sexual activity since the early 1990s, this trend does appear to signal a growing conservatism among young people on sexual matters. In its annual survey of college freshman, the Higher Education Research Institute has shown a decline from 52 percent to 42 percent between 1987 to 2001 of the number of respondents who agree with the statement, "If two people really like each other, it's all right for them to have sex if they've known each other for a very short time." The National Campaign Against Teen Pregnancy conducted a survey in which it asked, "When it comes to teens having sex over the past several years would you say that you have become more opposed, less opposed, or remained unchanged?" Twenty-eight percent of teens said they were more opposed, as compared with 9 percent who said they were less opposed.

Surveys consistently show that somewhere around two-thirds of teenagers who have had sex say they wish they had not. In the most recent example, the National Campaign asked, "If you have had sexual intercourse, do you wish you had waited longer?" Eighty-one percent of 12 to 14 year olds and 55 percent of 15 to 17 year olds answered yes. Some of these responses are undoubtedly influenced by the bedeviling "social desirability" factor, but the very fact that kids believe they should give a positive answer suggests that the abstinence message is not out of line with social attitudes. Interestingly, there are indications that adults are more likely to be skeptical of abstinence than teens. The National Campaign asked in a 2002 survey, "Do you think it is embarrassing for teens to admit they are virgins?" Thirty-nine percent of adults said yes, while only 19 percent of teens agreed, though this finding may conflict with a Kaiser Family Foundation survey showing 59 percent of kids agreeing with the statement, "There is pressure to have sex by a certain age."

What the data show

Regardless, wishes are not horses, and we are still left with the question of whether abstinence education actually makes kids abstain. The answer to that question is less clear. Just about everyone agrees that the decline in teen pregnancy that began in 1991 is partly attributable to a growing number of teenagers delaying sex, though there is vigorous disagreement about just how much can be chalked up to abstinence and how much to improved condom use. At any rate, a national decline in teen sexual activity cannot prove the impact of abstinence education per se, something that has been difficult to measure.

The key problem is finding well-designed research. The few early abstinence programs that did seem to show an impact on attitudes or behavior didn't use the sort of randomized control groups that more exacting researchers tend to trust. There are many studies of kids before and after attending a program, but either there is no control group, the control group comes from a different school, the sample size is too small, there was a follow-up only three months after the invention, but nothing longer term, or some combination of all of these.

"Emerging Answers," a 2001 review of the research on sex education sponsored by the National Campaign Against Teen Pregnancy, included only those programs that had been subjected to research with a rigorous experimental or quasi-experimental design. Douglas Kirby, the report's author and a senior researcher at ETR, an education research organization that also produces comprehensive sex curricula, was able to find only three abstinence programs that satisfied the study's requirements. (By contrast, there were 19 comprehensive programs that did so, of which 5 were considered successful.) And while none of the three abstinence programs could be shown to affect either sexual initiation, pregnancy rates, or condom use, the results do not lead to generalizable conclusions about abstinence

education. All three studies were of older-model programs, and as both Kirby's writings and Mathematica's research seem to confirm, straight didactic programs don't work with any message, abstinence or safe sex.

Another problem is that programs take time to test and refine. Up until two years ago there was little convincing evidence that comprehensive sex education was working. Four years before "Emerging Answers," Kirby wrote other less optimistic review of the research literature on sex education entitled "No Easy Answers," which concluded that "only a few programs have produced credible evidence that they reduced sexual risk-taking behavior," and even those results were limited to the short term.

Still, there are a few studies that provide what even the most scrupulous researchers might be willing to call "some evidence" that several abstinence programs are successful in getting kids to delay sexual initiation. One of the most intriguing, published in the Journal of Health Communication in 2001, looked at a community-based program called "Not Me, Not Now" in Monroe County, New York. In an effort to turn around high rates of teen pregnancy in and around the city of Rochester in the mid 1990s, the architects of "Not Me, Not Now" took a multifaceted approach to the problem: They spread the abstinence message through Internet sites, billboards, and community-sponsored events. Organizers also set up a youth-advisory panel, distributed 50,000 information packets for parents, and pushed abstinence curricula for middle schoolers. The results of the study show a decrease in the number of students who said they could "handle the consequences of intercourse" and a notable decline in sexual activity. Those who reported intercourse by the age of 15 dropped from 46.6 percent to 31.6 percent, and the rate of decline in teen pregnancy in Monroe surpassed that in comparison counties. But questions remain: Are students lying in their survey answers? Were there other interventions in the county that could explain the decline in teen pregnancy? These questions may yet yield firmer answers since "Not Me, Not Now" is one of the programs now being studied by Mathematica.

There are several reasons to anticipate that other abstinence programs will also have good results. The most suggestive finding in "Emerging Answers" is that service-learning programs that include time for contemplation and discussion are the most uniformly effective in getting adolescents to delay sexual initiation—even though they don't teach anything at all about sex. Kirby speculates that kids who are being supervised and mentored as they work in soup kitchens or hospitals develop close relationships with their teachers, increase their sense of competency, and gain a sense of self-respect from "the knowledge that they can make a difference in the lives of others." In general, Kirby finds that effective programs instill feelings of connectedness in kids. A number of earlier studies had shown that children who are more rooted in their peer group have earlier intercourse, while those more attached to their families and schools tend to begin having sex later. Connectedness, competency, and self-respect are precisely the goals of abstinence programs like Best Friends.

It's not just about sex

But the truth is, even if evidence emerges that one particular abstinence-education program drastically reduces teen pregnancy and STDs—or conversely, of a comprehensive program that makes teenagers use condoms 100 percent of the time—sex education will remain a flashpoint in the culture wars. What a society teaches its young about sex will always be a decision founded in cultural beliefs rather than science. In the case of sex education, those beliefs are not about efficacy; they are not even only about sex. They are in part about clashing notions of adolescence. Sexuality educators emphasize teens' capacity for responsible and rational choices and their right to opportunities for self-exploration. They see their role as empowering the young to make their own decisions. Abstinence educators imagine a more impressionable and erratic adolescent. They see their role as guiding the young.

The two camps also presume different notions of identity. Comprehensive sex educators place a great deal of emphasis on gender identity and sexual orientation. Abstinence-only educators, who for the most part don't mention homosexuality, locate identity in character as reflected through qualities like respect, self-control, and perseverance. And finally, there are conflicting notions of freedom at stake. Sexuality educators see freedom as meaning individual self-expression while abstinence proponents tend to understand freedom in a more republican sense—the capacity for personal responsibility that allows individuals to become self-governing family members and citizens.

But it is likely that for most Americans outside the culture-war zone these are not absolute distinctions. One of the most striking flaws of the entire sex-ed dispute is that both sides talk about 13 year olds in the same breath as they do 18 or for that matter 23 year olds. It's unlikely that most Americans see age differences as insignificant. According to Mathematica's interim report, a good deal of Title V money is being directed toward middle schools because there is a general consensus that younger teens need a strong message that they are not ready for sex. Perhaps because they believe that as kids age they develop a firmer sense of identity and have even achieved some measure of character, Americans are not as likely to think the same about older teenagers and young adults in their twenties. Certainly, abstinence until marriage seems an improbable outcome in a society where people marry on average at the age of 26, and where acceptance of premarital cohabitation is widespread. Still, in their appeal to kids' higher aspirations and need for meaningful connections, abstinence proponents are on to something that has been missing in the lives of many children of baby boomers. "My father wasn't a very responsible man. I want to be a better father when the time is right," the 18 year old son of divorced parents told the Indianapolis Star about his decision to remain abstinent. Comprehensive sexual education promises pleasure, but abstinence education pushes honor—and a surprising number of kids seem interested in buying.

KAY S. HYMOWITZ is a contributing editor to City Journal and author of Liberation's children (Ivan r. Dee, 2003).

Should Congress be giving more financial support to abstinence-only sex education? Yes

Abstinence is working to decrease teen pregnancy and is
building character among our nation's youth.

Kathleen Tsubata

The current tug-of-war between "abstinence-only" and "comprehensive" sexual-education advocates is distracting us from the real issue. We are in a war against forces far more unforgiving than we ever have encountered. We must look at what works to save lives. My work brings me to deal with teens every day, in public schools, churches and community organizations, teaching HIV/AIDS prevention. I train teens to teach others about this genocidal plague that is sweeping nations around the world and depleting continents of their most-productive population. I can tell you that most teens have a very superficial understanding of HIV and that many are putting themselves at risk in a wide variety of ways.

While teen pregnancy is serious, it is still, in one sense, the lesser evil. It's a difficult thing to bear a child out of wedlock, with the accompanying loss of education, financial stability and freedom. However, compared to HIV, it's a walk in the park. Make no mistake about it: The choice of sexual activity is a life-and-death matter, as Third World nations are finding out in stark terms.

Having multiple sexual partners is the No. 1 risk factor for contracting HIV and 19 percent of teens have had four or more sexual partners.

"So teach them to use condoms!" we are told. Studies indicate that condoms, if used correctly and consistently, may lower the transmission rate to 15 to 25 percent. That's not a fail-safe guarantee, as any condom manufacturer under litigation quickly would point out.

But there are two additional problems with condoms being the central pillar of HIV prevention. First, correct usage of condoms is hard to achieve in the dimly lit, cramped back seat of a car. Second, and more importantly, kids simply make decisions differently than adults. Janet St. Lawrence, of the Centers for Disease Control and Prevention (CDC), related the results of one behavioral study to me in a phone conversation last year. In that study, teens reported using a condom for their first sexual contact with someone, and subsequent contacts,

"until they felt the relationship was permanent," St. Lawrence said. Then they stopped using condoms. These teens were asked what defines a "permanent" relationship. "Lasting 21 days or longer," was their response. In other words, such a teen could start a relationship, initiate sex using a condom, decide after three weeks that it is "safe" to stop using a condom, break up and replay the whole cycle, convinced that this was responsible sexual behavior.

Teens are not realistic because they are young and not fully developed in key mental and emotional areas. They tend to imbue love with magical properties, as if the emotion is a sanitizing force, and that their trust can be shown by the willingness to take risks. Kids process information differently than adults. Parents know this. Saying "It's best not to have sex, but if you do, use a condom" is translated in their minds to "It's okay to have sex if you use a condom." Then, if they feel "this is true love," they convince themselves that even that is unnecessary. That's why during four decades of sex education we witnessed steep increases in sexual activity and the consequential increases in teen pregnancy, sexually transmitted diseases and poverty.

Only when abstinence education began in recent years did the numbers of sexually active teens go down - a full 8 percentage points from 54 percent of teens to 46 percent, according to the 2001 Youth Risk Behavior

Surveillance, published by the CDC. Simultaneously, teen pregnancies went down, abortions went down and condom use went up among those who were sexually active. Raising the bar to establish abstinence as the best method indirectly resulted in more-responsible behavior in general.

You would think such good news would have people dancing in the aisles. Instead, the safe-sex gurus grimly predict that increased abstinence education will result in teens giving in to natural urges without the benefit of latex. Or, the critics of abstinence-until-marriage education insisted that their programs (which pay lip service to abstinence) somehow reached teens more effectively than the programs that focused on abstinence. A third interpretation is that contraception, not abstinence, has lowered the numbers.

However, a study of lowered teen-pregnancy rates between 1991 and 1995 (published in Adolescent and Family Health by Mohn, Tingle et al., April 2003) showed that abstinence, not contraceptives, was the major cause of the lowered pregnancy rate. Another 1996 study, by John Vessey, of Northwestern University Medical School, followed up on 2,541 teens, ages 13 to 16, who completed an abstinence-education program. He reported that one year after completing the program, 54 percent of formerly sexually active teens no longer were sexually active. This puts to rest the idea that "once a teen has sex, they will continue to be sexually active."

It often is claimed that most parents want pro-contraceptive education for their kids. In fact, a nationwide Zogby International poll of 1,245 parents in February (see poll results at www.whatparentsthink.com) commissioned by the pro-abstinence Coalition for Adolescent Sexual Health found that when shown the actual content of both comprehensive and abstinence-only sex-education programs, 73 percent of parents supported abstinence education and 75 percent opposed the condom-based education, with 61 percent opposing the comprehensive sex-ed programs.

But what do teens themselves think? In a 2000 study by the National Campaign to Prevent Teen Pregnancy, 93 percent of the teens surveyed said there should be a strong message from society not to engage in sex at least until graduation from high school. Will abstinence education cause sexually active teens to be unable to find out about contraception? The small amount in abstinence-education funding requested by Congress ($135 million among three programs) is miniscule compared with the $379 million funding of only six of the 25 federal programs teaching contraceptive-based education. This is Goliath complaining that David is using up all the rocks.

But, in all good conscience, can we teach something that would put kids in danger of contracting HIV, even if at a somewhat-reduced risk? Can we glibly decide, "Oh, only 15 percent of users will die?" That's acceptable? The stakes simply are too high. Even one life is too important to lose. When we're talking about life and death, we can't settle for the soggy argument of "Kids are going to do it anyway." That's what used to be said about racial discrimination, drunk driving and cigarette smoking, but when people became serious about countering these behaviors, they receded. If we realize the necessity of saving every teen's life, we can't help but teach them that because sex is wonderful, powerful and life-changing, it must be treated with great care.

Sex is most pleasurable and joyful when there is no fear of disease, when both partners feel absolute trust in the other, when the possibility of a pregnancy is not a destructive one and when each person truly wants the best for the other. This takes self-development, investment, emotional growth, responsibility and a whole host of other elements a typical teen doesn't possess, unless they are guided. In reality, every person already is aware of the need to limit sexuality to certain times and places, like many activities. Sexuality is far more complex than the physical mechanics of orgasm. That stuff is pretty much automatic. It's far more important to know that orgasm is the perfectly engineered system for creating life, and for experiencing the fulfillment of love.

Abstinence isn't a vague ideal but a practical, feasible life skill. Studies show that kids who are able to say no to sex also can say no to drugs, alcohol and tobacco. The skills in one area automatically transfer to other areas of health. Learning to delay gratification can have positive impacts on academic goals and athletic accomplishments.

Without the soap-opera distractions of sex, kids feel more confident and free to enjoy the process of making friends, developing their own individuality and working on their dreams. That's why virtually no one looks back on the decision to be sexually abstinent and says "I wish I had never done that." But 63 percent of teen respondents who have had sex regretted it and said they wish they had waited, according to an International Communications Research of Media survey in June 2000 commissioned by the National Campaign to Prevent Teen Pregnancy. Further, 78 percent of the 12- to 17-year-old respondents said teens should not be sexually active, and only 21 percent thought sex for teens was okay if they used birth control.

Teens are telling us that they need support to resist the pressure to have sex. Even just making an abstinence pledge was found to delay sexual debut by 18 months on average, according to the National Longitudinal Study on Adolescent Health in 1997. And teens who know their parents have a strong belief and expectation of abstinence are far more likely to abstain, as shown in two 2002 studies released by the University of Minnesota Center for Adolescent Health and Development in which more than 80 percent of teens stayed abstinent when they knew their mothers strongly disapproved of premarital sex.

Even if it were only to end the spread of HIV/AIDS, that would be a valid reason to support abstinence education.

But teaching abstinence goes beyond preventing disease and unwanted pregnancy. It helps kids improve in the areas of self-esteem, academic attainments and future careers. It increases refusal skills toward drugs, alcohol and smoking. It equips teens with tools that they will use successfully throughout life, especially in their eventual marriage and family life. In other words, it has a positive ripple effect both in terms of their current and future life courses. In my estimation, that definitely is worth funding.

Tsubata is a regular contributor to the Washington Times as well as co-director of the Washington AIDS International Foundation. She teaches HIV/AIDS prevention in public schools and community venues and trains teens as peer educators. E-mail Kathleen Tsubata at kate@waifaction.org.

Should Congress be giving more financial support to abstinence-only sex education? No

Withholding information about contraception and teaching only abstinence puts sexually active teens at risk.

Cory Richards

Helping young people to understand the benefits of delaying sexual activity and to resist peer pressure is, and clearly should be, a cornerstone of sex education in the United States. Virtually no one disputes the importance of abstinence education. But support for abstinence-only education-which ignores or actually denigrates the effectiveness of contraceptives and condoms-is not based on scientific evidence; rather it is driven by a subjective moral and, for many, religious agenda. The nation's leading medical, public-health and educational organizations endorse sex education that includes positive messages about the value of delaying sexual activity along with information about condoms and contraceptive use to avoid sexually transmitted diseases (STDs) and unintended pregnancy. Public-opinion polls show that this also is the position of parents, teachers and young people themselves in the United States.

What does the evidence show?

- Teen-agers and young adults are at risk of unintended pregnancies and STDs for almost a decade between the time they initiate sexual activity and when they get married. By their 18th birthday, six in 10 teen-age women and nearly seven in 10 teen-age men have had sexual intercourse.
- Teen-age pregnancy happens. Nearly 900,000 American teen-agers (ages 15-19) become pregnant each year, and almost four in five (78 percent) of these pregnancies are unintended.
- Other countries do better. Despite recent declines, the United States has one of the highest teen-age pregnancy rates in the developed world. U.S. teen-agers are twice as likely to be-

come pregnant as teen-agers in England, Wales or Canada and nine times as likely as those in the Netherlands and Japan.

- Teen-agers and young adults are at risk of STDs and HIV/AIDS. Four million teen-agers acquire an STD annually. Half of the 40,000 new cases of HIV infection in the United States each year occur to individuals younger than age 25. This means that every hour of every day an average of two young people become infected with HIV.
- Contraceptives and condoms are effective. While it is true that successfully abstaining from sexual activity is the only 100 percent guaranteed way of preventing pregnancy and disease, abstinence can and does fail. Extensive research demonstrates that correct and consistent use of contraceptives, including condoms, radically reduces one's risk of pregnancy and disease among those who are sexually active.

Despite the clear need to help young people make safe decisions regarding sexual activity so that they can delay the initiation of sexual intercourse and protect themselves from unintended pregnancy and STDs when they become sexually active, U.S. policymakers continue to promote school-based, abstinence-until-marriage education that fails to provide accurate and complete information about condoms or other contraceptives.

Overall, federal and matching funding from states for abstinence education that excludes information about contraception has totaled more than $700 million since 1996. There is, on the other hand, no federal program dedicated to supporting comprehensive sex education. Federal law contains an extremely narrow eight-point definition of abstinence-only education that sets forth specific messages to be taught, including that sex outside of marriage for people of any age is likely to have harmful physical and psychological effects. Because funded programs must promote abstinence exclusively, they are prohibited from advocating contraceptive use. They thus have a choice: They either must refrain from discussing contraceptive methods altogether or limit their discussion to contraceptive failure rates. Further, in many cases federal law prevents these programs from using their private funds to provide young people with information about contraception or safer-sex practices. Yet even today, many policymakers remain unfamiliar with this extremely restrictive brand of abstinence-only education required by federal law.

Considerable scientific evidence shows that certain programs that include information about both abstinence and contraception help teen-agers delay the onset of sexual activity, reduce their number of sexual partners and increase contraceptive use when they do become sexually active. Indeed, leading medical, public-health and educational organizations, including the American Medical Association, the American Academy of Pediatrics, the American College of Obstetricians and Gynecologists and the National Institutes of Health, support sex-education programs that both stress abstinence and teach young people about the importance of protecting themselves against unintended pregnancy and disease when they become sexually active.

In contrast, there have been few rigorous evaluations of programs focusing exclusively on abstinence. None of these has found evidence that these programs either delay sexual activity or reduce teen pregnancy. Finally, research on virginity-pledge programs and HIV-prevention efforts suggests that education and strategies that promote abstinence but withhold information about contraceptives (and condoms, in particular) may have harmful health consequences by deterring the use of contraceptives when teens become sexually active.

Despite similar levels of sexual activity among American teen-agers and their counterparts in other developed countries, teen-agers in this country fare worse in terms of pregnancy and STDs. U.S. teenagers are less likely to use contraceptives, particularly the pill or other highly effective hormonal methods. U.S. teen-agers also have shorter relationships and thus more sexual partners over time, increasing their risk for STDs. Evidence from other developed countries, moreover, suggests that when teen-agers are provided with comprehensive education about pregnancy and STD prevention in schools and community settings, levels of teen-age pregnancy, childbearing and STDs are low. Adults in these other countries give clear and unambiguous messages that sex should occur within committed relationships and that sexually active teen-agers are expected to take steps to protect themselves and their partners from pregnancy and STDs.

On certain topics, there is a large gap between what sex-education teachers believe they should cover and what they actually are teaching. The great majority of sex-education teachers think that instruction should cover factual information about birth control and abortion, the correct way to use a condom and sexual orientation. However, far fewer actually teach these topics, either because they are prohibited from doing so or because they fear such teaching would create controversy. As a result, a startling one in four teachers believes they are not meeting their students' needs for information.

The gap between what sex-education teachers think should be covered and what they actually teach particularly is acute when it comes to contraception. Sex-education teachers almost universally believe that students should be provided with basic factual information about birth control, but one in four teachers are prohibited by school policies from doing so. Overall, four in 10 teachers either do not teach about contraceptive methods (including condoms) or teach that they are ineffective in preventing pregnancy and STDs.

What many students are being taught in sex-education classes does not reflect public opinion about what they should be learning. Americans overwhelmingly support sex education that includes information about both abstinence and contraception. Moreover, public-opinion polls consistently show that parents of middle-school and high-school students support this kind of sex education over classes that teach only abstinence.

Parents also want sex-education classes to cover topics that are perceived as controversial by many school administrators and teachers. At least three-quarters of parents say that sex-education classes should cover how to use condoms and other forms of birth control, as well as provide information on abortion and sexual orientation. Yet these topics are the very ones that teachers often do not cover. Finally, two out of three parents say that significantly more classroom time should be devoted to sex education.

Similarly, students report that they want more information about sexual-and reproductive-health issues than they are receiving in school. Nearly one-half of junior-high and high-school students report wanting more factual information about birth control and HIV/AIDS and other STDs, as well as what to do in the event of rape or sexual assault, how to talk with a partner about birth control and how to handle pressure to have sex. Young people also need to receive information sooner: More than one-quarter of students become sexually active before they receive even a rudimentary level of sex education such as "how to say no to sex."

Abstinence-only programs also can undermine students' confidence in contraception by providing unbalanced evidence of its ineffectiveness. These programs miss the opportunity to provide students with the skills they need to use contraceptives more, and more effectively. Instead students may leave the program thinking that pregnancy and STDs are inevitable once they begin having sex.

To be sure, promoting abstinence to young, unmarried people as a valid and realistic lifestyle choice should remain a key component of sex education. But those who argue that this is the only message that should be provided to young people are misguided. The evidence strongly suggests that sex in the teen-age years-and certainly prior to marriage, which now typically occurs in the mid-20s is and will continue to be common, both in this country and around the world. Undermining people's confidence in the effectiveness of condoms and other contraceptive methods as a means of scaring them out of having sex is just plain wrong. Protecting our young people requires a balanced approach that emphasizes all the key means of prevention including effective contraceptive and condom use, as well as delaying sex. Ultimately, only such a comprehensive approach will provide young people with the tools they need to protect themselves and to become sexually healthy adults.

Richards is senior vice president and vice president for public policy at the Alan Guttmacher Institute and editor of The Guttmacher Report on Public Policy. He writes and lectures widely on sexual- and reproductive-health-related public-policy concerns. Contact Cory Richards at policyworks@guttmacher.org.

Choosing Virginity

A New Attitude: Fewer teenagers are having sex. As parents and politicians debate the merits of abstinence programs, here's what the kids have to say.

BY LORRAINE ALI AND JULIE SCELFO

THERE'S A SEXUAL REVOLUTION GOING ON IN AMERICA, AND believe it or not, it has nothing to do with Christina Aguilera's bare-it-all video "Dirrty." The uprising is taking place in the real world, not on "The Real World." Visit any American high school and you'll likely find a growing number of students who watch scabrous TV shows like "Shipmates," listen to Eminem—and have decided to remain chaste until marriage. Rejecting the get-down-make-love ethos of their parents' generation, this wave of young adults represents a new counterculture, one clearly at odds with the mainstream media and their routine use of sex to boost ratings and peddle product.

According to a recent study from the Centers for Disease Control, the number of high-school students who say they've never had sexual intercourse rose by almost 10 percent between 1991 and 2001. Parents, public-health officials and sexually beleaguered teens themselves may be relieved by this "let's not" trend. But the new abstinence movement, largely fostered by cultural conservatives and evangelical Christians, has also become hotly controversial.

As the Bush administration plans to increase federal funding for abstinence programs by nearly a third, to $135 million, the Advocates for Youth and other proponents of a more comprehensive approach to sex ed argue that teaching abstinence isn't enough. Teens also need to know how to protect themselves if they do have sex, these groups say, and they need to understand the emotional intensity inherent in sexual relationships.

The debate concerns public policy, but the real issue is personal choice. At the center of it all are the young people themselves, whose voices are often drowned out by the political cacophony. Some of them opened up and talked candidly to NEWSWEEK about their reasons for abstaining from sex until marriage. It's clear that religion plays a critical role in this extraordinarily private decision. But there are other factors as well: caring parents, a sense of their own unreadiness, the desire to gain some semblance of control over their own destinies. Here are their stories.

The Wellesley Girl

ALICE KUNCE SAYS SHE'S A FEMINIST, BUT NOT THE "ARMY-boot-wearing, shaved-head, I-hate-all-men kind." The curly-haired 18-year-old Wellesley College sophomore—she skipped a grade in elementary school—looks and talks like what she is: one of the many bright, outspoken students at the liberal Massachusetts women's college. She's also a virgin. "One of the empowering things about the feminist movement," she says, "is that we're able to assert ourselves, to say no to sex and not feel pressured about it. And I think guys are kind of getting it. Like, 'Oh, *not* everyone's doing it'."

But judging by MTV's "Undressed," UPN's "Buffy the Vampire Slayer" and just about every other TV program or movie targeted at teens, everyone *is* doing it. Alice grew up with these images, but as a small-town girl in Jefferson City, Mo., most teen shows felt alien and alienating. "You're either a prudish person who can't handle talking about sex or you're out every Saturday night getting some," she says. "But if you're not sexually active and you're willing to discuss the subject, you can't be called a prude. How do they market to that?" The friend from back home she's been dating since August asked not to be identified in this story, but Alice doesn't mind talking candidly about what they do—or don't do. "Which is acceptable? Oral, vaginal or anal sex?" she asks. "For me, they're all sex. In high school, you could have oral sex and still call yourself a virgin.

Now I'm like, 'Well, what makes one less intimate than the other?'"

Alice, a regular churchgoer who also teaches Sunday school, says religion is not the reason she's chosen abstinence. She fears STDs and pregnancy, of course, but above all, she says, she's not mature enough emotionally to handle the deep intimacy sex can bring. Though most people in her college, or even back in her Bible-belt high school, haven't made the same choice, Alice says she has never felt ostracized. If anything, she feels a need to speak up for those being coerced by aggressive abstinence groups. "Religious pressure was and is a lot greater than peer pressure," says Alice, who has never taken part in an abstinence program. "I don't think there are as many teens saying 'Oh come on, everybody's having sex' as there are church leaders saying 'No, it's bad, don't do it. It'll ruin your life.' The choices many religious groups leave you with are either no sex at all or uneducated sex. What happened to educating young people about how they can protect themselves?"

The Dream Team

KARL NICOLETTI WASTED NO TIME WHEN IT CAME TO HAVING "the talk" with his son, Chris. It happened five years ago, when Chris was in sixth grade. Nicoletti was driving him home from school and the subject of girls came up. "I know many parents who are wishy-washy when talking to their kids about sex. I just said, 'No, you're not going to have sex. Keep your pecker in your pants until you graduate from high school'."

"If you're abstinent, it's like you're the one set aside from society because you're not 'doing it'."

AMANDA WING, 17,
who plans to stay a virgin until marriage

Today, the 16-year-old from Longmont, Colo., vows he'll remain abstinent until marriage. So does his girlfriend, 17-year-old Amanda Wing, whose parents set similarly strict rules for her and her two older brothers. "It's amazing, but they did listen," says her mother, Lynn Wing. Amanda has been dating Chris for only two months, but they've known each other for eight years. On a Tuesday-night dinner date at Portabello's (just across from the Twin Peaks Mall), Amanda asks, "You gonna get the chicken parmesan again?" Chris nods. "Yep. You know me well." They seem like a long-married couple—except that they listen to the Dave Matthews Band, have a 10:30 weeknight curfew and never go beyond kissing and hugging. (The guidelines set by Chris's dad: no touching anywhere that a soccer uniform covers.)

"Society is so run by sex," says Chris, who looks like Madison Avenue's conception of an All-American boy in his Abercrombie sweat shirt and faded baggy jeans. "Just look at everything—TV, movies. The culture today makes it seem OK to have sex whenever, however or with whoever you want. I just disagree with that." Amanda, who looks tomboy comfy in

baggy brown cords, a white T shirt and chunky-soled shoes, feels the same way. "Sex should be a special thing that doesn't need to be public," she says. "But if you're abstinent, it's like *you're* the one set aside from society because you're not 'doing it'."

The peer pressure in this town of 71,000 people in the shadow of the Rocky Mountains is substantially less than in cosmopolitan Denver, 45 minutes away. ("It figures you had to come all the way out here to find a virgin," one local said.) Chris joined a Christian abstinence group called Teen Advisors this year. "We watched their slide show in eighth grade and it just has pictures of all these STDs," he says. "It's one of the grossest things you've ever seen. I didn't want to touch a girl, like, forever." He now goes out once a month and talks to middle schoolers about abstinence. Amanda saw the same presentation. "It's horrible," she says. "If that doesn't scare kids out of sex, nothing will." Could these gruesome images put them off sex for life? Chris and Amanda say no. They're sure that whoever they marry will be disease-free.

To most abstaining teens, marriage is the golden light at the end of the perilous tunnel of dating—despite what their parents' experience may have been. Though Amanda's mother and father have had a long and stable union, Karl Nicoletti separated from Chris's mother when Chris was in fifth grade. His fiancée moved in with Chris and Karl two years ago; Chris's mother now has a year-and-a-half-old son out of wedlock. Chris and Amanda talk about marriage in the abstract, but they want to go to college first, and they're looking at schools on opposite sides of the country. "I think we could stay together," Chris says. Amanda agrees. "Like we have complete trust in each other," she says. "It's just not hard for us." Whether the bond between them is strong enough to withstand a long-distance relationship is yet to be seen. For now, Chris and Amanda mostly look ahead to their next weekly ritual: the Tuesday pancake lunch.

The Survivor

REMAINING A VIRGIN UNTIL MARRIAGE IS NEITHER AN EASY nor a common choice in Latoya Huggins's part of Paterson, N.J. At least three of her friends became single mothers while they were still in high school, one by an older man who now wants nothing to do with the child. "It's hard for her to finish school," Latoya says, "because she has to take the baby to get shots and stuff."

Latoya lives in a chaotic world: so far this year, more than a dozen people have been murdered in her neighborhood. It's a life that makes her sexuality seem like one of the few things she can actually control. "I don't even want a boyfriend until after college," says Latoya, who's studying to be a beautician at a technical high school. "Basically I want a lot out of life. My career choices are going to need a lot of time and effort."

Latoya, 18, could pass for a street-smart 28. She started thinking seriously about abstinence five years ago, when a national outreach program called Free Teens began teaching classes at her church. The classes reinforced what she already knew from growing up in Paterson—that discipline is the key to getting through your teen years alive. Earlier this year she dated a 21-year-old appliance salesman from her neighborhood, until Latoya heard that he was hoping she'd have sex with him. "We decided that we should just be friends," she explains, "before he cheated on me or we split up in a worse way."

So most days Latoya comes home from school alone. While she waits for her parents to return from work, she watches the Disney Channel or chills in her basement bedroom, which she's decorated with construction-paper cutouts of the names of her favorite pop stars, such as Nelly and Aaliyah. She feels safe there, she says, because "too many bad things are happening" outside. But bad things happen inside, too: last year she opened the door to a neighbor who forced his way inside and attempted to rape her. "He started trying to take my clothes off. I was screaming and yelling to the top of my lungs and nobody heard." Luckily, the phone rang. Latoya told the intruder it was her father, and that if she didn't answer he would come home right away. The man fled. Latoya tries not to think about what happened, although she feels "like dying" when she sees her attacker on the street. (Her parents decided not to press charges so she wouldn't have to testify in court.) Her goal is to graduate and get a job; she wants to stay focused and independent. "Boys make you feel like you're special and you're the only one they care about," she says. "A lot of girls feel like they need that. But my mother loves me and my father loves me, so there's no gap to fill."

The Beauty Queen

Even though she lives 700 miles from the nearest ocean, Daniela Aranda was recently voted Miss Hawaiian Tropic El Paso, Texas, and her parents couldn't be prouder. They've displayed a picture of their bikini-clad daughter smack-dab in the middle of the living room. "People always say to me 'You don't look like a virgin'," says Daniela, 20, who wears super-sparkly eye shadow, heavy lip liner and a low-cut black shirt. "But what does a virgin look like? Someone who wears white and likes to look at flowers?"

Daniela models at Harley-Davidson fashion shows, is a cheerleader for a local soccer team called the Patriots and hangs out with friends who work at Hooters. She's also an evangelical Christian who made a vow at 13 to remain a virgin, and she's kept that promise. "It can be done," she says. "I'm living proof." Daniela has never joined an abstinence program; her decision came from strong family values and deep spiritual convictions.

Daniela's arid East El Paso neighborhood, just a mile or so from the Mexican border, was built atop desert dunes, and the sand seems to be reclaiming its own by swallowing up back patios and sidewalks. The city, predominantly Hispanic, is home to the Fort Bliss Army base, breathtaking mesa views—and some of the highest teen-pregnancy rates in the nation. "There's a lot of girls that just want to get pregnant so they can get married and get out of here," Daniela says.

But she seems content to stay in El Paso. She studies business at El Paso Community College, dates a UTEP football player named Mike and works as a sales associate at the A'gaci Too clothing store in the Cielo Vista Mall. She also tones at the gym and reads—especially books by the Christian author Joshua Harris. In "Boy Meets Girl," she's marked such passages as "Lust is never satisfied" with a pink highlighter. She's also saved an article on A. C. Green, the former NBA player who's become a spokesman for abstinence. "My boyfriend's coach gave it to him because the other guys sometimes say, 'Are you gay? What's wrong with you?' It's proof that if a famous man like Green can do it, so can he."

"I feel that part of me hasn't been triggered yet," she says. "Sex is one of those things you can't miss until you have it."

LENÉE YOUNG, 19,
who has never had a boyfriend

Daniela has been dating Mike for more than a year. He's had sex before, but has agreed to remain abstinent with her. "He's what you call a born-again virgin," she says. "Or a secondary abstinent, or something like that. We just don't put ourselves in compromising situations. If we're together late at night, it's with my whole family."

Daniela knows about temptation: every time she walks out onstage in a bathing suit, men take notice. But she doesn't see a contradiction in her double life as virgin and beauty queen; rather, it's a personal challenge. "I did Hawaiian Tropic because I wanted to see if I could get into a bikini in front of all these people," she says. "I wasn't thinking, 'Oh, I'm going to win.' But I did, and I got a free trip to Houston's state finals. I met the owner of Hawaiian Tropic. It's like, wow, this is as good as it gets."

The Ring Bearer

Lenée Young is trying to write a paper for her Spanish class at Atlanta's Spelman College, but as usual she and her roommates can't help getting onto the subject of guys. "I love Ludacris," Lenée gushes. "I love everything about him. Morris Chestnut, too. He has a really pretty smile. Just gorgeous." But Lenée, 19, has never had a boyfriend, and has never even been kissed. "A lot of the guys in high school had already had sex," she says. "I knew that would come up, so I'd end all my relationships at the very beginning." Lenée decided back then to remain a virgin until marriage, and even now she feels little temptation to do what many of her peers are doing behind closed dormitory doors. "I feel that part of me hasn't been triggered yet," she says. "Sex is one of those things you can't miss until you have it."

Last summer she went with a friend from her hometown of Pittsburgh to a Silver Ring Thing. These popular free events meld music videos, pyrotechnics and live teen comedy sketches with dire warnings about STDs. Attendees can buy a silver ring—and a Bible—for $12. Then, at the conclusion of the program, as techno music blares, they recite a pledge of abstinence

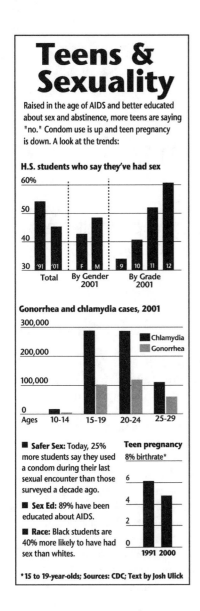

Teens & Sexuality

Raised in the age of AIDS and better educated about sex and abstinence, more teens are saying "no." Condom use is up and teen pregnancy is down. A look at the trends:

H.S. students who say they've had sex

Total: '91, '01
By Gender 2001: F, M
By Grade 2001: 9, 10, 11, 12

Gonorrhea and chlamydia cases, 2001

Chlamydia
Gonorrhea

Ages: 10-14, 15-19, 20-24, 25-29

■ **Safer Sex:** Today, 25% more students say they used a condom during their last sexual encounter than those surveyed a decade ago.

■ **Sex Ed:** 89% have been educated about AIDS.

■ **Race:** Black students are 40% more likely to have had sex than whites.

Teen pregnancy
8% birthrate*

1991, 2000

*15 to 19-year-olds; Sources: CDC; Text by Josh Ulick

Young was the only woman who said no, and everybody in the room was stunned. "Are you serious? We gotta find you a boyfriend!" But Lenée wasn't embarrassed. "I don't feel like I've missed out," she says. "I just feel like my time will come." Until then, she sports that shiny silver ring.

The Renewed Virgin

LUCIAN SCHULTE HAD ALWAYS PLANNED TO WAIT UNTIL HE was married to have sex, but that was before a warm night a couple of years ago when the green-eyed, lanky six-footer found himself with an unexpected opportunity. "She was all for it," says Lucian, now 18. "It was like, 'Hey, let's give this a try'." The big event was over in a hurry and lacked any sense of intimacy. "In movies, if people have sex, it's always romantic," he says. "Physically, it did feel good, but emotionally, it felt really awkward. It was not what I expected it to be."

While the fictional teens of "American Pie" would have been clumsily overjoyed, Lucian, raised Roman Catholic, was plagued by guilt. "I was worried that I'd given myself to someone and our relationship was now a lot more serious than it was before," he says. "It was like, 'Now, what is she going to expect from me?'" Lucian worried, too, about disease and pregnancy. He promised himself never again.

Lucian, now an engineering major at the University of Alberta in Canada, is a "renewed virgin." His parents are strong proponents of chastity, and he attended school-sponsored abstinence classes. But the messages didn't hit home until he'd actually had sex. "It's a pretty special thing, and it's also pretty serious," he says. "Abstinence has to do with 'Hey, are you going to respect this person?'" He has dated since his high-school affair, and is now hoping a particular cute coed from Edmonton will go out with him. "But I'll try to restrict myself to kissing," he says. "Not because I think everything else is bad. But the more you participate with someone, the harder it's going to be to stop."

It's not easy to practice such restraint, especially when those around him do not. Lucian lives in a single room, decorated with ski-lift tickets and a "Scooby-Doo" poster, in an all-male dorm, but he says most students "get hitched up, sleep around and never see each other again." Meanwhile he does his best to push his own sexual urges from his mind. "I try to forget about it, but I have to say it sucks. Homework is a good thing to do, and going out for a run usually works." He also goes to Sunday mass. Lucian figures he can hold out until he's married, which he hopes will be by the time he's 30. "I'm looking forward to an intimate experience with my wife, who I'll truly love and want to spend the rest of my life with," says Lucian. "It's kind of corny, but it's for real."

and don their rings. "My friend, who's also a virgin, said I needed to go so I could get a ring," Lenée says. "It was fun, like the music and everything. And afterwards they had a dance and a bonfire."

The idea of abstinence was not new to Lenée. In high school she participated in a program sponsored by the University of Pittsburgh Medical Center called Postponing Sexual Involvement. Her mother had discussed it with her—once—the week before she left for college. Two of her closest friends are also virgins; the trio jokingly call themselves The Good Girls Club. But student life can sometimes be a shock to her sensibilities. "Another friend of mine and this guy were talking about how they didn't use a condom. He said, 'I like it raw.' I was like, 'Oh, my goodness'."

And then there was the recent party that began with truth-or-dare questions. The first one: have you ever kissed a boy?

With SARAH DOWNEY and VANESSA JUAREZ

The Perils of Playing House

Living together before marriage seems like a smart way to road test the relationship. But cohabitation may lead you to wed for all the wrong reasons—or turn into a one-way trip to splitsville.

Nancy Wartik

Forget undying love or shared hopes and dreams—my boyfriend and I moved in together, a year after meeting, because of a potential subway strike. He lived in Manhattan, and I across the river in Brooklyn. Given New York City taxi rates, we'd have been separated for who knows how long. And so, the day before the threatened strike, he picked me up along with two yowling cats and drove us home. Six years, one wedding and one daughter later, we still haven't left.

Actually, if the strike threat hadn't spurred us to set up housekeeping, something else would have. By then, we were 99 percent sure we'd marry some day—just not without living together first. I couldn't imagine getting hitched to anyone I hadn't taken on a test-spin as a roommate. Conjoin with someone before sharing a bathroom? Not likely!

With our decision to cohabit, we joined the mushrooming ranks of Americans who choose at some point in their lives to inhabit a gray zone—more than dating, less than marriage, largely without legal protections. Thirty or 40 years ago, cohabitation was relatively rare, mainly the province of artists and other questionable types, and still thought of as "living in sin." In 1970 only about 500,000 couples lived together in unwedded bliss.

Now, nearly 5 million opposite-sex couples in the United States live together outside of marriage; millions more have done it at some point. Some couples do choose to live together as a permanent alternative to marriage, but their numbers are only a tiny fraction: More than 50 percent of couples who marry today have lived together beforehand. (At least 600,000 same-sex couples also cohabit, but their situation is different, since most don't have the choice to marry.)

"It's not this bad little thing only a few people are doing," says University of Michigan sociologist Pamela Smock. "It's not going away. It's going to become part of our normal, typical life course—it already is for younger people. They think it would be idiotic not to live with someone before

marriage. They don't want to end up the way their parents or older relatives did, which is divorced."

In my and my husband's case, the pre-matrimonial experiment seems to have worked out well. But according to recent research, our year of shacking up could have doomed our relationship. Couples who move in together before marriage have up to two times the odds of divorce, as compared with couples who marry before living together. Moreover, married couples who have lived together before exchanging vows tend to have poorer-quality marriages than couples who moved in after the wedding. Those who cohabited first report less satisfaction, more arguing, poorer communication and lower levels of commitment.

Many researchers now argue that our penchant for combining households before taking vows is undermining our ability to commit. Meaning, the precautions we take to ensure marriage is right for us may wind up working against us.

From toothbrush to registry

Why would something that seems so sensible potentially be so damaging? Probably the reigning explanation is the inertia hypothesis, the idea that many of us slide into marriage without ever making an explicit decision to commit. We move in together, we get comfortable, and pretty soon marriage starts to seem like the path of least resistance. Even if the relationship is only tolerable, the next stage starts to seem inevitable.

Because we have different standards for living partners than for life partners, we may end up married to someone we never would have originally considered for the long haul. "People are much fussier about whom they marry than whom they cohabitate with," explains Paul Amato, a sociologist at Penn State University and one of the theory's originators. "A lot of people cohabit because it seems like a good idea to share expenses and have some security and companionship, without a lot of commitment."

Couples may wind up living together almost by accident. "People move in their toothbrush, their underwear, pretty soon a whole dresser," says Marshall Miller, coauthor with his partner, Dorian Solot, of *Unmarried to Each Other: The Essential Guide to Living Together as an Unmarried Couple.* "Then someone's lease is up and since they're spending all their time together anyhow... "

Or, two people may move in together without a firm future plan because one partner isn't sure the other is good marriage material: He drinks too much; she gets really nasty during fights. Rather than commit, they take a trial run. Once they've shacked up, relatives start noodging: "So when are you going to get married already?" At friends' weddings, people ask, "When will it be your turn?"

"There's an inevitable pressure that creates momentum toward marriage," says Amato. "I've talked to so many cohabiting couples, and they'll say, 'My mother was so unhappy until I told her we were getting married—then she was so relieved.'" On top of the social pressure, Amato points out, couples naturally start making investments together: a couch, a pet—even a kid. Accidental pregnancies are more common among cohabiting couples than among couples who don't live together.

Once their lives are thoroughly entangled, some couples may decide to wed more out of guilt or fear than love. "I know a lot of men who've been living with women for a couple of years, and they're very ambivalent about marrying them," says John Jacobs, a New York City psychiatrist and author of *All You Need Is Love and Other Lies About Marriage.* "What sways them is a feeling they owe it to her. She'll be back on the market and she's older. He's taken up a lot of her time." Women in particular may be afraid to leave an unhappy cohabiting relationship and confront the dating game at an older age. "If you're 36, it's hard to take the risk of going back into the single world to look for another relationship," says Jacobs.

Younger people think it would be idiotic not to live with someone before marriage. They don't want to end up the way their parents did—divorced.

Charles, a 44-year-old New Yorker (who asked that his name be changed), admits that in his 30s, he almost married a live-in girlfriend of three years for reasons having little to do with love. The two moved in together six months after meeting when his sublet came to an end. "I thought it probably wasn't the best idea, but it was so much easier than looking for an apartment," Charles says. "I told myself: 'Keep trying, and maybe it will work.'"

Eventually his girlfriend insisted they either marry or break up, and he couldn't find the strength to leave. The two got engaged. Weeks before the date, Charles realized he couldn't go through with it and broke off the engagement. "Her father told me, 'I'm sorry horsewhips are a thing of the past,'" Charles recalls, still pained by the

Would You Be My...Roomate?

EVERYONE WHO'S MARRIED remembers how, when and where the momentous question was popped. But when two people move in together, they're often much more cavalier about it. "It's a bigger decision than a lot of couples realize," says Galena Kline, a research assistant at the Center for Marital and Family Studies at the University of Denver. "It's really going to change their life and relationship more than they might think. But a lot of couples don't necessarily communicate about it."

- **TALK, TALK, TALK:** Sitting down to discuss the feelings and expectations about living together before making a move is the best way for couples to ensure a good experience. It's helpful for partners to talk about topics ranging from the sublime to the mundane: marriage, kids, life goals—and who will take out the garbage or feed the cat.
- **FINANCIAL FIRST STEP:** Decide how you'll deal with money matters. "We don't recommend immediately combining your accounts," cautions Marshall Miller, coauthor with Dorian Solot of *Unmarried to Each Other.* Keeping money and credit separate initially, he says, removes an area of potential conflict during a time of adjustment and lets partners see how compatible their financial styles really are.
- **THE SHAKEDOWN:** If you want to test the waters before hiring a moving van, do a "trial cohabitation." Solot and Miller suggest living with your potential partner for a week or two, but caution, "Don't be enticed by fantasies of spending long, lazy days in bed followed by heartfelt conversations while you prepare dinner elbow to elbow, looking adorable . . . Give yourselves a real feel for the pressure of the morning dash, the low energy I-just-want-to-crash-in-front-of-the-TV evening and the negotiation over who will do the dishes." —*NW*

memory. Even now, he regrets moving in with her. "It was a terrible idea," he says. "You get entwined in each other's lives. If you're not sure you want to be entwined, you shouldn't put yourself in a position where it's definitely going to happen."

Some evidence indicates that women have less control over the progress of the cohabiting relationship. She may assume they're on the road to marriage, but he may think they're just saving on rent and enjoying each other's company. Research by sociologist Susan Brown at Bowling Green State University in Ohio has shown there's a greater chance cohabiting couples will marry if the man wants to do so. The woman's feelings don't have as much influence, she found: "The guy has got to be on board. What the woman wants seems to be less pivotal."

Cohabiting men may carry their uncertainty forward into marriage, with destructive consequences. A 2004 study by psychologist Scott Stanley, based on a national phone survey of nearly 1,000 people, found that men who had lived with their spouse premaritally were on average less committed to their marriages than those who hadn't. By contrast, cohabitation didn't seem to change how women felt about their partners.

Based on this finding and others, Stanley, director of the Center for Marital and Family Studies at the University of Denver and another originator of the inertia theory, believes women should be especially wary of moving in before getting engaged. "There are plenty of young men who will say, 'I'm living with a woman but I'm still looking for my soul mate,'" he says. "But how many women know the guy is thinking that way? How many women are living with a guy thinking he's off the market, and he's not?" Men also get trapped in troubled relationships, admits Stanley, but women are more likely to bear the brunt of ill-considered cohabitation decisions for the simplest reason—they are the ones who have the babies.

> Charles almost married a live-in girlfriend for reasons having little to do with love. "It was so much easier than looking for an apartment. I told myself: 'Keep trying, and it will work.'"

The cohabiting type

The inertia theory is not the only way to explain why couples who move in before marriage are less likely to stick it out for the long haul. There may also be something specific about the experience that actually changes people's minds about marriage, making it seem less sacrosanct. "A couple of studies show that when couples cohabit, they tend to adopt less conventional beliefs about marriage and divorce, and it tends to make them less religious," says Amato. That could translate, once married, to a greater willingness to consider options that are traditionally frowned upon—like saying "so long" to an ailing marriage.

Nonetheless, there's a heated debate among social scientists about whether the research to date has been interpreted properly or overplayed to some extent. Having a family income below $25,000, for example, is a stronger predictor of divorce in the first 15 years of marriage than having shared a premarital address. "Having money, a sense of an economically stable future, good communication skills, living in a safe community—all of those things are more important," says Smock.

Because it's impossible to directly compare the effects of marriage and cohabitation, there's just no way to prove cohabiters' higher divorce rates aren't a side effect of their other characteristics, says psychologist William Pinsof, president of the Family Institute at Northwestern University. They may just be less traditional people—less likely to stay in an unhappy marriage in observance of religious beliefs or for the sake of appearances. "Those who choose to live together before getting married have a different attitude about marriage to begin with. I think cohabiting is a reflection of that, not a cause of higher divorce rates," he says. One population of cohabiters also tends to have less money and lower levels of education, which in itself can strain a relationship.

In short, not everyone buys the idea that cohabitation itself is hazardous to your relationship. For some couples, it may serve a useful purpose—even when it lacks a happy ending. About half of all cohabiters split up rather than marry, and many of those splits save the parties involved from rocky marriages, miserable divorces or both.

That's the attitude Amy Muscoplat, 34, a children's librarian who lives in Santa Monica, California, now has about the man she lived with several years ago. She and Mr. X had dated for nine months when they got engaged; a few months later she gave up her rent-controlled apartment by the beach, sold most of her furniture, and the two moved in together. "We moved in in August, and by early September he flipped out," she says. "We were supposed to get married in early November. The invitations had gone out, and then he changed his mind. Living together was the reality check for him, the mirror that made him go, 'Gosh, this might not really work for me.'"

Though she and her family lost thousands of dollars when the wedding was called off, Muscoplat is grateful things fell apart when they did. If they hadn't moved in together, she says, "I think he might have been pushed to the same place at some later point, maybe some day down the road when I was pregnant. I have a religious take on it—God was really watching out for me and I dodged a bullet."

The debate over cohabitation is partly a rehash of the values and morals conflicts that tend to become political footballs in America today. But on one point, virtually all researchers agree: We need to understand the effects of cohabitation on children. Some 40 percent of all cohabiting households include kids—that's somewhere close to 3.5 million children living in homes with two unmarried opposite-sex grown-ups.

Cohabiting relationships, by their nature, appear to be less fulfilling than marital relationships. People who cohabit say they are less satisfied and more likely to feel depressed, Susan Brown has found. While the precarious finances of many cohabiters has something to do with it, Brown also points to the inherent lack of stability. Long-term cohabitation is rare: most couples either break up or marry within five years. "Cohabiters are uncertain about the future of their relationship and that's distressing to them," she says.

> People who cohabit say they are less satisfied and more likely to feel depressed.

As a result, cohabitation is not an ideal living arrangement for children. Emotionally or academically, the children of cohabiters just don't do as well, on average, as those with two married parents, and money doesn't fully explain the difference. The stress of parenting in a shakier living situation may be part of the problem, says Brown. "Stability matters. It matters for the well-being of children and adults alike," she adds. "We're better off with commitment, a sense that we're in it for the long haul."

The must-have discussion

Cohabitation rates may be skyrocketing, but Americans are still entirely enchanted with marriage. That's a sharp contrast with some Western societies—Sweden, France or the Canadian province of Quebec, for example—where cohabitation is beginning to replace marriage. In the United States, 90 percent of young people are still expected to tie the knot at some point.

Since most Americans are destined for marriage—and a majority will live together beforehand—how can we protect against the potentially undermining effects of cohabitation? Follow the lead of one subgroup of cohabiters: Those who make a permanent commitment to each other first. One study that tracked 136 couples through the initial months of marriage found that early intentions seem to make a big difference. About 60 of the couples in the study lived together before getting engaged, while the rest waited either until after they were engaged or after they were married to set up housekeeping. Ten months after the wedding, the group that had cohabited before being engaged had more negative interactions, less confidence about the relationship and weaker feelings of commitment than the other two groups. But the marriages of couples who had moved in together after getting engaged seemed just as strong as those who had moved in together after marrying.

Among other things, couples who get engaged before cohabiting probably have a clearer understanding of each other's expectations before they combine households. On that point, Mia Dunleavey, a 39-year-old online financial columnist living in Brooklyn, New York, can speak with the sadder-but-wiser voice of experience. In her late 20s, Dunleavey was involved with a man she hoped to marry. He reluctantly agreed to move in with her, spurred by the fact that his lease was running out, but he vacillated for so long about setting a wedding date that she finally ended the relationship. Soon after, she relocated across the country to move in with a new man she'd fallen in love with, only to find their living styles were utterly incompatible.

"When you leave the door open for quasi-commitment, quasi-commitment is what you get."

Back in New York again, she took stock. "I was terribly disappointed," Dunleavey says. "You have this faith that you're moving in with someone in order to deepen the commitment, and it doesn't necessarily happen at all. Those two things are not correlated."

"At that point, I said, 'Never ever, ever again,'" she continues. "Living together is a waste of time and energy. The piece of china you'd gotten from your mother gets broken in the move. My living-together experience was a catalog of lost and broken things, never mind my heart."

When she fell in love again, she did things differently. She moved in with her intended just two weeks before the wedding—because by that point, there was no question about their future together. "There was no take-it or leave-it," she says. "The commitment was the foundation of the marriage. Alas, my only experience of living with someone is that when you leave the door open for quasi-commitment, quasi-commitment is what you get."

Miller and Solot don't advise against cohabitation for couples without immediate plans to marry. But they do believe each partner needs to understand clearly what the other is thinking. "The most important thing is for people to treat moving in together as a serious decision, a major life choice," Miller says. "What does it mean to you both for the long and short term? If one person thinks living together means a quick path towards marriage and the other thinks it's just saving on rent and having a friend with benefits, there could be trouble. The important thing is to be on the same page."

As for my husband and me, we had this much going for us when we moved in together: We'd already discussed a lot of the important issues. We knew we wanted similar things: a family; a "for better or worse" kind of commitment; a partner who knew life had to stop on Sundays, when *Six Feet Under* or *The Sopranos* was on. Even before the ring, it was clear to me I'd found someone who'd be willing to work things through. And he has been.

Perhaps there's hope for us after all.

Nancy Wartik is a freelance writer living in New York City.

From *Psychology Today*, vol. 38, no. 4, July/August 2005, pp. 44, 46, 48, 50, 52. Copyright © 2005 by Sussex Publishers, Inc. Reprinted by permission.

UNIT 8

Problem Behaviors and Intervention

Unit Selections

Key Points to Consider

- Is there any relationship between teenage fatherhood and various indicators of deviant behavior?

- What are good interventions for teens who go through trauma and grief?

- Is capital punishment appropriate for adolescents? What does the Supreme Court say?

- How can school counselors help a teen who is self-injurious?

- What types of bullying occurs in schools today?

Student Website

www.mhcls.com/online

Internet References

Further information regarding these websites may be found in this book's preface or online.

Mental Health Net: Eating Disorder Resources
http://eatingdisorders.mentalhelp.net/

Mental Health Risk Factors for Adolescents
http://education.indiana.edu/cas/adol/mental.html

Questions & Answers about Child & Adolescent Psychiatry
http://www.aacap.org/about/q&a.htm

Suicide Awareness: Voices of Education
http://www.save.org/

Youth Suicide League
http://www.unicef.org/pon96/insuicid.htm

That adolescents can and do engage in high-risk behaviors is not subject to much debate. The statistics on adolescent fatalities demonstrate their risk-taking behavior. The leading causes of death in adolescents are tragic: accidents, suicide, and homicide. Alcohol use is frequently involved, particularly in motor vehicle accidents. About half of the fatal motor vehicle accidents involving an adolescent also involves a drunk peer driver.

Why adolescents engage in high-risk behaviors is much debated. Some researchers believe that adolescent risk taking is related to cognitive development. They propose that adolescents possess a sense of invulnerability. Adolescents believe they are special and unique; things that could happen to others could not possibly happen to them. Other researchers believe at best this may apply only to young adolescents. By their mid-teens a majority of adolescents are too sophisticated to consider themselves invulnerable. Despite this, however, adolescents still take more risks than do adults.

If older adolescents do not perceive themselves as invulnerable, than why do they take risks? There are several possible explanations. One proposal is that adolescents may not perceive the risk. For example, adults may have a better sense of how fast they can safely drive given differing road conditions. Adolescents, simply because they are inexperienced drivers, may not recognize when road conditions are dangerous and so may not adjust their speed. Adolescents may engage in riskier behaviors than adults simply because they have the time and energy. Many adolescents have free time, money, and a car. Access to these may allow adolescents to put themselves in dangerous situations. Adults may work, do more household chores, and take care of their children. These adults may not have time to drink, take drugs, or joy ride.

Adolescents may also be less adept than adults at extricating themselves from high-risk behavior. For example, adults who attend a party where drugs are consumed may be more comfortable declining offered drugs than adolescents or they may be able to leave the party without depending on transportation from others. Some researchers indicate that society may be somewhat to blame for adolescents' risk taking. If impoverished adolescents have no chance of obtaining meaningful work, have limited access to recreational activities, and have little encouragement to go to school, then participation in drug-related or violent behavior may be the only options open to them. It may be up to society to provide these adolescents with an increased number of safe choices.

Adolescent risk-taking activities can take many forms. The U.S. Public Health Service identifies several categories of behavior related to health risks for adolescents. Included are behaviors that may cause injuries, such as suicide and violence, use of tobacco or illicit drugs (including alcohol), and risky behaviors related to sexuality or eating disorders. All these can clearly threaten adolescents. Moreover, alcohol use seems to exacerbate many of the other risks, as indicated by the statistics on alcohol use and violent death. And drug use can be related to accidents, health problems, and violence. Violent behaviors are an increasing concern to society. Murder is the second leading cause of death in adolescence; it is the leading cause of

death for African American male teenagers. Suicide rates in young people have tripled since the 1950s. Eating disorders are another threat to adolescents. Millions of adolescents suffer from anorexia nervosa or bulimia in the United States.

In this unit, problem behaviors and interventions are presented. The first article investigates the relationship between teenage fatherhood and various indicators of deviant behaviors. Next we turn to an intervention program developed at schools to deal with trauma and grief. Intervention to help teens has been successful.

Claudia Wallis presents a most controversial topic related to a Supreme Court decision in which the court declared that capital punishment of a juvenile offender (under 18) to be unconstitutional. Although there may various views on this topic, the ruling of the Supreme Court has the final word.

High-risk behavior of self-imposed injury is most alarming. The next article presents strategies for school counselors' intervention for at risk students. And finally, Sandra Harris presents an interesting study of bullying at school among older adolescents.

Teenage Fatherhood and Involvement in Delinquent Behavior

Terence P. Thornberry, Ph.D., Carolyn A. Smith, Ph.D., and Susan Ehrhard, M.A.

The human life course is composed of a set of behavioral trajectories in domains such as family, education, and work (Elder, 1997). In the domain of family formation, for example, a person's trajectory might be described as being in the following states: single, married, divorced, remarried, and widowed. Movement along these trajectories is characterized by elements of both continuity and change. Continuity refers to remaining in a certain state over time (such as being married) while change refers to transitions to a new state (such as getting divorced).

The life course is expected to unfold in a set of culturally normative, age-graded stages. In American society, for example, the culturally accepted sequence is for an individual to complete his or her high school education prior to beginning employment careers and getting married, and all the former, especially marriage, are expected to precede parenthood. Despite these expectations, there is, in fact, a great deal of "disorder" in the life course (Rindfuss, Swicegood, & Rosenfeld, 1987). That is, many life-course transitions are out of order (i.e., parenthood before marriage) and/or off-time (i.e., either too early or too late).

A basic premise of the life-course perspective is that off-time transitions, especially precocious transitions that occur before the person is developmentally prepared for them, are likely to be disruptive to the individual and to those around the individual. Precocious transitions are often associated with social and psychological deficits and with involvement in other problem behaviors. Precocious transitions may also lead to additional problems at later developmental stages. This paper focuses on one type of precocious transition—teenage fatherhood—and investigates whether it is related to various indicators of deviant behavior.

Teen Fatherhood

Until recently, the study of teen parenthood has focused almost exclusively on becoming a teen mother, and relatively little attention has been paid to teenage fatherhood (Parke & Neville, 1987; Smollar & Ooms, 1988). Nevertheless, teen fatherhood appears to be associated with negative consequences, both to the father and child, that are similar to those observed for teen mothers

(Lerman & Ooms, 1993). These consequences include reduced educational attainment, greater financial hardship, and less stable marriage patterns for the teen parent, along with poorer health, educationally, and behavioral outcomes among children born to teen parents (Furstenberg, Brooks-Gunn, & Morgan, 1987; Hayes, 1987; Irwin & Shafer, 1992; Lerman & Ooms, 1993). Given these negative consequences, both to the young father and his offspring, it is important to understand the processes that lead some young men to become teen fathers while others delay becoming fathers until more developmentally normative ages.

One possibility is that becoming a teen father is part of a more general deviant lifestyle. If so, we would expect teen fatherhood to be associated with involvement in other problem behaviors, such as delinquency and drug use. There is some evidence for this hypothesis; teen fathering has been found to be associated with such problem behaviors as delinquency, substance use, and disruptive school behavior (Elster, Lamb, & Tavare, 1987; Ketterlinus, Lamb, Nitz, & Elster, 1992; Resnick, Chambliss, & Blum, 1993; Thornberry, Smith, & Howard, 1997). Some researchers suggest a common problem behavior syndrome underlying all these behaviors (Jessor & Jessor, 1977), a view consistent with Anderson's ethnographic data (1993). In the remainder of this paper, we explore the link between teen fatherhood and other problem behaviors, addressing two core questions:

1. Are earlier delinquency, drug use, and related behaviors risk factors for becoming a teen father?
2. Does teen fatherhood increase the risk of involvement in deviant behavior during early adulthood?

Research Methods

We examine these questions using data from the Rochester Youth Development Study, a multi-wave panel study in which adolescents and their primary caretakers (mainly mothers) have been interviewed since 1988. A representative sample from the population of all seventh- and eighth-grade students enrolled in the Rochester public schools during the 1987–1988 academic year was selected for the study. Male adolescents and students living in census tracts with high adult arrest rates were over-sampled based on the premise that they were more likely than other youth to be at risk for antisocial behavior, the main concern of the original study. Of the 1,000 students ultimately selected, 73% were male and 27% were female.

Because the chances of selection into the panel are known, the sample can be weighted to represent all Rochester public school students, and statistical weights are used here. The Study conducted 12 interviews with the sample members, initially at 6-month intervals and later at annual intervals. This analysis is based on the 615 men in the study who were interviewed in Wave 11, when their average age was 21. Twenty percent of these individuals are White, 63% are African American, and 17% are Hispanic. The interviews, which lasted between 60 and 90 minutes, were conducted in private, face-to-face settings with the exception of a small number of respondents who had moved away from the Northeast and were interviewed by telephone. Overall, 84% (615/729) of the total male sample was interviewed at Wave 11. Due to missing data generated by cumulating data across interview waves, the number of cases included in the models for the analysis varies from 551 to 611. There is no evidence of differential subject loss [see Thornberry, Bjerregaard, & Miles (1993), and Krohn & Thornberry (1999) for detailed discussions of sampling and data collection methods.]

Measurement of Teen Fatherhood

In Wave 11, respondents were asked to identify all of their biological children, including the name, birth date, and primary caregiver of each child. If the respondent fathered a child before his 20th birthday, he is designated a teen father. The validity of the respondent's self-reported paternity is suggested by the 95% agreement with the report provided by the respondent's parent in their interview at Wave 11.

Problem Behavior Variables

In predicting teen fatherhood, we examine the effects of delinquent beliefs, gang membership, and three forms of delinquent behavior. These measures are based on data from early waves of the study, generally between Waves 2–5, covering ages 13.5 to 15.5, on average. As such, these indicators of problem behaviors precede the age at which fatherhood began for this sample, and they can be considered true risk factors for teen fatherhood.

Delinquent beliefs asks the respondent how wrong it is to engage in each of eight delinquent acts, with responses ranging from "not wrong at all" to "very wrong." The measure used here is a dichotomous variable denoting whether the respondent was above or below the median value on the scale. Gang membership is a self-reported measure of whether or not the respondent reported being a member of a street gang (see Thornberry, Krohn, Lizotte, Smith, & Tobin, 2003).

Three variables are used to measure deviant behavior: drug use, which is an index of the respondent's use of 10 different substances; general offending, which is an index based on 32 items reflecting all types of delinquency; and violent offending, which is based on 6 items measuring violent crimes. For the risk factor analysis, all three indices are based on self-reported data and are trichotomized to indicate no offending, low levels of offending (below the median frequency), and high levels of offending (above the median).

These three indicators of offending are also measured during early adulthood (ages 20–22) in order to determine the effects of teen fatherhood on deviant behavior later in life. At this stage, they are simple dichotomies indicating offending versus non-offending.

Results

We present the results in three sections. The first examines the prevalence of teen fatherhood, and the second examines whether delinquency and related behaviors are significant risk factors for becoming a teen father. The final section focuses on whether the young men who became teen fathers, as opposed to those who did not, are more likely to engage in criminal behavior during early adulthood.

Prevalence of Teen Fatherhood

In the Rochester sample, 28% of the male respondents reported fathering a child before age 20. The age distribution at which they became fathers is presented in Figure 3.1. Seven subjects (1%) became fathers at age 15, truly a pre-

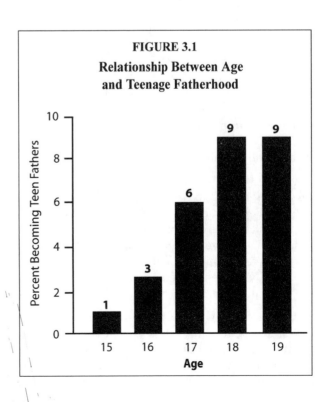

FIGURE 3.1

Relationship Between Age and Teenage Fatherhood

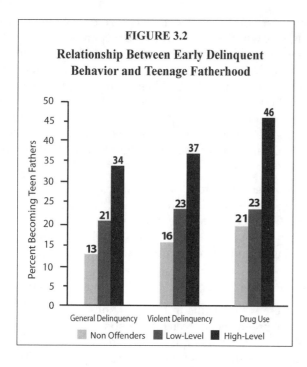

FIGURE 3.2

Relationship Between Early Delinquent Behavior and Teenage Fatherhood

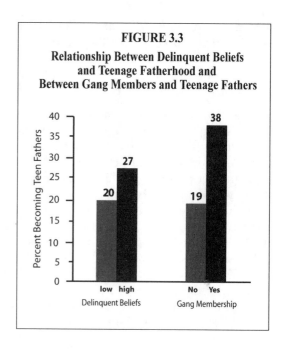

FIGURE 3.3

Relationship Between Delinquent Beliefs and Teenage Fatherhood and Between Gang Members and Teenage Fathers

cocious transition. The rate of fatherhood increased sharply from that point on. At 16, 3% of the sample became fathers; at 17, 6% did; and at both 18 and 19 years of age, 9% entered the ranks of the young fathers.

Risk Factors

The link between delinquent behavior and becoming a teen father is evident from the results presented in Figure 3.2. One-third (34%) of the high-level delinquents during early adolescence fathered a child before age 20, as compared to 21% of the low-level delinquents and only 13% of the non-delinquents. The same dose-response relationship can be seen for violent behavior: the prevalence of teen fatherhood increases from 16%, to 23%, to 37% across the three groups. The pattern is a little different for drug use. The prevalence of teen fatherhood for the non-users and the low-level users is about the same, 21% and 23% respectively, but the rate for the high-level drug users is substantially higher, 46%. All three of these relationships are statistically significant.

In Figure 3.3 we present bivariate results for two variables closely related to delinquency, holding delinquent beliefs and being a member of a street gang. Both relationships are statistically significant. Younger adolescents who have higher levels of pro-delinquent beliefs are more likely (27%) to become teen fathers than those who do not (20%). Finally, gang members are more likely (38%) to become teen fathers than non-members (19%).

To this point, we have simply investigated bivariate associations, that is, the link between delinquency, say, and teen fatherhood, without holding the effect of other potential explanatory variables constant. In a fuller investigation of this issue, Thornberry et al., (1997) examined

these relationships when the following variables were controlled: race/ethnicity, neighborhood poverty and disorganization, parent's education and age at first birth, family poverty level, recent life stress, family social support, parent's expectations for son to attend college, CAT reading achievement, early onset of sexual intercourse, and depression. When this was done, delinquent beliefs were no longer significantly related to teen fatherhood, but gang membership remained a significant and sizeable predictor of becoming a teen father. These two variables—delinquent beliefs and gang membership—were then added to the above list of controls when early adolescent delinquency, drug use, and violence were considered. General delinquency was no longer significantly related to the risk of teen fatherhood, but drug use and violent behavior were (figure not included).

Overall, it appears that early problem behaviors are a risk factor for teen fatherhood. This appears to be the case especially for the more serious forms of these behaviors—violence, high-level drug use, and gang membership.

Later Consequences

The final issue we investigate is whether becoming a teen father is associated with higher rates of criminal involvement during early adulthood, ages 20–22. The results are presented in Figure 3.4. Teen fathers, as compared to males who delayed the onset of parenthood until after age 20, are not significantly more likely to be involved in general offending or in violent offending during their early 20s. However, there is a significant bivariate relationship between teen fatherhood and later drug use. Of the teen fathers, 66% report some involvement with drug use as compared to 47% of those who delayed fatherhood. This relationship is not statistically significant once

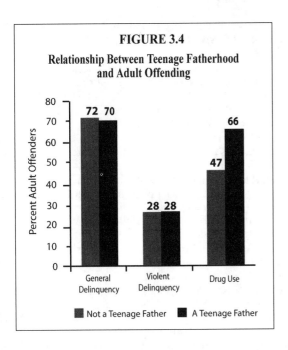

FIGURE 3.4

Relationship Between Teenage Fatherhood and Adult Offending

adolescent drug use is held constant (results not shown), however. The latter finding indicates that early adult drug use is more a reflection of continuing use than a later consequence of becoming a teen father.

Conclusion

This article investigated the relationship between teenage fatherhood and involvement in delinquency and related behaviors. Based on data from the Rochester Youth Development Study, it appears that an earlier pattern of problem behaviors significantly increases the risk of later becoming a teen father. This relationship is evident bivariately for the five indicators used in this analysis. Also, three of the relationships—violence, drug use, and gang membership—remain significant when the impact of a host of other important risk factors is held constant.

While earlier involvement in deviant behavior and a deviant lifestyle is related to the odds of becoming a teen father, teen fatherhood is not significantly related to later involvement in criminal conduct. At least during their early 20s, teen fathers are not more likely than those who delayed parenthood to be involved in general offending or in violent crime. They are more likely to use drugs, although that relationship is not maintained once prior drug use is controlled.

There is a clear link between teen fatherhood and earlier involvement in other deviant behaviors. Two kinds of explanations have been suggested for these effects. The first is that adolescent males immersed in a deviant lifestyle have many opportunities to develop a set of values and behaviors conducive to risky, adult-like adventures, some involving conquest and domination over others, including young women. This notion is supported by some ethnographic research (Anderson, 1993) and some gang

studies (for example, Covey, Menard, & Franzese, 1992). Second, research has also documented that about one-fifth of teenage males feel that impregnating a young woman would make them feel "more like a man" (Marsiglio, 1993). There may be so few avenues for positive identity formation, particularly among poor adolescents and adolescents of color, that having a child is no deterrent to potential goals. Involvement in deviant behaviors, including early fatherhood, may at best be a means of achieving adult status and positive recognition or at least a means of making a mark in a world where even survival is in doubt (Burton, 1995).

Implications

It seems evident that becoming a teen father is not an isolated event in the lives of these young men. It is systematically related to involvement in a deviant lifestyle and, in a broader analysis of these data (Thornberry et al., 1997), to a variety of other deficits. These results have a number of implications for prevention programs designed to delay the transition to fatherhood and to improve the lot of these young men and their offspring. First, these programs need to be prepared to deal with this constellation of behavior problems and how teen fatherhood is intertwined with them. Focusing simply on reducing teenage fatherhood, absent a consideration of the broader context in which it occurs, may not be very effective. Second, prevention programs should include, or at least be prepared to provide access to, services to reduce involvement in antisocial behaviors for these adolescent males. Third, programs to improve the parenting skills of these young fathers need to take into account their higher level of involvement in delinquency, drug use, and related behaviors. All of these behaviors have been shown to be related to less consistent, more erratic styles of parenting (Patterson, Reid, & Dishion, 1992) and efforts to improve effective parenting need to address these risk factors. Finally, programs and policies that try to maximize the teenage father's involvement in the rearing of his children need to be aware of the higher level of antisociality on the part of many of these young fathers. Insuring that risk to the young child is not elevated seems to be the first order of business.

Although there is a pronounced relationship between earlier antisocial behavior and the likelihood of becoming a teen father, we end on a somewhat more positive note. Not all antisocial adolescent males become teen fathers and not all teen fathers have a career of involvement in antisocial behavior. This relationship should not be painted with too broad a brush. Policies need to realistically assess the magnitude of the relationship and realistically take it into account when working with these men and their children.

Terence P. Thornberry, Ph.D., is Director of the Research Program on Problem Behavior at the Institute of Behavioral Science and Professor of Sociology, University of Colorado. He is the Principal Investigator of the Rochester Youth

Development Study, an ongoing panel study begun in 1986 to examine the causes and consequences of delinquency, drug use, and other forms of antisocial behavior. Professor Thornberry is an author of Gangs and Delinquency in Developmental Perspective and an editor of Taking Stock of Delinquency: An Overview of Findings from Contemporary Longitudinal Studies.

Carolyn A. Smith, Ph.D., is Professor in the School of Social Welfare, University at Albany. She holds an M.S.W. from the University of Michigan, and a Ph.D. from the School of Criminal Justice at the University at Albany. She has international social work practice experience in child and family mental health, and in delinquency intervention. Her primary research interest is in the family etiology of delinquency and other problem behaviors, and most recently the impact of child maltreatment on the life course.

Susan Ehrhard holds an M.A. in Criminal Justice and is currently a doctoral student at the School of Criminal Justice, University at Albany, as well as a Research Assistant for the Rochester Youth Development Study. Her research interests include the sociology of crime, restorative justice, and capital punishment.

References

Anderson, E. (1993). Sex codes and family life among poor inner-city youths. In R.I. Lerman & T.J. Ooms (Eds.), *Young Unwed Fathers: Changing Roles and Emerging Policies* (pp. 74-98). Philadelphia: Temple University Press.

Burton, L.M. (1995). Family structure and nonmarital fertility: Perspectives from ethnographic research. In K.A. Moore (Ed.), *Report to Congress on Out-of-Wedlock Childbearing* (pp. 147-166). Hyattsville, MD: U.S. Department of Health and Human Services.

Covey, H.C., Menard, S., & Franzese, R.J. (1992). *Juvenile Gangs.* Springfield, IL: Charles C. Thomas.

Elder, G.H., Jr. (1997). The life course and human development. In W. Damon (Ed.-in-Chief) & R.M. Lerner (Ed.), *Handbook of Child Psychology, Vol. 1: Theoretical Models of Human Development* (pp. 939-991). New York: Wiley.

Elster, A.B., Lamb, M.E., & Tavare, J. (1987). Association between behavioral and school problems and fatherhood in a national sample of adolescent fathers. *Journal of Pediatrics, 111,* 932-936.

Furstenberg, F.F., Brooks-Gunn, J., & Morgan, S.P. (1987). *Adolescent Mothers in Later Life.* New York: Cambridge University Press.

Hayes, C.D. (1987). *Risking the Future: Adolescent Sexuality, Pregnancy and Childbearing* (Vol. 1). Washington, DC: National Academy Press.

Irwin, C.E., Jr., & Shafer, M.A. (1992). Adolescent sexuality: Negative outcomes of a normative behavior. In D.E.

Rodgers & E. Ginzberg (Eds.), *Adolescents at Risk: Medical and Social Perspectives* (pp. 35-79). Boulder, CO: Westview Press.

Jessor, R., & Jessor, S.L. (1977). *Problem Behavior and Psychosocial Development.* New York: Academic Press.

Ketterlinus, R.D., Lamb, M.E., Nitz, K., & Elster, A.B. (1992). Adolescent nonsexual and sex-related problem behaviors. *Journal of Adolescent Research, 7,* 431-456.

Krohn, M.D., & Thornberry, T.P. (1999). Retention of minority populations in panel studies of drug use. *Drugs & Society, 14,* 185-207.

Lerman, R.I., & Ooms, T.J. (1993). Introduction: Evolution of unwed fatherhood as a policy issue. In R.I. Lerman & T.J. Ooms (Eds.), *Young Unwed Fathers: Changing Roles and Emerging Policies* (pp. 1-26). Philadelphia: Temple University Press.

Marsiglio, W. (1993). Contemporary scholarship on fathers: Culture, identity, and conduct. *Journal of Family Issues, 14,* 484-509.

Parke, R.D., & Neville, B. (1987). Teenage fatherhood. In S.L. Hofferth & C.D. Hayes (Eds.), *Risking the Future: Adolescent Sexuality, Pregnancy, and Childbearing, Vol. 2* (pp. 145-173). Washington, DC: National Academy Press.

Patterson, G.R., Reid, J.B., & Dishion, T.J. (1992). *Antisocial Boys.* Eugene, OR: Castalia Publishing Company.

Resnick, M.D., Chambliss, S.A., & Blum, R.W. (1993). Health and risk behaviors of urban adolescent males involved in pregnancy. *Families in Society, 74,* 366-374.

Rindfuss, R.R., Swicegood, C.G., & Rosenfeld, R. (1987). Disorder in the life course: How common and does it matter? *American Sociological Review, 52,* 785-801.

Smollar, J., & Ooms, T. (1988). *Young Unwed Fathers: Research Review, Policy Dilemmas, and Options: Summary Report.* U.S. Department of Health and Human Services, Washington, DC: U.S. Government Printing Office.

Thornberry, T.P., Bjerregaard, B. & Miles, W. (1993). The consequences of respondent attrition in panel studies: A simulation based on the Rochester Youth Development Study. *Journal of Quantitative Criminology, 9,* 127-158.

Thornberry, T.P., Krohn, M.D., Lizotte, A.J., Smith, C.A., & Tobin, K. (2003). *Gangs and Delinquency in Developmental Perspective.* New York: Cambridge University Press.

Thornberry, T.P., Smith, C.A., & Howard, G.J. (1997). Risk factors for teenage fatherhood. *Journal of Marriage and the Family, 59,* 505-522.

From *Prevention Researcher,* 11(4), November 2004, pp. 10-13. Copyright © 2004 by Integrated Research Services, Inc. www.tpronline.org Reprinted by permission.

School-Based Trauma and Grief Intervention for Adolescents

William R. Saltzman, Ph.D., Robert S. Pynoos, M.D., M.P.H., Christopher M. Layne, Ph.D., Alan M. Steinberg, Ph.D., and Eugene Aisenberg, Ph.D.

Juveniles are two times more likely than adults to be victims of serious violent crime and three times more likely to be victims of simple assault. A national survey of adolescents found that 23% reported having been both a victim of assault and a witness to violence and that over 20% of these individuals met lifetime criteria for post-traumatic stress disorder (PTSD).

Of particular concern to educators and health professionals is the considerable evidence indicating that adolescents exposed to violence are at increased risk for a spectrum of adverse psychosocial difficulties and functional impairments. These difficulties include reduced academic achievement; aggressive, delinquent, or high-risk sexual behaviors; and substance abuse and dependence. The burden of single and, frequently, multiple exposures to violence, may also be compounded by the traumatic death of a close friend or family member. In a city-wide survey of adolescents in Pasadena, California, 23% reported having an immediate or extended family member that died in a violent manner, and 48% reported having a friend that died in a violent manner. Recent studies indicate that the death of a family member or friend that occurs in violent or traumatic circumstances may lead to a form of "complicated bereavement" that may have a long-term impact on the development of children and adolescents.

An example of the way in which trauma and traumatic bereavement can interfere with academic performance is provided by Hector. Hector was standing next to a friend when the friend was killed in a drive-by shooting. Typically a quiet boy, Hector did not relate his experience to teachers or peers. Following his friend's murder, Hector's grades dropped sharply and his level of participation in school activities declined. He was afraid to leave his house or to ride his bicycle by the park or liquor store where his friend was killed. Hector experienced increasing difficulty with going about his daily activities. He startled whenever there were loud noises, he had diffi-culty sleeping, and he had intrusive images of his murdered friend. In school, he began to have, increasing test-taking anxiety and panic when called on to speak.

Such traumatic losses as Hector's impose a dual burden of post-traumatic stress reactions and bereavement, the interplay of which may complicate grief reactions. Research by Robert Pynoos and others has found that intrusive, distressing memories and emotions linked to the violent circumstances of the death, avoidance of cues linked to the death or to the deceased, and numbing of responsiveness may disrupt critical adaptive grieving processes. These processes include reminiscing, participating in grief rituals, processing painful emotions associated with accepting and adapting to the loss, and making meaning of the death.

These findings point to a need to provide trauma-exposed adolescents with access to specialized mental health services. The challenge to providing appropriate services to adolescents exposed to community violence has two major aspects. The first involves the need for a systematic, accurate, and efficient means of identifying youths with histories of severe trauma or loss who currently experience distress and functional impairment.

Traumatized youths do not generally seek professional assistance, and recruiting school personnel to refer trauma-exposed students can also leave many of these students unidentified.

The second aspect to providing appropriate services to adolescents exposed to community violence is to recruit and retain traumatized youths in appropriate treatment. Services must be easily accessible, engage the adolescent, and minimize attrition. According to school counselors and community mental health providers, as many as one half of the students referred by schools for mental health services in the community do not show up for treatment, and those who do frequently terminate prematurely.

This article describes the results of a school-based trauma- and grief-focused group psychotherapy program designed to address these two challenges.

Trauma- and Grief-Focused Treatment Protocol

This program was adapted from intervention programs developed by members of the University of California, Los Angeles (UCLA) Trauma Psychiatry Service. It was used in Armenia following the 1988 earthquake, in Southern California with adolescents traumatized by community violence, and in post-war Bosnia with severely war-exposed secondary school students.

The program consists of four primary components. The first is a triage self-report survey of community violence exposure and post-traumatic stress, depression, and grief symptoms. Students who endorse significant exposure and concurrent distress are then invited to participate in the second component, which consists of an individual screening interview. This interview is designed to verify the survey results; to explore functional impairments at school, home, and with peers; and to assist in determining appropriateness for individual or group psychotherapy. The third component is a pre-group clinical interview. This interview provides education about traumatic stress and complicated bereavement, initiates the construction of a shared vocabulary about the trauma or loss, and prepares the adolescent for group participation. The fourth component consists of a manual-driven trauma- and grief-focused group psychotherapy protocol that is based on five treatment foci developed by Robert Pynoos and his colleagues. The five foci are traumatic experiences, reminders of trauma and loss, the interplay of trauma and grief, post-trauma adversities, and developmental progression.

This study addressed four basic questions: What are the prevalence rates of different forms of trauma and traumatic loss exposure reported by students? What percentage of these students were appropriate candidates for specialized psychological services? How many students were in need of specialized mental health services but did not access it? And, was participation in trauma and grief-focused group psychotherapy associated with significant improvements in post-traumatic stress, depression, complicated grief symptoms, and academic performance?

Method

This program was implemented at two junior high schools located within a community characterized by chronic economic disadvantage and violent gang activity. Participants consisted of 812 students (41% of the school population) who were surveyed for trauma exposure and distress and 26 students who participated in the trauma- and grief-focused group psychotherapy program. Group participants were aged 11 to 14 years (average 12.6 years), 61% were boys, 68% Hispanic, 28% African American,

and 4% Caucasian. Parents gave active written consent for all aspects of this program.

The measures used in the self-report survey included a variety of reliable and valid self-report measures: the Community Violence Exposure Survey, the UCLA PTSD Reaction Index-Adolescent Version, the Reynolds Adolescent Depression Scale, and the Grief Screening Scale. Additionally, we used the UCLA Trauma-Grief Screening interview, which is designed for administration by a trained clinician. Grade point average (GPA) was used to assess school performance. Of the 812 students surveyed, approximately 14% reported significant trauma or loss exposure and current distress, these students were administered an individual screening interview. Students identified by the self-report and interview procedures as having serious psychological disturbances, substance abuse problems, or being at risk for harming self or others were referred to appropriate local agencies. Suspected child abuse or neglect was reported to the appropriate authorities as mandated by state laws. In recognition that group therapy was not appropriate for all students, a procedure was established for referring students to individual treatment. At the conclusion of the multi-stage screening process, 26 students were determined to be appropriate candidates for the group therapy protocol.

Once students were identified and selected for group treatment, and parental consent was received, five groups were formed. Each group was composed of five to seven students and two group leaders. Efforts were made to maximize the homogeneity of the groups according to whether the primary treatment issue centered on trauma versus traumatic death, the severity of the trauma or loss, and the student's general developmental level. Groups met once a week, for 20 weeks, on the school grounds during regular school hours. Each meeting lasted about 50 minutes.

Results

Results of the screening survey revealed high base rates of multiple forms of community violence exposure (see Table 1). Of the 812 students surveyed, 22% reported one or more items measuring direct victimization, 37% reported one or more incidents of witnessing severe violence, and 58% reported one or more items indicating that a close friend or family member had been either victimized or killed. Seventy-five (9.2%) of the students surveyed were administered individual screening interviews, and 58 (7.1%) of the students surveyed met criteria for inclusion in the treatment program. It was notable that only 14 (24%) of these students had previously been referred for mental health services. Of the 26 students who participated in the trauma- and grief-focused group psychotherapy programs 14 had initial levels of PTSD in the severe to very severe range. The mean pre-treatment GPA of this severe to very severe PTSD group fell in the D range and was significantly lower than the

Table 1
Prevalence of Exposure to Trauma and Traumatic Loss (N=812)

Type of Exposure	% Endorsed
Direct Victimization	
Badly hurt in violent incident (needed to see a doctor)	17
Stabbed or attacked with a knife or sharp object	6
Shot at with a gun	18
Shot with a gun	3
Choked, strangled, or smothered (not playing)	12
Tried to (or did) kidnap me	5
Been badly hurt in an accident (needed to see a doctor)	19
Witnessing	
Seen someone badly hurt or killed in a violent incident	22
Seen someone stabbed or attacked with a knife or sharp object	19
Seen someone shot or shot at with a gun	28
Seen someone choked, strangled, or smothered (not playing)	15
Seen someone kill someone else (on purpose)	3
Seen someone attempt to commit suicide	2
Family Member or Close Friend Victimized	
Family member was badly hurt in an accident	47
Family member was badly hurt in violent incident	21
Close friend was badly hurt in an accident or violent incident	51
Family member was killed in an accident	14
Family member was killed in a violent incident	10
Close friend was killed in an accident or violent incident	15
Family member or friend committed suicide	6
Threatened,	
Been threatened with serious physical harm	46
Been threatened with a weapon	38
Natural Disasters and Wars	
Lived in a war where there was fighting, people hurt, or dead bodies	4
Been in a big earthquake that badly damaged the building I was in	64
Been in another kind of disaster like a fire, hurricane, or flood	7

mean pre-treatment GPA of the other 12 group members, who had moderate PTSD scores and GPAs in the C range.

We found post-traumatic stress scores decreased significantly pre- to post-treatment. Of greater clinical relevance, the post treatment mean PTSD score (36.8) fell below the clinical cutoff of 40. In addition, of the seven students reporting histories of significant loss, complicated grief symptoms decreased significantly pre- to post-treatment. In contrast, depressive symptoms did not significantly decrease. GPA also improved significantly. There was no attrition among group members.

We also calculated a series of exploratory correlations to examine the relationship between pre-post change in scores and GPA. The correlations revealed that pre-post reduction in posttraumatic stress symptoms was associated with an improvement in GPA; on the other hand, pre-post depression change scores were not significantly associated with improvement in GPA.

Discussion

Before discussing the implications of this preliminary field trial, it is important to describe its methodological limitations. First, the participant sample was relatively small and not representative, in that 59% of the student body was not screened. Second, control groups were not used, making it impossible to rule out the effects of history, maturation, and regression to the mean. Third, a limited battery of treatment outcome measures was used that may not have captured important dimensions of change. For example, school staff noted reductions in disruptive and inappropriate behaviors among some of the participants in the program.

On the other hand, this study possesses a number of strengths. First, it contains a number of features that characterize well-controlled treatment outcome studies, including clearly defined target symptoms, the use of reliable and valid measures, and the use of a manual-driven and replicable treatment program. Second, group attendance was consistently high and there was no attrition of group members. Third, the intervention provided services to a heterogeneous participant group in a natural setting. Many group members in this study reported multiple exposures to trauma or loss and face adverse life circumstances characterized by chronic family dysfunction, parental substance abuse, severe economic hardship, frequent relocations, and changes in caretakers. Several members also possessed extensive histories of behavioral and psychological problems. Although the inclusion of such students in this study probably introduced considerable error variance, their participation was essential to providing an ecologically valid and welcome mental health service to the schools.

The results of the screening survey and screening interview provide some evidence that a significant number of secondary school students may need mental health services focusing specifically on trauma and loss. We view the finding that over 7% of the students screened met criteria for receiving specialized trauma and grief services, in combination with the finding that fewer than one quarter had been previously referred for services, as suggesting a need for a systematic, accessible, and specialized set of mental health services among this population of students.

One of the most notable findings of this study was its identification of significant barriers to receiving appropriate mental health services. These barriers existed at multiple levels, including at the school district level, which was reluctant to grant permission to survey students regarding potentially sensitive issues such as sexual abuse or exposure to domestic violence. In addition, less than one half (41%) of all parents let their children participate in the screening survey, and up to 16% of the parents who consented to the initial screening then refused to let their child receive specialized mental health services. A possible contributing factor to parents' reticence about involving their children may be their lack of knowledge concerning their children's traumatic exposure and related difficulties. In the individual interviews, almost half the students invited to participate in the group psychotherapy program reported that they had never disclosed their traumatic experiences to their parents. They cited various reasons for not doing so, including not wanting to worry their parents or fearing that their parents would learn that they had been in a forbidden place or in the company of people with whom they had been forbidden to associate. Efforts to counter this problem may take the form of outreach and education to parents and students focusing on the prevalence of traumatic exposure among youths in the community and the importance of seeking appropriate support and services.

A second important finding, although tentative, suggested that participation in trauma- and grief-focused group psychotherapy is linked to improvements in post-traumatic stress symptoms, complicated grief symptoms, and academic performance. It is notable that these improvements were observed among youths who had chronic PTSD, more than half of whom reported symptoms falling in the severe to very severe range. These improvements are not as large as those reported by J. March and colleagues on an efficacy study of group treatment for single-incident trauma involving youths with moderate PTSD and satisfactory academic functioning. However, the reduction of PTSD symptoms observed in this study moved students from the relatively severe level to moderate levels of distress. Moreover, the current intervention program was designed to treat students with severe levels of trauma exposure, associated distress, and functional impairment. Thus, one possible explanation for our more modest improvement in PTSD symptoms is that the group members had histories of multiple trauma or loss exposures, were exposed to ongoing community violence, and experienced chronic adverse living circumstances. A second explanation is that, as noted above, students with ongoing conduct problems were not excluded and may have introduced additional error variance.

A significant number of secondary school students may need mental health services focusing specifically on trauma and loss.

Two preliminary findings suggested that PTSD severity and school performance may be linked. First, group members with severe to very severe PTSD scores had a significantly lower mean GPA than members with moderate scores. Second, pre-post reduction in PTSD was correlated with pre-post improvement in GPA for all group members. These exploratory findings are consistent with observations that traumatized youths may experience breakdowns in key attentional and task-related skills that can jeopardize academic performance. Improvement in specific PTSD symptoms, including sleep disturbances, re-

activity to reminders, intrusive thoughts and images, hypervigilance and exaggerated startle, and avoidant behavior, may all contribute to increased attention and concentration, improved school attendance, increased classroom participation, less disruptive behavior, and less distraction in completing homework assignments. It is important to note that the improvement in GPA to a C range among many group members permitted them to resume participation in many school activities—including field trips and recreational activities—available only to students receiving passing grades. This improvement in functioning and consequent resumption of normal interpersonal and enrichment activities has important implications for promoting long-term development and adaptation.

The lack of reduction of depression scores is a complex issue. Concurrent chronic depression is a common feature of chronic PTSD among adolescents. This program did not include a specific depression module which may be necessary when concurrent depression is severe and chronic. The persistent depressive symptoms may have been linked to ongoing adverse circumstances in the students' lives. A.Y. Shalev and colleagues recommended that additional treatment for depression should be added after a primary PTSD intervention is completed. In cases of chronic PTSD and complicated bereavement, concurrent depression may also be related to the risk of depression associated with loss. Reduction of complicated grief reactions reduces preoccupation with the traumatic circumstance of the death and initiates an active grieving process that includes positive reminiscing.

An important aim of group treatment is to reduce trauma avoidant behaviors that curtail normal activities. This principle is illustrated by the case of Julia, a group member who expressed the intention that she would not attend her graduation because of her belief that "bad things happen to the people around me." Group discussion centered on this belief as a traumatic expectation or distorted view born out of her repeated traumatic experiences in which people around her were injured or killed. It became apparent that graduation served as a strong trauma reminder because Julia witnessed her uncle being fatally stabbed at a family birthday party after arguing with a family friend. The group then supportively challenged the accuracy of her belief and, through a structured exercise, explored the worst, best, and most likely outcome if her family members attended her graduation. Julia then shared her fears with her family, elicited their support, and made plans to attend her graduation. Overcoming her trepidation, she celebrated the event with her friends and family.

For Hector, our student highlighted at the beginning of this article, though he had never spoken in detail to anyone about his experience before he began treatment, his therapy group included students with similar experiences. In therapy, Hector was able to share his experience, participate in narrative exposure exercises, and use a number of

What to Expect After Trauma: Possible Reactions in Middle and High School Students

Compiled by Robin H. Gurwitch, Ph.D., Jane F. Silovsky, Ph.D., Shelli Schultz, Ph.D., Michelle Kees, Ph.D., and Sarah Burlingame, B.A.

Middle and High School Students Might Exhibit

1) Worries, fears, and anxiety about safety of self and others
2) Worries about re-occurrence or repercussions such as war or school violence
3) Changes in behavior:
   - Withdrawal
   - Irritability with friends, teachers, events
   - Anger outbursts and/or aggression
   - Changes in academic performance
   - Decrease in attention and concentration
   - Increase in hyperactivity
   - Absenteeism
4) Negative impact on issues of trust and perceptions of others, particularly those that are "different"
5) Increased sensitivity to sounds (e.g., sirens, planes, thunder, backfires, loud noises)
6) Repetitive thoughts and comments about death or dying (including suicidal thoughts)

Middle School Students Might Also Exhibit

1) Increased somatic complaints (e.g., headaches, stomach aches, chest pains)
2) Discomfort with feelings, particularly those associated with revenge
3) Repeated discussions of the event and increased likelihood to discuss the gruesome details

High School Students Might Also Exhibit

1) Increased risk for substance abuse, including drinking
2) Discomfort with feelings, particularly revenge, but also those of vulnerability
3) Discussion of events and reviewing of details

Changes at Home Might Include

1) Changes in sleep or appetite
2) Withdrawal
3) Lack of interest in usual activities (e.g., after-school activities, time with friends)
4) Increased negative behaviors (e.g., defiance) or emotions (e.g., sadness, fears, anger, worries)
5) Hate or anger statements
6) Denial of impact

Condensed and reprinted from "Reactions and Guidelines for Children Following Trauma/Disaster" (helping.apa.org/daily/ptguidelines.html) with permission from the author.

strategies to reduce his reactivity and exposure to trauma and loss reminders. As a result, his overall anxiety diminished and his grades returned to pre-trauma levels. One of his teachers noted, "Hector always used to seem so distracted, and he rarely completed his assignments. He got so nervous when I called on him that I stopped doing so. Now, he seems much more relaxed and present."

In conclusion, this field-trial study suggests that there is a sizable group of young adolescents with chronic severe PTSD and concurrent depression from severe trauma or loss experiences who are not typically identified or given appropriate therapeutic services. The results provide very preliminary support for a school-based model of case identification and trauma treatment that may reduce symptoms of distress and enable students to perform better at school.

William R. Saltzman, Ph.D., is at the Department of Educational Psychology at California State University, Long Beach, and the National Center for Child. Traumatic Stress at UCLA; Robert S. Pynoos, M.D., M.P.H., and Alan M. Steinberg, Ph.D., are at the National Center for Child Traumatic Stress at UCLA; Eugene Aisenberg, Ph.D., is at the University of Washington, School of Social Work; and Christopher M. Layne, Ph.D., is at Brigham Young University.

As seen in *Prevention Researcher,* April 2003, pp. 8-11; condensed from Saltzman et al, *Group Dynamics: Theory and Practice,* Vol. 5, 291-303, 2001.

Too Young to Die

The Supreme Court nixes the juvenile death penalty.
What that says about the Justices' thinking—and ours

Claudia Wallis

In his Norman, Okla., law office, attorney Steven Presson stores two unusual keepsakes. One is a leather pouch that holds the ashes of Sean Sellers, the only person executed for a crime committed as a 16-year-old since the death penalty was reinstated in the U.S. in 1976. Sellers—who murdered his mother, his stepfather and a store clerk—was dispatched by lethal injection in 1999, when he was 29. Presson's other memento is a plastic box containing the ashes of Scott Hain, who, it now seems fair to say, was the last juvenile offender to be executed in the U.S. Hain, sent to his death in 2003 at the age of 32, was 17 when he and a friend committed a grisly double murder.

Presson, who represented both boys, found it "very bittersweet" when the U.S. Supreme Court ruled last week that it was cruel and unusual to sentence anyone to death for crimes committed before the age of 18. "I'm happy for those on death row, but it came six years too late for Sean and two years too late for Scott," says Presson. "We've been arguing for decades that kids don't have the same moral culpability that adults have, and finally, finally, they listened."

It took 16 years for the high court to come around to Presson's point of view, by a narrow 5-to-4 vote. In 1989 the court ruled 5 to 4 the other way. Justice Antonin Scalia, who wrote the 1989 decision, argued that there was neither a "historical nor a modern societal consensus" forbidding capital punishment for 16- or 17-year-olds (though the court had found such a consensus for those under 16 a year earlier). Last week, however, Scalia was on the short side of the decision.

What changed? The views of Justice Anthony Kennedy, for one thing. While Kennedy voted with Scalia in 1989, he wrote a very different majority opinion this time around. Why did Kennedy change his mind? Legal tradition invites him to do so. Since 1958 the court has applied a flexible standard to interpreting the Eighth Amendment's ban on "cruel and unusual punishments." What we mean by the phrase, wrote then Chief Justice Earl Warren in *Trop v. Dulles*, depends on "the evolving standards of decency that mark the progress of a maturing society."

How do you know that society no longer believes in sentencing a 17-year-old killer to death? Kennedy's argument mirrors his reasoning in a 2002 decision that outlawed death sentences for the mentally retarded. He notes that since 1989 five states have banned capital punishment for juveniles, making the practice illegal in 30 states, including the 12 with an outright ban on executions. Second, Kennedy cites scientific literature showing that, like the retarded, adolescents lack mature judgment and a full appreciation of the consequences of their actions. They are also more vulnerable than adults to peer pressure. Third, Kennedy points out that only seven other countries have executed juvenile offenders since 1990, and all seven have repudiated the practice: "The United States now stands alone in a world that has turned its face against the juvenile death penalty."

"This reference to international practices is a very big deal," says Cass Sunstein, a constitutional scholar at the University of Chicago Law School, and is part of a surprising new trend in Supreme Court thinking. Overseas legal practices were also cited by the court in the 2002 ruling on the mentally retarded and in a 2003 decision overturning a Texas law banning gay sex. For his part, Scalia blasted his brethren for suggesting that "American law should conform to the laws of the rest of the world" and pointed out that the U.S. has unique legal traditions.

In the 12 states where juvenile offenders have been languishing, death sentences will be lifted for 72 offenders. That brought dismay to many victims' families. Martin Soto-Fong was 17 in 1992 when he and two accomplices robbed the El Grande Market in Tucson, Ariz., for $300 and shot three workers. Richard Gee, who lost a brother and an uncle that day, is not happy to see the murderer exit death row. "We had him at the gates of hell," he says, "and he got kicked back."

Adolescents Who Self-Injure:

Implications and Strategies for School Counselors

Victoria E. White Kress, Ph.D.; Donna M. Gibson and Cynthia A. Reynolds, Ph.D.

This article explores strategies for school counselors to use in intervening and managing adolescent students who engage in self-injurious behaviors. The school counselor's roles in intervention, referral, education, advocacy, and prevention are discussed. Implications and recommendations for school counselors are addressed.

In recent years, the media and popular literature have begun to address the issue of adolescent self-injurious behavior, and many counselors have had an increasing exposure to students who engage in these behaviors. Approximately 13% of adolescents sampled in one recent survey indicated that they engaged in self-injurious behaviors (Ross & Heath, 2002), and research has indicated that self-injury is becoming increasingly prevalent among adolescents (Hawton, Fagg, Simkin, Bale, & Bond, 1997). The incidence of self-injurious behaviors rises to 40% to 61% in adolescent inpatient settings and is ostensibly beginning earlier in the childhood and adolescent years (Conterio, Lader, & Bloom, 1998; Darche, 1990; DiClemente, Ponton, & Hartley, 1991).

Self-injurious behavior is discussed often with regard to the mentally retarded and developmentally disabled populations—people diagnosed with psychotic disorders, personality disorders, and dissociative identity disorder; however it is rarely addressed in discussions of the general adolescent population (Zila & Kiselica, 2001). This article focuses on self-injurious behaviors associated with adolescents in the non-severely mentally disabled population (e.g., mental retardation, schizophrenia, etc.). This article also is delimited to self-injurious behaviors involving self-cutting, interference with wound healing, scratching, and burning, but will not explore issues associated with hair pulling (e.g., trichotillomania), and extreme forms of self-injury (e.g., eye enucleation, amputation of body parts, breaking bones, etc.) as these are less commonly presented in school settings.

It is important to acknowledge that most cultures have forms of culturally acceptable and sanctioned self-injurious behaviors (Favazza, 1996). For example, among adolescents in Western culture, ear piercing, tattooing, and various forms of body piercing are becoming more commonplace. Deviant forms of self-injury are generally considered physically damaging and

occur in response to psychological crisis. These acts demonstrate a sense of disconnection and alienation from others; the line between socially sanctioned self-injury and deviant self-injury can be hazy (Dallam, 1997).

Self-cutting is one of the most common forms of self-injury found in the non-hospitalized population, followed by burning, pinching, scratching, biting, self-hitting, and interference with wound healing (Briere & Gil, 1998; Ross & Heath, 2002; Taiminen, Kallio-Soukainen, Nokso-Koivisto, Kaljonen, & Helenius, 1998). The areas that are most typically injured are the arms and wrists, legs, abdomen, head, chest, and genitals, respectively (Conterio et al., 1998; Zila & Kiselica, 2001). In the literature, many varied definitions abound as to what constitutes self-injury. In this article, self-injury will be defined as a volitional act to harm one's body without any intention to die as a result of the behavior (Simeon & Favazza, 2001; Yarura-Tobias, Neziroglu, & Kaplan, 1995).

In many ways, the current awareness of self-injurious behaviors parallels the appreciation of eating disorders that developed in the 1970s and 1980s. At that time, anorexia and bulimia were thought to be rare and interesting conditions, but as public and professional awareness increased, many people began to seek help (Conterio et al., 1998). Despite an increasing awareness of adolescent self-injurious behavior, little is known about what treatments work best with this population (Zila & Kiselica, 2001).

The age at which people first begin to engage in self-cutting behaviors varies; however, these behaviors usually begin in middle adolescence (Herpertz, 1995), with the freshman year of high school being the average age of the first self-injurious behaviors (Ross & Heath, 2002; Favazza & Conterio, 1989). One study found that mental health professionals identified 18 as the average age their clients last engaged in self-cutting behaviors (Suyemoto & MacDonald, 1995). Thus, with regard to self-injury, school counselors are in a unique position to intervene as these behaviors typically begin, and often end, during the adolescent years.

Gender issues may also be present with regard to rates of self-injury. It is commonly stated that females are more likely to engage in self-injury than males. In one study of self-injurious adolescents, 64% were female and 36% were males (Ross

& Heath, 2002). Indeed, most studies have indicated the majority of hospitalized self-injuring patients are female (Herpertz, 1995). However, Briere and Gil (1998), using a community sample, found no gender differences with regard to self-injurious behaviors. The belief that females are more likely to engage in self-injury may be related to researchers' use of samples including help-seeking clinical populations, hospitalized patients, and sexual abuse and incest survivor populations; samples that are more likely to be comprised of females. Higher rates of male self-injury in community samples may be due to different definitions of self-injury with some researchers including deliberate recklessness and risk-taking behaviors in which males may be more likely to engage (Ross & Heath).

Many theories have been proposed concerning the etiology and function of self-injurious behaviors. Generally, theories of the etiology of self-injury tend to be based on biological, psychological, and sociological explanations. From a biological perspective, the seratonergic system has been implicated in the pathophysiology of self-injury (Dallam, 1997; Simeon et al., 1992) as well as the idea that the endorphin rush associated with self-injury can lead to an addiction to the behavior (Pies & Popli, 1995). Among mental health professionals, one of the more popular psychological theories (Suyemoto & MacDonald, 1995) involves the ability of self-injury to regulate emotions. The psychodynamic-oriented emotional dysregulation theory holds that self-injury is the result of anger turned inward on the self (Feldman, 1988) and that the self-injury results in emotional catharsis (Crowe & Bunclark, 2000). Similarly, Linehan's (1993) biosocial emotional dysregulation theory holds that self-injury in person's diagnosed with borderline personality disorder occurs secondary to a person being highly sensitive and reactive to emotional stimuli, yet having a deficit in emotion regulation skills. In other words, people who self-injure have an inability to distract themselves from their emotional experiences; thus the person self-injures as an attempt to modulate or cope with strong emotions.

Research investigations indicate that people who self-injure have identified the following as reasons for engaging in self-injurious behaviors: (a) feeling concrete pain when psychic pain is too overwhelming; (b) reducing numbness and promoting a sense of being real; (c) keeping traumatic memories from intruding into the consciousness; (d) affect modulation; (e) receiving support and caring from others; (f) discharge of anger, anxiety, despair, and expression of disappointment; (g) gaining a sense of control; (h) self-punishment for perceptions of being bad; and (i) an enhancement of self-esteem (Himber, 1994; Shearer, 1994).

Various life factors and clinical correlates are related to self-injurious behaviors in adolescents. Self-injury is often associated with childhood sexual abuse and subsequent posttraumatic stress disorder reactions (Darche, 1990; Favazza & Rosenthal, 1993; Ghaziuddin, Tsai, Naylor, & Ghaziuddin, 1992; Langbehn & Pfohl, 1993), as well as sexual assault/rape (Greenspan & Samuel, 1989), anxiety and depression (Ross & Heath, 2002) and eating disorders (Cross, 1993).

There are many correlates and predictors that are indicative of self-injurious behavior. Conterio et al. (1998) noted that other life conditions including loss of a parent, childhood illness, physical abuse, marital violence, and familial self-injury are related to self-injury. However, a history of sexual abuse and family violence are the best predictors of self-injury. Research also identifies adolescents' experiences that trigger self-mutilation, including the following: a recent loss, peer conflict and intimacy problems, body alienation or dissociation related to abuse, and impulse control problems (Conterio et al.; Welch, 2001). Indeed, all of these correlates can be useful in identifying at-risk adolescents for the purposes of intervention and prevention (Walsh & Rosen, 1988).

Many times, school counselors become aware of students' self-injurious behaviors prior to families and persons outside of the school setting. The school counselor's first awareness that a student is self-injuring can come from many sources: observations or physical indicators of self-injury, information reported to the counselor by the student, concerns of teachers and parents reported to counselor, or finally, other students reporting a peer's self-injury.

The dynamics of adolescent self-injurious behaviors and implications and strategies for school counselors in working with this population are important to understanding these behaviors. School counselors' functions as providers of interventions, referral agents, advocates, and as educators and prevention agents of student self-injurious behavior are essential in helping these adolescents.

SCHOOL COUNSELORS' ROLE IN INTERVENING AND MANAGING SELF-INJURIOUS BEHAVIORS

According to Dahir, Sheldon, and Valiga (1998), the heart of the National Standards for school counseling programs is a focus on student success being equated with academic development, career development, and personal/social development. Therefore, in terms of facilitating student success, school counselors have an important role to play in ensuring that students are safe and that they have the resources they need to develop in all of the aforementioned areas. School counselors can help facilitate student success by providing interventions, and referrals as well as acting as advocates, educators, and prevention agents with regard to student self-injurious behaviors.

Intervention

Most adolescents who self-injure are evasive about their role in the injury, attempt to avoid attention and embarrassment, and frequently wear clothes that hide their injuries (Alderman, 2000). Physical indicators of self-injury include numerous unexplained scars, burns or cuts. The scars are often more prevalent on the arm opposite the student's dominant hand and are more likely on the forearm at an angle. Some non-threatening questions that can be helpful in eliciting information about injuries are: "What is this from?"; "Could you say more about this?"; "Have you had accidents like this before?"; "What were you thinking or feeling prior to the accident?"; "Have you found a pattern to these accidents?"; and, "How did you feel after the accident?" (Barstow, 1995; Dallam, 1997).

The primary goal for school counselors intervening with self-injuring students is to help them create a safe environment. As many students who self-injure have been physically and sexually abused and thus have a history of adults abusing their power and disregarding their needs, it may be difficult for the student to trust the counselor. Therefore, care should be taken in fostering a strong alliance with the student. An emphasis on structure, consistency, and predictability can be stressed and modeled in the counseling relationship. Developing a plan with the student that emphasizes the students' taking responsibility for behaviors and making the safest decisions possible is one method for accomplishing this goal. A detailed safety plan should be developed including identifying self-injury triggers, physical cues, and reducers related to self-injury; exploring safe people and safe places to go when wanting to self-injure; and the deliberate avoidance of objects which could be used to self-injure (e.g., paper clips, staples, erasers, sharp objects). This plan should serve to help stabilize the student and to provide structure and support until community-based counseling can begin. Techniques that can be used in helping the student manage self-injurious impulses include increasing feeling awareness and recognition, increasing coping skills to be used in managing feelings, encouraging the use of self-soothing techniques such as relaxation exercises, and encouraging the use of a safe [place] (Kehrberg, 1997).

Research has indicated that two important factors contribute to a cessation of self-injury (Dallam, 1997). The first factor that contributes to a cessation of self-injury is developing an ability to identify and express feelings verbally. The second factor contributing to a decrease in self-injury is learning to use behavioral alternatives to self-injury. The short-term safety plan could be used as a means of fostering the students' development of impulse control and a sense of control in managing the self-injurious behaviors (Kehrberg, 1997). Encouraging the student to be around others when wanting to injure can be helpful, as self-harm is rarely done when others are nearby (Dallam).

Safety issues should also be explored with the student including the importance of not bringing dangerous objects such as razor blades or knifes to school. Students should be instructed on the dangers of using rusty blades or sharing blades with other people who self-injure so as to prevent disease transmission (Dallam, 1997; DiClemente et al., 1991). DiClemente et al. found that 61% of a hospitalized sample of adolescents self-injured, and of that sample, 27% reported that they had shared cutting implements with other adolescents. Clearly, school counselors can play an important role in educating students about the issues associated with sharing cutting implements.

One serious complication of self-injury is the possibility of accidental death as a result of damage inflicted on the body. Thus, in assessing a student's self-injury, it is important to consider the severity of the behaviors as well as possible medical complications. If there is any concern that the student has infections or is engaging in self-injury of a severe and chronic nature (e.g., infections secondary to recurrent cutting, etc.) that could cause severe medical complications, the student should be referred to a physician for an assessment.

To facilitate student safety, issues related to suicide should be assessed. Counselors should consider (a) an assessment of depression, helplessness, and hopelessness; (b) suicidal ideation, plan and intent, preparation and access to a means of suicide, and past attempts; (c) social support; (d) family history of suicide; and (e) recent stressors. It is important to note that suicide and self-injury are not necessarily related. Indeed, self-injury should only be thought of as suicidal if the student indicates intent to die. It should be noted however, that the link between suicide and self-injury is complicated; one can have suicidal ideation and self-injure and not be considered suicidal (Simeon & Favazza, 2001). An over-reactive stance could alienate students and fracture a developing student/counselor alliance.

The school counselor could provide support during aftercare and could be involved in helping to arrange home tutoring if needed. School counselors might also suggest modifications of the students schedule if needed through the use of a 504 plan. This type of plan allows students identified with a physical or mental impairment, yet not qualified for specialized education, to receive accommodations in their school schedule to receive help for the impairment. For example, the self-injuring student may need to leave class for counseling sessions, follow-up medical care, behavior modification scheduled checks, and time-out sessions to practice cognitive-behavioral intervention techniques. The 504 plan is an agreed upon arrangement between school, parent, and student.

Finally, an important part of a school counselor's intervention plan for self-injurious students is to follow their ethical duty in assessing and, if necessary, reporting the situation. School counselors are obligated to assess the student's behavior in doing harm to him or herself. Legally, school counselors are obligated to contact the student's parents or local authorities in helping the student. Although this task may appear clear, it is often difficult to decipher the severity of behavior and the intent of the self-injury. Part of the process should include assessing the family situation and determining if the student is safe in his or her home environment. If appropriate, parents should be called to the school and appropriate referral information should be given. However, parents should not be the first contacted if issues of abuse are part of the student's report. Following school protocol, the local social service agency or police should be contacted if abuse is suspected.

Referral Issues

In discussing the role of school counselors, Baker (2001) stated that their scope of practice primarily includes the intervention and prevention of mental and emotional disorders, but not the diagnosis and treatment of disorders. Thus, school counselors play an important role in the referral of students to qualified professionals. School counselors can make either a partial or a complete referral (Baker). A complete referral would involve dissociating from the student's case, and a partial referral would involve some continued involvement with the student while he or she works with outside mental health professionals. A referral for inpatient or out-patient treatment would be appropriate, and should be done in a sensitive manner so that the student does not feel abandoned or refuses to go. School counselors need to be knowledgeable of the practitioners and treatment centers that have specific training in the management of self-injury. If possible, the school counselor might use an in-service day to visit local treatment facilities and determine the steps a student would go through in receiving treatment. When counselors are aware of what the treatment process is like, they can better help students and their families in making decisions and developing intervention plans.

Once the student begins work with a community mental health professional, the counselor can collaborate with the community professional and can continue to play a role in the student's treatment process (e.g., being a safe person the student can talk to when wanting to injure). If the student goes for inpatient treatment, the school counselor could be involved in continuing the educational process through arranging in home tutoring or collaborating with the educational tutor at the residential center or hospital.

Advocacy and Education

Advocating for students, and educating school personnel are important roles of school counselors (Baker, 2001). Through advocacy and education, school counselors can help to dispel myths and break down stereotypes regarding self-injury.

School counselors can advocate for students through faculty in-services and parenting groups, and speaking in health classes to students regarding self-injury. It is important to inform staff, parents, and students that self-injury does not mean someone is crazy, but can be understood as a means of attempting to help one's self. In particular, educating school faculty regarding the etiology and function of self-injury can help in dispelling the myth that people who self-mutilate are attention seeking. Dispelling myths can help students gain access to support and needed services both within the school and in the outside community. For example, a teacher who is aware a student is self-injuring may not report self-injury as he or she may perceive it as trivial or as a way for the student to receive attention. With education, the teacher may be more likely to seek help for the student and to make the school counselor aware of the situation.

Education of staff and teachers is one manner in which school counselors can advocate for students who self-injure. By educating faculty about self-injury, they should feel more comfortable in managing the issue of self-injury. Also, educating faculty on ways to approach or manage student self-disclosure of self-injury can be helpful. In particular, the physical education teacher and the school nurse may be of critical importance in identifying and monitoring students who self-injure.

Advocating for students by educating faculty about the fact that self-injury is not equated with suicidality is also very important. Strong personal reactions to self-injury can lead to reactionary stances and extreme measures such as unnecessary hospitalizations, pulling students out of school, or suspending students. Educating faculty and administrators on the differences between self-injury and suicide attempts can help in avoiding unnecessarily restrictive actions.

Prevention

Conterio et al. (1998) and Welch (2001) have noted that loss, childhood illness, physical and sexual abuse, marital violence, familial self-injury, peer conflict and intimacy problems, and impulse control problems are all related to self-injury. Thus, for the purposes of prevention, school counselors should consider these variables when targeting at-risk students. As with the issue of intervention, prevention efforts can include helping students to express and identify their feelings, while also developing healthy behavioral coping skills. Group counseling and counselor outreach activities that encourage at-risk students' development of these aforementioned skills may be helpful in preventing self-injury. Prevention efforts can also occur by providing pamphlets and handouts to students. Materials concerning self-injury can be distributed through health classes or directly through the school counseling office.

A sequence of events in which a person inflicts self-injurious behaviors and is imitated by others in the environment is referred to as contagion of self-injurious behaviors (Walsh & Rosen, 1985). The issue of contagion has received some attention in the research literature (Rosen & Walsh, 1989; Ross & McKay, 1979; Taiminen et al., 1998; Walsh & Rosen) Initial research indicated that in hospital and residential treatment settings, adolescents tend to imitate self-injurious behaviors. Self-injurious acts followed in 25 residents at a residential facility indicted that these acts are bunched or clustered in time across subjects, suggesting that adolescents in a residential setting trigger the self-injurious behaviors in each other (Walsh & Rosen). These findings suggest that a group process variable or social factors may contribute to the behavior in participants who already self-injure or are at risk for self-injuring. Walsh and Rosen noted that labeling self-injury as a behavior that is likely to be imitated actually decreases self-injury as many adolescents, for developmental reasons, do not want to be perceived as being imitative or be labeled as followers.

Similar to Walsh and Rosen (1985), Taiminen et al. (1998) have suggested adolescents' weak egos and diffuse identities make them susceptible to various forms of identification including self-injuring and refer to this phenomena as "rites of togetherness" (p. 215). Through intensive study (i.e., interviewing methods and empirical observation), Rosen and Walsh (1989) came to similar conclusions. They stated that adolescents in a residential setting engaged in contagious self-injury as a "concrete display of affinity between two people" (p. 657). Rosen and Walsh observed the following: (a) individuals involved in contagious self-injury are highly enmeshed; (b) they have difficulty with conventional forms of intimacy; (c) they find deviate acts (e.g., shared self-injury) to be compelling and exciting. Rosen and Walsh concluded that when contagious self-injury occurs, it is important to use interventions that target specific dyads. It is important to help the adolescents express emotions and negotiate intimacy in more normative ways.

When this is not possible, it may be necessary to isolate the person being modeled from the rest of the group.

While the aforementioned studies all involved adolescents in residential treatment settings, Fennig, Carlson, and Fennig (1995) described their experiences consulting in a public school setting regarding a situation where an outbreak of self-mutilation occurred. They expressed concerns that this phenomenon may be more frequent in educational systems than reported. In describing their experiences they made the following observations: (a) the majority of students involved in the outbreak did not demonstrate any overt psychopathology and were not identified as emotionally disturbed; (b) the only overt sign of problems associated with self-injury was a drop in grades; (c) several initiators with more severe psychopathology seemingly induced the behavior in more passive students and all had anxiety and depressive related traits; (d) isolation of the more severely disturbed initiators was most effective in lowering the severity and frequency of the phenomenon.

While these suggestions are narrative and have not been empirically scrutinized, school counselors facing similar situations can use this information. Combined, the research related to contagion implies that social factors may contribute to the development and maintenance of self-injurious behavior. A related issue is to differentiate initiation self-mutilating behaviors of gangs or cliques from self-injuring behaviors related to psychopathology. Although both types of behaviors are significant, intervention and referral can take different directions. If an ostensible contagion situation occurs, consultation with other professionals may be necessary.

PERSONAL REACTIONS

Counselors may have many strong feelings when faced with student self-injurious behaviors. Alderman (2000) stated that the typical clinician treating a client who self-mutilates is often left feeling a combination of helplessness, guilt, anger, betrayal, disgust, and sadness. Self-injury has been identified as the most distressing client behavior encountered in clinical practice and the behavior that many professionals find most traumatizing to encounter (Gamble, Pearlman, Lucca, & Allen as cited in Deiter & Peralman, 1998).

Writers on self-injury frequently address the issue of counselors' need to manage their personal reactions towards clients who self-injure. Issues such as the time and emotional investment required in working with this population, the strong reactions of counselors to self-injury, and the limits these reactions place on counselors' ability to work with clients have been noted (Levenkron, 1998; Zila & Kiselica, 2001). Self-injury is sometimes viewed as being manipulative or "attention seeking" (Simcon & Favazza, 2001). Counselors may sometimes feel frustrated with self-injury and may want to attempt to control the student by forcing him or her to stop engaging in the self-destructive behavior, or by lecturing or debating the problems associated with self-injury. A personal awareness and understanding of one's intentions when working with students who self-injure can be helpful in facilitating successful interventions. Avoiding attempts to control the student or tell him or her

to stop the behavior can facilitate student empowerment as well as prevent potential power struggles. A constant monitoring of personal reactions combined with ongoing consultation and supervision can help in ensuring that counselors maintain an objective perspective when working with this population (Deiter & Pearlman, 1998).

CONCLUSIONS

Self-injury is an increasing trend that has not been adequately addressed in the literature. Preliminary research indicates that the etiology, function, and interventions associated with self-injury are diverse and varied; counselors know little and must be careful, deliberate, and thoughtful in working with this population.

Counselors can serve as powerful advocates to students who self-injure through challenging a culture that may contribute to adolescents' challenges and by hearing adolescents stories, validating their experiences, and providing a safe refuge. Counselors can also play a role in intervening and preventing self-injury; educating teachers, parents, and students; and making referrals to specialists who can help the self-injuring student. On a more macro-cultural level, counselors can serve to fight oppressive cultural systems that serve to disempower adolescents and hamper their voices by providing an environment that fosters self-expression and the use of positive coping skills (Conterio et al., 1998; Zila & Kiselica, 2001).

References

Alderman, T. (2000). Helping those who hurt themselves. The Prevention Researcher, 7(4), 43-46.

Baker, S. B. (2001). School counseling for the twenty-first century (3rd ed.). Upper Saddle River, NJ: Prentice Hall.

Barstow, D. G. (1995). Self-injury and self-mutilation: Nursing approaches. Journal of Psychosocial Nursing and Mental Health Services, 33(2), 19-22.

Briere, J., & Gil, E. (1998). Self-mutilation in clinical and general population samples: Prevalence, correlates, and functions. American Journal of Orthopsychiatry, 68, 609-620.

Conterio, K., Lader, W., & Bloom, J. K. (1998). Bodily harm: The breakthrough healing program for self-injurers. New York: Hyperion.

Cross, L.W. (1993). Body and self in feminine development: Implications for eating disorders and delicate self-mutilation. Bulletin of the Menninger Clinic, 57, 41-67.

Crowe, M., & Bunclark, J. (2000). Repeated self-injury and its management. International Review of Psychiatry, 12(1), 49-54.

Dahir, C. A., Sheldon, C. B., & Valiga, M. J. (1998). Vision into action: Implementing the national standards for school counseling. Alexandria, VA: American School Counselor Association.

Darche, M. A. (1990). Psychological factors differentiating self-mutilating and non-self-mutilating adolescent inpatient females. Psychiatric Hospital 21(1), 31-35.

Dallam, S. J. (1997). The identification and management of self-mutilating patients in primary care. The Nurse Practitioner, 22, 151-164.

Deiter, R J., & Pearlman, L. A. (1998). Responding to self-injurious behavior. In P. M. Kleespies (Ed.), Emergencies in mental health practice: Evaluation and management (pp. 235-257). New York: Guilford.

DiClemente, R. J., Ponton, L. E., & Hartley, D. (1991). Prevalence and correlates of cutting behavior: Risk for HIV transmission. Journal of the American Academy of Child and Adolescent Psychiatry, 30, 735-738.

Favazza, A. R. (1996). Bodies under siege: Self-mutilation and body modification in culture and psychiatry (2nd ed.). London: John Hopkins.

Favazza, A. R., & Conterio, K. (1989). Female habitual self-mutilation. Acta Psychiatrica Scandinavica, 79, 283-289.

Favazza, A. R., & Rosenthal, R. J. (1993). Diagnostic issues in self-mutilation. Hospital and Community Psychiatry, 44, 134-140.

Feldman, M. D. (1988). The challenge of self-mutilation, a review. Comprehensive Psychiatry, 29, 252-269.

Fennig, S., Carlson, G. A., & Fennig, S. (1995). Letter to the editor: Contagious self-mutilation. Academy of Child and Adolescent Psychiatry, 34, 402-403.

Ghaziuddin, M., Tsai, L., Naylor, M., & Ghaziuddin, N. (1992). Mood disorders in a group of self-cutting adolescents. Acta Paedopsychiatrica, 55, 103-105.

Greenspan, G. S., & Samuel, S. E. (1989). Self-cutting after rape. American Journal of Psychiatry, 146, 789-790.

Hawton, K., Fagg, J., Simkin, S., Bale, E., & Bond, A. (1997).Trends in deliberate self-harm in Oxford, 1985-1995. British Journal of Psychiatry, 171, 556-560.

Herpertz, S. (1995). Self-injurious behaviour: Psychopathological and nosological characteristics in subtypes of self-injurers. Acta Psychiatrica Scandinavica, 91, 57-68.

Himber, J. (1994). Blood rituals: Self-cutting in female psychiatric inpatients. Psychotherapy, 31, 620-631.

Kehrberg, C. (1997). Self-mutilating behavior. Journal of Child and Adolescent Psychiatric Nursing, 10(3), 35-40.

Langbehn, D. R., & Pfohl, B. (1993). Clinical correlates of self-mutilation among psychiatric inpatients. Annals of Clinical Psychiatry, 5, 45-51.

Levenkron, S. (1998). Cutting: Understanding and overcoming self-mutilation. New York: W. W. Norton.

Linehan, M. M. (1993). Cognitive behavioral therapy of borderline personality disorder. New York: Guilford.

Pies, R.W., & Popli, A. P. (1995). Self-injurious behavior: Pathophysiology and implications for treatment. Journal of Clinical Psychiatry, 56, 580-588.

Rosen, R. M., & Walsh, B.W. (1989). Patterns of contagion in self-mutilation epidemics. American Journal of Psychiatry, 146, 656-658.

Ross, S., & Heath, N. (2002). A study of the frequency of self-mutilation in a community sample of adolescents. Journal of Youth and Adolescence, 31(1), 67-77.

Ross, R. R., & McKay, H. B. (1979). Self-mutilation. Lexington, MA: DC Heath.

Shearer, S. L. (1994). Phenomenology of self-injury among inpatient women with borderline personality disorder. Journal of Nervous and Mental Disease, 182, 524-526.

Simeon, D., & Favazza, A. R. (2001). Self-injurious behaviors: Phenomenology and assessment. In D. Simeon & E. Hollander (Eds.), Self-injurious behaviors: Assessment and treatment (pp. 1-28). Washington D.C.: American Psychiatric Press.

Simeon, D., Stanley, B., Frances, A., Mann, J. J., Winchel, R., & Stanley, M. (1992). Self-mutilation in personality disorders: Psychological and biological correlates. American Journal of Psychiatry, 149, 221-226.

Suyemoto, K. L., & Macdonald, M. L. (1995). Self-cutting in female adolescents. Psychotherapy, 32, 162-171.

Taiminen, T. J., Kallio-Soukainen, K., Nokso-Koivisto, H., Kaljonen, S., & Helenius, H. (1998). Contagion of deliberate self-harm among adolescent inpatients. Journal of the American Academy of Child and Adolescent Psychiatry, 37, 211-217.

Walsh, B.W., & Rosen, R. (1985). Self-mutilation and contagion: An empirical test. American Journal of Psychiatry, 142, 119-120.

Walsh, B.W., & Rosen, R. (1988). Self-mutilation: Theory, research, and treatment. New York: Guilford.

Welch, S. S. (2001). A review of the literature on the epidemiolooogy of parasuicide in the general population. Psychiatric Services, 52, 368-375.

Yarura-Tobias, J. A., Neziroglu, R. A., & Kaplan, S. (1995). Self-mutilation, anorexia, and dysmenorrhea in obsessive compulsive disorder. International Journal of Eating Disorders, 17, 33-38.

Zila, L. M., & Kiselica, M. S. (2001). Understanding and counseling Self-mutilation in female adolescents and young adults. Journal of Counseling and Development, 29, 46-52.

Victoria E. White Kress Ph.D., is an assistant professor, Department of Counseling, Youngstown State University, Youngstown, OH. E-mail: vewhite@ysu.edu.

Donna M. Gibson Ph.D., is an assistant professor, School of Education, The Citadel, Charleston, SC.

Cynthia A. Reynolds Ph.D., is an assistant professor, Counseling and Special Education, University of Akron, OH.

From *Professional School Counseling*, Vol. 7, Issue 3, February 2004, pp. 195-201. Copyright © 2004 by American School Counselor Association (ASCA). Reprinted by permission.

Bullying at School Among Older Adolescents

Sandra Harris, Ph.D.

The Justice Department's Bureau of Justice Statistics and the Department of Education's National Center for Education Statistics (2001) reported that overall juvenile crime rates have dropped since 1992 from 48 crimes per 1,000 students ages 12 through 18 to 33 per 1,000 students. At the same time, data indicated that students who said they were victims of any crime of violence or theft at school decreased from 10% to 8%. However, before the 2003-04 school year had even completed the first quarter, there had been school shootings in and around Chicago and Minnesota, gang feuds in Arizona, stabbings in Texas and Florida, apparent murder-suicides in California and Kentucky; and armed students in standoffs in Washington and California (Toppo, 2003).

Many argue that school violence is a product of a sense of escalating alienation and rage that seems to exist in many of today's young people. The fuel for this violence is often considered to be school bullying. In fact, a 2002 report by the Families and Work Institute interviewed 2,000 students and found that small things, such as teasing, often trigger serious episodes of violence. On school campuses, studies have found anywhere from 20% to 30% of students are frequently involved in bullying incidents either as the victim or the bully (Juvonen, Graham, & Schuster, 2003). Consequently, high school students report that bullying has seriously affected their physical, social, and academic well-being.

Bullying is intentionally harmful, aggressive behavior of a more powerful person or group of people directed repeatedly toward a less powerful person, usually without provocation. The most common form of bullying among adolescents is verbal—name calling and hurtful teasing. Bullying also includes threatening gestures, hitting, stealing, spreading rumors, intentionally excluding others, and using weapons to threaten or harm. Sexual harassment is another harmful form of bullying that increases in adolescence. In fact, Stein (1995) has noted that even as early as kindergarten there appears to be bullying conduct with sexual overtones.

High school bullies tend to pick on students who don't fit in. Boys tend to select victims who are physically weak, who are short tempered, based on who their friends are, or by their clothing. Girls, on the other hand, choose victims based on looks, emotionalism, being overweight, or who get good grades.

Being a victim of school bullying causes students to feel less connected with the high school, which often leads to poor physical health, lowered participation in extra-curricular events, violence, substance use, and suicide (Resnick et al., 1997). The ability to form natural relationships is often impaired and this rejection by peers often leads to emotional disturbances in adulthood (Ross, 1996). In high school, victims of bullying are more anxious than their high school peers, are likely to be targeted for racism or actions that cross traditionally accepted gender behaviors (such as sexual orientation), and have poorer relationships with classmates and feel lonelier than bullies, especially boys (Nansel et al., 2001).

> *High school students are more likely to bully with ridicule, rejection, and other forms of emotional abuse, rather than using physical bullying.*

While bullies demonstrate some of the same characteristics as their victims, they are more likely to be depressed than their victims; hold higher social status than victims; use alcohol and smoke; have poorer academic achievement and perceive a poorer school climate. They are more likely to manifest defiant behavior (Nansel et al., 2001) and are more likely to have racist attitudes (Ross, 1996). The students that seem to be the most seriously affected by bullying are the bully/victims. Bully/victims are more likely to smoke, drink and have poorer academic achievement than victims; and have poorer relationships with classmates and are lonelier than bullies (Nansel et al., 2001). They also need to retaliate following acts of aggression against them (Glover et al., 2000).

Study Design

It has only been within the last few years that bully studies have been done in the United States and many of these studies have concentrated on children and young adolescents. Since 2000, my colleagues and I have conducted several studies on bullying. For this article, I used data from students in grades 8–12 to gain an understanding of bullying among older adolescents.

<table>
<thead>
<tr><th colspan="4">Table 1.
What Kind of Bullying Do Students Observe at School?</th></tr>
<tr><th></th><th>Never</th><th>Sometimes</th><th>Often</th></tr>
</thead>
<tbody>
<tr><td>Being Called Names</td><td>485 (26%)</td><td>880 (47%)</td><td>503 (27%)</td></tr>
<tr><td>Being Left Out of Activities</td><td>607 (33%)</td><td>792 (43%)</td><td>441 (24%)</td></tr>
<tr><td>Teasing</td><td>697 (37%)</td><td>846 (45%)</td><td>320 (17%)</td></tr>
<tr><td>Hit/Kicked</td><td>999 (53%)</td><td>665 (35%)</td><td>211 (11%)</td></tr>
<tr><td>Threatened</td><td>1,082 (58%)</td><td>619 (33%)</td><td>178 (9%)</td></tr>
</tbody>
</table>

Note. n=1,893
Because stealing and sexual harassment were not included in earlier surveys, those categories are not reported here.

<table>
<thead>
<tr><th colspan="4">Table 2.
Where Do Students Observe Bullying at School?</th></tr>
<tr><th></th><th>Never</th><th>Sometimes</th><th>Often</th></tr>
</thead>
<tbody>
<tr><td>Classroom</td><td>315 (17%)</td><td>1,162 (62%)</td><td>398 (21%)</td></tr>
<tr><td>Lunchroom</td><td>473 (25%)</td><td>1,051 (56%)</td><td>348 (19%)</td></tr>
<tr><td>At Break</td><td>556 (32%)</td><td>879 (50%)</td><td>319 (18%)</td></tr>
<tr><td>Extracurricular Events</td><td>676 (36%)</td><td>977 (52%)</td><td>215 (12%)</td></tr>
<tr><td>Initiations of Clubs/Athletics</td><td>924 (50%)</td><td>786 (42%)</td><td>147 (8%)</td></tr>
<tr><td>On the Way Home from School</td><td>1,137 (61%)</td><td>602 (32%)</td><td>123 (7%)</td></tr>
<tr><td>On the Way to School</td><td>1,279 (70%)</td><td>465 (25%)</td><td>83 (5%)</td></tr>
</tbody>
</table>

Note. n=1,893
Because students frequently wrote in "restrooms" and "hallways" these locations were added to later surveys, but those categories are not reported here.

Participants in the study included 1,893 students in grades 8–12. Ethnic breakdown of participating students was 11% African American, 22% Hispanic, and 77% Anglo. Fifty-one percent were boys and 49% girls. Twenty-two percent of the participants were in the 8th grade, 53% were in the 9th grade, 14% were in the 10th grade, 8% were in the 11th grade, and 3% were in the 12th grade.

A diverse group of schools were represented. They were located in rural and suburban areas in Texas, Georgia, and Nebraska, and sizes varied from a small school of 250 students to a large high school of 1,500 students. Schools were selected based on convenience to the researchers and willingness of administrators to permit the studies. None of the school leaders thought that they had a problem with bullying.

The survey sought to gather data regarding the types of bullying that occurred, where bullying took place, how safe students felt at school, how bullying made them feel, who they told when they were bullied, and how interested they felt their teachers and administrators were in stopping bullying. Surveys were administered in English classes or in physical education classes by the regular classroom teacher from 1999–2004. Since the survey was revised several times during this time frame, only selected questions on each survey were used. The survey has a reliability alpha of .69, which is appropriate.

Findings

What kind of bullying do students observe at school? As can be seen from Table 1, the most common form of bullying at school was being called names, followed by being left out of activities and teasing. Other studies have reported similar findings, noting that high school students are more likely to bully with ridicule, rejection, and other forms of emotional abuse, rather than using physical bullying (Juvonen et al., 2003).

Where do students observe bullying at school? When students were asked how often they observed bullying in certain school locations, surprisingly, 83% identified the classroom as a place where bullying occurred at least sometimes. Seventy-four percent of the students reported that the lunchroom was a place where bullying occurred at least sometimes. (See Table 2).

Student Experiences Being Bullied. While 60% of students indicated that they were never bullied at school, an alarming 16% reported that they were bullied at least once a week, while 24%

reported being bullied less than once a week. When students were asked how it made them feel when they were bullied at school, 15% admitted that it made them feel angry, and 16% said they felt sad and miserable. Thirty-four percent of students indicted that it did not bother them when they were bullied.

We asked students who they would tell if they were bullied or if they became aware of someone being bullied. Forty-six percent said they would tell a friend, 27% would tell their mother, and 14% would tell their father. However, only 13% of students would tell a teacher or an administrator.

Only half of the students responded to the next question which asked if students had told someone about being bullied and, if so, what happened. Nearly 37% reported that when they told, things got better. However, 17% said they never told anyone that they had been bullied, 37% reported that nothing changed even though they told, and 9% admitted that when they told the bullying only became worse.

A critical element in reducing bullying is the leadership of adults.

How safe do students feel at school? Despite the high reported occurrences of bullying, 39% of students reported that they always felt safe at school, and 45% indicated that they usually felt safe. However, 16% of students admitted that they did not feel very safe when they were at school. Consequently, 9% of students reported that they had even stayed home from school at least once because of bullying and 14% said they had considered staying home.

How interested is the faculty? When asked if administrators were interested in stopping bullying at school, 24% of students did not think that they were; while 34% admitted that they were not sure how administrators felt about this. Only 42% of students believed that administrators were interested in stopping bullying. Students felt nearly the same way about their teachers, with 22% admitting that they did not think teachers were interested in stopping bullying and 33% were not sure how their teachers felt. Only 45% felt that teachers were interested in stopping bullying.

The Dismal Conclusions

This study looked at 1,893 self-reports of older adolescents about bullying and findings suggested the following conclusions:

- Three out of four students are aware of name-calling, students being left out of activities, and teasing at least sometimes at school
- Bullying happens at many places on the campus, even locations where there is teacher supervision, such as the classroom

Bullying at School Among Older Adolescents

- Nearly one-third of students admit that being bullied causes them to feel sad and miserable, or angry
- A small percentage of students tell school faculty about being bullied; and when they do tell, for more than one-third, nothing changes, and for a small but significant number of students, things get worse
- Over one-half of students are not convinced that administrators or teachers are interested in stopping bullying

What Can We Do About Bullying at School?

A critical element in reducing bullying is the leadership of adults. Lazarus (1996) identified the importance of adults in helping young people cope with stressful situations. Likewise in the early 1970s, Daniel Olweus led Sweden and Norway to implement an anti-bullying campaign characterized by adult involvement as a critical component. Two years later, incidents of bullying had been reduced by 50% (Olweus, 1993). Yet, too often, teachers cannot identify bullies or victims at school (Leff, Kupersmidt, Patterson & Power, 1999). Due in part to a lack of trust in adults, students very rarely break the "code of silence" to "rat" on bullies. Furthermore, studies indicate that adults are not viewed by students as being committed to reducing bullying at school (Rigby, 1996). In fact, teachers are not even sure if other teachers are committed to reducing bullying, nor, they admit, do they know how to help when they do become aware of bullying (Harris & Willoughby, 2003).

Building on the importance of adult involvement, the following model for reducing bullying at school is recommended (Harris & Willoughby, 2003)

- **Be Aware.** Adults must first recognize bullying as harmful and a precursor to more severe forms of school violence.
  Strategies: participate in training to recognize bullies and victims; survey students, teachers, and parents regularly to identify kinds of bullying and locations on campus that are high risk; increase supervision; and develop school policies that define bullying.
- **Build Trusting Relationships.** Adults must develop a culture of trust and respect on the campus.
  Strategies: Talk with students in class discussions about bullying; encourage students to share how bullying makes them feel; be responsive to bullies' needs, as well as victims' needs; and show students that adults care about student achievement and about personal achievements.
- **Accept the Challenge to Provide Support.** Adults must be willing to accept the challenge to provide support for all students.
  Strategies: Accept the responsibility to advocate for students

in need; present a united front that establishes behavior guidelines that emphasize bullying is not acceptable behavior; encourage students to tell when bullying occurs; involve parents; and be encouraged to support one another in preventing and intervening in bully situations.

- **Know How to Help.** Adults must have the skills to be able to respond appropriately to bullying situations.
  Strategies: Work collaboratively with school and community personnel to adopt school policies with anti-bully guidelines; create policies that address appropriate consequences that include counseling for the bully, as well as the victim; participate in training that provides strategies for supporting students.

Conclusion

Bullying breeds violence. It teases, torments, and taunts. While many young people ignore bullying or overcome it, some succumb to the pain it inflicts. Most suffer in silence, but a few turn to horrible acts of school violence, such as 15 year old Charles "Andy" Williams. He brought a revolver to school, fired 30 bullets, and killed two schoolmates and wounded 13 others. His father later said, "[they] accused him of being gay… they made fun of him for being a country boy, for his big ears. It didn't matter what he did, they made fun of him" (Booth & Snyder, 2001, A1, A6). When adults are aware, when they build trusting relationships, when they accept the challenge to provide support, and when they have the skills to know how to help hurting students, schools will be safer for everyone.

References

Booth, W., & Snyder, D. (2001). No remorse, no motive from shooting suspect. *San Antonio Express-News,* March 7, A1, A6.

Bureau of Justice Statistics and DOE National Center for Education Statistics. (2001). *Indicators of School Crime and Safety.* Washington, D.C.: Author.

Glover, D., Gough, G., Johnson, M., & Cartwright, N. (2000). Bullying in 25 secondary schools: Incidence, impact and intervention. *Educational Research, 42,* 141–156.

Harris, S., & Petrie, G. (2002). *Bullying: The Bullies, the Victims, the Bystanders.* Lanham, MD.: The Scarecrow Press, Inc.

Harris, S., & Willoughby, W. (2003). Teacher perceptions of student bullying behaviors. *ERS Spectrum, 21*(3), 11–18.

Juvonen, J., Graham, S., & Schuster, M. (2003). Bullying among young adolescents: The strong, the weak, and the troubled. *Pediatrics, 112*(6), 1,231–1,237.

Lazarus, R. (1966). *Psychological Stress and the Coping Process.* New York: McGraw-Hill.

Leff, S., Kupersmidt, J., Patterson, C., & Power, T. (1991). Factors influencing teacher identification of peer bullies and victims. *The School Psychology Review, 28*(3), 505–517.

Nansel, T., Overpeck, M., Pilla, R., Ruan, W., Simons-Morton, B., & Scheidt, P. (2001). Bullying behaviors among U.S. youth: Prevalence and association with psychosocial adjustment. *Journal of American Medical Association, 285*(16), 2,094–2,100.

Olweus, D. (1993). *Bullying at School.* Cambridge, MA: Blackwell Publishers, Inc.

Resnick, M., Bearman, P., Blum, R., Bauman, K., Harris, K., Jones, J. et al. (1997). Protecting adolescents from harm: Findings from the National Longitudinal Study on Adolescent Health. *Journal of the American Medical Association, 278,* 823–832.

Rigby, K. (1996). *Bullying in Schools: And What To Do About It*. London: Jessica Kingsley Publishers.

Ross, D. (1996). *Childhood Bullying and Teasing: What School Personnel, Other Professionals, and Parents Can Do*. Alexandria, VA.: American Counseling Association.

Stein, N. (1995). Sexual harassment in school: The public performance of gender violence. *Harvard Educational Review, 65*, 145–162.

Toppo, G. (2003, October 21). Troubling days at U.S. schools. *USA Today*, 1A,2A

Sandra Harris *received her Ph.D., in Educational Leadership from the University of Texas, Austin. She has more than 30 years of experience as a teacher and administrator and is currently an associate professor of educational leadership at Lamar University in Beaumont, Texas. She is the co-author of the book:* Bullying: The Bullies, the Victims, the Bystanders *(Scarecrow Press, 2003).*

From *Prevention Researcher*, Vol. 11, No. 3, September 2004, pp. 12-14. Copyright © 2004 by Integrated Research Services, Inc. www.tpronline.org. Reprinted by permission.

Index

Index

Test Your Knowledge Form

We encourage you to photocopy and use this page as a tool to assess how the articles in *Annual Editions* expand on the information in your textbook. By reflecting on the articles you will gain enhanced text information. You can also access this useful form on a product's book support Web site at *http://www.mhcls.com/online/*.

NAME: _____ DATE: _____

TITLE AND NUMBER OF ARTICLE: _____

BRIEFLY STATE THE MAIN IDEA OF THIS ARTICLE:

_____

LIST THREE IMPORTANT FACTS THAT THE AUTHOR USES TO SUPPORT THE MAIN IDEA:

_____

WHAT INFORMATION OR IDEAS DISCUSSED IN THIS ARTICLE ARE ALSO DISCUSSED IN YOUR TEXTBOOK OR OTHER READINGS THAT YOU HAVE DONE? LIST THE TEXTBOOK CHAPTERS AND PAGE NUMBERS:

_____

LIST ANY EXAMPLES OF BIAS OR FAULTY REASONING THAT YOU FOUND IN THE ARTICLE:

_____

LIST ANY NEW TERMS/CONCEPTS THAT WERE DISCUSSED IN THE ARTICLE, AND WRITE A SHORT DEFINITION:

We Want Your Advice

ANNUAL EDITIONS revisions depend on two major opinion sources: one is our Advisory Board, listed in the front of this volume, which works with us in scanning the thousands of articles published in the public press each year; the other is you—the person actually using the book. Please help us and the users of the next edition by completing the prepaid article rating form on this page and returning it to us. Thank you for your help!

ANNUAL EDITIONS: Adolescent Psychology

ARTICLE RATING FORM

Here is an opportunity for you to have direct input into the next revision of this volume.
We would like you to rate each of the articles listed below, using the following scale:

1. **Excellent: should definitely be retained**
2. **Above average: should probably be retained**
3. **Below average: should probably be deleted**
4. **Poor: should definitely be deleted**

Your ratings will play a vital part in the next revision.
Please mail this prepaid form to us as soon as possible.
Thanks for your help!

RATING	ARTICLE
	1. Harnessing the Energies of Youth
	2. On (not) "Coloring in the Outline" (Transformations from Youth Through Relationships)
	3. The Future of Adolescence: Lengthening Ladders to Adulthood
	4. Why do Kids Eat Healthful Food?
	5. Body Image: How Do You See Yourself?
	6. What Makes Teens Tick
	7. Medicating Young Minds
	8. The Biology of Risk Taking
	9. Wearing Out Their Bodies?
	10. Sense of Belonging to School: Can Schools Make a Difference?
	11. Challenges and Suggestions for Safe Schools
	12. Healthier Students, Better Learners
	13. The 100 Best High Schools in America
	14. Safe Schools for the Roller Coaster Years
	15. The New College Dropout
	16. The Perils of Higher Education
	17. Studies Reveal Strengths, Weaknesses in Improving Rates of High School Graduation and College Completion for Low-Income
	18. The New Cheating Epidemic
	19. What Empathy Can Do
	20. Fostering Social-Emotional Learning in the Classroom
	21. A Mother's Story
	22. The Consequences of Insufficient Sleep for Adolescents: Links Between Sleep and Emotional Regulation
	23. Support Network Eases Problems for Parents and Out-of-Control Teens
	24. Learning to Chill: Overloaded at School and Overscheduled at Home
	25. A Nation of Wimps
	26. Prevention of Domestic Violence During Adolescence
	27. Adolescents from Maritally Violent Homes
	28. Who's Killing Kids' Sports?

RATING	ARTICLE
	29. Risky Business: Exploring Adolescent Risk-Taking Behavior
	30. Family, Religious, School, and Peer Influences on Adolescent Alcohol Use
	31. Alcohol Use Among Adolescents
	32. Terrorism, The Media, and Distress in Youth
	33. What to Tell Kids About Sex
	34. Should Congress be Giving More Financial Support to Abstinence-Only Sex Education? YES
	35. Should Congress Be Giving More Financial Support to Abstinence-Only Sex Education? NO
	36. Choosing Virginity
	37. The Perils of Playing House
	38. Teenage Fatherhood and Involvement in Delinquent Behavior
	39. School-Based Trauma and Grief Intervention for Adolescents
	40. Too Young to Die
	41. Adolescents Who Self-Injure: Implications and Strategies for School Counselors
	42. Bullying at School Among Older Adolescents

(Continued on next page)

BUSINESS REPLY MAIL
FIRST CLASS MAIL PERMIT NO. 551 DUBUQUE IA

POSTAGE WILL BE PAID BY ADDRESEE

McGraw-Hill Contemporary Learning Series
2460 KERPER BLVD
DUBUQUE, IA 52001-9902

NO POSTAGE
NECESSARY
IF MAILED
IN THE
UNITED STATES

Ililuilillmilliiiillililiilliiiiililill

ABOUT YOU

Name   Date
_____   _____

Are you a teacher? ☐   A student? ☐
Your school's name
_____

Department
_____

Address   City   State   Zip
_____

School telephone #
_____

YOUR COMMENTS ARE IMPORTANT TO US!

Please fill in the following information:
For which course did you use this book?
_____

Did you use a text with this ANNUAL EDITION?   ☐ yes ☐ no
What was the title of the text?
_____

What are your general reactions to the *Annual Editions* concept?
_____

Have you read any pertinent articles recently that you think should be included in the next edition? Explain.
_____

Are there any articles that you feel should be replaced in the next edition? Why?
_____

Are there any World Wide Web sites that you feel should be included in the next edition? Please annotate.
_____

May we contact you for editorial input? ☐ yes ☐ no
May we quote your comments? ☐ yes ☐ no